AGAINST RACE

AGAINST RACE

Imagining Political Culture
beyond the Color Line

PAUL GILROY

THE BELKNAP PRESS OF
HARVARD UNIVERSITY PRESS
Cambridge, Massachusetts
2000

Library of Congress Cataloging-in-Publication Data

Gilroy, Paul.
Against race : imagining political culture beyond the color line / Paul Gilroy.
p.   cm.
Includes bibliographical references and index.
ISBN 0-674-00096-X (alk. paper)
1. Race awareness—Political aspects. 2. Racism—Political aspects. 3. Blacks—Politics
and government. 4. Blacks—Social conditions. 5. Political culture. 6. Fascism. I. Title.

HT1521 .G524 2000
305.8'00973—dc21   99-052340

For Vron Ware
and in memory of my friend Nick Robin,
routed cosmopolitans both

CONTENTS

AGAINST RACE

At first thought it may seem strange that the anti-Semite's outlook should be related to that of the Negrophobe. It was my philosophy professor, a native of the Antilles, who recalled the fact to me one day: "Whenever you hear anyone abuse the Jews, pay attention, because he is talking about you." And I found that he was universally right—by which I meant that I was answerable in my body and my heart for what was done to my brother. Later I realized that he meant, quite simply, an anti-Semite is inevitably anti-Negro.

—FRANTZ FANON

The modern times that W. E. B. Du Bois once identified as the century of the color line have now passed. Racial hierarchy is still with us. Approaching that conundrum, this book addresses some of the continuing tensions associated with the constitution of political communities in racialized form. It considers patterns of conflict connected to the consolidation of *culture lines* rather than color lines and is concerned, in particular, with the operations of power, which, thanks to ideas about "race," have become entangled with those vain and mistaken attempts to delineate and subdivide humankind.

Against Race should be read as a cautious contribution to another larger task that often seems impossible and misguided. This involves the slow work of making black European mentalities equipped for the perils of the twenty-first century. That grand-sounding but ultimately parochial obligation is complemented by some conjuring with the transitional yearning for what we should probably call a "planetary humanism." Elements of that elusive mindset have been allied to nonracial, transblack histories and are imagined here from an assertively cosmopolitan point of view that challenges the version of these themes currently being offered by occultists, mystics, and conspiracy theorists. Perpetual peace is off the menu for the time being; nonetheless, racial difference provides a new and timely test for the democratic character of all today's cosmopolitan imaginings.

I have had to recognize personal motivation for turning to the relationship between "race" and fascism. I was born in 1956, the year of British folly in Suez and of the Hungarian uprising against Soviet tyranny. My first real geopolitical apprehensions came one fateful morning in 1962 when I sobbed into my cornflakes because I thought the world would end in a nuclear fireball before I could get back home after school. At that point, I was, I thought, exactly as old as the cold war itself. Britain's strict rationing of food had ended by that time, but the shadows cast by the war and by the unfulfilled promise of a comprehensive welfare-state that followed it, were enduring.

As children, we could still see where the bombs had fallen. My own memory tells me that I was a militaristic child, but this must have been a wider generational affliction. I certainly spent much of my childhood re-enacting the glories of the Second World War. The leafy fringes of north London provided the battlegrounds across which I marched my troops and flew my imaginary Battle of Britain aircraft. We preferred these games to alternative pastimes like cowboys and Indians because we savored the fact that we always had right on our side. Our faceless, unremittingly evil enemies were Hitler's Nazis and, inspired by what we read in comics like *Eagle* and *Swift* as well as the stronger fare to be found in places like the barbershop, we harried and slaughtered them wherever they could be located: in parks, gardens and wastelands, or the disused air-raid shelters that were unearthed all around us. This may seem to have been an eccentric pursuit for a black boy, but it was entirely unproblematic. No white playmate ever questioned the right of us not-yet-postcolonials to play that game.

I knew from an early age that West Indian and other colonial service personnel had participated bravely in the anti-Nazi war. I admired and appreciated the portraits of my uncle and his wife in their wartime uniforms, which hung, enshrined, in one corner of their sitting room. I knew that he had crewed a bomber, but my sense of the romantic potential involved in that heroic history was more likely to have been supplied by Capt. W. E. Johns and his ilk. It remained uncomplicated by the details of the conflict itself. I didn't dare to ask these real veterans much about what their wars had entailed. They did not usually speak about that time to children.

I read the piles of literature that my parents had accumulated on the war, its causes, conduct, and consequences. I did this, not to play better wargames, but because I felt an obligation to know. Knowledge of that war and its horrors was central to an unspoken compact that we made with the adult world. The memory of the conflict was one of the first places where the edge of childhood could be detected. Following these studies, often conducted in secret, I felt confident in a brash, ten-year-old way that I understood what had happened. I remember being especially perplexed when, on one weekend historian's walk through the desolate and bomb-damaged riverside areas of the old City of London, my father and I encountered the encircled lightning-flash insignia of the British Union of Fascists painted carefully on a wall alongside the, by then, traditional injunction to Keep Britain White. Weren't fascists the same as Nazis, I asked him? What were they doing here? Were they still around? How could *they* be English people? How could *English* people be Fascists? Was their exciting lightning-flash the same sort of thing as the hated but fascinating swastika?

My father's attempts at comprehensive reassurance did not convince me. At that point, I felt a little disadvantaged when other children proudly recounted their parents' wartime exploits. My father, a twenty-year-old student when war was declared, had chosen another testing path. He said that no government could compel him to kill another human being and became a conscientious objector undertaking various types of decidedly unglamorous war-work that made him vulnerable to the hatred and resentment of many. His principled stance was interpreted as cowardice, and he was informally punished for it. He and I finally glimpsed a Gas Identification Officer's badge, like the one he had worn while checking bomb-damaged buildings for evidence of chemical attack, in a dusty glass case upstairs at the Imperial War Museum. At the time, I mistakenly felt that it compared poorly with the German helmets, daggers, and bullets that were the most prestigious trophies in the symbolic economy of re-membrance. My mother, in any case younger, was equally unsatisfactory as a source of war lore. The conflict had certainly been registered in what was then British Guiana. Although the idea that a German victory would mean the reintroduction of slavery had been circulated there, along with the imperial propaganda newsreels, the war was not central to her life prior to migration.

The world of my childhood included the incomprehensible mystery of the Nazi genocide. I returned to it compulsively like a painful wobbly tooth. It appeared to be the core of the war, and its survivors were all around us. Their tattoos intrigued me. Their children were our playmates and school friends. It was they who counseled our carless family against the pleasures of riding in Volkswagens and they who introduced us to the subtle delights of poppy-seed cake. It was clear, too, that some Jewish families had opened their homes to West Indian students who had been shut out from much commercially rented property by the color-bar. I struggled with the realization that their suffering was somehow connected with the ideas of "race" that bounded my own world with the threat of vio-lence. Michael Franks, my school friend who wore a prayer shawl under his clothes in spite of the ridicule it brought upon him when we changed for P.E. class, was especially acute in diagnosing the casual anti-semitism of some of our teachers who had, of course, all distinguished themselves in the real manly business of war against the evil Germans.

I now know that these contradictions were the first puzzles from which this project stemmed. They were supplemented and refined when, as part of the new, global media constituency for black America's civil rights strug-gles, we saw that familiar swastika flying again: this time alongside the Confederate flags and burning crosses of affirmative but declining segregationism. This too was an interpretative challenge. What "theory" of racial difference, of racial prejudice, could explain these transcultural pat-terns of identification? The teddy boys who terrified me as a child and their successors, the skinheads who hounded me through my teenage years, did not invoke Hitler's name or cause. To have done so then would have been an unthinkable treason to the concentrated English identities they were celebrating and defending against alien encroachments. They spoke and acted in the name of another belligerent nationalism, but it was only later, in the 1970s, that conditions changed and a new skinhead chant of "Sieg heil" made their unanimist hopes explicit if not exactly clear. By then the cosmopolitan landscape of my London childhood had expanded to include substantial numbers of South African refugees and exiles whose stories of antiracist activism brought new twists into my bewildered understanding of raciology. In what sense, we wondered, was Hendrik Verwoerd a fascist? While that question hung unanswered in my adolescent mind, the outer-national energy of black power and the momentum of late-1960s counterculture loudly and plausibly leveled the charge of fascism yet again, this time against American imperialism and domestic policy.

Political battles over the significance of local neo-fascists and their ultranationalist ideology surfaced again in the mass antiracist movement of the 1970s. It seems extraordinary now, but the opposition to them was deeply divided by disagreements over the place of "race" in their thinking. To make matters worse, the populism of what was after all an anti-Nazi league, seemed to play down the routine racism of the British state and its institutional agencies: police, housing, and education. That imaginative intervention broke the potential bond between Europe's young people and a mass racist movement. The neo-fascists were relegated to the fringes, but they are now once again on the march across Europe. Outside its fortifications, authoritarian irrationalism, militarism, and genocide have become part of how desperate people answer the destructive impact of globalization on their lives.

As living memory dies out, the idea of just, anti-Nazi war is being recovered, commemorated, and struggled over, but we must ask hard, uncomfortable questions about the forms this commemoration takes. Is the presence of nonwhites—West Indians, African Americans, and other colonial combatants—being written out of the heroic narratives that are being produced in this, the age of apologies and overdue reparations? Before that memory dies, we must inquire what impact the war against fascism and Nazi race-thinking had upon the way that black intellectuals understood themselves, their predicament, and the fate of Western culture and civilization. What role might their stories have if we could write a different history of this period, one in which they were allowed to dwell in the same frame as official anti-Nazi heroism? This book is not yet that history, but I hope that it will be a part of its precondition.

Even more important, what place should the history and memory of past conflicts with fascism have in forging the minimal ethical principles on which a meaningful multiculturalism might be based? Answering that question takes us into an initial confrontation with the idea of "race" and the raciological theories to which it has given rise.

Indirectly, then, this essay seeks to engage the pressures and demands of multicultural social and political life, in which, I argue, the old, modern idea of "race" can have no ethically defensible place. If that line of argument sounds overly familiar, I should note that it concludes, though it cannot complete, the critical consideration of nationalism and its modes of belonging that was conducted in some of my earlier work. This time it is intended to clarify and build upon the discussion of intercultural histories that was offered before in a provisional form. These long-standing interests have had to be combined with more urgent priorities. In particular, they have been transformed by my apprehensions about the growing absence of ethical considerations from what used to be termed "antiracist" thinking and action. Revitalizing ethical sensibilities in this area requires moving away from antiracism's tarnished vocabulary while retaining many of the hopes to which it was tied.

This mixture of concerns is part of the answer tentatively offered below to the authoritarian and antidemocratic sentiments and styles that have recurred in twentieth-century ultranationalism. I am prepared to accept that they have figured even in the black political cultures constituted where victimized people have set out in pursuit of redress, citizenship, and autonomy. Too often in this century those folk have found only the shallowest comfort and short-term distraction in the same repertory of power that produced their sufferings in the first place. My enduring distaste for the ethnic absolutisms that have offered quick ethnic fixes and cheap pseudo-solidarities as an inadequate salve for real pain, means that I do not see contact with cultural difference solely as a form of loss. Its inevitable interactions are not approached here in terms of the elemental jeopardy in which each sealed and discrete identity is supposedly placed by the destructive demands of illegitimate "transethnic" *relation*. I borrow that critical term from the work of the Martiniquean writer, Edouard Glissant. His creative use of it brings a concern with what has been relayed together with a critical interest in relative and comparative approaches to history and culture and attention to what has been related in both senses of that word: kinship and narration. Approaching the issue of relation in this spirit requires a sharp departure from all currently fashionable obligations to celebrate incommensurability and cheerlead for absolute identity. The preeminent place of black cultures in the glittering festivities that have been laid on to accompany recent phases in the globalization of capital and the entrenchment of consumerism is not for me either a surprise or a source of unalloyed joy. I argue that this apparent triumph clearly exhibits patterns that originated in European fascism and that it remains tainted by the same ambiguities, especially where "race" is invoked. I suggest, not only that these formations need to be recognized as having been marked by their frightful origins in the aestheticization and spectacularization that replaced politics with easier, unanimist fantasies, but also that they retain the power to destroy any possibility of human mutuality and cosmopolitan democracy.

This interest in the latent and often unrecognized legacies of fascism's great cultural revolution is a major theme in what follows. It is but one example of how the argument below is directed toward a number of more general political problems not usually associated with the critical theories of "race." I oppose the fashionable reluctance to face the fundamental differences marked in Western history and culture by the emergence and entrenchment of biopolitical power as means and technique for managing the life of populations, states, and societies. I suggest that this damaging refusal has been closely associated with an equally problematic resistance to any suggestion that there might be links between those characteristically modern developments and the fundamental priority invested in the idea of "race" during the same period. By challenging the dismissive responses, which would disregard the full, constitutive force of racial divisions, I have tried to place a higher value upon the cosmopolitan histories and transcultural experiences whereby enlightenment aspirations might eventually mutate in the direction of greater inclusivity and thus greater authority. My fundamental point is that the promise of their completion in happily non-Eurocentric forms can be glimpsed only once we have worked through the histories of extremity associated with raciology's brutal reasonings.

This essay is divided into three overlapping sections. The first part deals with the key abstractions, "race," belonging, and identity, which organize the argument as a whole. It has a utopian tone, but that should not disguise its practical purposes. It departs from the idea that genetic determinism and the nano-political struggles of the biotech era have transformed the meaning of racial difference. This new situation demands a renewed critique of race-thinking. It also requires ethical resources that can be drawn from histories of suffering, in particular from the memory of the 39–45 war, reconceptualized on a different scale. The modes of belonging articulated through appeals to the power of sovereign territory and the bonds of rooted, exclusive national cultures, are contrasted with the different translocal solidarities that have been constituted by diaspora dispersal and estrangement.

In Part II, attention turns toward cultural aspects of the fascist revolution. The reader is asked first, to consider some of its disturbing traces in the present, and second, to see where and how they have entered black Atlantic cultures in motion toward globalization. This commercial and political order is decreasingly amenable to the racial codes of earlier times and has unexpectedly given the black body a new prestige. Black Atlantic cultures are not being singled out for harsh and negative evaluation; indeed, their vernacular forms have supplied a joyful, playful, and vulgar opposition that fascism cannot subordinate. My point is different: if ultranationalism, fraternalism, and militarism can take hold, unidentified, among the descendants of slaves, they can enter anywhere. Past victimization affords no protection against the allure of automatic, prepolitical uniformity.

Part III inquires into the components of a cosmopolitan response to the continuing dangers of race-thinking. It argues that the occult, militaristic, and essentialist theories of racial difference that are currently so popular, should be seen as symptoms of a loss of certainty around "race." Their powerful appeal can be repudiated only if we break the restraining hold of nationalist history and its frozen past upon our political imaginations. Only then can we begin to reorient ourselves toward the future.

|

RACIAL OBSERVANCE, NATIONALISM, AND HUMANISM

Since race is not a mere word, but an organic living thing, it follows as a matter of course that it never remains stationary; it is ennobled or it degenerates, it develops in this or that direction and lets this or that quality decay. This is a law of all individual life. But the firm national union is the surest way to protect against going astray: it signifies common memory, common hope, common intellectual nourishment; it fixes firmly the existing bond of blood and impels us to make it ever closer.

—HOUSTON STEWART CHAMBERLAIN

1

THE CRISIS OF "RACE" AND RACIOLOGY

It is indeed the case that human social and political organization is a
reflection of our biological being, for, after all, we are material biological objects developing under the influence of the interaction of
our genes with the external world. It is certainly not the case that
our biology is irrelevant to social organization. The question is,
what part of our biology is relevant?

—RICHARD LEWONTIN

A genuine revolution of values means in the final analysis that our
loyalties must become ecumenical rather than sectional. Every nation must now develop an overriding loyalty to mankind as a whole
in order to preserve the best in their individual societies.

—MARTIN LUTHER KING, JR.

It is impossible to deny that we are
living through a profound transformation in the way the idea of "race" is
understood and acted upon. Underlying it there is another, possibly
deeper, problem that arises from the changing mechanisms that govern
how racial differences are seen, how they appear to us and prompt specific
identities. Together, these historic conditions have disrupted the observance of "race" and created a crisis for raciology, the lore that brings the
virtual realities of "race" to dismal and destructive life.

Any opportunities for positive change that arise from this crisis are circumscribed by the enduring effects of past catastrophe. Raciology has saturated the discourses in which it circulates. It cannot be readily re-signified or de-signified, and to imagine that its dangerous meanings can be easily re-articulated into benign, democratic forms would be to exaggerate the power of critical and oppositional interests. In contrast, the creative acts involved in destroying raciology and transcending "race" are more than warranted by the goal of authentic democracy to which they point. The political will to liberate humankind from race-thinking must be complemented by precise historical reasons why these attempts are worth making. The first task is to suggest that the demise of "race" is not something to be feared. Even this may be a hard argument to win. On the one hand, the beneficiaries of racial hierarchy do not want to give up their privileges. On the other hand, people who have been subordinated by race-thinking and its distinctive social structures (not all of which come tidily color-coded) have for centuries employed the concepts and categories of their rulers, owners, and persecutors to resist the destiny that "race" has allocated to them and to dissent from the lowly value it placed upon their lives. Under the most difficult of conditions and from imperfect materials that they surely would not have selected if they had been able to choose, these oppressed groups have built complex traditions of politics, ethics, identity, and culture. The currency of "race" has marginalized these traditions from official histories of modernity and relegated them to the backwaters of the primitive and the prepolitical. They have involved elaborate, improvised constructions that have the primary function of absorbing and deflecting abuse. But they have gone far beyond merely affording protection and reversed the polarities of insult, brutality, and contempt, which are unexpectedly turned into important sources of solidarity, joy, and collective strength. When ideas of racial particularity are inverted in this defensive manner so that they provide sources of pride rather than shame and humiliation, they become difficult to relinquish. For many racialized populations, "race" and the hard-won, oppositional identities it supports are not to be lightly or prematurely given up.

These groups will need to be persuaded very carefully that there is something worthwhile to be gained from a deliberate renunciation of "race" as the basis for belonging to one another and acting in concert. They will have to be reassured that the dramatic gestures involved in turning against racial observance can be accomplished without violating the precious forms of solidarity and community that have been created by their protracted subordination along racial lines. The idea that action against racial hierarchies can proceed more effectively when it has been purged of any lingering respect for the idea of "race" is one of the most persuasive cards in this political and ethical suit.

Historians, sociologists, and theorists of politics have not always appreciated the significance of these sometimes-hidden, modern countercultures formed by long and brutal experiences of racialized subordination through slavery and colonialism and since. The minor, dissident traditions that have been constituted against the odds amid suffering and dispossession have been overlooked by the ignorant and the indifferent as well as the actively hostile. Some initiates, who should certainly know better, have even rejected and despised these formations as insufficiently respectable, noble, or pure. Nonetheless, vernacular cultures and the stubborn social movements that were built upon their strengths and tactics have contributed important moral and political resources to modern struggles in pursuit of freedom, democracy, and justice.[1] Their powerful influences have left their imprint on an increasingly globalized popular culture. Originally tempered by the ghastly extremities of racial slavery, these dissident cultures remained strong and supple long after the formalities of emancipation, but they are now in decline and their prospects cannot be good. They are already being transformed beyond recognition by the uneven effects of globalization and planetary commerce in blackness.

Where the dangers represented by this historic decline have been recognized, the defense of communal interests has often mobilized the fantasy of a frozen culture, of arrested cultural development. Particularity can be maintained and communal interests protected if they are fixed in their most authentic and glorious postures of resistance. This understandable but inadequate response to the prospect of losing one's identity reduces cultural traditions to the simple process of invariant repetition. It has helped to secure deeply conservative notions that supply real comfort in dismal times but do little justice either to the fortitude and the improvisational skills of the slaves and their embattled descendants or to the complexities of contemporary cultural life.

We need to understand the appeal of the idea of tradition in this context. Where it is understood as little more than a closed list of rigid rules that can be applied consciously without interpretation or attention to particular historical conditions, it is a ready alibi for authoritarianism rather than a sign of cultural viability or ethical confidence. Indeed, the defense of tradition on these grounds can, as we shall see, open a door to ultraconservative forms of political culture and social regulation.

In identifying these problems and moving beyond them, I shall try to show that the comfort zone created in the fading aura of those wonderful cultures of dissidence is already shrinking and that the cultures themselves are not as strong, complex, or effective as they once were. They do still occasionally flicker into spectacular life, urging desperate people to stand up for their rights and giving them a potent political and moral language with which to do it. However, there is no reason to suppose that they will be able to withstand all the destructive effects of globalization and localization, let alone the corrosive power of substantive political disagreements that have arisen over the nature of black particularity and its significance relative to other contending identity-claims: religion, sexuality, generation, gender, and so on.

The dissident traditions inaugurated by the struggle against slavery, a struggle for recognition as human rather than chattel, agent and person rather than object, have already been changed by translocal forces, both political and economic, that bear heavily on the symbolic currency of "race." This situation is another fundamental part of the crisis of raciology. It provides further inducements to recognize that the current disruption of race-thinking presents an important opportunity. There is here a chance to break away from the dangerous and destructive patterns that were established when the rational absurdity of "race" was elevated into an essential concept and endowed with a unique power to both determine history and explain its selective unfolding.

If we are tempted to be too celebratory in assessing the positive possibilities created by these changes in race-thinking and the resulting confusion that has enveloped raciology, we need only remind ourselves that the effects of racial discourses have become more unpredictable as the quality of their claims upon the world have become more desperate. This is a delicate situation, and "race" remains fissile material.

A CRISIS OF RACIOLOGY

Any inventory of the elements that constitute this crisis of raciology must make special mention of the rise of gene-oriented or genomic constructions of "race." Their distance from the older versions of race-thinking that were produced in the eighteenth and nineteenth centuries underlines that the meaning of racial difference is itself being changed as the relationship between human beings and nature is reconstructed by the impact of the DNA revolution and of the technological developments that have energized it.[2] This book is premised upon the idea that we must try to take possession of that profound transformation and somehow set it to work against the tainted logic that produced it. In other words, the argument here unfolds from the basic idea that this crisis of "race" and representation, of politics and ethics, offers a welcome cue to free ourselves from the bonds of all raciology in a novel and ambitious abolitionist project.

The pursuit of liberation from "race" is an especially urgent matter for those peoples who, like modern blacks in the period after transatlantic slavery, were assigned an inferior position in the enduring hierarchies that raciology creates. However, this opportunity is not theirs alone. There are very good reasons why it should be enthusiastically embraced by others whose antipathy to race-thinking can be defined, not so much by the way it has subordinated them, but because in endowing them with the alchemical magic of racial mastery, it has distorted and delimited their experiences and consciousness in other ways. They may not have been animalized, reified, or exterminated, but they too have suffered something by being deprived of their individuality, their humanity, and thus alienated from species life. Black and white are bonded together by the mechanisms of "race" that estrange them from each other and amputate their common humanity. Frantz Fanon, the Martiniqean psychiatrist and anticolonial activist whose work frames these concerns, observed this dismal cycle through its effects on the lives of men: "the Negro enslaved by his inferiority, the white man enslaved by his superiority alike behave in accordance with a neurotic orientation."[3] Dr. Martin Luther King, Jr., another influential pathologist of "race," whose work counterpoints Fanon's own, was fond of pointing out that race-thinking has the capacity to make its beneficiaries inhuman even as it deprives its victims of their humanity.[4]

Here, drawing implicitly upon the combined legacies of King and Fanon, his sometime interlocutor, a rather different, postracial and postanthropological version of what it means to be human might begin to take shape. If this radically nonracial humanism is to be placed upon more stable foundations than those provided by King's open-minded and consistent Christianity or Fanon's phenomenological, existential, and psychoanalytic interests, it must be distinguished from earlier, less satisfactory attempts to refigure humankind. Its attempt at a comprehensive break from those traditions of reflection is signaled fundamentally by a refusal to be articulated exclusively in the male gender. From this angle, the precious, patient processes that culminate in community and democracy do not exist only in the fraternal patterns that have proved so durable and so attractive to so many. The ideal of fraternity need no longer compromise or embarrass the noble dreams of liberty and equality. This willfully ungendered humanism is not reducible to demands for equality between men and women or even for reciprocity between the sexes. Those revolutionary ideas are already alive and at large in the world. They can be complemented by a change of the conceptual scale on which essential human attributes are being calculated.

This change, in turn, entails the abolition of what is conventionally thought of as sexual division. Minor differences become essentially irrelevant. The forms of narcissism they support need not retain their grip upon the world. If that aim seems to be an unduly utopian or radical aspiration, we would do well to recall the important practical example of these principles currently being pursued by the military organizations of the over-developed world. Forced by recruitment shortfalls and other demographic changes to accept the possibility that women are just as physically capable of front-line combat duties as their male counterparts, these organizations have undertaken a partial but nonetheless significant de-masculinization of soldiery. While Demi Moore was being incarnated as GI Jane, Western military organizations were conducting a number of technical studies of exactly how the female body can be modified by exercise and training so that its physical potential for military activities can be optimized. Scientists at Britain's Ministry of Defence Research Agency have, for example, outlined a form of basic training, cryptically known as "personnel selection standards," for their new female recruits. The British Army has emphasized that it cannot eliminate intrinsic physical differences such as hip size and varying proportions of fat and muscle; however, "initial results from the new training regime have, on average, added 2 lbs more muscle while removing 6 lbs of fat." One British officer said: "Brute strength is not a great part of military life in the 1990s."[5] Comparable strategies are also being revealed on the other side of scarcity in the underdeveloped parts of the planet. The active and enthusiastic contribution of women to the genocide of Tutsi and the killing of Hutu political opponents that took place in Rwanda during 1994 provides one warning against any desire to celebrate these changes as inherently progressive.[6]

Perhaps, pending the eventual sublation of governmental militarism, the ideal of military genderlessness can enhance our understanding of moral and civic agency. As a sign of transition, it hints at a universality that can exist in less belligerent forms. There need be no concessions to the flight from embodiment that has been associated with the consolidation of abstract, modern individuality.[7] Here, the constraints of bodily existence (being in the world) are admitted and even welcomed, though there is a strong inducement to see and value them differently as sources of identification and empathy. The recurrence of pain, disease, humiliation and loss of dignity, grief, and care for those one loves can all contribute to an abstract sense of a human similarity powerful enough to make solidarities based on cultural particularity appear suddenly trivial.[8]

Some other features of this pragmatic, planetary humanism can be tentatively enumerated. Though most political philosophers who consider these questions have ignored this possibility or failed to recognize its truly subversive force, I would suggest that a certain distinctiveness might also be seen to emerge through the deliberate and self-conscious renunciation of "race" as a means to categorize and divide humankind. This radically nonracial humanism exhibits a primary concern with the forms of human dignity that race-thinking strips away. Its counteranthropological and sometimes misanthropic orientation is most powerfully articulated where it has been accompanied by a belated return to consideration of the chronic tragedy, vulnerability, and frailty that have defined our species in the melancholic art of diverse poetic figures from Leopardi and Nietzsche to Esther Phillips and Donny Hathaway. Its signature is provided by a grim determination to make that predicament of fundamentally fragile, corporeal existence into the key to a version of humanism that contradicts the triumphal tones of the anthropological discourses that were enthusiastically supportive of race-thinking in earlier, imperial times.

This is not the humanism of existentialists and phenomenologists, short-sighted Protestants or complacent scientists. Indeed, mindful of raciological associations between past humanisms and the idea of progress, this humanism is as unfriendly toward the idea of "race" as it is ambivalent about claims to identify progress that do not take the de-civilizing effects of continuing racial division into account. I want to show that important insights can be acquired by systematically returning to the history of struggles over the limits of humanity in which the idea of "race" has been especially prominent. This humanism is conceived explicitly as a response to the sufferings that raciology has wrought. The most valuable resources for its elaboration derive from a principled, cross-cultural approach to the history and literature of extreme situations in which the boundaries of what it means to be human were being negotiated and tested minute by minute, day by day. These studies of the inhumanity inspired by and associated with the idea of "race" are not, of course, confined to slavery or the brutal forms of segregation that followed it. They have arisen from numerous episodes in colonial history and from the genocidal activities that have proved to be raciology's finest, triumphant hours. They are especially worthwhile, not because the suffering of the victims of extreme evil offers easy lessons for the redemption of the more fortunate; indeed, we cannot know what acute ethical insights the victims of race-thinking may have taken with them in death. The victims of these terrors are necessarily mute, and if there are any survivors, they will be beset by guilt, shame, and unbearably painful and unreliable memories. They will not be the best guides to the moral and political lessons involved in histories of pointless suffering, but they may still be able to yield important insight into the moral dilemmas of the present. We should therefore pay attention to the doubts that the most eloquent and perceptive survivors of systematic inhumanity have thrown on the value of their own testimony. We must be alert to its unspoken conventions and genres, for there are tacit rules governing the expectations of the reading publics that have formed around these painful, moving words and texts.

However, in an unprecedented situation in which ambivalence reigns and general laws of ethical conduct are difficult to frame, this legacy of bearing witness should not be spurned as a distraction from the laborious tasks of documentation and historical reconstruction. It is far better to make this dubious testimony our compass and to seek our bearings in the words of witnesses than to try vainly to orient ourselves with the unreliable charts supplied by covertly race-coded liberal or even socialist humanisms, which, if they did not steer us into this lost position, have offered very few ideas about how we might extricate ourselves from it and find ourselves again without the benefit of racial categories or racial lore.

GENES AND BODIES IN CONSUMER CULTURE

The contemporary focus on the largely hidden potency of genes promotes a fundamental change of scale in the perception and comprehension of the human body. This change is not an automatic product of only the most recent scientific developments and needs to be connected to an understanding of techno-science, particularly biotechnology, over a longer period of time. Its impact upon the status of old, that is, essentially eighteenth-century, racial typologies has been inexcusably neglected by most writers on "race."

The tragic story of Henrietta Lacks, an African-American mother of five from Baltimore who died of cervical cancer at the age of thirty-one in October 1951, can provide important orientation as we move away from the biopolitics of "race" and toward its nano-politics. Cells taken without consent from Lacks's body by Dr. George Gey, a cell biologist at the Johns Hopkins Hospital, were grown in tissue culture and have been used since then in countless scientific experiments all over the world. The cell-line extracted from her cancer, now known as HeLa, was the first human tumor cell-line to be cultivated. It had a number of unusual properties. The unprecedentedly virulent cells grew rapidly and proliferated, invading adjacent cultures and combining unexpectedly with other organisms in the labs where they were in use.[9] They were soon being marketed as a "research organism" and have proved to be an indispensable tool in the burgeoning biotech industry.

The Lacks case raises important issues about when material of this type extracted from a body can be considered human tissue and the point at which it is to be identified alternatively as a form of property that belongs, not to the person in whose body it began, but to the commercial interests involved in selling it for private profit. The story of HeLa cells is also instructive for the confusion that was created when enzymes that suggested Mrs. Lacks's "blackness" revealed themselves, confounding and perplexing researchers who had assumed her "whiteness" or had, more importantly, failed to think raciologically about her legacy or their own research. This episode can be used to mark the point at which an important threshold in thinking about "race" was crossed. The message conveyed by commerce in HeLa cells exceeds even the old familiar tale in which black patients have sometimes been abused and manipulated by the white doctors employed to treat them. It would appear that race-defying cells, the body's smallest vital component, have become absolutely central to controversies over the limit and character of species life.

At the risk of sounding too anthropocentric, I would suggest that the cultivation of cells outside the body for commercial and other purposes is an epoch-making shift that requires a comprehensive rethinking of the ways we understand and analyze our vulnerable humanity. Like the speculative manipulation of genetic material between various species that has followed it with unpredictable and possibly dangerous results for all human beings, this change suggests a wholly new set of boundaries within which humanity will take shape. The "engineering" of transgenic animals and plants, some of which have supposedly benefited from the insertion of human genes into their DNA, is a related phenomenon that has also been the subject of intense debate about its potentially catastrophic consequences. The international and therefore necessarily "transracial" trade in internal organs and other body parts for transplant, sometimes obtained by dubious means, is another pertinent development. The challenges that have arisen from the manipulation and commerce in all aspects of human fertility, including the vividly contentious issue of whether mothers of one "race" might perversely choose to bear babies of another, represent yet another key change, while a number of recent attempts to patent or hold copyright in organisms, cells, and other elements of life itself would be the final sign that we have to adjust our conceptions of life and our mutable human nature.[10]

All these changes impact upon how "race" is understood. Awareness of the indissoluble unity of all life at the level of genetic materials leads to a stronger sense of the particularity of our species as a whole, as well as to new anxieties that its character is being fundamentally and irrevocably altered. With these symptomatic developments in mind, it is difficult to resist the conclusion that this biotechnological revolution demands a change in our understanding of "race," species, embodiment, and human specificity. In other words, it asks that we reconceptualize our relationship to ourselves, our species, our nature, and the idea of life. We need to ask, for example, whether there should be any place in this new paradigm of life for the idea of specifically *racial* differences.

The well-known and surprisingly popular portrait of human beings as an essentially irrelevant transitory medium for the dynamic agency of their supposedly selfish genes is not the only morally and politically objectionable consequence of emergent, genomic orthodoxy. It, too, has fundamental implications for the coherence of the idea of "race" and its relationship to the increasingly complex patterns of natural variation that will no doubt be revealed in a geographically distributed species and the endlessly varying but fundamentally similar individuals who compose it. The specification of significant differences can only be calculated within specific scales, what the physicist Ilya Prigogine calls "domains of validity."[11] Sadly, however much common sense and popular comprehension of "race" lag behind these developments, they do not mean that ideas of "race" based upon immediate appearance have become instantly redundant, acquiring a residual status that contrasts sharply with the conspicuous power they enjoyed previously in the ages of colonial empires, mass migration, and mass extermination.

As actively de-politicized consumer culture has taken hold, the world of racialized appearances has become invested with another magic. This comes courtesy of developments like the proliferation of ever-cheaper cosmetic surgery and the routine computer enhancement and modification of visual images. These changes, which build upon a long history of technical procedures for producing and accentuating racial differences on film,[12] undermine more than the integrity of raciological representation. They interact with other processes that have added a conspicuous premium to today's planetary traffic in the imagery of blackness. Layer upon layer of easily commodified exotica have culminated in a racialized glamour and contributed an extra cachet to some degree of nonspecific, somatic difference. The perfect faces on billboards and screens and in magazines are no longer exclusively white, but as they lose that uniformity we are being pressed to consider and appreciate exactly what they have become, where they fit in the old hierarchy that is being erased, and what illicit combination of those familiar racial types combined to produce that particular look, that exotic style, or that transgressive stance. The stimulating pattern of this hyper-visibility supplies the signature of a corporate multiculturalism in which some degree of visible difference from an implicit white norm may be highly prized as a sign of timeliness, vitality, inclusivity, and global reach.

A whole new crop of black models, stylists, photographers, and now, thanks to the good offices of Spike Lee, a black advertising agency, have contributed to this change of climate in the meaning of racialized signs, symbols, and bodies. The stardom of prominent iconic figures like Tyson Beckford, Tyra Banks, and, of course, Lee himself supplements the super-human personalities and conspicuous physical attributes of the latest heroic wave of black athletes who built connections to the emerging planetary market in leisure, fitness, and sports products. In that domain, blackness has proved to be a substantial asset. What Fanon, pondering the iconic stardom of Joe Louis and Jesse Owens, called "the cycle of the biological"[13] was initiated with the mythic figure of The Negro: either unthinkingly lithe and athletic or constitutionally disposed to be lethargic and lazy. That modern cycle may also be thought of as terminating in the space of black metaphysicality. Zygmunt Bauman has argued that the primal scene of postmodern social life in the overdeveloped world is being staged in a distinctive private relation to one's own corporeality, through a disciplinary custodianship that can be specified as the idea of the body "as task."[14] This has unexpected consequences where the ideal of physical prowess, to which blacks were given a special title in exchange for their disassociation from the mind, assumes an enhanced significance.

It is best to be absolutely clear that the ubiquity and prominence currently accorded to exceptionally beautiful and glamorous but nonetheless racialized bodies do nothing to change the everyday forms of racial hierarchy. The historic associations of blackness with infrahumanity, brutality, crime, idleness, excessive threatening fertility, and so on remain undisturbed. But the appearance of a rich visual culture that allows blackness to be beautiful also feeds a fundamental lack of confidence in the power of the body to hold the boundaries of racial difference in place. It creates anxiety about the older racial hierarchies that made that revolutionary idea of black beauty oxymoronic, just as it requires us to forget the political movement that made its acknowledgment imperative. It is as though these images of nonwhite beauty, grace, and style somehow make the matter of "race" secondary, particularly when they are lit, filtered, textured, and toned in ways that challenge the increasingly baffled observer's sense of where racial boundaries might fall. In this anxious setting, new hatreds are created not by the ruthless enforcement of stable racial categories but from a disturbing inability to maintain them. Conforming enthusiastically to wider social patterns, the surface of black bodies must now be tattooed, pierced, and branded if they are to disclose the deepest, most compelling truths of the privatized ontology within. The words "Thug Life" famously inked onto the eloquent torso of the late Tupac Shakur, like the hexa-grams, Oriental characters, cartoon pictures, and other devices sported by a host of stars—Treach, Foxy Brown, and Dennis Rodman, to name only three—conform to this trend and have the additional significance of showing the world how far from the color black these muscled black bodies really are.

It should be clear that the shape-shifting and phenotype-modifying antics that abound in the world of black popular culture did not culminate in the strange case of Michael Jackson.[15] His physical transformation of himself ushered in this new phase of creative possibilities. Playful mut(il)ation did not contradict either his affirmation of an African-American heritage or his well-publicized distaste for Africa itself. Similar patterns enjoy a far more insidious afterlife in the antics of the legions of models, athletes, and performers whose beauty and strength have contributed to the postmodern translation of blackness from a badge of insult into an increasingly powerful but still very limited signifier of prestige. The on-going activities of this group in the worlds of television, music, sports, fashion, entertainment, and, above all, advertising supply further proof that as far as "race" is concerned, what you see is not necessarily what you get.

All these developments stem from and contribute to the same uncertainties over "race." They help to call the self-evident, obvious authority of familiar racialized appearances, of common-sense racial typologies, into question. Bodies may still be the most significant determinants in fixing the social optics of "race,"[16] but black bodies are now being seen—figured and imaged—differently. Thanks to Adobe Photoshop® and similar image-processing technologies, skin tones can be more readily manipulated than the indelibly marked musculatures that sell the sweated and branded products of Tommy Hilfiger, Calvin Klein, Timberland, and Guess in the glossy pages of overground publications like *Vibe* and *The Source* that trade widely in aspects of black culture but are not primarily addressed to any black reading public. This crisis has ensured that racialized bodies represented as objects—objects among other objects—are never going to be enough to guarantee that racial differences remain what they were when everyone on both sides of the line between white and colored knew what "race" was supposed to be.

These timely occurrences should be placed in the context of the leveling forces of placeless development and commercial planetarization. The meaning and status of racial categories are becoming even more uncertain now that substantial linguistic and cultural differences are being flattened out by the pressures of a global market. Where cultural continuity or overlap is recognized between different racialized groups, the smallest cultural nuances provide a major means of differentiation. Once the course of the mainstream is diverted through marginal, underexploited cultural territory, an emphasis on culture can readily displace previous attention to the receding certainties of "race." In these conditions, the relationship between cultural differences and racial particularity gets complex and fraught. Culture, no less than Mrs. Lacks's valuable cells, becomes akin to a form of property attached to the history and traditions of a particular group and regulated by anyone who dares to speak in its name. This can produce some odd conflicts over the assignment of fragments that resist all disciplinary powers. One small illustration springs to mind from the workings of the British political system. Much to the disgust of the Labour Party's black members of Parliament, Bernie Grant and Paul Boateng, who wanted to place it in other political traditions, some of Bob Marley's music was employed as the curtain raiser for a fringe meeting of the European Movement (UK) at the 1996 Conservative Party conference. The person responsible for this grave affront to Marley's inherent socialism was Sir Teddy Taylor, an eccentric, Euro-skeptic but reggae-loving right-winger who explained to the media that he "thought the song ["Three Little Birds"] summed up the Tory policy on Europe."[17]

The emphasis on culture as a form of property to be owned rather than lived characterizes the anxieties of the moment. It compounds rather than resolves the problems arising from associating "race" with embodied or somatic variation. Indeed, we must be alert to circumstances in which the body is reinvested with the power to arbitrate in the assignment of cultures to peoples. The bodies of a culture's practitioners can be called upon to supply the proof of where that culture fits in the inevitable hierarchy of value. The body may also provide the preeminent basis on which that culture is to be ethnically assigned. The body circulates uneasily through contemporary discussions of how one knows the group to which one belongs and of what it takes to be recognized as belonging to such a collectivity. Differences within particular groups proliferate along the obvious axes of division: gender, age, sexuality, region, class, wealth, and health. They challenge the unanimity of racialized collectivities. Exactly what, in cultural terms, it takes to belong, and, more importantly, what it takes to be recognized as belonging, begin to look very uncertain. However dissimilar individual bodies are, the compelling idea of common, racially indicative bodily characteristics offers a welcome short-cut into the favored forms of solidarity and connection, even if they are effectively denied by divergent patterns in life chances and everyday experience.

Even more pernicious symptoms of the crisis of raciology are all around us. They are more pronounced in Europe now that the racial sciences are no longer muted by the memories of their active complicity in the genocide of European Jews. The special moral and political climate that arose in the aftermath of National Socialism and the deaths of millions was a transitory phenomenon. It has receded with the living memory of those frightful events. The Nazi period constitutes the most profound moral and temporal rupture in the history of the twentieth century and the pretensions of its modern civilization. Remembering it has been integral to the politics of "race" for more than fifty years, but a further cultural and ethical transition represented by war-crimes trials, financial reparations, and a host of national apologies is irreversibly under way. It aims to place this raciological catastrophe securely in an irrecoverable past, what Jean Améry called "the cold storage of history," designed more to be cited or passed en route to other happier destinations rather than deliberately summoned up, inhabited, or mourned in an open-ended manner. Official restitution promotes a sense of closure and may be welcomed as a sign that justice has been belatedly done, but it may also undercut the active capacity to remember and set the prophylactic powers of memory to work against future evils. The effects of trauma may be modified if not moderated by the passage of time. They are also vulnerable to the provision of various forms of compensation: substantive and vacuous, formal and informal, material and symbolic.

This is not a straightforward conflict between a culturally sanctioned public obligation to remember and a private desire to forget the unforgettable. The manner, style, and mood of collective remembrance are absolutely critical issues, and the memory of racial slavery in the New World is not the only history of suffering to have been belittled by the power of corrosive or trivializing commemoration. One small example suffices here. The slaves in Steven Spielberg's courtroom drama *Amistad* arrive at their Cuban auction block fresh from the horrors of the Middle Passage. They are buffed: apparently fit and gleaming with robust good health. They enjoy the worked-out and pumped-up musculature that can only be acquired through the happy rigors of a postmodern gym routine. Against the grain of white supremacy's indifference and denial, the Middle Passage has been deliberately and provocatively recovered, but it is rendered in an impossible and deeply contentious manner that offers only the consolation of tears in place of more challenging and imaginative connections. It may be that those coveted abdominal muscles are now deemed to be an essential precondition for identifying with the superhuman figures of heroes like Spielberg's Joseph Cinqué.[18]

There has never been spontaneous consensus over how to commemorate and memorialize histories of suffering. Significant discrepancies have been apparent, for example, between the ways that African Americans and Ghanaians have approached the conservation of fortified sites of slave-trading activity that have recently become places of pilgrimage and cultural tourism for some of the more affluent daughters and sons of the Atlantic diaspora.[19] In the very same moment that these sharp divisions have appeared inside what we were once urged to see as a single "racial" group, a torrent of images of casual death and conflict have been transmitted instantaneously from all over the African continent. For some, these dismal reports have ushered in nostalgia for the orderly world of colonial empires and threatened to make savagery something that occurs exclusively beyond the fortified borders of the new Europe. Through genocide in Rwanda and slaughter in Congo and Burundi, civil strife in Liberia, Sierra Leone, and Nigeria, corruption and violence in Kenya, Uganda, Sudan, and Mozambique, government by terror has been associated once again with infrahuman blackness reconstituted in the "half-devil, half-child" patterns favored by older colonial mentalities.[20] Attempts to emphasize that many of the architects of mass killing in Rwanda and Bosnia were educated to the highest standards of the Western humanities have not achieved the same prominence.[21] Placing some of them on trial for war crimes or for the genocidal activities involved in their crimes against humanity has raised more difficult questions about the specificity and uniqueness of earlier mass killing and the central place of the "race-thinking" that has recurrently been featured as a means to justify more recent episodes.[22]

Interestingly, the important work of South Africa's Truth Commission has mobilized a version of the history of Apartheid that accentuates its political affinities as well as its concrete historical connections to the criminal governance of the Nazi period.[23] With these connections underlined, Apartheid's elaborate theories of cultural and tribal difference can be swiftly reduced to the bare bones of raciology that originally warranted them and dispatched Broederbond commissioners back to Europe during the 1930s in pursuit of an appropriate ethnic content for the ideal white culture that was being actively invented.[24]

An even blend of those deceptively bland terms "ethnicity" and "culture" has emerged as the main element in the discourse of differentiation that is struggling to supersede crude appeals to "race" by asserting the power of tribal affiliations. These timely notions circulate in more specialized language, but any sense that they bring greater precision into the task of social division is misleading. The culturalist approach still runs the risk of naturalizing and normalizing hatred and brutality by presenting them as inevitable consequences of illegitimate attempts to mix and amalgamate primordially incompatible groups that wiser, worldlier, more authentically colonial government would have kept apart or left to meet only in the marketplace. The unfolding of recent postcolonial history has sent out a less nostalgic and more challenging message: if the status of "race" can be transformed even in South Africa, the one place on earth where its salience for politics and government could not be denied, the one location where state-sponsored racial identities were openly and positively conducted into the core of a modern civic culture and social relations, then surely it could be changed anywhere. If it is as mutable as that, what then does racial identity comprise?

The widespread appearance of forms of ultranationalist race-thinking that are not easily classified as either biologistic or cultural but which seem to bear the significant imprint of past fascism is another dimension to the crisis of raciology. In Britain, today's patriotic neo-fascists are still undone by the memory of the 39–45 war, torn between their contradictory appeals to the figures of Churchill on one side and Hitler on the other. The French Front Nationale has included a full complement of Holocaust deniers and apologists for colonial brutality, but it also managed to stand black and Jewish candidates in the elections of May 1997. The most prominent of these, Hugette Fatna, the organization's secretary for France's overseas territories, proudly declaimed, "I'm black and proud of it . . . I'm a free woman, and I accept my difference,"[25] as though democratic denunciations of her then leader, Jean-Marie Le Pen, as a racist, required her to deny it. In other places, the loquacious veterans of Apartheid's death squads have protested at length that, speaking personally, they are not themselves inclined to antiblack racism. The Italian-born Belgian broadcaster Georges Ruggiu faces a trial for crimes against humanity as a result of being arrested and charged with complicity in the 1994 genocide of Tutsis. His inflammatory programs on Radio Mille Collines famously compared the Hutu assault to the French Revolution. Thus, in their genocidal confrontation with the African proxies of "Anglo-Saxon" geo-political ambition, the francophone killers seemed to have imagined themselves as an extension of the French nation to which they were bound. Gérard Prunier has described this as "the Fashoda syndrome."[26]

The advocates of these unsettling varieties of racialized politics have been forced to become fluent in the technical, anthropological language of ethnicity and culture. Their opinions are also likely to be leavened with mechanistic determinism and neurotic hyper-patriotism. Nonetheless, these obvious ties to past raciologies should not be allowed to obscure the fact that the language produced by this crisis of race-thinking differs from its predecessors. When facing these new phenomena, what we used to be able to call an antiracist opposition must involve more than merely establishing the secret lineage that associates these contemporary groups with their radically evil, authentically fascist antecedents. What Primo Levi, with characteristic precision, referred to as "the silent Nazi diaspora" continues to go about its strategic work, but soon, mobilizing the fragmentary memories of Hitlerism will not be enough to embarrass its activists, never mind defeat them. Nazism and other related versions of populist ultranationalism have found new adherents and, more worryingly, new bands of imitators in all sorts of unlikely locations. The glamour of that particular political style and its utopian charge will be explored later on. They, too, have increased as emotional, psychological, and historical distance from the events of the Third Reich has grown.

All these factors contribute to a situation in which there are diminishing moral or political inhibitions against once more invoking "race" as a primary means of sorting people into hierarchies and erecting unbridgeable chasms around their discrete collective identities. Why, then, describe this situation as a crisis of raciology rather than its crowning glory? It is a crisis because the idea of "race" has lost much of its common-sense credibility, because the elaborate cultural and ideological work that goes into producing and reproducing it is more visible than ever before, because it has been stripped of its moral and intellectual integrity, and because there is a chance to prevent its rehabilitation. Prompted by the impact of genomics, "race," as it has been defined in the past, has also become vulnerable to the claims of a much more elaborate, less deterministic biology. It is therefore all the more disappointing that much influential recent work in this area loses its nerve in the final furlong and opts to remain ambiguous about whether the idea of "race" can survive a critical revision of the relationship between human beings and their constantly shifting social nature.[27]

Whether it is articulated in the more specialized tongues of biological science and pseudo-science or in a vernacular idiom of culture and common sense, the term "race" conjures up a peculiarly resistant variety of natural difference. It stands outside of, and in opposition to, most attempts to render it secondary to the overwhelming sameness that overdetermines social relationships between people and continually betrays the tragic predicaments of their common species life. The undervalued power of this crushingly obvious, almost banal human sameness, so close and basically invariant that it regularly passes unremarked upon, also confirms that the crisis of raciological reasoning presents an important opportunity where it points toward the possibility of leaving "race" behind, of setting aside its disabling use as we move out of the time in which it could have been expected to make sense.

There is a danger that this argument will be read as nothing more than a rather old-fashioned plea for disabusing ourselves of the destructive delusions of racism. Injunctions of that kind have been a recurrent feature of some liberal, religious, socialist, and feminist pronouncements on these matters since the term "race" was first coined. While I value that political pedigree, I want to try to be clear about exactly where this line of thought departs from its noble precursors in those traditions that have contributed so extensively to the ideas and the practice of antiracism. All the earlier arguments conform to the same basic architecture. They posit the particular, singular, and specific against the general, universal, and transcendent that they value more highly. In contrast, the approach I favor attempts to break up these unhappy couples. It has less to say about the unanswerable force of claims to singularity and particularity that have fueled ethnic absolutism.

Instead, it directs attention toward the other side of these simultaneous equations. We should, it suggests, become concerned once again with the notion of the human into which reluctant specificity has been repeatedly invited to dissolve itself. My position recognizes that these invitations would be more plausible and attractive if we could only confront rather than evade the comprehensive manner in which previous incarnations of exclusionary humanity were tailored to racializing codes and qualified by the operation of colonial and imperial power. In other words, the alternative version of humanism that is cautiously being proposed here simply cannot be reached via any retreat into the lofty habits and unamended assumptions of liberal thinking, particularly about juridical rights and sovereign entitlements. This is because these very resources have been tainted by a history in which they were not able to withstand the biopolitical power of the race-thinking that compromised their boldest and best ambitions. Their resulting failures, silences, lapses, and evasions must become central. They can be reinterpreted as symptoms of a struggle over the boundaries of humanity and then contribute to a counterhistory that leads up to the rough-hewn doorway through which any alternative conception of the human must pass. This can only be attained after a wholesale reckoning with the idea of "race" and with the history of raciology's destructive claims upon the very best of modernity's hopes and resources. A restoration of political culture is the evasive goal of these operations.

Another curious and perplexing effect of the crisis of raciology is a situation in which some widely divergent political interests have been able to collaborate in retaining the concept and reinvesting it with explanatory power. Strange alliances and opportunistic connections have been constructed in the name of ethnic purity and the related demand that unbridgeable cultural differences be identified and respected. This desire to cling on to "race" and go on stubbornly and unimaginatively seeing the world on the distinctive scales that it has specified makes for odd political associations as well as for less formal connections between raciological thinkers of various hues. In doing battle against all of them and their common desire to retain and reinflate the concept so that it becomes, once again, a central political and historical reference point, we must be very clear about the dimensions of this moment and the significant discrepancies that have arisen between different local settings. We should recognize that "race" has been given a variety of accents. Problems of compatibility and translation have been multiplied by the globalization of culture in which local codes may have to fight against the encroachments of corporate multiculturalism if they are to retain their historic authority and explanatory power. For example, America's distinctive patterns of color consciousness may not be anything other than a fetter on the development of the planetary market in health, fitness, leisure, and sports products mentioned above. Certain common features, like the odd prestige attached to the metaphysical value of whiteness, do recur and continue to travel well, but they too will be vulnerable to the long-term effects of this crisis. Some distinctive local patterns undoubtedly persist, but their anachronistic longevity compounds the problem. Where communication becomes instantaneous, the crisis of racial meaning is further enhanced by the way attachments to the idea of "race" develop unevenly and remain primarily associated with the context of overdevelopment.

We cannot remind ourselves too often that the concept of "race" as it is used in common-sense, everyday language to signify connectedness and common characteristics in relation to type and descent is a relatively recent and absolutely modern invention. Though it would be foolish to suggest that evil, brutality, and terror commence with the arrival of scientific racism toward the end of the eighteenth century, it would also be wrong to overlook the significance of that moment as a break point in the development of modern thinking about humanity and its nature. Even prescientific versions of the logic of "race" multiplied the opportunities for their adherents to do evil freely and justify it to themselves and to others. That problem was compounded once confused and unsystematic race-thinking aspired to become something more coherent, rational, and authoritative. This threshold is important because it identifies the junction point of "race" with both rationality and nationality. It is the beginning of a period in which deference toward science, scientists, and scientific discourses around "race" began to create new possibilities and orchestrate new varieties of knowledge and power centered on the body, what Foucault identifies as "political anatomy."

The story of how this change was influenced by imperatives of colonial trade and government and shaped by growing imperial consciousness, how it was endorsed and then challenged by the developing science of anthropology, discredited by the catastrophic consequences of racial science, silenced by the aftereffects of Nazi genocide only to gain another commanding voice in the wake of Watson and Crick, is a familiar one. But the most recent phases in this process—which we have already seen is not simply and straightforwardly reducible to the resurgence of biological explanations—have not been understood adequately.

BEYOND THE NEW RACISM

Some years ago, a loose group of scholars in which the English philosopher Martin Barker was especially influential began, in recognition of changed patterns in the way the discourse of racial difference was employed in politics, to speak about the emergence of what they called a New Racism. This racism was defined by its strong culturalist and nationalist inclinations. Whereas in the past raciology had been arrogant in its imperial certainty that biology was both destiny and hierarchy, this persuasive new variant was openly uncomfortable with the idea that "race" could be biologically based. Consciousness of "race" was seen instead as closely linked to the idea of nationality. Authentic, historic nations had discrete cultural fillings. Their precious homogeneity endowed them with great strength and prestige. Where large "indigestible" chunks of alien settlement had taken place, all manner of dangers were apparent. Conflict was visible, above all, along cultural lines. Of course, these regrettably transplanted aliens were not identified as inferior, less worthy, or less admirable than their "hosts." They may not have been infrahuman, but they were certainly out of place. The social, economic, and political problems that had followed their mistaken importation could only be solved by restoring the symmetry and stability that flowed from putting them back where they belonged. Nature, history, and geopolitics dictated that people should cleave to their own kind and be most comfortable in the environments that matched their distinctive cultural and therefore national modes of being in the world. Mythic versions of cultural ecology were invented to rationalize the lives of these discrete national and racial identities. The Germans became a people in their forests, whereas the British were a nation whose seafaring activity shaped their essential inner character. In all cases, fragments of self-evident truth nourished the fantasies of blood and belonging,[28] which in turn demanded an elaborate geopolitical cartography of nationality.[29]

The culturalist arguments of the New Racism enjoy a lingering residual appeal. Similar patterns appeared in a number of different settings.
They were evident in Britain, where cultural difference rather than biological hierarchy emerged as the core substance of the nation's
postcolonial racial problems. They were audible in the United States,
where five great raciocultural agglomerations (Asians, blacks, Hispanics,
whites, and Native Americans) appeared and took on many of the fateful
characteristics associated with eighteenth-century racial groups; and they
were evident also in parts of Europe where conflicts between migrant
workers and their resentful hosts were re-articulated as the grander cultural and religious opposition between Christian universalism and resurgent Islamic fundamentalism.

The historic role of these culturalist notions in the consolidation and
development of Apartheid in South Africa ought to be obvious. The wider
shifts from biology to culture, from species to ethnos, from rigid, predictable hierarchy toward the different perils represented by a cultural alterity
that was as fascinating as it was contaminating were all to some extent
pre-figured in the constitution of the Apartheid system. Whether or not
these forms of power and authority were broadly representative of colonial
governance in general cannot be settled here.[30] The pernicious fiction of
separate but equal identities based in discrete homelands was an important
marker of a change in which the idea of contending national and ethnic
traditions was employed to legitimate and rationalize the move from natural to cultural hierarchies. This shift was not, of course, an absolute
change. Nature and culture may have functioned as neatly exclusive poles
in the models of early modern thought, but as the organic overtones of the
word "culture" reveal, the boundaries between them have always been porous. The New Racism endorsed the annexation of the idea of natural difference by the claims of mutually exclusive, national cultures that now
stood opposed to one another. In the political geometry of nation-states,
culture was offset not by nature but by other cultures. What seems new
about the New Racism, twenty years after this insight was first employed,
is not so much the tell-tale emphasis on culture that was its intellectual
hallmark but the way its ideologues refined the old opposites—nature and
culture, biology and history—into a new synthesis: a bioculturalism that,
as Barker had pointed out, drew its deterministic energy from the intellectual resources supplied by sociobiology.[31]

When this point is made, it is always necessary to emphasize that there are many subtle shadings between the biological and the cultural and that the culturalist versions of racial discourse—though superficially more benign than the cruder force of biological "race" theory—are no less vicious or brutal for those on the receiving end of the cruelties and terrors they promote. With these important qualifications in mind, it is better to say that the starting point of this book is that the era of that New Racism is emphatically over. This should not be interpreted as a suggestion that we are therefore traveling back toward some older, more familiar version of biological determinism. To be sure, a genomic reworking of biology has reemerged to supply the dominant pessimistic motifs in talk about "race," but the mere presence of what is better understood as a post-biological perspective does not confirm my diagnosis. There are several new versions of determinism abroad. They place and use the human body in a number of contrasting ways. The impatient manner in which other, less mechanistic, varieties of social and historical explanation are silenced by genomics betrays the transfiguration of bio-logic into something unanticipated: a nonwholistic micromechanism in which organisms are to be engineered, tooled, and spliced and human life takes on qualities associated with the dead, menacing, but compliant world of machines.

This change of perspective demonstrates that today's raciology is no longer confined to the cognitive and perceptual habits of political anatomy. It has been drawn by technological and conceptual changes toward ever-smaller scales. Thus what appears to be the *re*birth of biologism is not in fact the resurgence of older colonial and imperial codes that accentuated hierarchy rather than simple difference but part of a bigger contemporary transformation in the ways that people conceptualize the relationship between nature, culture, and society, between their freedom and their human agency. The status of "race" is inevitably transformed by this. Yes, we are once again in a period in which social and cultural differences are being coded according to the rules of a biological discourse, but it cannot be emphasized enough that this latest raciological regime differs from its predecessors. We must not approach it as though it represents a retreat behind the culturalist ambitions of the old, that is, the New, Racism. It is a distinctive phenomenon that needs to be apprehended and countered as such. "Race" can no longer be ossified, and, as may have been anticipated, it is the gene-centeredness of this discourse that defines its deterministic approach to human action in general and the formation of racial groups in particular.[32]

The history of scientific writing about "races" has involved a long and meandering sequence of discourses on physical morphology. Bones, skulls, hair, lips, noses, eyes, feet, genitals, and other somatic markers of "race" have a special place in the discursive regimes that produced the truth of "race" and repeatedly discovered it lodged in and on the body. The historian of science Londa Schiebinger has demonstrated how the study of bodily components and zones first helped to focus the racializing gaze, to invest it with real scientific authority and to bring "race" into being in strongly gendered forms while simultaneously producing an understanding of gender and sex that saturated the interconnected discourses of "race," nation, and species.[33] The textbooks of classical, eighteenth-century raciology were studded with images. Their argumentation proceeded swiftly from illustration to illustration. The enduring power of the best-known visual material—depictions of Caucasian and Nordic heads or of the various skulls to be measured, drawn, and classified—was more than an iconic counterpoint to the inscription of respectable racial science. It raises the interesting possibility that cognition of "race" was never an exclusively linguistic process and involved from its inception a distinctive visual and optical imaginary. The sheer plenitude of racialized images and icons communicates something profound about the forms of difference these discourses summoned into being. Racial differences were discovered and confirmed in fragmentary selections of physical characteristics. Because the combination of phenotypes chosen to identify a "race" so actively generated the chosen racial categories, antiraciological thinking was soon alerted to the way that particular criteria varied within the selected groups as well as between them. My concern here is not with the well-known history of those necessarily doomed attempts to produce coherent racial categories by picking representative combinations of certain phenotypes: lips, jaws, hair texture, eye-color, and so on. It is far more interesting that this race-producing activity required a synthesis of logos with icon, of formal scientific rationality with something else—something visual and aesthetic in both senses of that slippery word. Together they resulted in a specific relationship to, and mode of observing, the body.[34] They fixed upon a certain variety of perception that favored particular representational scales and could only follow on from the isolation, quantification, and homogenization of vision. Foucault is the most famous explorer of the epistemological consequences that accompanied the institutionalization of this anthropological gaze and its "autonomization of sight."[35]

Whether the distinguishing marks, organs, and features were discovered on the external surface of the body or were thought to dwell somewhere inside it where the hidden properties of racially differentiated blood, bone, and sinew were imagined to regulate social and cultural manifestations, the modern idea of race favored a specific representational scale and operated within the strictest of perceptual limits. We can call that distinctive ratio the scale of comparative anatomy. The idea of "race" leaked quite rapidly from the lofty confines where that scale was first codified and calibrated, but it always worked best in conjunction with those ways of looking, enumerating, dissecting, and evaluating. Abstract and metaphysical, "race" defined and consolidated its accidental typologies. In moving toward the empirical and the concrete, it (re-)produced a set of methods, regulated a certain aesthetics,[36] and quietly delimited the field in which color-coded ethics would operate. The most compelling truths of political anatomy were produced "performatively" from the hat that raciological science provided, like so many startled rabbits in front of an eager, noisy crowd. The idea of "race" enjoyed its greatest power to link metaphysics and scientific technology under those conditions. Reinforced by belief in separate and opposing national cultures, it would later inspire the colonial anthropologies that succeeded the earliest versions of scientific raciology. Our situation is demonstrably different. The call of racial being has been weakened by another technological and communicative revolution, by the idea that the body is nothing more than an incidental moment in the transmission of code and information, by its openness to the new imaging technologies, and by the loss of mortality as a horizon against which life is to be lived.

Blackness can now signify vital prestige rather than abjection in a global info-tainment telesector where the living residues of slave societies and the parochial traces of American racial conflict must yield to different imperatives deriving from the planetarization of profit and the cultivation of new markets far from the memory of bondage. In 1815 Cuvier, who would eventually dissect her, commissioned melancholy portraits of Saartjie Baartman depicted from several angles in a peculiarly empty landscape by Léon de Wailly. Almost two centuries later, a different encounter with the limits of black humanity has been provided by the dubious pleasures of the animated movie *Space Jam*. Baartman's earth-bound infrahumanity has been replaced by the larger-than-life presence of a godly Michael Jordan, who collaborates in a bright extraterrestrial pas de deux with Bugs Bunny—the reductio ad absurdum of African trickster tale telling. When Jordan takes wing to persuade us that a black man can fly, can we agree that the eighteenth-century perceptual regimes that first gave us "race" have been superseded along with many of their epistemological and metaphysical pretensions? Now that the microscopic has yielded so comprehensively to the molecular, I want to ask whether these outmoded representational and observational conventions have been left behind. This would mean that much of the contemporary discourse animating "races" and producing racialized consciousness is an anachronistic, even a vestigial, phenomenon. Screens rather than lenses now mediate the pursuit of bodily truths. This is a potent sign that "race" should be approached as an afterimage—a lingering effect of looking too casually into the damaging glare emanating from colonial conflicts at home and abroad.

Disregarding for a moment the obvious dangers represented by contemporary eugenic ambitions, which neither employ the word "eugenic" nor coincide with divisions derived from the old racial categories, I want to argue that the perceptual and observational habits that have been associated with the consolidation of today's nano-science might also facilitate the development of an emphatically postracial humanism. Genomics may send out the signal to reify "race" as code and information, but there is a sense in which it also points unintentionally toward "race's" overcoming. This cannot be a single, bold act of creativity, a triumphant, once-and-for-all negation. It must be more like a gradual withering away arising from growing irrelevancy. At the smaller than microscopic scales that open up the body for scrutiny today, "race" becomes less meaningful, compelling, or salient to the basic tasks of healing and protecting ourselves. We have a chance, then, to recognize the anachronistic condition of the idea of "race" as a basis upon which human beings are distinguished and ranked. We can draw an extra measure of courage from the fact that proponents of the idea of "races" are further than ever from being able to answer the basic question that has confounded them since the dawn of raciology: if "race" is a useful way of classifying people, then how many "races" are there? It is rare nowadays to encounter talk of a "Mongoloid race."

We have already had to appreciate that it may coincide with the political desires of some people inside the imagined community of a racialized group to proceed on the basis of given or automatic unanimity and to approach their own "race" as a single, undifferentiated magnitude bound together not by the superficialities of history or language, religion or conquest, but by some underlying, essential similarity coded in their bodies. Here, of course, science and the everyday world of racial, I would prefer to say *racializing,* talk, part company and mysticism and occultism take over. The political language used to describe and justify these models of belonging has also been partially updated. Notions of the essential unity of particular "races" have similarly moved on with the times, sometimes acquiring a New Age gloss and a matching therapeutic language. We will see that these "essentialist" and "primordialist" outlooks have become all the more vicious by virtue of the wounds they have acquired as the idea of a fundamental, shared identity has been challenged by the appearance of sharp intraracial conflicts.

In the overdeveloped world, de-industrialization and brutal economic differentiation have complicated this situation still further. Everywhere, struggles arising from family, gender, and sexuality have also been clearly visible within the same groups that used to be identified as unitary racial communities. The impact of these factors of division has been intensified by shifts that have occurred in the relationship between "race" and the principle of nationality. The latter has lost some of its appeal and much of its complexity because it has been assimilated too swiftly either to the idea of closed, exclusive racialized cultures or to the biological determinisms that reduce behavior, sociality, and common interests to information inscribed in cells or arrangements of molecules.

As far as black political cultures are concerned, in the period after emancipation, essentialist approaches to building solidarity and synchronized communal mobilization have often relied upon the effects of racial hierarchy to supply the binding agent that could in turn precipitate national consciousness. Routine experiences of oppression, repression, and abuse—however widespread—could not be transferred into the political arena from which blacks were barred. Instead they became the basis for dissident cultures and an alternative public world. Togetherness produced under these conditions was inherently unreliable. Its instability added to the attractiveness of the authoritarian solutions that offered shortcuts to solidarity, especially where everyday consciousness of racial difference fell short of the models of nationhood that had been borrowed wholesale from the Europe-centered history of the dominant group. Where the political chemistry of nation, race, and culture came together to produce these alarming results, the rebirth of fascist thinking and the reappearance of stern, uniformed political movements was not far away, as we shall see. These developments have not always been marked by the convenient emblems shamelessly borne by fascisms in the past.

ECOLOGY, ETHICS, AND RACIAL OBSERVANCE

The word "ecology" was coined in 1866 by Ernst Haeckl, the German disciple of Darwin and Lamarck who would become known for his zoology and his ultranationalist critique of the dysgenic effects of Western civilization.[37] The elaboration of the term in the development of racial science before and during Nazi rule should be acknowledged before it can be engaged here. It can be connected in profound ways to the notions of Lebensraum (living-space) that figured in but were not created by the racist population policies and agricultural and scientific planning of the Nazi period.[38] What can only be called "ecological sensibilities" have an elaborate role in the geo-organic, biopolitical, and governmental theories of the German geographers Friedrich Ratzel and Karl Haushofer and the early-twentieth-century Swedish geopolitician Rudolf Kjellén.[39] These writers supplied important conceptual resources to Nazi racial science, helping it to conceptualize the state as an organism and to specify the necessary connections between the nation and its dwelling area. We invest differently in this approach as a result of having to face its historic associations with that raciology, as well as Hitlerism and sundry other attempts to deduce the ideal form of government from organic analogies.[40] Today, building self-consciously on attempts by the botanist Sir Alfred George Tansley to theorize the ecosystem via patterned interaction between organisms and habitats in the widest possible sense, an even more complex sense of interactivity governing relations between human beings and their environments has been prompted by the more acute critics of genetic determinism. A refined ecological perspective complements those critiques with a complex, chaotic, and resolutely nonreductive organicism. This confounds mechanistic notions of cause and effect and objects loudly to the reduction of individual human particularity to the "maps" of its DNA sequences. Richard Lewontin spoke from the critical perspective he describes as a "reverse Lamarckian position" when he emphasized that

> it takes more than DNA to make a living organism . . . the organism does not compute itself from its DNA. A Living organism at any moment in its life is the unique consequence of a developmental history that results from interaction of and determination by internal and external forces. The external forces, what we usually think of as "environment," are themselves partly a consequence of the activities of the organism itself as it produces and consumes the conditions of its own existence. Organisms do not find the world in which they develop. They make it. Reciprocally, the internal forces are not autonomous, but act in response to the external. Part of the internal chemical machinery of a cell is only manufactured when external conditions demand it . . . Nor is "internal" identical with "genetic."[41]

A similar sensitivity to the complexity of these interactive processes can be useful when we move from focusing on the immediate environments in which individual organisms exist and turn instead to the ecological conditions in which relations between agents/actors are staged. This attention to intersubjectivity can be supplemented by yet another idea. It is drawn from Frantz Fanon's phenomenological study of "epidermalized" embodiment and directly inspired by his bitter Hegelian discovery that the curse of racial domination is the condition, not of being black, but of being black in relation to the white.[42] The ontological complexities of the black predicament that Fanon uncovered in the workings of colonial power are no longer, if they ever were, exclusively confined to those contested locations. Indeed, the political and cultural changes I have described as part of the crisis of "race" have carried into the core of contemporary concerns the same anxieties about the basis upon which races exist. I am suggesting that the only appropriate response to this uncertainty is to demand liberation not from white supremacy alone, however urgently that is required, but from all racializing and raciological thought, from racialized seeing, racialized thinking, and racialized thinking about thinking. There is one other overriding issue associated with these utopian aspirations. However reluctant we may feel to take the step of renouncing "race" as part of an attempt to bring political culture back to life, this course must be considered because it seems to represent the only *ethical* response to the conspicuous wrongs that raciologies continue to solicit and sanction.

Making this ethical point has an additional significance. Students of "race" have not always been sufficiently alive to the ethical dimensions of our own practice, particularly when analyzing the recurrent association between raciology and evil. This overdue reform of our own thinking has become imperative as the memory of the Nazi genocide has ceased to form the constellation under which we work. The deliberate wholesale renunciation of "race" proposed here even views the appearance of an alternative, metaphysical humanism premised on face-to-face relations between different actors—beings of equal worth—as preferable to the problems of inhumanity that raciology creates. If this metaphysics ultimately acquires a religious cast, as in the very different cases presented by the more philosophical writings of Martin Luther King, Jr., on one hand and the work of the philosopher Emmanuel Levinas on the other, it can be rescued from the worst excesses of idealism if only it is recognized as incorporating a provocative attempt to reactivate political sensibilities so that they flow outside the patterns set for them in a world of fortified nation-states and antagonistic ethnic groups. The spaces in which "races" come to life are a field from which political interaction has been banished. It is usually replaced by enthusiasm for the cheapest pseudo-solidarities: forms of connection that are imagined to arise effortlessly from shared phenotypes, cultures, and bio-nationalities. This is a period in which the easy invocation of "race" supplies regular confirmation of the retreat of political activity, defined here not as statecraft but as the exercise of power in a reasoned public culture capable of simultaneously promoting both self and social development. If we choose the testing route I favor, toward the evasive goal of multicultural democracy, the rehabilitation of politics requires bold and expansive gestures. The demand for liberation from "race" becomes still more eloquent in the special context provided by this ethical and political project. It becomes an essential prerequisite if we are to give effective answers to the pathological problems represented by genomic racism, the glamour of sameness, and the eugenic projects currently nurtured by their confluence.

OBSERVING "RACE"

Once the dimensions of the crisis of raciology have been fully appreciated, we can turn to the other principal aim of this opening chapter: to question and explore some of the tensions arising from a critical consideration of how "race" is beheld. This is intended to contribute to an account of how the signs and symbols of racial difference have become apparent. As you may anticipate, the "postracial" stance I have been trying to develop does not admit the integrity of any avowedly natural perceptual schemes. It does not concede the possibility that "race" could be seen spontaneously, unmediated by technical and social processes. There will be individual variation, but that is not "race." There is no raw, untrained perception dwelling in the body. The human sensorium has had to be educated to the appreciation of racial differences. When it comes to the visualization of discrete racial groups, a great deal of fine-tuning has been required.

This stage of the argument is underpinned by a desire to link the historical and critical study of raciologies and "racial" metaphysics to the new histories of visuality and perception that are being produced. It seeks to connect them with some timely critiques of absolute or integral ethnic identity and the genealogies of subjectivity with which it has been associated. Above all, I want to link the critical study of "race" with an equally critical understanding of the technoscientific means that have fostered and mediated particular relations with our racialized selves in the modern past. The founding *absurdity* of "race" as a principle of power, differentiation, and classification must now remain persistently, obstinately in view. That initial move is, as I don't need to remind you, patently out of fashion. "Race"-entrenching pragmatism has been allied with the simplistic versions of racial phenomenology mistakenly attributed to Fanon by critics who seek a leak-proof ontology in his work. These developments have been complemented by the appeal of articulate but brittle traveling nationalisms firmly rooted in African-American circumstances, as well as by cynicism and opportunism. These interlinked tendencies agree that the cold, corporeal fact of "race" cannot and should not be theorized out of sight in the very ways that I propose.

You are still feeling doubtful. Perhaps it will help to appreciate that aspects of "race" as it has been understood in the past are already being conjured away by new technologies of self and of species being, and that the use of those technologies, particularly in the medical field, has already precipitated significant political consequences. The old, modern representational economies that reproduced "race" subdermally and epidermally are today being transformed on one side by the scientific and technological changes that have followed the revolution in molecular biology, and on the other by a similarly profound transformation in the ways that bodies are imaged. Both have extensive ontological implications. Bodies are now routinely opened up to new forms of scrutiny by multidimensional medical imaging that uses ultrasound and electromagnetic radiation as well as light, natural and artificial. Have you, has your body, your child's body, ever been scanned? Do you recognize its changing optic density? If so, perhaps you could consider that development another compelling sign that we have begun to let the old visual signatures of "race" go. Having waved them farewell, we may do a better job of countering the injustices that they brought into being if we make a more consistent effort to de-nature and de-ontologize "race," thereby disaggregating raciologies.

This is not an easy option. It necessitates the reconstitution of antiracist hopes. In future, they will have to operate easily across the boundaries erected between text and discourse, spectacle and performance. They will have to move outside the angles of vision, the truth-seeking strategies, the moral and political choices that still offer too many hostages to the normative claims of raciology. This line of attack on racial observance demands frank reflection on the interest in reifying "race" that has repeatedly arisen in academic analysis—something that was not possible when the link between antiracist politics and interventionist scholarship was stronger and closer than it is today. Pursuing this path leads back to the hard work involved in identifying and exploring the political technologies that govern our relation to our selves, our humanity, and our species. As suggested, these tasks take us beyond the discourses and the semiotics of "race" into a confrontation with theories and histories of spectatorship and observation, visual apparatuses and optics. They ask us to rethink the development of a racial imaginary in ways that are more distant from the reasoned authority of logos and closely attuned to the different power of visual and visualizing technologies. The politics of "race" has relied upon and coordinated both.

I have already alluded to the profound transformations in the ways the body is understood, experienced, and observed that followed the emer-

gence of molecular biology. The use of computers as modeling and imaging technologies prosthetically extending sight onto nano-scales can be
linked to the impact of digital processing and other allied approaches to
the body that allow it to be seen and understood in new ways, principally
as code and information. We must be especially attentive to the ways in
which the body is being imaged in approaches to health and disease, which
have a paramount importance in the workings of contemporary culture.
These new ways of seeing, understanding, and relating to ourselves point
once again to the possibility that the time of "race" may be coming to a
close even while racisms appear to proliferate.

Michel Foucault's early work explored significant historical precedents for the contemporary emergence of new fields of visibility that operate on nano-scales. However, he is both an inspiring and a frustrating
guide to recent changes in seeing, observing, and knowing the racialized
body. For all his great historical insight into the problem of the individual
observer as a locus of knowledge, the formation of epistemologies with
novel investments in observation, and the shift "signaled by the passage
from geometrical optics of the seventeenth and eighteenth centuries to
the physiological optics, which dominates both scientific and philosophical discussion of vision in the nineteenth century,"[43] he seems to have
been insufficiently attuned to the significance of protracted struggles over
the raciological disunity of mankind that attended the emergence of
biopolitics. The human and the infrahuman emerged together, and "race"
was the line between them.

Regrettably, Foucault was not really interested in the meaning of racial
differences or in the tests that they provided for eighteenth-century "nom-
ination of the visible" and other related attempts to "bring language as
close as possible to the observing gaze."[44] Although his analysis, which
witnesses the birth of biopower, seems ripe for a decisive confrontation
with the idea of "race," this never happens. To put it simply, he identified
the figure of man as both the pivot and the product of the new relationship
between words and things but then moved too swiftly toward a sense of
modern humanity as unified by its immiserating passage from sanguinity
to sexuality. He failed, for example, to consider how the idea that *Asiaticus
luridus, Americanus rubescus,* and *Afer niger* were less than human might
have affected this transformation and its epistemic correlates. Perhaps he
was not haunted, as I believe we should still be, by the famous image of an

orangutan carrying off a Negro girl that provides the frontispiece for Linnaeus' *Genuine and Universal System of Natural History*. The central, inescapable problem in that famous picture is the suggested kinship between these sub- and infrahuman species rather than the fact that their conflictual interrelation is gendered and figured through the trope of rape. The picture's historic setting and the interpretative puzzle it presents point to the unresolved issue of how "race" interrelates with sex, gender, and sexuality—something that is further than ever from being settled and that defines a new and urgent need for future work. The picture's relation to that foundational text of raciology raises other uncomfortable matters: the characteristics of the new, post-Vesalian semiotics of the body, and the relationship between text and image in the performative constitution of "races" that was not one in which words were simply or consistently able to dominate the images—icons—that went far beyond any merely illustrative function.

The extensive debate as to whether Negroes should be accorded membership in the family of mankind (a group whose particularity was inaugurated, proved, produced, and celebrated by the transformed relationship between words and things that crystallized at the end of the eighteenth century) might have been more central to the formation and reproduction of modern scientific thinking than Foucault appreciated. I raise this, neither to pillory him nor to reopen discussion of how that process has been reconstructed by historians of science, but rather because his study of that fateful change in the workings of science and the production of truth is an important resource in our own situation, where comparable changes in the technologies of the body can be observed.

Nobody fills old skulls with lead shot these days. It bears repetition that the truths of racial difference are being sought by other means and produced by technologies that operate on other, less immediate scales. The semiosis of anthropology has been transformed several times since the high point of skull-filling activity. Here, we must acknowledge the impact of vernacular observational codes that have a tangential or ambivalent relationship to racial science proper. There are "one drop of blood" rules with their unsentimental disjunctions between insides and outsides, "pencil tests" and other shadowy technologies of alterity that purport to discover symptoms of degeneration in the special tones of pink and red to be found at the base of fingernails. However, with Kuhn's history and philosophy of science in our book bags, we comprehend the contingencies of truth-seeking, the pressures of institutional location, the active power of language to shape inquiry, and the provisional status of all scientific enterprises.

Let me propose that the dismal orders of power and differentiation —defined by their persistent intention to make the mute body disclose and conform to the truths of its racial identity—can be roughly periodized. The critical notion of "epidermalization" bequeathed to our time by Frantz Fanon is valuable here. It was born from a philosopher-psychologist's phenomenological ambitions and their distinctive way of seeing as well as of understanding the importance of sight. It refers to a historically specific system for making bodies meaningful by endowing them with qualities of "color." It suggests a perceptual regime in which the racialized body is bounded and protected by its enclosing skin. The observer's gaze does not penetrate that membrane but rests upon it and, in doing so, receives the truths of racial difference from the other body. Whatever phrenology and physiognomy may have meant to Hegel, an enthusiastic reader of Lavater, the skull beneath the skin is now an irrelevancy. This is not the scale of comparative anatomy that arose in moving from natural history to the science of biology. The skin has no independent life. It is not a piece or component of the body but its fateful wrapping. Dermo-politics succeeded biopolitics. Both preceded nano-politics.[45]

Fanon's term "epidermalization" deserves a wider application than its firmly colonial origins would suggest. Emmanuel Chukwudi Eze and Christian M. Neugebauer have reminded us recently that Immanuel Kant's *Physische Geographie* said more than his contemporary celebrants like to admit about the distinctive attributes of tough Negro skin and the practical problems it presented to slave husbandry when pain had to be inflicted on stock with a split bamboo cane.[46] Like Hegel's well-known opinions on the aesthetic deficiencies and intellectual limitations of the Negro, these sentiments can be thought of as exemplifying epidermal thinking in its emergent forms. In an era in which colonial power had made epidermalizing into a dominant principle of political power, Fanon used the idea to index the estrangement from authentic human being in the body and being in the world that colonial social relations had wrought. For him epidermalized power violated the human body in its symmetrical, intersubjective, social humanity, in its species being: in its fragile relationship to other fragile bodies and in its connection to the redemptive potential dormant in the wholesome or perhaps suffering corporeality. What he glimpsed as a "real dialectic between (the) body and the world" might be re-articulated, in a less triumphal mode, as our being toward death.[47]

Fanon's notion supplies an interesting footnote to the whole history of racial sciences and the exclusive notions of color-coded humanity that they specified. How many skin colors are there? How exactly, scientifically, is skin shade supposed to correspond to the variety of "races"? You may recall that Buffon had counted thirty races of dogs. Linnaeus, Kant's ideal reader, thought that *Homo sapiens* included four varieties, whereas the other species that constituted the genus *Homo* had its own numerous sub-species, including *Homo troglodytes.* Kant identified four races of man: the white, the black, the Hun, and the Hindustani. All these raciologists dealt differently with the question of whether the variations they noted within races were as significant as the differences that might exist between them.

In the period since, these distinctively modern raciologies with their strong scientific flavors have joined hands with common-sense perception and made the external surface of the body the focus of their inquiring gaze. When the body becomes absolutely penetrable, and is refigured as the transient, epiphenomenon of coded invisible information, that aesthetic, that gaze, and that regime of power are irrecoverably over. The idea of epidermalization points toward one intermediate stage in a critical theory of body scales in the making of "race." Today skin is no longer privileged as the threshold of either identity or particularity. There are good reasons to suppose that the line between inside and out now falls elsewhere. The boundaries of "race" have moved across the threshold of the skin. They are cellular and molecular, not dermal. If "race" is to endure, it will be in a new form, estranged from the scales respectively associated with political anatomy and epidermalization.

We have been made more skeptical than ever about the status of easily visible differences and are now obliged to ask on what scale human sameness and human diversity are to be calibrated. Can a different sense of scale and scaling form a counterweight to the appeal of absolute particularity currently celebrated under the fading sign of "race"? Can it answer the seductions of self and kind projected onto the surface of the body but stubbornly repudiated inside it by the proliferation of invisible differences that produce catastrophic consequences where people are not what they seem to be? In the instability of scale that characterizes our time, how is racialized and racializing identity being imagined? Is there still place for "race" on the new scale at which human life and human difference is contemplated? We can cut this long story short by posing the central question even more starkly. What does that long-lived trope "race" mean in the age of molecular biology?

We have seen that on their journey away from modernity's inaugural catastrophes, raciological ways of organizing and classifying the world have retained a special baggage of perspectival inclinations, perceptual habits, and scalar assumptions. Their anthropologies depended and still depend upon observations that cannot be wholly disassociated from the technological means that have both fostered and mediated them. This is where anatomical scale was first broken. Long ago, microscopes transformed what could be seen, but the latest technologies for observing on smaller and smaller scales changed the threshold of visibility and contributed to an enhanced sense of the power of the unseen and the unseeable. The eugenic ravings of Francis Crick, the Nobel–Prize-winning co-discoverer of DNA, demonstrate exactly how the change of scale involved in the founding of molecular biology and the redefinition of life in terms of information, messages, and code was recognized as having cataclysmic moral and political consequences.[48] Biopolitics laid the foundations for and was superseded by "nano-politics."

Skin, bone, and even blood are no longer the primary referents of racial discourse. If the modern episteme was constituted through processes that forsook the integrity of the whole body and moved inside the threshold of the skin to enumerate organs and describe their functional relationship to an organic totality, the situation today is very different. The same inward direction has been maintained and the momentum increased. Forget totality: the aspiration to perceive and explain through recourse to the power of the minute, the microscopic, and now the molecular has been consolidated. In a space beyond comparative anatomy and all dermo-political concerns, the body and its obvious, functional components no longer delimit the scale upon which assessments of the unity and variation of the species are to be made. The naked eye was long ago recognized to be insufficient to the tasks of evaluation and description demanded by the beleaguered condition of everyday life and the popular eugenic answers to its manifold problems. It is more than technological changes that make what was hitherto invisible not only visible but also decisive.

Nuclear magnetic resonance spectroscopy (NMR), positron emission tomography (PET), and computerized tomography (CT) are several of the technical innovations in medical imaging that have transformed the relationship between the seen and the unseen. Whether it is the IBM logo being spelled out in atoms of xenon or a less specific dream of gaining control over the big world "by fiddling with the nanoscale entities of which it is composed," the movement is always in one direction: downward and inward. Our foundational question should be this: Where do these changes leave the idea of racial difference, particularly when it cannot be readily correlated with complex genetic variation? Current wisdom seems to suggest that up to six pairs of genes are implicated in the outcome of skin "color." They do not constitute a single switch.

Several years ago Stephen Lawrence, a young black man, was brutally murdered by several young white men at a bus stop in South East London. His tragic death was but one fatality in a sequence of racial attacks that had been perpetrated in the same area. Two others, Rolan Adams and Rohit Duggal, had been killed in comparable circumstances, but it was the Lawrence murder that became a landmark in the politics of "race" in Britain.[49]

The whole story of political action around these and other similar deaths cannot be recapitulated here. For these limited purposes, it is enough to say that a small but dynamic movement grew up around these terrible tragedies and that the actions of the bereaved families and their various groups of supporters took place both inside and outside the formal institutions of government, publicity, and legislation. Tactical actions were intended to project anger, amplify grief, win support, change consciousness, and raise money for legal fees. Political initiatives included a demand for the justice that had been effectively denied when police, courts, and prosecutors refused to act with speed and diligence against the attackers. They also encompassed a demand for sympathy for the plight of the families in their loss and their sadness that has left a substantial mark on the life of our nation. These actions articulated a further sequence of supplementary demands: for recognition of the seriousness of the offense and for acknowledgment of the humanity of the victims and the distinctively unwholesome nature of the brutal offenses that had left them to die on the pavement while their blood drained away. A government-sponsored judicial inquiry into Lawrence's murder and the way the police and the criminal justice system had responded to it raised the disturbing issue that "institutional racism" had conditioned the workings of Britain's government agencies.

Although most aspects of the forbiddingly complex case of Stephen Lawrence cannot be explored here, that does not mean they have been forgotten. There are also solid moral and political reasons why that bitter episode and the events that followed it should not be used as illustrative material on the way toward a more general and inevitably speculative argument about the nature of racial categories and the limits of racialized explanation. Nevertheless, that is what I wish to do.

The British National Party—an openly neo-fascist group—had been very active in the area where Stephen Lawrence was murdered. Their national headquarters was close to the spot where he died, and it was not surprising that the group's presence in the neighborhood and its possible role in legitimating white supremacist terror there became the focus of political activity directed toward the police and the local state. In the names of antifascism and antiracism, activists demanded that the party's well-fortified headquarters be shut down. There were tactical divisions within the campaign as to how this might be achieved. One group favored localized direct action, another preferred to pursue more familiar patterns of protest. Rather than march against the bunker, they chose to make their public demands in the central area of the city where government buildings are located and where the media would attend. Another, local demonstration was held outside the fortified building. This action was animated by the suggestion that if the authorities were unable to move against the group and their headquarters (which had become powerful symbols of the malevolent forces of racism and fascism), antiracist demonstrators would do so. This demonstration, held on Saturday, October 16, 1993, pitted a large number of protesters against a considerable formation of police in riot gear that had been deployed to protect the neo-fascists from the wrath of the antiracists.

The details of the violence that followed are interesting but not essential to the points being explored here. As a result of the physical confrontation between these groups, forty-one demonstrators were injured. Nineteen police officers were treated for their injuries, and four of them spent the night in the hospital. Conflict over the behavior of the marchers erupted after the event. This was something more than the routine cycle of mutual denunciation. In particular, the police claimed that antiracist marchers had singled out black officers and made them special targets for hostility and attack. One of these policemen, deployed by his superiors in defense of the rights of an organization that does not recognize him as belonging to the national community or upholding its laws, was Constable Leslie Turner. Turner said he had been attacked because he was black. He told the newspapers, "It was white demonstrators. There were no black people there that I could see. They singled me out as being a traitor." Whatever his thoughts to the contrary, it is possible that Officer Turner's plight might well have been worse if there had been larger numbers of black protesters around that day. On the scale of human suffering that ends with brutal murder, his experiences are slight, even trivial. His story of victimage may even have been fabricated to win new legitimacy for a dubious police operation. But I want to proceed as if, almost irrespective of what really happened, there was indeed a measure of truth in what he said about that demonstration. What if he *was* attacked as a traitor? What kind of traitor would he have been? What if he *was* assaulted by angry people on the basis that by being a black police officer he had somehow violated the political position that they imagined to match his uniformed black body? What is the currency of what are sometimes called "coconut," "choc-ice," or "oreo cookie" ontologies with their strict and pernicious divisions between "inside" and "outside"? What if the mob was not alive to the irony of his being deployed in defense of the local neo-Nazis? What if they, too, succumbed to the vicious logic of race-thinking?

I am telling this tale here in order to conjure up some of the substantive problems lodged in the way people conceptualize and act upon racial difference. If dedicated antiracist and antifascist activists remain wedded to the most basic mythologies and morphologies of racial difference, what chance do the rest of us have to escape its allure? If the brutal simplicity of racial typology remains alive even in the most deliberate and assertive of antifascist gestures, then perhaps critical, avowedly "anti-essentialist" intellectuals are asking too much when we inquire about the renunciation of "race," or when we aspire to polychromatic and multiethnic utopias in which the color of skin makes no more difference than the color of eyes or hair. It would probably be inappropriate to assume too much common ground between this readership and those anti-Nazi demonstrators. But it is not illegitimate to inquire into where professional and academic interests might resonate in this narrative. Have we, too, become complicit in the reification of racial difference? What has happened to the antiracist assumptions that governed our scholarly activities in previous times? Have they been beaten back by the gains of postbiological determinism, which is claiming the right to account for human behavior back from the social sciences? This argument should not be misunderstood. It seeks to initiate a period of reflection and clarification about our intellectual, ethical, and political projects in the critical scholarship of "races" and raciologies.

I am alive to all the ironies of my position. I understand that taking antipathy toward "race" beyond the unstable equilibrium represented by my liberal use of scare quotes might be viewed as a betrayal of those groups whose oppositional, legal, and even democratic claims have come to rest on identities and solidarities forged at great cost from the categories given to them by their oppressors. But to renounce "race" for analytical purposes is not to judge all appeals to it in the profane world of political cultures as formally equivalent. Less defensively, I think that our perilous predicament, in the midst of a political and technological sea-change that somehow strengthens ethnic absolutism and primordialism, demands a radical and dramatic response. This must step away from the pious ritual in which we always agree that "race" is invented but are then required to defer to its embeddedness in the world and to accept that the demand for justice requires us nevertheless innocently to enter the political arenas it helps to mark out.

Simply to raise these issues may be to violate a tacit scholarly agreement. The link between antiracist practice and intellectual work in this area is certainly not what it was twenty years ago, and yet there are precious few reflections on the changes signaled along the road that leads through municipal antiracism and beyond it into the barren terrain where work on "race" is overshadowed by privatized, corporate multiculturalism and cultures of simulation in which racial alterity has acquired an important commercial value. This just might be a suitable time to break the foundational oscillation between biology and culture, to open the closed circuit that analyses of what we used to call the New Racism have become. It will be more fruitful in future to trace the history of racial metaphysics—or rather of a metaphysical raciology—as an underlying precondition for various versions of determinism: biological, nationalistic, cultural, and now, genomic.

It has become commonplace to remark that, however noble, the idea of antiracism does not communicate any positive or affirmative notes.

What, after all, are antiracists in favor of? What are we committed to and how does it connect with the necessary moment of negativity that defines our political hopes? There are difficulties in framing those objectives, utopian and otherwise. I see this as another small symptom of the larger, chronic condition involved in the crisis of "race" and attempts to escape it by refiguring humanism. The history of racism is a narrative in which the congruency of micro- and macrocosm has been disrupted at the point of their analogical intersection: the human body. The order of active differentiation that gets called "race" may be modernity's most pernicious signature. It articulates reason and unreason. It knits together science and superstition. Its specious ontologies are anything but spontaneous and natural. They should be awarded no immunity from prosecution amid the reveries of reflexivity and the comfortable forms of inertia induced by capitulation to the lazy essentialisms that postmodern sages inform us we cannot escape.

2

MODERNITY AND INFRAHUMANITY

In the present century, black people are believed to be totally different from whites in race and origin, yet totally equal to them with regard to human rights. In the sixteenth century, when blacks were
thought to come from the same roots and to be of the same family
as whites, it was held, most of all by Spanish theologians, that with
regard to rights blacks were by nature and Divine Will greatly inferior to us. In both centuries, blacks have been bought and sold and
made to work in chains under the whip. Such is ethics; and such is
the extent to which moral beliefs have anything to do with actions.

—GIACOMO LEOPARDI

African colonial possessions became the most fertile soil for the
flowering of what became the Nazi elite. Here (they) had seen with
their own eyes how peoples could be converted into races and how
. . . one might push one's own people into the position of the master
race.

—HANNAH ARENDT

The concept of modernity brings to
mind the interpenetration of capitalism, industrialization, and democracy.
It directs attention toward the emergence of modern government, the appearance of nation-states, and numerous other social and cultural changes.

Earth's place in the cosmos and the relationship between Europe and the rest of the planet were transformed, as was unquestioned acceptance of the account of human origins provided by the Bible. Other changes, in the registration of time, the experience of urban living, the configuration of public and private spheres, and the distinctive quality of both modern individuality and modern ethical life, have inspired large volumes of philosophical, sociological, and historical commentary. The development of territorial sovereignty and the cultural and communicative apparatuses that corresponded to it stand out amid this flux. They, too, were bound up with the struggle to consolidate the transparent working of the national states and governmental powers to which the term modernity refers.[1] That combination promoted a new definition of the relationship between place, community, and what we are now able to call "identity."

Modernity defined a new role for its citizen soldiers that merits recognition as what I want to call a "distinctive ecology of belonging."[2] A special formula for the relationship between territory, individuality, property, war, and society was dramatized in this historical phase. It emerged, for example, in the founding myth of Robinson Crusoe, who conserved and created culture, self, and wealth, mingling his labor and ingenuity with the opportunities furnished by God and nature to the industrious and the rational on his tropical island kingdom.[3] The ethical boundaries of that colonial modernity were memorably signaled by the fact that Crusoe felt free to take the lives of the natives, "whose barbarous customs were their own disaster," irrespective of the divine sanction that ordained their life of savagery.[4] His example helps to demonstrate how the reach of the European world and its distinctive resources of violence emerge in this consideration of modernity as a major issue, not only for the history of capitalist commerce, but also for historical understanding of national government and the geopolitical projection of states as discrete cultures arranged in antagonistic national units.[5] From this perspective, modernity can also be used to introduce the problems posed by the relationship of capitalism, industrialization, and democracy to the emergence and consolidation of systematic race-thinking. The concept frames these inquiries into the connection between rationality and irrationality by directing attention toward the links between racial typologies and the heritage of the Enlightenment. It makes that fateful compact fundamental to the task of grasping how knowledge and power produced the truths of "race" and nation close to the summit of modern reflections on individuality, subjectivity, and ontology, time, truth, and beauty.[6]

The emergence of "race" as a major means of differentiation and division is an important reminder that making politics aesthetic was not a governmental strategy that originated in twentieth-century fascism.[7] The historian George Mosse did more than anyone to draw attention to the aesthetic criteria employed in the earliest versions of raciology that reconciled art and science into a sharply graded conceptualization of the human species.[8] The same racialized hierarchy shaped the standards whereby the power and actions of state and government could be compared, evaluated, and enjoyed. Hegel's anthropological view of the Ashanti and their kingly rituals suggests that colonial settings provided manifold opportunities to exercise the confident comparative ambitions of this modern political imagination. Africans were, by his judgment, not only prehistoric but prepolitical also:[9]

> Turning our attention in the next place to the category of *political constitution*, we shall see that the entire nature of this race is such as to preclude the existence of any such arrangement. The standpoint of humanity at this grade is mere sensuous volition with energy of will; since universal spiritual laws (for example, that of the morality of the Family) cannot be recognised here.[10]

These observations arise in Hegel's elaborate presentation of how geography conditions history. He presents modernity mediated by "race" as both period and region. Today the history of colonization and conquest that modernity encompasses raises an important sequence of critical questions. What was the geopolitical scale on which Europe-centered modernity was traced, inscribed, and projected? Where, if anywhere, did its representational conventions begin to break down?

We need to ponder how our understanding of modernity inside and beyond Europe might benefit from a change in the resonance of the key terms "history" and "culture." Their transformation might also be understood as contributing to the decisive reorientation I called for in the previous chapter. It has important consequences for our comprehension of the relationship between the universal and the particular coded into the ethical and political constellation under which we anatomize not "race" but raciology. To put it another way, in what sense does modernity belong to a closed entity, a "geo-body"[11] named Europe? What forms of conscious-ness, solidarity, and located subjectivity does it solicit or produce? What might modernity comprise if the unspoken link with European planetary consciousness[12] was broken, stretched, or even tested? The last question suggests that the operations of historical consciousness become more than merely national phenomena. They were racialized most effectively and comprehensively where historicality became the exclusive attribute of cer-tain favored and selected populations. Racially differentiated groups no longer shared the same present. The dominant groups could enlist the ir-resistible momentum of history on their side and treat their apparently anachronistic subordinates as if they belonged to the past and had no fu-ture. For those of us who are engaged in studying the historical develop-ment of raciological thought, this break in the apprehension of time was especially significant.

Although "race"-thinking certainly existed in earlier periods,[13] moder-nity transformed the ways "race" was understood and acted upon. I am broadly sympathetic to the account that emerges from the rich work of re-cent historians of the "race" idea. From various political standpoints, many of them have argued that "race" as we comprehend it now simply did not exist until the nineteenth century.[14] Though it is presented as a perma-nent, inevitable, and extrahistorical principle of differentiation, there is, they suggest, nothing automatic about "race" and the differences it makes. Consciousness of "race" is most constructively apprehended as a specific social product, the outcome of historical processes that can be mapped in detail. Eric Voegelin, who has an especially thoughtful approach to the ge-nealogies of "race," warns critical historians who venture into this terrain about the particular conceptual problems they are likely to encounter:

> A symbolic idea like the race idea is not a theory in the strict sense of the word. And it is beside the mark to criticize a symbol, or a set of dogmas, because they are not empirically verifiable. While such criticism is correct it is without meaning, because it is not the func-tion of an idea to describe social reality but to assist in its constitu-tion. An idea is always "wrong" in the epistemological sense, but this relation to reality is its very principle.[15]

The point is well made. It yields a view of "race" as an active, dynamic idea or principle that assists in the constitution of social reality. It is a short step from appreciating the ways that particular "races" have been historically invented and socially imagined to seeing how modernity catalyzed the distinctive regime of truths, the world of discourse that I call "raciology." In other words, the modern, human sciences, particularly anthropology, geography, and philosophy, undertook elaborate work in order to make the idea of "race" epistemologically correct. This required novel ways of understanding embodied alterity, hierarchy, and temporality. It made human bodies communicate the truths of an irrevocable otherness that were being confirmed by a new science and a new semiotics just as the struggle against Atlantic racial slavery was being won.

Although it is not acknowledged as often as it should be, the close connection between "race" and modernity can be viewed with special clarity if we allow our understanding of modernity to travel, to move with the workings of the great imperial systems it battled to control. Though they were centered on Europe, these systems, both exploitative and communicative, extended far beyond Europe's geo-body. Anthropology and geography are usually understood as the terminal points of the cognitive aspects of colonial modernity's social and cultural revolution, but its effects were not confined to the consolidation of these new disciplinary perspectives. The same fundamental change in comprehending "race" was given philosophical gravity by the notion that character and talent could be distinguished unevenly and had been distributed by nature along national and racial lines. Kant's famous discussion of national and racial characteristics in section four of "Observations on the Feeling of the Beautiful and the Sublime" has been brilliantly analyzed by the philosopher Ronald Judy. It provides a valuable point of departure here.[16] The figure of "The Negro" appears in Kant's text in a famous citation from David Hume:

> The Negroes of Africa have by nature no feeling that rises above the trifling. Mr. Hume challenges anyone to cite a single example in which a Negro has shown talents, and asserts that among the hundreds of thousands of blacks who are transported elsewhere from their countries, although many have been set free, still not one was ever found who presented anything great in art or science or any other praiseworthy quality, even though among the whites some continually rise aloft from the lowest rabble, and through superior gifts earn respect in the world. So fundamental is the difference be-

tween these two races of man, and it appears to be as great in regard
to mental capacities as in color.[17]

Kant's movements from body to mind, from color to mental capacity,
might now be recognized as symptoms of a "race" consciousness that went
to the core of his thinking about agency and subjectivity, democracy and
mutuality. He did not announce that Negroes had been deprived of all
humanity. He accorded them a grudging, associate membership in the
human family and allocated them to the lowest positions within a single,
nominally inclusive species stratified by the workings of natural law
against racial assimilation. His raciological ideas blend the physical and
the metaphysical into a powerful and elaborate argument which, as we will
see, sits awkwardly alongside the compelling features of his cosmopolitanism. His ideas were developed in a number of texts from the same period,
most notably in his 1798 *Anthropology from a Pragmatic Point of View* and
his 1775 essay "On the Different Races of Man." They are too little read
these days, perhaps because they are deemed to embarrass or even compromise the worthy democratic aspirations to which the critical Kant also
gave such enduring expression. Calling for more complex responses than
the squeamishness evident in contemporary distaste for enlightened discussions of "race," these discomforting writings communicate the ways
that the consolidation of modern raciology required enlightenment and
myth to be intertwined. Indeed, they reveal theories of culture, "race," and
nation as supplying the logic and mechanism of their dangerous interconnection. This confluence matters to the argument here because it presents
equally distressing links between raciology and statecraft and shows how
modern political theory was being annexed by the imperatives of colonial
power even in its emergent phase. It bears repetition that Kant's warnings
against the perils of racial intermixture derive their urgency from European imperial projects and enlist the potency of natural law in the important cosmo-political work of keeping racial groups apart:

> Thus we can judge with probability that the intermixture of races
> (caused by large-scale conquests), which gradually extinguishes
> their characteristics, does not seem beneficial to the human
> race—all pretended philanthropy notwithstanding . . . Instead of
> assimilation, which was intended by the melting together of various
> races, Nature has here made a law of just the opposite. In a nation of

the same race (for example, of the white race), instead of allowing the characters to develop constantly and progressively toward resembling one another, whereby ultimately only one and the same portrait would result as in prints taken from the same copperplate, Nature has preferred to diversify infinitely the characters of the same stock.[18]

However beautiful they appear to their beneficiaries, Kant's democratic hopes and dreams simply could not encompass black humanity. The Negro remained locked out of the circle of intersubjective relations. Another of his memorable incidental observations on slave husbandry informs his eager readers that "blacks are . . . so talkative that they must be driven apart from each other with thrashings."[19] This interesting aside shows how readily the rational application of violence to the enslaved and the colonized followed from these attempts to bring their "race" into focus as a properly philosophical object rather than merely a matter of typology. The implicit setting for these compromised scientific operations was the slave plantation, which here seems to point toward the institution of another modern locus of power: the concentration camp. Both constituted exceptional spaces where normal juridical rules and procedures had been deliberately set aside. In both, the profit motive and its economic rationalities were practically qualified by the geopolitical imperatives of racialized hierarchy. It is easy to overlook how colonial societies and conflicts provided the context in which concentration camps emerged as a novel form of political administration, population management, warfare, and coerced labor.[20]

Before proceeding, we should acknowledge the difficulties involved in making Kant stand in for the Enlightenment as a whole. It should also be stressed that he does not himself conceive of genocide or endorse its practice against Negroes, Jews, or any other variety of people. Having made exactly these important qualifications, Berel Lang has opened a promising critical path into these difficult aspects of Kant's work. As part of an attempt to reconstruct the philosophical prehistory of the Nazi genocide, he has made a judicious evaluation of Kant's theories of community, ethics, and mutuality. This survey is integral to what Lang identifies as "affiliation" (a mode of linking ideas that is "stronger than analogy or likeness although more oblique than that of direct physical causality").[21] He demonstrates how national limits could readily be applied to the formal universalizing mechanisms that regulate the conduct of moral agents in Kant's system. These precious mechanisms rely on recognition. If people were not recognized as being endowed with the particular corporeal or cultural attributes that signaled their possession of a universal self to a community of equals, the rules of moral and civic conduct might, reasonably enough, not apply to them. If, to put it even more bluntly, their "race," religion, color, or nationality deprived them of access to that precious, universal human selfhood, they would clearly be in grave jeopardy.[22]

The value of an argument like Lang's was underlined by Kant himself in some pithy observations on the defects his pragmatic anthropology had divined within the English national character. Kant acknowledges the possibility that national boundaries and cultural difference might intrude into moral and political conduct, though in the case of the English, the question of color, so important to him elsewhere, does not disrupt his criticism of the resulting double standard. The petty force of national difference stands in sharp contrast to the absolute divisions marked out by "race":

> For his own countrymen the Englishman establishes great benevolent institutions unheard of among all other peoples. But the foreigner who has been driven to England's shores by fate, and has fallen into dire need, will be left to die on the dunghill because he is not an Englishman, that is not a human being.[23]

From sharply contrasting political standpoints, the post-1945 writings of Aimé Césaire and Hannah Arendt might also be used to support a negative verdict on the more grandiose modern pretensions that Kant has been made to represent. Arendt, for example, memorably raises the troubling issue of Adolf Eichmann's courtroom claim to have been guided by Kantian precepts during his service to Hitler. By identifying Eichmann's stance as an obvious distortion of Kant's own thinking, she diverges sharply from Lang's more nuanced line of thought. However, her caustic argument begs the question of whether any other ambiguities in Kant's influential formulations could have fostered their reduction to what Eichmann described as a version of Kant for the "household use of the little man."[24] Although Césaire does not share Arendt's faith in ancient models of political activity, his concerns intersect with hers. He presents

Hitler and Hitlerism as the culmination of modern patterns of formal humanism and philosophic renunciation. He condemns what he dismisses as "pseudo-humanism" because "for too long it has diminished the rights of man . . . its concept of those rights has been—and still is—narrow and fragmentary, incomplete and biased and, all things considered, sordidly racist."[25]

Both these combative thinkers have important things to say about the complex and delicate processes that culminated in the governmental order of the modern nation that was also an imperial state. They are alert to the fact that this new pattern of power rewrote the rules of political and ethical conduct according to novel principles that were opposed to ancient and modern notions of political rationality, self-possession, democracy, and citizenship.

Shadowing both Arendt and Voegelin, Ivan Hannaford has pointed to the way that modern notions of "race" were articulated in some rather free and contentious translations of key texts by Aristotle and other ancient writers at the start of the nineteenth century. In an important but hardly comforting argument, he suggests that wherever the modern idea of "race" took hold, a characteristic perversion of the principles of democratic politics was the result. These arguments do not mean that the political and ethical resources supplied by these modern traditions should be disposed of lightly. Rather, the point of departure for this chapter is the still heretical notion that modernity's new political codes must be acknowledged as having been compromised by the raciological drives that partly formed them and wove a deadly, exclusionary force into their glittering universal promises. I hope it is not too obvious to underline and repeat Césaire's central point. The ideal of humanity, too restrictively defined, emerged from all this in filleted form. It was not only something that was to be monopolized by Europe; it could exist only in the neatly bounded, territorial units where true and authentic culture could take root under the unsentimental eye of ruthlessly eugenic government.

A theory of nations had rationalized many of these peculiar notions long before they were turned into matters of political and racial science. That theory was founded, as Claude Lefort has pointed out, on the unanimist principle articulated through the idea of "the people as one." It therefore denied "that division is constitutive of society" and accentuated the interchangeability and disposability of the nation's members—its population.[26] In time, they would also be discovered to exist in the strict organic patterns of a natural hierarchy that continued and extended the premodern typologies of race-thinking in the direction of a totalizing biosocial science. The nation could then be seen as a political body in which diverse but functionally interrelated components were subjected to a higher logic resulting from their combination. Though it was shaped by the residues of both, this was not the contractual unity of the commonwealth or the spiritual unity of the church but a violent, organic entity of a new type manifest above all in the workings of the state, which could demand the sacrifice of individual life in the service of collective goals. In sharp contradistinction to mechanized conceptualizations of modern government, raciology required the state to be an organism, rooted in and acting upon the volk. The strongly Kantian work of Houston Stewart Chamberlain synthesized these ideas into a theoretical form in his influential two-volume study *The Foundations of the Nineteenth Century.* Henceforth, freedom would be located in a private, inner world rather than in any opportunities created by modern social and political institutions. This inner freedom required a voluntary submission to outward political authority that could be justified in turn as a matter of biological necessity.[27] The commitment to an organic ordering of humankind was important also because it endorsed the claims of racial science to observe, organize, and regulate the social body. Chamberlain, an Aryanist and sterling inspiration to the raciological fantasies of the National Socialists, also stands for the easy racialization of the European ideal and reminds us that alongside Hellenism and Hebraism we should acknowledge the stubborn presence of Nordicism and Aryanism.

If we appreciate the constitutive force of raciology on the thinking of nationalists, we can interpret Chamberlain's work as he wanted it to be understood: as a strong bridge between Kant and Hitler over which that noble hero, the Teutonic Plato, could drive his historic battle chariot through the chaos of racelessness. Chamberlain's anti-semitism points toward our own period where he disavows hatred of the Jews in favor of the apparently more lofty goal of Aryan self-love. It allowed praise of the authentic Eastern Jews while articulating special scorn for those who dressed themselves up as what they were not and what they could never become. According to him, properly organic political links between "race" and nation could only be constructed via a state that maintained and strengthened Aryan racial traits in carefully planned ethnological operations analogous to the scientific work of that shepherd of racialized being, the livestock breeder:

> Horses and especially dogs give us every chance of observing that the intellectual gifts go hand in hand with the physical; this is specially true of the moral qualities: a mongrel is frequently very clever, but never reliable; morally he is always a weed. Continual promiscuity between two pre-eminent animal races leads without exception to the destruction of them both. Why should the human race form an exception?[28]

"Race" was blurred, but that lack of clarity in its relation to nationality was a positive asset. The idea was soon secured as a central philosophical, economic, and historical concept. In some national traditions, it could summon up a political ontology so fundamental(ist) that it supplied a ruthless logic to the unfolding of history itself.[29] Place, territory, and location were ontologized and history reconceptualized in elaborate geographical and geopolitical designs. Inferior and no longer merely different, other races were completely excluded from its compass and became prehistoric as well as extracultural. Their exclusion by means of a racialized rationality had the clearest implications for the cosmopolitan folly of imagining human beings to be an essentially undifferentiated collectivity.

The concept of historicality was strongly associated with these attempts to differentiate the status of peoples, their cultures, fates, destinies, and different racial and national spirits. The idea circulates through modern discourse on the lives and characteristics of nations, on their transition into nation-states, and on the cultural patterns that attended it. Historicality is a modern notion in that it presupposes a *politics* of time: making connections between ontology, nationality, and theories of racial difference. It is associated not only with the idea of authenticity and the national principle but with the elevation of "race" to a determining position in theories of history, especially those that pronounce upon war and conflict, naturalizing them in the convenient idea of specifically race-based imperial conflict. Historicality thus conveys the raciological rationalization of history. Hegel understood the implications of this point when, in expounding upon the place of Africa and Africans in his geographical theory of history, he wrote these words: "The peculiarly African character is difficult to comprehend, for the very reason that in reference to it we must give up the principle which naturally accompanies all *our* ideas—the category of universality."[30] The statement conveys his grasp of exactly how raciology restricted the scope of the modern political imaginary. Translated thus into ethics and primal ontology, "race" would become so potent in shaping human affairs that the necessarily unnatural world of formal politics could only seem trivial and insubstantial by comparison.

Historians of ideas, particularly those influenced by the account of the constitution of the human sciences found in Michel Foucault's early work, have added to his arguments about the history of the figure of "Man" and its appearance at the focal point of modern knowledge. I have already suggested that Foucault's antihumanist arguments have been diminished by his failure to link them to an explicit consideration of the history of racial slavery and other colonial adventures in which the brutal exclusionary character of Western humanism was apparent. However, it is possible to develop Foucault's insights into the moment where philosophy became anthropology in other directions that contribute to contemporary controversies over "race." Important work in tune with the Foucauldian approach, if not always with Foucault's own politics, has been done by Edward Said, Bernard McGrane, Anthony Pagden, and a number of others. It has gone beyond suggesting that the plausibility of enlightenment as a modern project should be assessed in the context of its contingent political choices, for example, John Locke's practical involvement in the colonization of the New World. Instead, this growing body of work prompts consideration of whether enlightened modernity may have been compromised if not undone by its tolerance of and collusion with the rational irrationalism of emergent racial sciences. This is another way of saying that enlightenment pretensions toward universality were punctured from the moment of their conception in the womb of the colonial space. Their very foundations were de-stabilized by their initial exclusionary configuration: by the consistent endorsement of "race" as a central political and historical concept and by the grave violence done to the central image of man by the exigencies of colonial power, which offered a path toward the prison of exotic status as the only escape route from terror.

Anti-semitism and the other raciologies that conditioned this shift in modern consciousness emerge from all this as unavoidable questions in the history of Occidental knowledge. Paul Lawrence Rose, Martin Bernal,

and Mosse have all suggested that these manifestations cut the philosophical discourse of modernity to the quick. The contentious and stimulating
work of these writers should not be passed over rapidly. The lucidity and
force of their arguments, about the destructive capacity of nationalism, the
formative significance of anti-semitism, and the impact of hellenomaniacal fantasy on the writing of history and the conduct of European
political culture in the nineteenth century, deserve more patient and
thoughtful responses than they have so far received. These challenges to
orthodoxy become even more important when they are linked to the results of work done on the place of "race" and slavery in the same period by
scholars writing about the Americas, as well as to material produced on the
relationship between Europe and its imperial holdings in Africa and Asia.
We know, not least from the valiant efforts of Arendt and Césaire, that
this body of work can be used speculatively to produce for what we call
"fascism" an intellectual lineage very different from the genealogy that has
been more conventionally associated with that term. Even if that provocative revision cannot be secured at this point, there is a strong suggestion
that our understanding of the relationship between the civilizing process
and the catalogue of barbarity that is secreted in the pages of its heroic narrative will need to be rethought so that it takes the modern dynamics of
the colonial world more comprehensively into account.[31]

I have already said that the racialization of the nation-state and the
consequent transformations of the national community involved a comprehensive negation and repudiation of politics as it had been practiced in
the past. Caught between geopolitical statecraft on one side and imperialist propaganda on the other, politics no longer involved the ideal of managing inescapable plurality and multiplicity in a clearly demarcated, public
realm for which the participants took joint responsibility. We must also
consider the possibility that the idea of citizenship was transformed once
the unanimity of the mass could be orchestrated from above by governmental machines. The growth of propaganda, along with the consequent
debasement of the public sphere, was only one of a number of technical
and communicative innovations that conveyed the extent of profound
changes that coincided with the peak of European imperial power.

Of course, the effects of these developments were not confined to the
victims of raciology who had in any case been deterred from cultivating or
exercising themselves in any polity. I want to emphasize again that this

change had important consequences for the supposed beneficiaries of the new racial hierarchies as well.[32] Their self-consciousness was, as Fanon would have put it, amputated at the point where the seductions of raciology emerged in popular and geopolitical forms. In many cases, they were offered an ideology of superiority, the glamour of whiteness, or Aryan-ness, for example, as a form of practical compensation for the loss of that universal humanity. Today, surveying that development affords a good means to observe the transformation of the nation-state into a new type of collective body, integrated metaphysically and culturally as well as politically, and to observe the place of racial discourse in securing that outcome.

Michel Foucault confronted exactly this issue in those tantalizing pages toward the end of the first volume of his *History of Sexuality*, where he presents modernity as the progression from anatomo-politics of the human body to a biopolitics of the population. Forced by the scale of this important task to reflect upon the legacy and power of fascism, he writes:

> Beginning in the second half of the nineteenth century, the thematics of blood was sometimes called on to lend its entire historical weight toward revitalising the type of political power that was exercised through the devices of sexuality. Racism took shape at this point (racism in its modern, "biologizing" statist form): it was then that a whole politics of settlement (peuplement), family, marriage, education, social hierarchisation, and property, accompanied by a long series of permanent interventions at the level of the body, conduct, health and everyday life, received their color and their justification from the mythical concern with protecting the purity of the blood and ensuring the triumph of the race. Nazism was doubtless the most cunning and the most naive (and the former because of the latter) combination of the fantasies of blood and the paroxysms of a disciplinary power.[33]

We need to extend this line of argument further still, initially by enumerating the scientific principles upon which populations were to be divided and ranked by "race." However, in seeking to understand the sacralization this process involved and its conspicuous spiritual aspects, we should not underplay the mystical and irrational counterpoints to scientific raciology. Especially when it was closely tied in with the workings of imperial nations, the concept of "race" can be appreciated as a successor to what Voegelin calls previous "body ideas"—the political body represented by the Greek polis, and the idea of the mystical body of the Christian church. Right at the summit of imperial power, the combined impact of anthropology, raciology, and nationalism further reduced the already truncated civic functioning of the nation-state. The nation was then invested with characteristics associated with biocultural kinship in which new forms of duty and mutual obligation appeared to regulate relationships between members of the collective, while those who fell beyond the boundaries of the official community were despised, reviled, and subjected to entirely different political and juridical procedures, especially if they did not benefit from the protection of an equivalent political body. In fulfillment of the organic imperative, the integrity of imperial nations was actively re-imagined to derive from the primordial particularity of premodern tribes.[34] I want to call the resulting national and governmental formations "camps." That name emphasizes their territorial, hierarchical, and militaristic qualities rather than the organic features that have been more widely identified as the key ingredient in the antidote they supplied to mechanized modernity and its dehumanizing effects.[35]

MODERNITY, DIFFERENCE, AND POLITICAL CORRECTNESS

Universality, reason and progress, modernity and enlightenment: these glorious ideas were once the sturdy cornerstones of an all-conquering Occidental mentality. They have recently registered the shock of the postmodern critique of knowledge, truth, and science. Amid the ruins, more modest activities, both academic and political, have transformed our understanding of the role of intellectuals and helped to specify the character of our times. I would suggest that the critical force of these deliberately postmodern arguments is strongest, not where they point toward an urgently needed sociology of postmodernity, but where they have addressed the history of the relationship of knowledge to power and domination and converged on the problems of legitimacy that arose where the partial and the particular opted to represent themselves as the totalizing and the transcendent. They have articulated a compelling indictment of those forms of truth-seeking which imagined themselves to be eternally and placelessly valid. These critical orientations toward the processes they reconstitute as the politics of truth take many conflicting forms. Sadly, much of the time they are no more hospitable to the critique of race-thinking than are their modern foes. However, there is nothing to be gained from denying either their seriousness or their value in pressing an evangelical or overly innocent modernity toward greater clarity about its own desires and greater consistency in the fulfillment of the promises held out by its own glorious rhetoric.

Some of the most powerful versions of these arguments have been found in the works of feminist critics of epistemology who have recognized the significance of "race" as a factor of social division. I am thinking in particular of the work of Donna Haraway and Sandra Harding. They and many of their peers have supplemented a lengthy tradition that dissents from the objectivist conceits of the more triumphalist versions of both the natural and the human sciences. Their post-Kuhnian sociologies of science reflect upon the history of truth-seeking activities with a less innocent eye that is more mindful of contingency and more sharply attuned to the power of language, no longer regarded as a transparent medium. Another chorus of voices, raised in pursuit of a sustainable relationship with the finite natural resources of our planet and a more cautious and respectful attitude toward the biosphere upon which we all rely, has extended the critique of these ways of finding and producing truth in another direction and underscored their destructive character. This important work has reconceptualized the relationship between nature and culture outside the binary nineteenth-century pattern that still dominates in this area. How that relationship has been historically associated with the language of racial typology and the production of races as historical actors by means of anthropological and geographical discourse is something that should be of the greatest concern to peoples whose position on the ladder of evolution is projected as being closer to the ground than to the stars.

With these connections in mind, I want to add another register to the critical commentaries on the history of scientific mentalities. This critique emphasizes their connection to the rational irrationality of "race" and reductive accounts of the interplay of natural and cultural difference. It can be found in several places but is perhaps most strongly audible in the dissenting voices of many black intellectuals of the western hemisphere.

These were, and remain, people who have been shaped, nurtured, and trained by the West. Yet their sense of its promise was formed by a profound disenchantment. In response to their encounters with the fateful linkage of racialized knowledge and power and the ideologies of inhumanity it creates, these people have cultivated a distinctive variety of dissident consciousness. The characteristic location of being in, but not completely of, Western modernity lent their work bitter flavors. They are discernible even where their criticisms of race-coded civilization were inconsistent, and any distaste for the benefits of progress from which they have been barred was tempered by the irrepressible dream of human reconciliation beyond the veil of color and the violence that keeps its tantalizing, diaphanous folds in place. Their traveling and wandering, voluntary as well as coerced, induced them to work with different notions of culture, which was recognized as a fluid and mutable phenomenon.

The words of one member of this loosely organized but nonetheless self-conscious group, the African-American historian, sociologist, and activist W. E. B. Du Bois, suggest that the group had developed its own translocal and cosmopolitan conversations about the value of modernity and progress before equivalent patterns of disaffection were consolidated in Europe in the aftermath of the 1914–1918 war in a process to which Jewish writers and artists made such notable contributions:[36]

> So woefully unorganized is sociological knowledge that the meaning of progress, the meaning of swift and slow in human doing, and the limits of human perfectibility, are veiled, unanswered sphinxes on the shores of science.

In the period following the abolition of racial slavery, this itinerant group generated an important series of dialogues with other dissenting traditions of thought and action—religious, socialist, nationalist, feminist, and psychoanalytic—within the broad philosophical framework of post-enlightenment thinking about sociality and history, democracy and justice. Frantz Fanon spoke for that dissenting formation, from a position inside and against the larger cultural and intellectual structures that had shaped his consciousness. As both beneficiary and victim of European progress in its blood-stained imperial mode, he demanded national liberation for colonial peoples but linked that project of revolutionary reconstruction to the deliberate production of a new conception of humanity:

It is a question of the Third World starting a new history of Man, a history which will have regard to the sometimes prodigious theses which Europe has put forward, but which will also not forget Europe's crimes, of which the most horrible was committed in the heart of man, and consisted of the pathological tearing away of his functions *and the crumbling away of his unity* . . . For Europe, for ourselves and for humanity, comrades, we must turn over a new leaf, we must work out new concepts, and try to set afoot a new man.[37]

There is far more to Fanon's exhortation than an attempt to transcode the Jacobin imaginary into the idiom of colonial conflict. His charge against Europe raises a problem to which we will return repeatedly below. It is not merely that European imperial powers wrongfully deprived colonial subjects of their humanity, but that Europe has perpetrated the still greater crime of despoiling humanity of its elemental unity as a species. Fanon's call for the institution of an anticolonial and nonracial universalism is a significant gesture that reveals his links to the modern political traditions of the Western world even in his greatest gestures of disavowal. What is most important about this stance is his insistence that this precious universalism can only be bought at the price of a reckoning with colonial modernity. It takes shape only in the process of facing the antinomies of modernity revealed in the social order of the colony, which was emphatically not that of the metropole until the Nazi genocide brought it back home. His words articulate a reminder that between the fortified encampments of the colonizers and the quarters of the colonized there were other locations. These in-between locations represent, not disability and inertia, but opportunities for greater insight into the opposed worlds that enclosed them. There, the double-consciousness required by the everyday work of translation offered a prototype for the ethically charged role of the interpreter with which our most imaginative intellectuals have answered the challenges of postmodern society.

I want to stop short of suggesting that the preeminent position of that Western political culture is irrecoverable because the confidence and authority of epistemological and moral claims staked in this tradition will never be restored. Instead, I would argue first that a partial and pragmatic restoration or reform can proceed only if the depths of this tradition's difficulties with "race" are fully appreciated, and second, that a sustained engagement with these problems would have to acknowledge that the recurrence of terror and barbarity communicates more than a lapse from more exalted standards of rational conduct. We need to consider the circumstances in which the application of terror can emerge as a rational, legal, or acceptable option. What varieties of rationality sanction raciological brutality? How has the category of the human, which, as we have just seen, Fanon would have us purge and redeem, circulated in those lofty attempts to differentiate epistemology and morality, aesthetics and ethics? Racial and ethnic rhetorics, nationalist metaphysics, and imperial fantasies became intrinsic to colonial modernities at home and abroad. As the history of colonial conflicts suggests, European enlightenment's universal aspirations were undermined where they have been reinterpreted as tied to local and parochial preoccupations or read ethnohistorically so that their portentous, timeless promises appear context-bound and are associated with the desires of particular populations in particular predicaments.

Once the exclusionary character of modernity's loudly trumpeted democratic aspirations has been flushed out of the cover provided by inclusive, humanistic rhetoric, the image of humanity that arose in the interval between these contradictory messages can then be denounced as a fraud. Sometimes, of course, this duplicity has been perpetrated unknowingly. It may even have been voiced by many who have not been the enemies of freedom. Nonetheless, a fraud it remains and a fraud it can be demonstrated to be if assessments of it are conducted from a position in which "race" appears at the center rather than on the fringes of reflection. I propose this denunciation, not to endorse the power of "race" as a category for comprehending human social and historical development. Indeed, to reinflate the concept so that it remains a meaningful and powerful one would be to replicate the very failing that I am trying to illuminate. Recognizing the power of raciology, which is used here as a shorthand term for a variety of essentializing and reductionist ways of thinking that are both biological and cultural in character, is an essential part of confronting the continuing power of "race" to orchestrate our social, economic, cultural, and historical experiences.

We have the pioneering work of Max Weinreich, Robert Proctor, and Benno Mueller Hill to thank for outlining the enthusiasm for National Socialism evident among German academics during the 1930s. Their revelations do not exhaust the issue of raciology's impact on modern knowledge and other ethical problems associated with this significant manifestation of "political correctness." The image of Bertrand Russell and other socialists mired in their desire to implement eugenic schemes and the eloquent anti-semitism of too many figures in the very best traditions of the European humanities increase the dimensions of this problem. It is compounded by the undignified and sometimes absurd postures that recent scholars and commentators have assumed in trying to defend the indefensible. Their stances have often trivialized the issues involved in taking the power of "race" to heart.

Julian Young's extraordinary exposition of Martin Heidegger, though admirably clear and rigorous according to some academic protocols, is worth singling out here as an ideal type for this sort of immoral indifference to the power of race-thinking. Young is rare among Heidegger's numerous apologists because he appreciates that a comprehensive defense of his academic inspiration cannot duck a philosophical confrontation with the idea of "race." However, his zeal to get Heidegger off the hook by, for example, showing him to be an unexpectedly articulate critic of racism rather than a practitioner of its more metaphysical varieties, takes the intended defense of his hero into deeper water. The final price of Heidegger's rehabilitation is Young's flat denial that Nazism could have had "doctrinal" coherence. More important for these purposes, Young introduces a definition of racism so restrictive and narrowly biological in character that it forces a large wedge between volkism, nationalism, and the scientific errors he regards as racism proper. Rather than delve into modernity's cultural and metaphysical forms of race-thinking, Young ignores the extensive literature that undermines his credibility and pronounces sagely: "biological racism is the only kind there is."[38]

Focusing on the pathetic and embattled figure of Heidegger even when caught on one of his regular visits to his old chum Eugen Fischer, arguably Germany's leading racial scientist, risks diverting attention from the wider arguments I have tried to engage. It is not, after all, a matter of damning a whole tradition of inquiry because those who gave it direction, vigor, and critical insight were, by some inappropriate contemporary definition, racist, misogynist, homophobic, elitist, or indifferent to suffering. The choice is not, or rather should not be, between setting aside this work because of its taint, embracing it on the basis that its raciological character is a minor irritation or distraction from its other qualities, and following Young's bold signposts into an absurd denial that it has anything whatever to do with "race."

Heidegger is a potential distraction because the racism and anti-semitism, ethnic absolutism, and ultranationalism that are evident in the history of the human sciences are not only personal issues that can be ade-quately illuminated according to the restricted dimensions supplied by any individual life. Collusion in the personalization and individualization of these political commitments and their presentation as quirky or eccentric deviations are certainly wrong given the ubiquity and frequency of these problems. They are also wrong for more fundamental reasons. These reac-tions risk the hijacking of principled critique, which then gets diverted so that, as both Primo Levi and Richard Rorty have put it in different con-texts, the noble desire for comprehension of the unacceptable, the evil and the wrongful, can begin to damage the different imperatives of justice.[39] In that dangerous location we can easily lose our sense of what is right or fair in a welter of distracting detail—the fine grain of an individual life inevita-bly produces a cluttered complexity that may not be helpful. It is worth pointing out that something of this sort has certainly happened in the no-torious cases of Leni Reifenstahl and Heidegger, whose life histories were amended by their own attempts to project sanitized autobiographical nar-ratives. They scrambled to demonstrate that their particular, ideal versions of National Socialism were, in the first case, entirely unpolitical, and in the second, could not have been associated with mere biological racism, de-spite the fact that the evidence needed to assess this question is obviously unavailable. We need not always defer to the authority of biographies and the veracity effects of those particular forms of truth telling.

More sympathetic defenses of modern philosophical traditions and their capacity to unlock the world have been mounted by many well-inten-tioned voices. The best of them have urged us not to be tempted to dispose of reason but rather to criticize its instrumentalization; not to become skeptical of the ideal of enlightenment but to recognize its debasement in contemporary society; not to retreat from the space of a public culture but to enter that space and demand that its custodians fulfill the promises made in the luminous rhetoric that helped constitute it. To put it simply, we have been told by many of the most eminent and disciplined minds of our time that it is not these ideas that are to be found wanting, but their inadequate implementation and instrumentalization. We need more of them and not, as the postmodern critics might say, less of their immodest aspirations. In counterfactual ways, their enduring power has been reasserted and made indispensable to contemporary democracy. If we are to defend the least bad political and economic systems against the encroachments of organized, militant, and sometimes terroristic irrationalism, we need a resurgent democracy that can only operate if these pivotal concepts are deployed. This must be done with real conviction so that cosmopolitans and democrats can articulate substantive hopes, not engage in cynical or "strategic" borrowings from the well-stocked arsenal of resurgent liberalism.

The battle against revitalized fascisms, nationalism, regionalism, fundamentalism, and particularism can only be fought if we are able, with confidence, to employ the best of these ideas and the secular moral systems of modernity in which they have been so prominently voiced. The nation-state remains the most promising means to produce this result. Even if modernity's finest principles were soiled in the past by their relationship to the rational irrationalisms of racism and anti-semitism, that does not mean they cannot be reworked in the future, where conditions are necessarily different. In a passionate and thoughtful essay that makes exactly this type of argument, the philosopher Gillian Rose offered a simple analogy drawn from interpersonal intimacy as a key to understanding what is at stake in these conflicts. If you were betrayed by a friend you cared about, she asks, would that put you off the idea of friendship itself? Her interesting analogy is not applicable in all cases. Suppose instead that the initial intimacy against which any subsequent rupture is to be measured was neither long nor deep but born of painful necessity. Suppose also that there are not good grounds to accord "reason" the initial status of a friend because it has always been encountered under the signature of power as the product of coercive force. However much we may want to defend the potential of reason, and recognize its plural, historical forms, many of us would not want to concede that we should privilege the singular, local codes through which the ideal becomes powerful. At the very least, those codes have lost some of their credibility thanks to the histories of suffering with which they have been associated.

It is not only unreason, barbarism, antiquity, and primitivity that have promoted destruction, evil, and violence. Indeed, Zygmunt Bauman has argued that we should, in considering the limits of theodicy in our late modern time, acknowledge that the principles upon which our complex social and political systems operate allow for unprecedented opportunities for people to do the wrong thing. They multiply the possibilities in which evil can be done and is done more easily by people who are not in themselves evil, brutal, or blindly animated by hatred. The way back toward the idea of universal standards of morality, truth, and justice must, of necessity, be more complex than the direction suggested by Rose's provocative argument. I want to show that the ability to keep the issue of "race" in the forefront of one's thinking is essential if arguments against the principled, thoughtful, but fundamentally mistaken position adopted by thinkers like Rose are to be sustained. The comfort and confidence in her response have been dearly bought. Their price is the exclusion of "race." Even if we choose, like Rose, not to recognize how "race" acquired an epistemological value, the history of the idea and its strange trajectory, between the rational and the irrational, the scientific and the religious, the physical and the metaphysical, the popular and the elitist, poses a special variety of political and moral problems.

ALTERNATE MODERNITY, MODERNITY ELSEWHERE

I have hinted that Arendt, Césaire, and a good many other brave writers have faced these issues before. Their investigations were animated by the moral obligation to consider the connections that might exist between the genocidal terrors perpetrated inside Europe and the patterns of colonial and imperial slaughter that preceded them under Europe's colors but outside its Continental boundaries, its geo-body.[40] That question should remain in mind, but it cannot be answered hastily here. Instead, noting that the political logic of "race" works within a distinctive temporal and spatial framework that made empire a vital force within as well as without, here as well as there, I want to pursue another line of inquiry. It is oriented by the idea that blacks have borne witness to Europe's failings not just as colonized peoples in distant conquered and exploited lands, but at the other end of the imperial chain, inside Europe as citizens, bystanders, and sojourners.[41] This witnessing has sometimes been undertaken in the names of modernity and culture. Furthermore, there is the additional possibility that a history of this activity might be important today. There is a chance that it can be set to work in usefully complicating the history of raciology.

Employed explicitly, it might help to connect the presence of colonial peoples in Europe to the history of Europe's Jews and other vulnerable minorities conceptualized, plotted, and projected on a different non-national scale. It might usher in and give value to some of the alternate and devalued experiences of modernity that were organized through "race" and to the dissident democratic cultures to which struggles against race-thinking have made such extensive contributions. I proceed from these premises to ask what conceptual schemes around the idea of modernity—thankfully disabused of its fake innocence and Europe-centered solipsism—might foster the recognition of this historic convergence.

Responding to this stiff challenge requires a renewed critique of the idea of "race" itself—one hopes its death as a principle of moral and political calculation—but it cannot end with that. There have to be further confrontations, on one side with the human body represented as the fundamental repository of the order of racial truth, and on the other, with the idea of culture itself. The latter task asks us to identify again the distinctive rationalities, logics, metaphysics, pathologies, and possibilities of a more complex cultural ecology: one that sees species life as the outcome of interplay between communicative systems and the environments they incorporate but also modify and transcend.

While racisms endure, a distinctive understanding of identity does emerge from serious consideration of the dense, hybrid, and multiple formations of postcolonial culture in which translation is simultaneously both unremarkably routine and charged with an essential ethical significance. In its simplest form this understanding of solidarity, selfhood, and subjectivity might be congruent with a problem that the great humanist Jean Améry enumerated when he spoke long ago of the condition he described as the simultaneous "necessity and impossibility of being a Jew." A comparable state of being and not belonging has already been named by black thinkers as well versed as Améry in the esteemed traditions of speculative thought from which they were sometimes excluded by racial typology. They called it double consciousness.

The work of writers around the problematic of Négritude, Senghor and Fanon as well as Césaire, provides one of many possible entry points into this field. Their work is special not because they transcoded the Hegelian speculations of African Americans like Du Bois into a different moment, a different standpoint, but because, as Sandra Adell has so brilliantly shown, the black identities they argued with and argued over were partly created with a strange combination of conceptual tools provided by such unlikely figures as Leo Frobenius and even Heidegger.[42] Like many circum-Atlantic blacks, this group pondered Hitler's fragmentary pronouncements in *Mein Kampf* on the Negro and the perils of intermixture. During the 1930s, they followed the beleaguered position of European Jews attentively and pondered the relationship between the familiar patterns of pre-genocidal terror and discrimination against the German Jews and the different but certainly comparable situation to be found both in the Jim Crow Southern states and in their less formal, Northern approximations. Having savored Jesse Owens's victories at the 1936 Olympics, they recoiled when he pronounced upon the greatness of Hitler at a Republican Party rally. They cheered loudly when noble, heroic black manhood in the form of Joe Louis defeated Max Schmeling in that historic second fight.

These important examples were raised initially by Fanon. They point forward out of their time toward a transformation in the meaning and status of the black male body and some unprecedented patterns of identification and desire that became routine in the swoosh-emblazoned age of Michael Jordan's planetary stardom. More than any other figure, Fanon carried the anxieties and insights of his black Atlantic peers into subsequent political generations. It is often forgotten that he pronounced himself an antifascist patriot and, after a long journey back to the Fatherland against the injunctions of the Vichy government, went into battle against the Nazis on French soil and was decorated with the Croix de Guerre for his brave conduct in the valley of Doubs near Besançon. There is an obvious danger that these suggestive connections may appear to be nothing more than an accumulation of discrepant anecdotes. And yet, even in an untheorized condition they may be able to yield something morally and politically significant for both our present and Europe's cosmopolitan future. Assessing this necessitates one further round of speculation. Why does it remain so difficult for so many people to accept the knotted intersection of histories produced by this fusion of horizons? Before this question can begin to be answered, I would also like to suggest that these strands of modern history have become entangled irrespective of whether their association is viewed as a convenient, popular, or attractive outcome for those who can conceive of history only in ethnic, national, or racial terms. This loudly post-anthropological approach to complex, profane cultures cannot be expected to please nationalists or apostles of purity whatever their ethnic backgrounds. Oblique linkage warranted by critiques of raciology is unlikely to be appreciated as a convenient or easy phenomenon. It may not fit straightforwardly into the settled, orthodox patterns that regulate cultural criticism and historiography. Indeed, the connections we may be able to establish between countercultures of modernity and the profane counterpowers they animate are often regarded not with a healthy suspicion but with open discomfort and what, thanks to Zygmunt Bauman, we now know to be a "proteophobic" unease. This is because of the threat they are imagined to pose to the integrity of the groups whose solidarity the writing of history from ethnonational and racial perspectives is required to serve.

These counterhistorical narratives disturb the sediment over which the streams of modernity have flowed. What was transparent becomes murky. Previously unseen patterns of motion are revealed. It becomes possible to seek answers to what ought to have been obvious questions. What, for example, was the impact of Disraeli's fundamentalist view of "race" on the nineteenth-century African-American intellectuals who adapted his theories to their own needs and circumstances? How many of the ordinary men and women who became functionaries and supporters of the National Socialist cause had previously served in the German colonial forces or had other experiences of Germany's blood-soaked imperial adventures in South West Africa, Tanganyika, New Guinea, or China?[43] What did Léopold Sédar Senghor mean when he spoke of Nazism as having brought him to his senses? How could Norbert Elias, the most subtle and perceptive of sociological minds, be unable to recognize in more than one lone sentence that Germany had possessed an empire at all, something made obvious by even the most cursory reading of *Mein Kampf?* Hitler's book bears the deep imprint of popular racial science. He is known to have read the celebrated textbook on that subject published by Eugen Fischer and his associates Erwin Baur and Fritz Lenz when he was imprisoned in Landsberg. Lenz, who appreciated how Hitler had made race hygiene an important element of state policy, reviewed *Mein Kampf* for the journal *Der Rassenhygiene.* He noted with pride that the Führer had borrowed many of his ideas and claimed further that the direct means of transmission had been supplied by Julius Friedrich Lehmann, the textbook's publisher, who had personally presented Hitler with a copy of the second edition. Lenz's son Wilhelm, another racial scientist based this time at the University of Posen, worked for Alfred Rosenberg's civil administration in Riga and energetically applied his father's race theory to the task of assessing the racial composition of the Lettish population with a view to their eventual re-volking.[44]

Inspired by material like this, many observers have recognized that European Jews and colonial peoples have been connected by the transnational workings of raciology and governmental race-hygiene. Against the myopic logic that can comprehend the sufferings of these groups only in particularistic terms, they have been associated in numerous ways by their incarnation in racial metaphysics and their serial service as "others" in the "manicheism delirium" that distinguished the colonial order. The essential point is that these connections can now be made to point toward an altogether different, de-centered understanding of European history. Beyond that, they anticipate a set of cosmopolitan ethical obligations that try, not to transcend nationality, but rather, self-consciously and deliberately to set its claims aside in favor of more honest and worthy pursuits. They aspire, for example, to reconceptualize history so that the modernizing force of raciology can be recognized as having been intrinsic to the operations of power and government. Perhaps this approach will also be less deferential than is currently fashionable toward the technologies of territoriality that created Europe's imaginary unity. Perhaps it will see Europe instead as a fictive, less integral, and more extended configuration. The creative possibilities that flow from this change can be underlined by this useful example drawn from the French imperial setting:

> De Gaulle, in London, spoke of treason, of soldiers who surrendered their swords even before they had drawn them. All this contributed to convincing the West Indians that France, their France, had not lost the war but that traitors had sold it out . . . One then witnessed an extraordinary sight: West Indians refusing to take off their hats while the Marseillaise was being played. What West Indian can forget those Thursday evenings when on the Esplanade de la Savane, patrols of armed soldiers demanded silence and attention while the national anthem was being played? What had happened?[45]

We have become so accustomed to reading this sort of tale as a manifestation of an identity crisis visited on the colonized that we can miss the significance of the event for the colonizers and readily underestimate the impact of the image of an "antifascist," authentically national, and yet thoroughly colonial voice for Europe itself. Fanon's fellow Martiniqueans were not so immersed in the values of their colonizers that they were unable to distinguish the authentic culture of their parent-nation from its transitory political perversion by Vichy's collaborators with National Socialism. We need to ask how their reaction against Nazism was produced from the conditions of their colonial subordination. How would their later demands for national liberation be informed by exposure to fascists and their colonial supporters? Fanon was not alone among diaspora blacks in puzzling over the meanings of these unanticipated identifications and pondering their significance for religious belief, for secular humanism, for Western civilization and the prospect of its nonracial rehabilitation. Colonial modernity called the boundaries around Europe's national cultures into question. But the official portrait of the nation as an integrated unit subject to hierarchical distinctions under a political regime grounded on the idea of contiguous territory remained untroubled even when colonial parts of it, like Fanon's Martinique and Senghor's Senegal, were remote. National territory was bound to its colonies by more than governmental authority. Culture and language, biology and "race" were all elements of the imperial constitution. This model of belonging to a political body created profound problems for its colonial members, who were barred by "race" and color from assuming their rightful places in the family romance of the imagined community.

NATIONS, ENCAMPMENTS, AND FASCISM

As the example of Martinique makes clear, fascism's militarism and fraternalism changed the character of its national communities. However, the transformation of European nation-states into martial camps did not always coincide with the rise of fascism as a distinctive political and cultural technology. That process of consolidation and authoritarian reintegration should not be identified exclusively with the exceptional patterns exhibited where fascists triumphed. Colonial domination suggests that this process had a longer history and a more general significance. The nationalization, rationalization, and militarization of government communicated not only the entrance of "race" into the operations of modern political culture but also the confluence of "race" and nation in the service of authoritarian ends.

It should be apparent that modern nation-states have sometimes constituted camps in a straightforward descriptive sense. The organized work of disciplining and training citizens has had to coexist with less formal, involutionary complexes in which the fantastic idea of transmuting heterogeneity into homogeneity could be implemented and amplified outward as well as inward. Where "race" and nation became closely articulated, with each order of discourse conferring important legitimation on the other, the national principle can be recognized as having formed an important bond between different and even opposing nationalisms. The dominant varieties were bound to the subordinate by their shared notions of what nationality entailed. The forms of nationalism that invoke this mode of belonging exemplify camp-thinking. They have distinctive rules and codes, and however bitterly their various practitioners may conflict with each other, a common approach to the problem of collective solidarity is betrayed by shared patterns of thought about self and other, friend and stranger; about culture and nature as binding agents and about the technological institution of political collectivities to which one can be compelled to belong.

The recurrence of unexpected connections between avowedly sworn foes defines one axis of "race" politics in the twentieth century. What is more properly termed the (anti-)politics of "race" is deeply implicated in the institution of these national camps and the emergence of nationalized statecraft as an alternative to the traditional conceptions of political activity. Politics is reconceptualized and reconstituted as a dualistic conflict between friends and enemies. At its worst, citizenship degenerates into soldiery and the political imagination is entirely militarized. The exaltation of war and spontaneity, the cults of fraternity, youth, and violence, the explicitly antimodern sacralization of the political sphere, and its colonization by civil religion involving uniforms, flags, and mass spectacles, all underline that these camps are fundamentally martial phenomena. They are armed and protected spaces that offer, at best, only a temporary break in unforgiving motion toward the next demanding phase of active conflict.

Marx and Engels appropriated this idea of political solidarity in opposition to the power of nation-states when, at the start of *The Communist Manifesto,* they described the world they saw progressively divided "into two great hostile camps . . . facing each other." The class-based identification of the countryless proletarians was thus also a matter of camp-thinking—a mode of solidarity so powerful that it broke the historic allegiance of their universal class, industrial workers, to its respective national bourgeoisies. They saw antagonistic social forces more profound than those of the nation constituted in this distinctive arrangement. It would be foolish to deny that the internal organization of class consciousness and class struggle can also foster what Alexander Kluge and Oscar Negt, in their discussion of the history of the proletarian public sphere, call a "camp mentality." They contrast the oppositional but nonetheless antidemocratic moods fostered in the sealed-off space of the class-based camp with the openness that a living public culture can accumulate even in the most beleaguered circumstances. Although Kluge's and Negt's concerns differ from mine in that they are directed toward histories of class and party as sources of camp-thinking, it should be obvious that the solidarity of the camp can be constituted and fortified around dimensions of division other than class.

The camp mentalities constituted by appeals to "race," nation, and ethnic difference, by the lore of blood, bodies, and fantasies of absolute cultural identity, have several additional properties. They work through appeals to the value of national or ethnic purity. Their biopolitical potency immediately raises questions of prophylaxis and hygiene, "as if the (social) body had to assure itself of its own identity by expelling waste matter."[46] They incite the regulation of fertility even more readily than they command the labor power of their affiliates. Where the nation is a kin group supposedly composed of uniform and interchangeable family groups, the bodies of women provide the favored testing grounds for the principles of obligation, deference, and duty that the camp/nation demands. The debates about immigration and nationality that continually surface in contemporary European politics have regularly presented the intrusions of blacks, Moslems, and other interlopers as an invasion. They can be used to illustrate each of these unsavory features.

Though it may produce spectacular results, the camp mentality of the nationalists is betrayed by its crude theories of culture and might even be defined by the veneration of homogeneity, purity, and unanimity that it fosters. Inside the nation's fortifications, culture is required to assume an artificial texture and an impossibly even consistency. The national camp puts an end to any sense of cultural development. Culture as process is arrested. Petrified and sterile, it is impoverished by the national obligation not to change but to recycle the past continually in an essentially unmodified mythic form. Tradition is reduced to simple repetition.

In his unwholesome nineteenth-century raciological inquiry into the meaning of nationality, Ernst Renan famously argued that there was an active contradiction between the demands of nation-building and those of authentic historical study. The nation and its new temporal order involved, for him, socialized forms of forgetting and historical error. These can be identified as further symptoms of the camp mentality. An orchestrated and enforced amnesia supplies the best climate in which the national camp's principles of belonging and solidarity become attractive and powerful. We will see in the next chapter that the national camp demands the negation of diaspora not least because the latter places a premium on commemorative work. The diaspora opposes the camp where it becomes comfortable in the in-between locations that camp-thinking deprives of any significance.

For the members of the ethnic, national, or racial camp, chronic conflict, a war in the background, latent as well as manifest hostility, can legitimize stern patterns of discipline, authority, and deference. The camp always operates under martial rules. Even if its ideologues speak the language of organic wholeness, it is stubbornly a place of seriality and mechanical solidarity. As it moves toward the totalitarian condition of permanent emergency, the camp is shaped by the terrifying sense that anything is possible.

Deliberately adopting a position between camps of this sort is not a sign of indecision or equivocation. It is a timely choice. It can, as I hope the diaspora example in the next chapter will make clear, be a positive orientation against the patterns of authority, government, and conflict that characterize modernity's geometry of power. It can also promote a rich theoretical understanding of culture as a mutable and traveling phenomenon. Of course, occupying a space between camps means also that there is danger of encountering hostility from both sides, of being caught in the pincers of camp-thinking. Responding to this perilous predicament involves rethinking the practice of politics that is always debased where the nation-state operates under camp rules. We are immediately required to move outside the frustrating binary categories we have inherited: left and right, racist and antiracist. We need analyses that are alive to the fluidity and contingency of a situation that seems to lack precedents. If we are to operate in these new circumstances, it helps to approach the problem of encampment from another angle, not as a means to comprehend the geopolitical interrelation of space, identity, and power with modern raciology, but as emblematic sociological and historical features of a volatile period.

I have already identified these national camps as locations in which particular versions of solidarity, belonging, kinship, and identity have been devised, practiced, and policed. Now I want to turn away from the camp as a *metaphor* for the pathologies of "race" and nation and move toward reflection upon actual camps and the political and cultural logics that produced them. These camps were and are a political technology—concrete institutions of radical evil, useless suffering, and modern misery—rather than odious, if somehow routine, expressions of the bad habits of power. To identify a connection between these very different kinds of camp—in effect between levels of racism and nationalism regarded as normal and the exceptional state represented by genocidal fascisms—may be dismissed as oversimple, even far-fetched. In recent British history, nationalism has sometimes been part of the best populist responses to the menacing neo-fascisms that have been exposed as alien and unpatriotic. Many writers, including Hannah Arendt, have also counterposed the stable juridical institutions of the nation-state to the anarchy and violence of the colonies where raciology was first codified and institutionalized as a principle of government. However, I want to invoke a different case for the value of that linkage. This orientation is today supported by the bewildering tangles of recent postcolonial and postimperial history.[47] It is also a perspective that, as Aimé Césaire made clear long ago, went provocatively to the bottom of the relationship between civilization and barbarism. Its general message is certainly confirmed, for example, in the recent history of Rwanda, where, in conjunction with modern cultural technologies, the civilizing mission of colonial power hardened precolonial conflicts into full-fledged ethnic absolutism fueled equally by the imperatives of raciology and francophony. There, too, the emergence of camp-thinking, militaristic, camp-style nationality, and encamped ethnicity—the key features of the first kind of camps—have been implicated in the institution of camps of the second variety: first genocidal death spaces in which victims were assembled and then, bewilderingly, the refugee camps in which yesterday's killers became victims and reached out to seek aid and compassion.

Understanding this situation entails more than just seeing camps as epiphanies of catastrophic modernity and focusing on the extensive colonial precedents for genocidal killing in Europe. It necessitates recognizing our own postmodern predicament: we are caught not only between national camps but amid the uncertainties and anxieties that the condition of permanent emergency associated with the second type of camp both feeds on and creates. Drawing upon his own memories of suffering as he moved toward eloquent demands for justice, Primo Levi wisely recommended exactly this reorientation. He presents it most clearly at the conclusion of his reflections on the role of the collaborators and other victims of Nazi violence whose persecutors made them complicit in their own destruction and the destruction of their kin and their communities. Facing these recurrent abominations, Levi suggests that this stance should now be part of what it means to adopt a healthy and alert, properly ethical attitude amid chronically corrupting circumstances:

> The fever of our western civilisation that "descends into hell with trumpets and drums," and its miserable adornments are the distorting image of our symbols of social prestige . . . we . . . are so dazzled by power and prestige as to forget our essential fragility: willingly or not we come to terms with power, forgetting that we are all in the ghetto, that the ghetto is walled in, that outside the ghetto reign the lords of death and that close by the train is waiting.[48]

Levi's argument should not be an open license to indulge in paranoia. It loses none of its force when we appreciate that the trains are not necessarily being loaded right now in our own neighborhoods. Fascism is not permanently on the brink of assuming terroristic governmental power. His point is far more subtle. If we wish to live a good life and enjoy just relations with our fellows, our conduct must be closely guided not just by this terrible history but by the knowledge that these awful possibilities are always much closer than we like to imagine. To prevent their reappearance, we must dwell on them and with them, for they have become an essential moral resource: a compass sensitive to the demanding, individualizing, anti-ethical field of postmodernity. Levi's shocking insight is compounded by the fact that there are no more acceptable excuses for the failure to become completely familiar with the institutional life of camps. We do not have to become inmates to appreciate that their testimony calls out to us and we must answer it. This means being alive to the camps out there now and the camps around the corner, the camps that are being prepared.

With another sage version of strategic postmodern universality in mind, Zygmunt Bauman has suggested that our unstable time could one day be remembered as "The Age of Camps." For him, camps are confirmation of the fact that cruelty has been modernized, sundered from modern morality. Bauman, for whom a reconfigured humanism is neither explicitly post-anthropological nor postcolonial, makes no secret of his Europe-centeredness. He has Auschwitz and the gulags in mind rather than events in Windhoek, Kigali, Dili, and Katanga. For him the murderous accomplishments of the gardening state do not extend to the genocidal activities of Theodor Leutwein and Lothar Von Trotha among the Herero people of German South West Africa.[49] Although his case is weakened by this oversight, there is nonetheless something valuable and eminently translatable in Bauman's polemical observations, especially if they do not prompt simplistic speculation about some easily accessible essence of modernity.

In moving toward more modest goals, I want to acknowledge the grave dangers that are involved in instrumentalizing extremity. However, I will set those important inhibitions cautiously aside in pursuit of the way that the twentieth century's camps ruptured modern time so comprehensively that remembering them enforces a "before" and an "after." They afford significant points of entry into a new ethical and cultural climate associated with the repudiation of modernity's more extravagant but nonetheless color-coded promises. Adorno's acute sense of the unhappy obligations that these novel circumstances placed upon the committed artist have a wider applicability. They should be studied carefully by the would-be committed academic lest "political reality is sold short for the sake of political commitment; that decreases the political impact as well."[50]

In that spirit, I want to take the risk of identifying camps—refugee camps, labor camps, punishment camps, concentration camps, even death camps—as providing opportunities for moral and political reflection in the careful, cautious sense described by the philosopher Stuart Hampshire, who employs a consideration of Nazism as a means to refine his understanding of justice.[51] Other courageous writers, particularly the German sociologist of the concentration camps Wolfgang Sofsky and the Ugandan political philosopher Mahmood Mamdani, who has insightfully applied the concept of fascism to his careful study of Idi Amin's Uganda, can guide and inspire this research into the historical and practical connections between ultranationalism and the emergence of the infrahuman life forms that the institution of these camps is guaranteed to produce.[52] To link together the very different historical examples to which this diverse body of work is addressed is already to have transgressed against the prescriptive uniqueness invoked to protect the special status of the Nazi genocide. Without being drawn deeply into the question of what, if anything at all, might constitute a common denominator at the experiential level, we can observe that the camp and its extreme wrongs have been associated with the transformation of justice and with important attempts to clarify and restore the normal moral and historical order of modernity once the state of emergency has become an everyday reality. A condition of social death is common to camp inmates in regimes of unfreedom, coercion, and systematic brutality. If genocide is not already under way, the raciology that energizes camp-thinking brings it closer and promotes it as a solution. Let me be absolutely clear: the death factory is not itself a camp—its inmates are unlikely to be alive long enough for camp rules to be engaged. But camps gain something from their proximity to the death factory and other places of organized mass killing. Tadeusz Borowski's extraordinary work springs to mind as our most vivid exploration of the articulation of the camp and the death factory. We can proceed heuristically by arguing that the camp is not always a death factory, though it can easily become one, and that the death factory is one possible variation on the patterns of rational administration that the camp initializes. The procedures of the death factory might also be thought of as partially derivative of the camps that preceded them in Europe and outside it. The definitive statement of this argument is found, of course, in Césaire's angry and moving *Discourse on Colonialism.*

The second type of camp delivers us to the gray zone where the boundaries of humanity are negotiated by force. They are especially important because they have provided some stern tests for the role and stance of the critical intellectual. Jean Améry, Primo Levi's most profound, though not his most unsettling, interlocutor—that title is reserved for Borowski—describes the profound shock of discovering the redundancy of his own egg-head learning in the camp, where, without technical or practical skills, and devoid of religious certainties, intellectuals were less well equipped and more vulnerable than many of their fellows. Under these conditions, their characteristic commitment to an overly abstract humanity amounted to a disability:

> Not only was rational-analytic thinking in the camp and particularly in Auschwitz of no help, but it led straight into a tragic dialectic of self-destruction . . . First of all the intellectual did not so easily acknowledge the unimaginable conditions as a given fact as did the nonintellectual. Long practice in questioning the phenomena of everyday reality prevented him from simply adjusting to the realities of the camp, because these stood in all-too-sharp a contrast to everything that he had regarded until then as possible and humanly acceptable.[53]

Améry's acute commentaries on the temperamental and physical incapacity of intellectuals in camp conditions can be cited again for what they reveal about the specific vulnerability of intellectuals, not to the bodily demands of the camp regime, but to its "philosophical" character and the dynamics of its absolute power. One powerful passage in which Améry illuminates the mechanisms of that total power in ways that extend far beyond his own particular case is worth quoting at length:

> More than his unintellectual mates the intellectual in the camp was lamed by his historically and sociologically explicable deeper respect for power; in fact, the intellectual always and everywhere has been totally under the sway of power. He was, and is, accustomed to doubt it intellectually, to subject it to his critical analysis, and yet in the same intellectual process to capitulate to it. The capitulation became entirely unavoidable when there was no visible opposition to the hostile force. Although outside gigantic armies might battle the destroyer, in the camp one heard of it only from afar and was really unable to believe it. The power structure of the SS state towered up

before the prisoner monstrously and indomitably, a reality that could not be escaped and therefore finally seemed *reasonable*. No matter what his thinking may have been on the outside, in this sense here he became a Hegelian: in the metallic brilliance of its totality the SS state appeared as a state in which the idea was becoming reality.

It is interesting too that Améry, for whom Fanon's work provided a constant point of reference and dialogue, was driven to discover the power of even limited counterviolence in the restoration of the dignified humanity of which he had been deprived: it facilitated the countermovement from infrahumanity back toward the recognizable subjectivity that would count in Kant's democratic equations. In making that case, he points to another of those resonant connections which often produces hesitation, shuffling, and embarrassed silences. In these circumstances, it should be noted that, against the wishes of essentialists and biopoliticians, his emaciated body did not spontaneously manifest the absolute truths of its Jewish "racial" otherness. His words are all the more notable because their contribution to the phenomenology of embodiment and autonomy makes no concessions to the veracity of raciological differences:

> Painfully beaten, I was satisfied with myself. But not, as one might think, for reasons of courage and honor, but only because I had grasped well that there are situations in life in which our body is our entire self and our entire fate. I was my body and nothing else: in hunger, in the blow that I suffered, in the blow that I dealt. My body, debilitated and crusted with filth, was my calamity. My body when it tensed to strike, was my physical and metaphysical dignity. In situations like mine, physical violence is the sole means for restoring a disjointed personality. In the punch I was myself—for myself and for my opponent. What I later read in Frantz Fanon's *Les damnés de la terre*, in a theoretical analysis of the behaviour of colonised peoples, I anticipated back then when I gave concrete form to my dignity by punching a human face. To be a Jew meant the acceptance of the death sentence imposed by the world as a world verdict. To flee before it by withdrawing into oneself would have been nothing but a disgrace, whereas acceptance was simultaneously the physical revolt against it. I became a person not by subjectively ap-

pealing to my abstract humanity but by discovering myself within the given social reality as a rebelling Jew and by realising myself as one.[54]

We should note that there are difficulties involved in attempting to translate this individual gesture and insight into the very different terms and rules of statecraft. It is also essential to appreciate that Améry, no less than Fanon, with whom his work is in such profound dialogue, sublimated these problems through his "existential tie" to a national liberation and state-building project that sits uneasily alongside his equally passionate advocacy of a radical humanism. Both were decisively shaped by his experiences at the hands of the Nazis. The latter was a well-known and powerful corrective to the formal antihumanism of the cold war Left, something Améry regarded as trivializing. I would suggest that the value of his response has increased amid contemporary attempts to reconfigure the ethical and political integrity of the Left at the end of the twentieth century. His poignant reflections on the idea of home, on the complexities of identity and identification, and on the philosophical resources available to renew humanistic critique without falling into the patterns set by the compromised race-friendly and masculinist humanisms of the past remain inspiring even when their commitment to the conceptual constellation of the classical Enlightenment seems overblown. His clarion call for a return to the values of the Enlightenment looks rather different, however, once we appreciate that it was the outcome of a long and patient detour through the genocidal barbarities that racial science, raciological reason, and exclusionary humanity had made possible. These were not to be transcended by dialectical or any other means. They were to be passionately preserved, worked upon, and actively remembered so that they could guard against the inevitable future perils that simplistic, innocent notions of progress just simply cannot entertain.

Améry's extraordinary account of his experiences in Auschwitz Monowitz and other camps might be instructively placed alongside the reflections of Léopold Sédar Senghor. Like Dedan Kimathi and Ahmed Ben Bella, Senghor is a convenient representative of the generation of colonial intellectuals who faced fascism on the battlefield and then used their confrontations with it to clarify their approaches to freedom and democracy, culture and identity. Senghor's work exhibits a similar pattern in which fervent humanism is combined with, but somehow not contradicted by, a romantic ethnic particularity and an appreciation for cultural syncretism and transcultural symbiosis. The Senegalese poet, statesman, resistance fighter, socialist, and influential theorist of Négritude, hybridity, and cultural intermixture was captured with fellow members of the Colonial Infantry at La Charité-sur-Loire in June 1940. Saved from a racist massacre at the moment of surrender by the intervention of a French officer, Senghor was confined for two years in German prison camps, principally Frontstalag 230, near Poitiers. In these camps, Senghor met other troops who had come into combat direct from Africa and whose social backgrounds were very different from his own elite formation. Senghor sought comfort in the traditional songs, poems, and stories of his fellow Africans and in the classic works of European philosophy and literature. Neither of these experiences redeemed the camp, but they did help him to reconstitute his sense of humanity out of absolutism's reach but still under its nose. He describes how his re-reading—particularly of Goethe—triggered a "veritable conversion" that enabled him to live with the complex transcultural patterns of his own hybrid mentality and to see that complex commingling as something more than the loss and betrayal we are always told it must be. His comprehension of the relationship between the particular and the universal was thus enhanced along with his understanding of Négritude itself. In one postwar essay, "Goethe's Message to the New Negroes," he describes how, while standing at the camp's barbed wire, he arrived at these important insights under the uncomprehending gaze of a Nazi sentinel:

> I had been in the camp for "colonial" prisoners of war for one year . . . My progress in German had at last enabled me to read Goethe's poetry in the original . . . The defeat of France and of the West in 1940 had, at first, stupefied black intellectuals. We soon awoke under the sting of the catastrophe naked and sober . . . It is thus, I thought close to the barbed wire of the camp, that our most incarnate voice, our most Negro works would be at the same time our most human . . . and the Nazi sentry looked me up and down with an imbecilic air. And I smiled at him, and he didn't understand.
> Strange meeting, significant lesson.[55]

The poetry that Senghor produced at the camp would be published as the volume *Hosties Noires*. It was smuggled out of the compound to his friend Georges Pompidou by another of the guards, a German soldier who had formerly been Professor of Chinese at the University of Vienna.[56] Strange meeting indeed. These are only tiny examples. Many more could be drawn from the brave and strange lives of other, perhaps lesser known, black witnesses to European barbarity. Their complex consciousness of the dangers of camp-thinking and good understanding of the antitoxins that can be discovered and celebrated in crossing cultures—mixing and moving between—provide important resources which today's postcolonial peoples will require if we are to weather the storms that lie ahead.

Today the need to find an answer to globalization has stimulated some new and even more desperate varieties of camp-thinking. One of the many things that examples drawn from the generation that faced fascism can communicate is an invitation to contemplate the precarious nature of our own political environments. Reflecting on the brutal context in which these testimonies were first uttered, and thinking about the institutional patterns that fitted around them, makes it easier to grasp that we inhabit a beleaguered niche in what used to be, but is no longer, a state of emergency. The ubiquity of the camp in our mediascape conveys the routinization of the exceptional and our habituation to it. Modernity is besieged. As democracy, as creativity, and as cosmopolitan hope it is pitted against a moribund system of formal politics and its numbing representational codes, against the corrosive values of economic rationality and the abjection of postindustrial urban life. The persistence of fascism and the widespread mimicry of its styles constitute only the most alarming sign that modernity's best culture is assailed from all sides by political movements and technological forces that are working toward the erasure of ethical considerations and the deadening of aesthetic sensibilities. The resurgent power of racist and racializing language, of raciology, is a strong link between the perils of our own dangerous time and the enduring effects of the past horrors that continue to haunt us in Europe. Modernity is on trial and fascism is on hold. We can dispute the value of the term "postmodernity" as an interpretative device turned toward these novel conditions. However that debate is resolved, the camp experiences I have recovered and, I hope, briefly commemorated, are addressed to it, if only because they promote a reflexive, untrusting perspective toward the truth-claims made by modernity's overly complacent advocates, as well as by its sworn foes and their latter-day inheritors.

Although it helps to appreciate that the achievements of modernity are in continual jeopardy, it might be even more important to be able to welcome their incomplete and suspended state. Perhaps it is possible to recognize in that vulnerable condition the first stirrings of a serious response to the wrongs that raciology has repeatedly sanctioned in the "age of camps." The complex responses and layered identities of the black itinerants who witnessed Europe's genocidal catastrophe and were forced by their own formation to connect it to colonial history will be resumed in later chapters. Meanwhile, the concept of modernity remains invaluable in developing the change of orientation I favor as a response to the complex situation their journeys bring into focus. First, it draws the discussion of fascism away from the beguiling idea of a German sonderweg and the sense that Germany alone represents the immoral hub of eliminationist anti-semitism. Second, we have seen that as a temporal and qualitative category, modernity introduces a number of philosophical and historical problems at the center of which lies the fundamental issue of the relationship between racial nationalism, government, and rationality. The articulation of reason and history arises as a problem particularly where we recognize disputes about the scale upon which history should operate and, consequently, about the claims of religious, national, regional, or ethnic particularity upon our understanding.

Much has been written recently about that fateful shift from species to ethnos and the transformed understanding of humanity and its limits that took root in its wake. The Jew is only one of a number of figures of particularity that took on a new shape in that moment of transformation by becoming an object of raciology. It is important to recognize that, as with "the Negro," another obvious contender in the dynamic interplay of modernity, selfhood, and alterity, representations of the Jew have a lengthy history and that modern inventions, elaborations, and projections of that figure were reworked from ample materials inherited from a previous time in which the cosmos, the global, and the divine were quite differently configured.

In conclusion, let us once again make Améry our guide in approaching the relationship between modernity and enlightenment, which becomes pivotal at this point in the history of anti-semitisms and other racisms. His strong commitment to the goals of enlightenment was tempered by recognition of the inescapable power of emotions that could not, and should not, be silenced. The ensuing desire to reconcile rebellious passion with dispassionate justice in a combination that could simultaneously both fulfill and transcend the laws of enlightenment was articulated precisely so that shallow rationalism would not triumph and thereby, as he put it, "place the incomprehensible in the cold storage of history." His words underline how much more thinking we have still to do, especially those of us who do not have the living, embodied memory of these terrors as our torment and our incentive to know modernity better. We are led to a sense of the ethical and political gains that result from keeping a conversation about the value of modernity going.

Améry's closing sentences to the preface of the 1977 reissue of *At the Mind's Limits* describe this difficult stance, which, for all its worthy hopes, does not seem to have assisted him in the difficult work of finding life endurable. In response to his stringent demands, it seems worth trying to clarify the level of abstraction at which the concept of modernity operates most productively. I have tried to suggest that there are worthwhile critical observations to be made about the scale of analysis with which it has been most readily associated. Thinking of modernity as a region rather than a period generates additional urgent questions: Can we proceed confident that modernity is not a handy and exclusive codeword for social relations in certain favored parts of Europe? Can an engagement with translocal histories of suffering help to accomplish the shift from Europe-centered to cosmopolitan ways of writing history? More controversially, how do we keep the duality of modernity as progress and catastrophe, civilization and barbarism, at the forefront of our deliberations? How does placing racisms at the center of our thinking transform our command of those dualities? Does it help to address enlightenment through its vernacular codes as an ethnohistorical phenomenon? Should it become nothing much more than the distinctive burden of particular groups, which, though it points beyond their particularity to an emergent universalism, has grave difficulties in making this desirable adjustment? Here we confront substantive political questions for which superficial methodological disputes are an inadequate cloak. Are metahistorical, philosophical, and sociological speculations undone by microhistorical narratives which add so much texture and local color that generalization becomes impossible and we become politically inert, secure in the confidence that we have the best interpretation of the available data?

It may be better to welcome a change of scale and work toward a more complex picture in a longer time frame, perhaps also within a conceptual scheme that reorients our thinking away from the glamour of ethnos and redirects it to what used to be called "the problem of species being." This could be presented as an exercise in strategic universalism.

I am not scorning the historian's craft, nor need the change I propose here mean that modernity always slips back in time toward Luther and the invention of moveable type, or Columbus and the revolution in European world consciousness. As the humanities recoil from the charge of politicization, the favored response to these pressures lies in the time-honored refusal to acknowledge the complicity of rationality and barbarity. A conservative complacency seeks quietly to reinstate the innocent, unreflexive universalisms—liberal, religious, and ethnocentric. Here the concept of postmodernity might provide a useful supplementary means to mark the irretrievable loss of that innocence in truth-seeking and history-writing for which the histories of blacks and Jews in the modern Western world provide the best, that is the most inhumane, examples.

3

When first he opens his eyes, an infant ought to see the fatherland, and up to the day of his death he ought never to see anything else. Every true republican has drunk in love of country, that is to say love of law and liberty, along with his mother's milk. This love is his whole existence; he sees nothing but the fatherland, he lives for it alone; when he is solitary, he is nothing; when he has ceased to have a fatherland, he no longer exists; and if he is not dead, he is worse than dead.

—ROUSSEAU

If things aren't going too well in contemporary thought, it's because there's a return . . . to abstractions, back to the problem of origins, all that sort of thing . . . Any analysis in terms of movements, vectors, is blocked. We're in a very weak phase, a period of reaction. Yet philosophy thought that it had done with the problem of origins. It was no longer a question of starting or finishing. The question was rather, what happens "in between"?

—GILLES DELEUZE

We have seen that the uncertain and divided world we inhabit has made racial identity matter in novel and powerful ways. But we should not take the concept of identity and its multiple associations with "race" and raciology for granted. The term "identity" has recently acquired great resonance, both inside and outside the academic world. It offers far more than an obvious, common-sense way of talking about individuality, community, and solidarity and has provided a means to understand the interplay between subjective experiences of the world and the cultural and historical settings in which those fragile, meaningful subjectivities are formed. Identity has even been taken into the viscera of postmodern commerce, where the goal of planetary marketing promotes not just the targeting of objects and services to the identities of particular consumers but the idea that any product whatsoever can be suffused with identity. Any commodity is open to being "branded" in ways that solicit identification and try to orchestrate identity.[1]

In this chapter I want to show that there is more at stake in the current interest in identity than we often appreciate. I would also like to uncover some of the complexities that make identity a useful idea to explore if we can only leave its obviousness behind and recognize that it is far from being the simple issue that its currency in both government and marketplace makes it appear to be. Where the word becomes a concept, identity has been made central to a number of urgent theoretical and political issues, not least belonging, ethnicity, and nationality. Racialized conflicts, for example, are now understood by many commentators as a problem of the incompatible identities that mark out deeper conflicts between cultures and civilizations. This diagnosis sets up or perhaps confirms the even more widespread belief that the forms of political conflict with which racial division has been associated are somehow unreal or insubstantial, secondary or peripheral. This is something I intend to dispute. The new popularity of identity as an interpretative device is also a result of the exceptional plurality of meanings the term can harness. These diverse inflections—some of which are adapted from highly specialized academic usage—are condensed and interwoven as the term circulates. We are constantly informed that to share an identity is to be bonded on the most fundamental levels: national, "racial," ethnic, regional, and local. Identity is always bounded and particular. It marks out the divisions and subsets in our social lives and helps to define the boundaries between our uneven, local attempts to make sense of the world. Nobody ever speaks of a human identity. The concept orients thinking away from any engagement with the basic, anti-anthropological sameness that is the premise of this book. As Judith Butler puts it in her thoughtful reflection on the concept: "it seems that what we expect from the term *identity* will be cultural specificity, and that on occasion we even expect *identity* and *specificity* to work interchangeably."[2]

The same troubling qualities are evident where the term has been employed to articulate controversial and potentially illuminating themes in modern social and political theory. It has been a core component in the scholarly vocabulary designed to promote critical reflection upon who we are and what we want. Identity helps us to comprehend the formation of that perilous pronoun "we" and to reckon with the patterns of inclusion and exclusion that it cannot help creating. This situation is made more difficult once identity is recognized as something of a problem in itself, and thereby acquires an additional weighting. Calculating the relationship between identity and difference, sameness and otherness is an intrinsically political operation. It happens when political collectivities reflect on what makes their binding connections possible. It is a fundamental part of how they comprehend their kinship—which may be an imaginary connection, though nonetheless powerful for that.

The distinctive language of identity appears again when people seek to calculate how tacit belonging to a group or community can be transformed into more active styles of solidarity, when they debate where the boundaries around a group should be constituted and how—if at all—they should be enforced. Identity becomes a question of power and authority when a group seeks to realize itself in political form. This may be a nation, a state, a movement, a class, or some unsteady combination of them all. Writing about the need for political institutions and relationships at the dawn of our era, Rousseau drew attention to the bold and creative elements in the history of how disorganized and internally divided groups had been formed into coherent units capable of unified action and worthy of the special status that defined the nation as a political body. Reflecting on the achievements of heroic individual leaders as builders of political cultures that could "attach citizens to the fatherland and to one another," he noted that the provision of a unifying common identity was a significant part of this political process. Significantly for our purposes, his example was taken from the history of the Children of Israel:

(Moses) conceived and executed the astonishing project of creating a nation out of a swarm of wretched fugitives, without arts, arms, talents, virtues or courage, who were wandering as a horde of strangers over the face of the earth without a single inch of ground to call their own. Out of this wandering and servile horde Moses had the audacity to create a body politic, a free people . . . he gave them that durable set of institutions, proof against time, fortune and conquerors, which five thousand years have not been able to destroy or even alter . . . To prevent his people from melting away among foreign peoples, he gave them customs and usages incompatible with those of other nations; he over-burdened them with peculiar rites and ceremonies; he inconvenienced them in a thousand ways in order to keep them constantly on the alert and to make them forever strangers among other men.[3]

In outlining elements of the political technology that would eventually produce the nation as a fortified encampment, Rousseau drew attention to the old association between identity and territory. Moses' achievement is viewed as all the more impressive because it was accomplished without the binding power of shared land. Rousseau underlined that the varieties of connection to which our ideas of identity refer are historical, social, and cultural rather than natural phenomena. Even at that early point in the constitution of modernity, he recognized that work must be done to summon the particularity and feelings of identity that are so often experienced as though they are spontaneous or automatic consequences of some governing culture or tradition that specifies basic and absolute differences between people. Consciousness of identity gains additional power from the idea that it is not the end product of one great man's "audacity" but an outcome of shared and rooted experience tied, in particular, to place, location, language, and mutuality.

When we think about the tense relationship between sameness and difference analytically, the interplay of consciousness, territory, and place becomes a major theme. It afford insights into the core of conflicts over how democratic social and political life should be organized at the start of the twenty-first century. We should try to remember that the threshold between those two antagonistic conditions can be moved and that identity-making has a history even though its historical character is often systematically concealed. Focusing on identity helps us to ask in what sense the recognition of sameness and differentiation is a premise of the modern political culture that Rousseau affirmed and which his writings still help us to analyze.

The dizzying variety of ideas condensed into the concept of identity, and the wide range of issues to which it can be made to refer, foster analytical connections between themes and perspectives that are not conventionally associated. Links can be established between political, cultural, psychological, and psychoanalytic concerns. We need to consider, for example, how the emotional and affective bonds that form the specific basis of raciological and ethnic sameness are composed, and how they become patterned social activities with elaborate cultural features. How are they able to induce conspicuous acts of altruism, violence, and courage? How do they motivate people toward social interconnection in which individuality is renounced or dissolved into the larger whole represented by a nation, a people, a "race," or an ethnic group? These questions are important because, as we have seen, grave moral and political consequences have followed once the magic of identity has been engaged tactically or in manipulative, deliberately oversimple ways. Even in the most civilized circumstances, the signs of sameness have degenerated readily into emblems of supposedly essential or immutable difference. The special appeal of individuality-transcending sameness still provides an antidote to the forms of uncertainty and anxiety that have been associated with economic and political crises. The idea of fundamentally shared identity becomes a platform for the reverie of absolute and eternal division.

The use of uniforms and other symbols to effect the sameness that identity only speaks about has sometimes been symptomatic of the process in which an anxious self can be shed and its concerns conjured away by the emergence of a stronger compound whole. The uniforms worn in the 1930s by fascists (and still worn by some fascist groups today) produced a compelling illusion of sameness both for members of the group and for those who observed their spectacular activities. The British Union of Fascists, one of the less-successful black-shirted organizations from that period, argued that their garb was all the more attractive to adherents when contrasted with the conflict and bitterness created by class-based divisions that were tearing the nation apart from within:

> (The "blackshirt") brings down one of the great barriers of class by removing differences of dress, and one of the objects of Fascism is to break the barriers of class. Already the blackshirt has achieved within our own ranks that classless unity which we will ultimately secure within the nation as a whole.[4]

We will explore below how the ultranationalist and fascist movements of the twentieth century deployed elaborate technological resources in order to generate spectacles of identity capable of unifying and coordinating inevitable, untidy diversity into an ideal and unnatural human uniformity. Their synthetic versions of fundamental identity looked most seductive where all difference had been banished or erased from the collective. Difference within was repressed in order to maximize the difference between these groups and others. Identity was celebrated extravagantly in military styles: uniforms were combined with synchronized body movement, drill, pageantry, and visible hierarchy to create and feed the comforting belief in sameness as absolute, metaphysical invariance. Men and women could then appear as interchangeable and disposable cogs in the encamped nation's military machine or as indistinguishable cells in the larger organic entity that encompassed and dissolved their individuality. Their actions may even be imagined to express the inner spirit, fate, and historicality of the national community. The citizen was manifested as a soldier, and violence—potential as well as actual—was dedicated to the furtherance of national interests. That vital community was constituted in the dynamic interaction between marchers moving together in austere time and the crowds that watched and savored the spectacle they created. In disseminating these valuable political effects, identity was mediated by cultural and communicative technologies like film, lighting, and amplified sound. These twentieth-century attributes were only partly concealed by the invocation of ancient ritual and myth.

The biblical stories of nation-building that demonstrate divine favor and the moral sanctions it supplies to worldly political purposes have been invoked by many different nationalist groups. The Afrikaners of South Africa provide one especially interesting and unwholesome example of how Rousseau's "peculiar rites and ceremonies" need not always serve a benign purpose. Their ethnically minded ideologues systematically invented an Afrikaner identity during the period that saw the rise of fascist movements elsewhere. They provided their political community with its own version of Christianity and a repertory of myths that were the basis for the elaborate political drama that summoned their historic nation into racialized being:

> The most dramatic event in the upsurge of Afrikaner nationalism
> was the symbolic ox-wagon trek of 1938, which celebrated the vic-

tory of the Great Trek. Eight wagons named after voortrekker heroes such as Piet Retief, Hendrik Potgeiter and Andres Pretorius traversed South Africa by different routes . . . before they converged on a prominent hill overlooking Pretoria. There, on 16th December 1938, the centenary of the battle of Blood River, which marked the defeat of the Zulu kingdom, more than 100,000 Afrikaners—perhaps one tenth of the total Afrikaner people—attended the ceremonial laying of the foundation stone of the Voortrekker Monument. Men grew beards, women wore voortrekker dress, for the occasion . . . (they) knelt in silent prayer . . . The ceremony concluded with the singing of *Die Stem van Suid Afrika; God Save the King* had been excluded.[5]

Today's ubiquitous conflicts between warring constituencies that claim incompatible and exclusive identities suggest that these large-scale theatrical techniques for producing and stabilizing identity and soliciting national, "racial," or ethnic identification have been widely taken up. The reduction of identity to the uncomplicated, militarized, fraternal versions of pure sameness pioneered by fascism and Nazism in the 1930s is now routine, particularly where the forces of nationalism, "tribalism," and ethnic division are at work. Identity is thus revealed as a critical element in the distinctive vocabulary used to voice the geopolitical dilemmas of the late modern age. Where the power of absolute identity is summoned up, it is often to account for situations in which the actions of individuals and groups are being reduced to little more than the functioning of some overarching presocial mechanism. In the past, this machinery was often understood as a historical or economic process that defined the special, manifest destiny of the group in question. These days, it is more likely to be represented as a prepolitical, sociobiological, or biocultural feature, something mysterious and genetic that sanctions especially harsh varieties of deterministic thinking.

In this light, identity ceases to be an ongoing process of self-making and social interaction. It becomes instead a thing to be possessed and displayed. It is a silent sign that closes down the possibility of communication across the gulf between one heavily defended island of particularity and its equally well fortified neighbors, between one national encampment and others. When identity refers to an indelible mark or code somehow written into the bodies of its carriers, otherness can only be a threat. Identity is latent destiny. Seen or unseen, on the surface of the body or buried deep in its cells, identity forever sets one group apart from others who lack the particular, chosen traits that become the basis of typology and comparative evaluation. No longer a site for the affirmation of subjectivity and autonomy, identity mutates. Its motion reveals a deep desire for mechanical solidarity, seriality, and hypersimilarity. The scope for individual agency dwindles and then disappears. People become bearers of the differences that the rhetoric of absolute identity invents and then invites them to celebrate. Rather than communicating and making choices, individuals are seen as obedient, silent passengers moving across a flattened moral landscape toward the fixed destinies to which their essential identities, their genes, and the closed cultures they create have consigned them once and for all. And yet, the desire to fix identity in the body is inevitably frustrated by the body's refusal to disclose the required signs of absolute incompatibility people imagine to be located there.

Numerous cross-cultural examples might be used to illustrate this point. Reports from the genocide in Rwanda repeatedly revealed that identity cards issued by the political authorities were a vital source of the information necessary to classify people into the supposedly natural "tribal" types that brought them either death or deliverance. There, as in several other well-documented instances of mass slaughter, the bodies in question did not freely disclose the secrets of identity:

> Many Tutsis have been killed either because their ID cards marked them out as a Tutsi or because they did not have their card with them at the time and were therefore unable to prove they were not a Tutsi . . . To escape the relentless discrimination they suffered, over the years many Tutsis bribed local government officials to get their ID card changed to Hutu. Unfortunately, this has not protected them . . . The Tutsi give-aways were: one, being tall and two having a straight nose. Such criteria even led hysterical militias to kill a number of Hutus whose crime was "being too tall for a Hutu." Where there was doubt about the person's physical characteristics or because of the complaints that too many Tutsis had changed their card, the Interahamwe called upon villagers to verify the "tutsiship" of the quarry in question.[6]

Similar events were still being reported four years later when the genocidal assault against the Tutsis had been rearticulated into the civil war in Congo—a conflict that had already drawn in several other states and that appeared to provide the key to stability in the region. Under the presidency of Laurent Kabila, people whose physical characteristics made them suspect were still being openly murdered.[7] It is important to remember, however, that the linguistic markers of residual colonial conflict between anglophone and francophone spheres of influence were also implicated in sustaining the killing.

These fragments from a history of unspeakable barbarity underline how the notion of fixed identity operates easily on both sides of the chasm that usually divides scholarly writing from the disorderly world of political conflicts. Recently, identity has also come to constitute something of a bridge between the often discrepant approaches to understanding self and sociality found on the different sides of that widening gulf. As a theme in contemporary scholarship, identity has offered academic thinking an important route back toward the struggles and uncertainties of everyday life, where the idea of identity has become especially resonant. It has also provided the distinctive signatures of an inward, implosive turn that brings the difficult tasks of politics to an end by making them appear irrelevant in the face of deeper, more fundamental powers that regulate human conduct irrespective of governmental superficialities. If identity and difference are fundamental, then they are not amenable to being re-tooled by crude political methods that cannot possibly get to the heart of primal ontologies, destinies, and fates. When the stakes are this high, nothing can be done to offset the catastrophic consequences that result from tolerating difference and mistaken attempts at practicing democracy. Difference corrupts and compromises identity. Encounters with it are just as unwelcome and potentially destructive as they were for Houston Stewart Chamberlain. They place that most precious commodity, rooted identity, in grave jeopardy.

When national and ethnic identities are represented and projected as pure, exposure to difference threatens them with dilution and compromises their prized purities with the ever-present possibility of contamination. Crossing as mixture and movement must be guarded against. New hatreds and violence arise not, as they did in the past, from supposedly reliable anthropological knowledge of the identity and difference of the Other but from the novel problem of not being able to locate the Other's difference in the common-sense lexicon of alterity. Different people are certainly hated and feared, but the timely antipathy against them is nothing compared with the hatreds turned toward the greater menace of the half-different and the partially familiar. To have mixed is to have been party to a great betrayal. Any unsettling traces of hybridity must be excised from the tidy, bleached-out zones of impossibly pure culture. The safety of sameness can then be recovered by either of the two options that have regularly appeared at the meltdown point of this dismal logic: separation and slaughter.

IDENTITY, SOLIDARITY, AND SELFHOOD

The political language of identity levels out distinctions between chosen connections and given particularities: between the person you choose to be and the things that determine your individuality by being thrust upon you. It is particularly important for the argument that follows that the term "identity" has become a significant element in contemporary conflicts over cultural, ethnic, religious, "racial," and national differences. The idea of collective identity has emerged as an object of political thinking even if its appearance signals a sorry state of affairs in which the distinctive rules that define modern political culture are consciously set aside in favor of the pursuit of primordial feelings and mythic varieties of kinship that are mistakenly believed to be more profound. At the same time, individual identity, the counterpart to the collective, is constantly negotiated, cultivated, and protected as a source of pleasure, power, wealth, and potential danger. That identity is increasingly shaped in the marketplace, modified by the cultural industries, and managed and orchestrated in localized institutions and settings like schools, neighborhoods, and workplaces. It can be inscribed in the dull public world of official politics where issues surrounding the absence of collective identity—and the resulting disappearance of community and solidarity from social life—have also been discussed at great length by politicians on different sides of the political divide.

Other aspects of identity's foundational slipperiness can be detected in the way that the term is used to register the impact of processes that take place above and below the level at which the sovereign state and its distinctive modes of belonging are constituted. The growth of nationalisms and other absolutist religious and ethnic identities, the accentuation of regional and local divisions, and the changing relationship between supranational and subnational networks of economy, politics, and information have all endowed contemporary appeals to identity with extra significance. Identity has come to supply something of an anchor amid the turbulent waters of de-industrialization and the large-scale patterns of planetary reconstruction that are hesitantly named "globalization."[8] It would appear that recovering or possessing an appropriately grounded identity can provide a means to hold these historic but anxiety-inducing processes at bay. Taking pride or finding sanctuary in an exclusive identity affords a means to acquire certainty about who one is and where one fits, about the claims of community and the limits of social obligation.

The politicization of gender and sexuality has enhanced the understanding of identity by directing attention to the social, familial, historical, and cultural factors that bear upon the formation and social reproduction of masculinity and femininity. Two groups of agents are bound together by the centripetal force of the stable, gendered identities that they apparently hold in common. But the anxious, disciplinary intensity with which these ideas are entrenched seems to increase in inverse proportion to the collapse of family and household structures and the eclipse of male domestic domination. In these important areas, the concept of identity has nurtured new ways of thinking about the self, about sameness, and about solidarity. If abstract identity and its thematics are on the verge of becoming something of an obsessive preoccupation in the overdeveloped countries, this novel pattern communicates how political movements and governmental activities are being reconstituted by a change in the status and capacity of the nation-state.[9]

This transformation also reveals something important about the workings of consumer society.[10] The car you drive and the brand of clothing or sports shoes that you wear may no longer be thought of as accidental or contingent expressions of the arts of everyday life and the material constraints that stem from widening inequalities of status and wealth. Branded commodities acquire an additional burden when they are imagined to represent the private inner truths of individual existence or to fix the boundary of communal sensibilities that have faded from other areas of public or civic interaction. Though it involves some over-simplification, we can begin to unpack the idea of identity so that it reveals several overlapping and interconnected problems that are regularly entangled in the more routine contemporary uses of the term. The first of these is the understanding of identity as subjectivity. Religious and spiritual obligations around selfhood were gradually assimilated into the secular, modern goal of an ordered self operating in an orderly polity.[11] This historic combination was supplemented by the idea that the stability and coherence of the self was a precondition for authoritative and reliable truth-seeking activity. That idea has itself been queried as truth has emerged as something provisional and perspectival that is seldom amenable to the application of placeless, universal laws. The forms of uncertainty that characterize our more skeptical time still emphasize the perils that flow from the lack of a particular variety of self-consciousness and self-cultivation.

When subjectivity is placed in command of its own mechanisms and desires, a heavy investment is made in the idea of identity and the languages of self through which it has been projected. The demise of the certainties associated with religious approaches to understanding oneself and locating oneself in a properly moral relationship to other selves endowed with the same ethical and cognitive attributes has had lasting consequences. The idea of a pre-given, internal identity that regulates social conduct beyond the grasp of conscious reflection has been valuable in restoring elements of increasingly rare and precious certainty to a situation in which doubt and anxiety have become routine. It has also been closely associated with the consolidation of a genomic raciology that promotes forms of resignation in which we are encouraged to do nothing while we wait for those decisive natural differences to announce their presence. These specifications are contradicted by the effects of technological acceleration arising from digital processing and computer-mediated communications. They mean that individual identity is even less constrained by the immediate forms of physical presence established by the body. The boundaries of self need no longer terminate at the threshold of the skin.[12]

The distance that an individual identity can travel toward others and, via technological instruments, become present to them has increased and the quality of that interaction has been transformed by a culture of simulation that has grown up around it. No longer finding uniformity and unanimity in symbols worn on or around the body, like the black shirt, the fascistic political identity cultivated by today's ultranationalist and white supremacist groups can be constituted remotely and transnationally over the Internet through computerized resources like the Aryan Crusader's Library, an on-line networking operation run from the United States but offered worldwide to anyone with a computer and a modem. Governments and corporations are promoting these technological resources as engines of modernized commerce and tools of democracy, but access to them is sharply skewed by poverty, inequality, and a variety of cultural and political factors.[13] That does not, however, mean that the cultural processes they animate and encourage remain confined to the privileged layers where they are most obviously apparent. They can be situated in their wider social setting:

> In the story of constructing identity in the culture of simulation, experiences on the Internet figure prominently, but these experiences can only be understood as part of a larger cultural context. That context is the story of eroding boundaries between the real and the virtual, the animate and the inanimate, the unitary and the multiple self, which is occurring both in advanced fields of scientific research and in the patterns of everyday life. From scientists trying to create artificial life, to children "morphing" through a series of virtual personae, we shall see evidence of fundamental shifts in the way we create and experience human identity.[14]

This uncertain, outward movement, from the anxious body-bound self toward the world, leads us to a second set of difficulties in the field of identity. This is the problem of sameness understood here as intersubjectivity. Considering identity from this angle requires recognition of the concept's role in calculations over precisely what counts as the same and what as different. This in turn raises the further question of recognition and its refusal in constituting identity and soliciting identification. The theme of identification and the consequent relationship between sociology, psychology, and even psychoanalysis enter here and add layers of complexity to deliberations about how selves—and their identities—are formed through relationships of exteriority, conflict, and exclusion. Differences can be found within identities as well as between them. The Other, against whose resistance the integrity of an identity is to be established, can be recognized as part of the self that is no longer plausibly understood as a unitary entity but appears instead as one fragile moment in the dialogic circuits that Debbora Battaglia has usefully called a "representational economy":

> . . . there is no selfhood apart from the collaborative practice of its figuration. The "self" is a representational economy: a reification continually defeated by mutable entanglements with other subjects' histories, experiences, self-representations; with their texts, conduct, gestures, objectifications.[15]

Building on this insight, the argument below takes shape around a third line of questioning: How does the concept of identity provide a means to speak about social and political solidarity? How is the term "identity" invoked in the summoning and binding of individual agents into groups that become social actors? For these purposes, considering identity requires a confrontation with the specific ideas of ethnic, racialized, and national identity and their civic counterparts. This departure introduces a cluster of distinctively modern notions that, in conjunction with discourses of citizenship, have actively produced rather than given a secondary expression to forms of solidarity with unprecedented power to mobilize mass movements and animate large-scale constituencies. The full power of communicative technologies like radio, sound recording, film, and television has been employed to create forms of solidarity and national consciousness that propelled the idea of belonging far beyond anything that had been achieved in the nineteenth century by the industrialization of print and the formalization of national languages.[16]

Contemporary conflicts over the status of national identity provide the best examples here. To return to the South African case for a moment, Nelson Mandela's historic inaugural speech as State President illustrated both the malleability of nationalist sentiment and some of the enduring tensions around its radical constitution. Working to produce an alternative content for the new nonracial, postracial, or perhaps antiracial political identity that might draw together the citizenry of the reborn country on a new basis beyond the grasp of racializing codes and fantasies of favored life as a people chosen by God, President Mandela turned to the land—common ground—beneath the feet of his diverse, unified, and mutually suspicious audience. Significantly, he spoke not only of the soil but of the beauty of the country and offered the idea of a common relationship to both the cultivated and the natural beauty of the land as elements of a new beginning. This, for him, was the key to awakening truly democratic consciousness. A transformed relationship between body and environment would transcend the irrelevancies of Apartheid South Africa's redundant racial hierarchies:

> To my compatriots, I have no hesitation in saying that each one of us is as intimately attached to the soil of this beautiful country as are the famous jacaranda trees of Pretoria and the mimosa trees of the bushveld.
>
> Each time one of us touches the soil of this land, we feel a sense of personal renewal ... That spiritual and physical oneness we all share with this common homeland explains the depth of pain we all carried in our hearts as we saw our country tear itself apart in a terrible conflict.[17]

Whether these laudable claims were a plausible part of rebuilding South African nationality remains to be seen. What is more significant for our purposes is that territory and indeed nature itself are being engaged as a means to define citizenship and the forms of rootedness that compose national solidarity and cohesion. President Mandela's words were powerful because they work with the organicity that nature has bequeathed to modern ideas of culture. In that blur, Mandela constructed an ecological account of the relationship between shared humanity, common citizenship, place, and identity. The speech subverted traditional assumptions with its implication that Apartheid was a brutal violation of nature that could be repaired only if people were prepared to pay heed to the oneness established by their connection to the beautiful environment they share and hold in common stewardship.

The alternative argument set out below recognizes the socioecological dynamics of identity-formation. However, it asks you to consider what might be gained if the powerful claims of soil, roots, and territory could be set aside. You are invited to view them in the light of other possibilities that have sometimes defined themselves against the forms of solidarity sanctioned by the territorial regimes of the nation-state. We will see that the idea of movement can provide an alternative to the sedentary poetics of either soil or blood. Both communicative technology and older patterns of itinerancy ignored by the human sciences can be used to articulate placeless imaginings of identity as well as new bases for solidarity and synchronized action. With these possibilities in mind, I want to suggest that considering the de-territorialized history of the modern African diaspora into the western hemisphere and the racial slavery through which it was accomplished has something useful to teach us about the workings of identity and identification and, beyond that, something valuable to impart about the claims of nationality and the nation-state upon the writing of history itself.

Shut out from literacy on the pain of death, slaves taken from Africa by force used the same biblical narratives we have already encountered to comprehend their situation and, slowly and at great emotional cost, to build what might be understood as a new set of identities. They, too, imagined themselves to be a divinely chosen people. This meant that the suffering visited upon their proto-nations in bondage was purposive and their pain was oriented, not merely toward heavenly freedom, but toward the moral redemption of anyone prepared to join them in the just cause of seeking political liberty and individual autonomy. These themes are nowhere more powerfully articulated than in the work of Martin Luther King, Jr. Writing amid the conflicts of the 1960s that would eventually claim his life, about the difficulties experienced by black Americans whose allegiance to America was broken by their lack of political rights and economic opportunities, he had the following to say about what we would now recognize as identity. (He, too, mobilized the biblical mythology of the chosen people to articulate his political choices and hopes):

> Something of the spirit of our slave forebears must be pursued today. From the inner depths of our being we must sing with them: "Before I'll be a slave, I'll be buried in my grave and go home to my Lord and be free." This spirit, this drive, this rugged sense of somebodyness is the first and vital step that the Negro must take in dealing with his dilemma . . . To overcome this tragic conflict, it will be necessary for the Negro to find a new self-image . . . The Pharaohs had a favorite and effective strategy to keep their slaves in bondage: keep them fighting among themselves . . . But when slaves unite, the Red Seas of history open and the Egypts of slavery crumble.[18]

We must be cautious because there are now considerable political gains to be made from being recognized as possessing an identity defined exclusively by this and other histories of ineffable suffering. Dr. King did not exploit that association, but those who followed in his wake have not always been so scrupulous. The identity of the victim, sealed off and presented as an essential, unchanging state, has become, in the years since his murder, a prized acquisition not least where financial calculations have sought to transform historic wrongs into compensatory monies.[19] This problem has not been confined to black politics with its demands for reparations and other forms of financial restitution for slavery in the Americas. From Palestine to Bosnia, the image of the victim has become useful in all sorts of dubious maneuverings that can obscure the moral and political questions arising from demands for justice. And yet, for all its pragmatic or strategic attractions, the role of the victim has its drawbacks as the basis of any political identity. With characteristic insight, James Baldwin described some of them in a discussion of the meaning of racial terror and its impact upon identity:

> I refuse, absolutely, to speak from the point of view of the victim. The victim can have no point of view for precisely so long as he thinks of himself as a victim. The testimony of the victim as victim corroborates, simply, the reality of the chains that bind him— confirms, and, as it were consoles the jailer.[20]

Baldwin cautions us against closing the gap between identity and politics and playing down the complexities of their interconnection. His words locate the trap involved in hoping that what is lazily imagined to be shared identity might be straightforwardly transferred into the political arena. With his help we can apprehend the many dangers involved in vacuous "me too-ism" or some other equally pointless and immoral competition over which peoples, nations, populations, or ethnic groups have suffered the most; over whose identities have been most severely damaged; and indeed over who might be thought of as the most de-racinated, nomadic, or cosmopolitan and therefore more essentially "modern" or paradigmatically "postmodern" peoples on our planet. However, with Baldwin's warning still in mind, there is much to be learned by foregrounding that experience of being victimized and using it to challenge the willful innocence of some Europe-centered accounts of modernity's pleasures and problems. That difficult operation yields more than a coda to the conventional historical and sociological stories of modern development. Perhaps a changed sense of what it means to be a modern person might result from this reassessment?

The careful reconstruction of those half-hidden, tragic narratives that demonstrate how the fateful belief in mutually impermeable, religious, racial, national, and ethnic identities was assembled and reproduced was briefly addressed in the previous chapter. It fits in well with the archaeological work already being done to account for the complex cultures and societies of the New World and their relationship to the history of European thought, literature, and self-understanding.[21] The significance of colony and empire is also being reevaluated and the boundaries around European nation-states are emerging as more porous and leakier than some architects of complacently national history would want to admit. These discoveries support the demand for a decisive change of standpoint. Again it seems that to comprehend the bleak histories of colonial and imperial power that besmirch the clean edifice of innocent modernity and query the heroic story of universal reason's triumphal march, we must shift away from the historiographical scale defined by the closed borders of the nation-state. If we are prepared to possess those histories and consider setting them to work in divining more modest and more plausible understandings of democracy, tolerance for difference, and cross-cultural recognition than currently exist, this historical argument can redirect attention toward some of the more general contemporary questions involved in thinking about identity in the human sciences. Histories of the violence and terror with which modern rationality has been complicit offer a useful means to test and qualify the explanatory power of theories of identity and culture that have arisen in quieter, less bloody circumstances. Perhaps those theories also derive from the more complacent scholarly ways of thinking about power common to temperate climes. The idea that possessing a particular identity should be a precondition or qualification for engaging in this kind of work is trivial. The intellectual challenge defined here is that histories of suffering should not be allocated exclusively to their victims. If they were, the memory of the trauma would disappear as the living memory of it died away.

This proposed change of perspective about the value of suffering is not then exclusively of interest to its victims and any kin who remember them. Because it is a matter of justice, it is not just an issue for the wronged "minorities" whose own lost or fading identities may be restored or rescued by the practice of commemoration. It is also of concern to those who may have benefited directly and indirectly from the rational application of irrationality and barbarity. Perhaps above all, this attempt to reconceptualize modernity so that it encompasses these possibilities is relevant to the majority who are unlikely to count themselves as affiliated with either of the principal groups: victims and perpetrators. This difficult stance challenges that unnamed group to witness sufferings that pass beyond the reach of words and, in so doing, to see how an understanding of one's own particularity or identity might be transformed as a result of a principled exposure to the claims of otherness.[22]

THE ROOTLESS COSMOPOLITANISM
OF THE BLACK ATLANTIC

Let us imagine that the study of African diaspora identity in the modern, Western world begins with an understanding of the lives of exemplary eighteenth-century figures of whom Olaudah Equiano, Ignatius Sancho, and Phillis Wheatley are the best known.[23] Equiano was a seafarer and a political activist in pursuit of the abolition of slavery who has left us his autobiography, which occupies a primary place in the literary enterprises of this group. He was born in what we would now call Nigeria in the middle of the eighteenth century, then kidnapped as a child and shipped across the Atlantic as a slave. Equiano passed between several masters in different parts of the Americas. His passage from chattel to free man and the processes of self-making that it entailed are communicated in the most obvious way by the proliferation of names under which he was known during different stages of his life—first Michael, then Jacob, and eventually Gustavus Vassa, an appellation borrowed from a celebrated Swedish patriot.

Wheatley, a distinguished poet, celebrity, and eloquent eyewitness to the political upheavals of the American revolutionary war against the British, was Equiano's contemporary. She had been taken from Senegambia as a girl, arrived in Boston in 1761 swathed in a piece of dirty carpet, and was named after the slaver in which she had made her ocean crossing. The absence of her front teeth made observers guess her to be about seven years of age. She was bought by Susannah and John Wheatley for Susannah's use in their home. Having noted Phillis's exceptional predisposition to learn, her owners segregated her from other slaves, appointed their eighteen-year-old daughter as the girl's first tutor, and then decided to have her educated more systematically. She repaid their investments in her mental capacity with a torrent of extraordinary poetry that reflects upon her personal transformation from African to American as well as upon the morality of the wider system that had fostered it. Wheatley was the first black person to publish a book. Her 1773 volume *Poems on Various Subjects, Religious and Moral* was published in London by a printer who had been skeptical of the *bona fides* of its black author. It has been placed by many critics at the head of a distinctive tradition of African-American literary creativity.

Like Equiano and many other ex-slaves and their descendants who would follow in their wakes, Wheatley crossed the Atlantic several times, not only as a slave, but as a free woman. Her journeying took her to London, where she moved in some exalted social circles and, as Peter Fryer has pointed out, against the expectations of her hosts bravely made her abolitionist sympathies known.[24] Sir Brook Watson, later to be a Lord Mayor of London, presented her with an edition of *Paradise Lost,* and she received a significant patronage from Selina Hastings, the countess of Huntington, a wealthy, prominent, and well-connected figure in the Methodist evangelical movement and the woman to whom Wheatley dedicated her book. Wheatley's poems were widely acclaimed, reviewed, and debated not only for their own qualities, but also, as Henry Louis Gates, Jr., has emphasized, for what they were thought to reveal about the intellectual and imaginative capacities of blacks in general. At the age of twenty-three and after fifteen years as a slave, she was freed on the death of her mistress but was unable to publish a second volume of the poetry that she had hawked door to door to raise money to support herself in freedom. This later work was likely to have been less constrained by the obligations of servitude than its predecessor.

It may be significant for our thinking about the workings of identity that although Equiano was involved in a scheme to resettle eighteenth-century London's unwanted blacks in Sierra Leone, neither he nor Wheatley ever returned to the African homelands from which their long journeys through slavery had begun.

This pair has left an interesting collection of published material through which we can consider the effects of relocation, displacement, and forced transition between cultural codes and habits, language, and religion. Their works are especially valuable for several reasons. The authors belonged to the generation that suffered the trauma of the Middle Passage and in which the physical and psychological effects of that brutal disjunction must have been at their most intense. More significantly, though, through their conspicuous mastery of genre, style, and expressive idiom their texts demand from us a sophisticated grasp of cultural syncretism, adaptation, and intermixture. We can, of course, identify elements in Wheatley's work which betray the residual presence of African animistic religion or sun worship. And although we can locate African words and accurate ethnological detail in Equiano's narrative, his work, like Wheatley's, was also influenced by Pope and Milton. They ask to be evaluated on their own terms as complex, compound formations. They should not be valued only as means to observe the durability of African elements or dismissed as an inadequate mixture, doomed always to be something less than the supposedly pure entities that first combined to produce it. Their legacy is most valuable as a mix, a hybrid. Its recombinant form is indebted to its "parent" cultures but remains assertively and insubordinately a bastard. It reproduces neither of the supposedly anterior purities that gave rise to it in anything like unmodified form. Here, at least, identity must be divorced from purity.

Transcultural mixture alerts us not only to the syncretic complexities of language, culture, and everyday modern life in the torrid areas where racial slavery was practiced, but also to the purity-defying metamorphoses of individual identity in the "contact-zones" of an imperial metropolis.[25] Even under those conditions, identity was the compound result of many accretions. Its protean constitution did not defer to the scripts of ethnic, national, racial, or cultural absolutism.

Like Wheatley's elegies, Equiano's absorbing autobiography yields many precious insights into modern racial slavery and illuminates some of the changes in consciousness and outlook that attended the African slaves as they negotiated the trauma, horror, and violence of forced rupture from home and kin that Orlando Patterson has called "natal alienation."[26] Equiano labored long and hard in a number of different New World locations in order to be able to buy his freedom from his owner. Before this was eventually accomplished in the service of Robert King, a Philadelphia Quaker, he had visited England and served on board warships of the Royal

Navy, participating in several battles against the French. He traveled throughout the Mediterranean, went to the Arctic as part of John Phipps's expedition in 1773, and journeyed among the Musquito Indians of Central America, an encounter that demonstrates to his readers exactly how far the narrator's once-African identity had come from anything that might be described as noble savagery.

No doubt, the rendering of Equiano's life story was tailored to the expectations and conventions of an abolitionist reading public. It certainly describes abuse, injustice, and exploitation, but it also shows him to have been treated with some decency and a measure of trust by masters for whom, both within and against the force of his servitude, he was able to develop significant affection and intimacy. Trapped on a boat on the Thames at Deptford in 1762 and locked in an unexpected confrontation with one master, whom, he tells his readers, he had "loved like a son," Equiano was desperate to gain the safety of the city on the river banks where both men knew that his freedom would be secured. He found himself instead being sold from one owner to another within sight of the shore he was unable to reach.

Equiano gradually acquired not only skills with which to improve his lot as a seaman and a trader but also an elaborate and complex critical consciousness that was able to analyze as well as describe his experiences and the system they exemplified. He became fervently Christian and, exactly as Wheatley had done, used the moral categories of that faith to denounce the immoral trade in human beings that had torn him from Africa and in which he had himself participated as a reluctant crewman on voyages where slaves were the cargo. His economic good fortune and astute management of his own finances made him a free man and a strong advocate on behalf of thrift, diligence, and disciplined Protestant endeavor. A radical Methodism touched his life as well as Wheatley's. It provided an appropriate toolbox with which he could dismantle the Christian pieties that had already been rendered hollow by their indifference to the plight of slaves.

There were other, alternative forms of Christianity around that yield clues as to the ways in which Equiano and Wheatley thought of themselves as children of God and human beings, sinners, workers, and patriots, free men and women whose vivid sense of freedom was conditioned by the fact that they had also been enslaved. The frontispiece of Equiano's

1789 autobiography *The Life of Olaudah Equiano or Gustavus Vassa the African* shows him in his Sunday best holding his Bible open to the Book of
Acts 12:4. That citation and the other scriptural references with which he
embellished his text are important pointers toward the precise character of
Equiano's Protestant outlook. Chapter 7 of his tale describes a formative
encounter with the evangelical, "great awakening" Methodism of George
Whitefield that had enjoyed a significant presence within antislavery
thinking and a pronounced influence upon the black antislavery activism
of the time.[27] Wheatley signaled some of the same affiliations in a widely
circulated poem commemorating Whitefield's death in August 1772. It
recalled that he had made a special point of urging blacks to accept their
Christian salvation and reproduced some of his appeals for general recognition of Christ as an "impartial" savior:

> He pray'd that grace in ev'ry heart might dwell,
> He long'd to see America excel;
> He charged its youth that ev'ry grace divine
> Should with full lustre in their conduct shine . . .
> " . . . Take him, ye *Africans,* he longs for you,
> *Impartial Saviour* is his title due:
> Wash'd in the fountain of redeeming blood,
> You shall be sons, and kings, and priests to God."[28]

For Methodists of this group, the Pauline view fully stated in Galatians
3:26–29 was central to the ideal of a properly Christian community[29]:

> For ye are all children of God by faith in Christ Jesus.
> For as many of you as have been baptized into Christ have put
>   on Christ.
> There is neither Jew nor Greek, there is neither bond nor
>   free, there is neither male nor female: for ye are all one
>   in Christ Jesus.
> And if ye be Christ's, then are ye Abraham's seed, and heirs
>   according to the promise.

One of the most aggressive and unsympathetic whites with whom
Equiano came into conflict is presented as abusing him for being "one of
St. Paul's men."[30] The superficial differences of gender and social status,
race and caste, marked on the body by the trifling order of man, were to be

set aside in favor of a relationship with Christ that offered a means to transcend and thereby escape the constraints of mortality and the body-coded order of identification and differentiation we now call "phenotype." There is also here something of a plea for the renunciation of specific defining characteristics associated with and articulated through the body. These are the same qualities that might today be thought of as constituting the most fixed and unchangeable forms of identity. They were lost, or rather left behind, at the point where Equiano's distinctive African body was immersed in the welcoming, baptismal waters of his new Christian faith. Perhaps what we should recognize as a new "identity" was constituted along with a new analysis of slavery in that fateful immersion. For him, slavery became a useful experience, morally and analytically as well as individually. It was a gift from God that redeemed suffering through the provision of wisdom:

> I considered that trials and disappointments are sometimes for our good and I thought God might perhaps have permitted this, in order to teach me wisdom and resignation. For he had hitherto shadowed me with the wings of his mercy and by his invisible, but powerful hand, had brought me the way I knew not.[31]

Thanks to the density of her allusions and the compression of the poetic form in which she wrote, Wheatley's ambivalence about her journeying through cultures and between identities is a more evasive quarry. Her poetry has been argued over in detail precisely because commentators find it hard to assess the relationship between her command of English neo-classicism, her enthusiasm for the American revolutionary struggle, and those few moments when unexpectedly strident denunciations of slavery erupted from her pen. An appreciation of the divine providence that took her from the darkness of her African life is combined with forthright assertions of the injustice and immorality of the slave trade and less frequent affirmations of an autonomy that preceded the fateful contact with whites and their world. The African-American poet and critic June Jordan is surely acute in drawing attention to the powerful assertion of autonomy that leaps out halfway through "On Being Brought from Africa to America," a poem that Wheatley had published when she was only sixteen years old:

> 'Twas mercy brought me from my Pagan land,
> Taught my benighted soul to understand

That there's a God, that there's a *Saviour* too:
Once I redemption neither sought nor knew.
Some view our sable race with scornful eye,
"Their color is a diabolic die."
Remember, *Christians, Negroes,* black as *Cain,*
May be refin'd, and join th' angelic train.

Equiano, Wheatley, and their many peers are also important to contemporary considerations of racialized identity because they dwelled in different locations. Significant portions of their itinerant lives were lived on British soil, and it is tempting to speculate here about how an acknowledgment of their political and cultural contributions to England, or perhaps to London's heterocultural life, might complicate the nation's portraits of itself. This decidedly monochromatic representation operates too often to exclude or undermine the significance of black participation and to minimize the power of colonial and imperial circuitry in determining the internal patterns of national life.

Tension about where to put the eighteenth-century blacks is connected not only to a color-coded British nativism that is indifferent if not actively hostile to the presence of slaves and ex-slaves, but also to another conceptual problem. This more profound conflict can be made visible in the contrast between encamped nations, rooted in one spot even if their imperial tendrils extend further, and the very different patterns of itinerant dwelling found in the transnational, maritime adventures of Equiano and celebrated in the cross-cultural creativity of Wheatley. The commemorative modes appropriate to this very different ecology of belonging reveal themselves in the oppositions between geography and genealogy, between land and sea. The latter possibility prompts a partial reversal of the myth in which Britannia held dominion over the waves. We can begin to perceive the sublime force of the ocean, and the associated impact of those who made their temporary homes on it, as a counterpower that confined, regulated, inhibited, and sometimes even defied the exercise of territorial sovereignty.[32]

It is not surprising that in his search to find historical precedents that could explain the character of the African idyll from which he had been snatched by unjust transnational trade in human flesh, Equiano turned once more to his Bible. In an interesting move that also repudiated the race-minded theories of those who used the biblically based Hamitic hypothesis[33] to present blackness as a curse and implicate it in justifications of slavery, he argued that Africans were descended not from Noah's accursed son, whose punishment entailed what could be read as a legitimation for slavery, but from the union of Abraham and Keturah. This bold claim was backed up with citations from contemporary scholarly work. It is combined with another assertion that recurs in the literature and political commentary produced by enslaved Africans and their descendants. Equiano suggests that there is one significant historical precedent for the mores and conduct of the African people from which he was wrongfully taken:

> . . . here I cannot forbear suggesting what has long struck me very forcibly, namely the strong analogy, which even by this sketch, imperfect as it is, appears to prevail in manners and customs of my countrymen and those of the Jews, before they reached the Land of Promise, and particularly the Patriarchs, while they were yet in that pastoral state which is described in Genesis—an analogy which alone would induce me to think that the one people had sprung from the other . . . As to the difference of colour between Eboan Africans and the modern Jews, I shall not presume to account for it.[34]

This "analogy" is evidence that the force of emergent raciology had touched Equiano's modern self-consciousness. It can be used in turn to introduce a discussion of the idea of diaspora, which, transcoded from its biblical sources and often divorced from the Jewish traditions in which it is primarily articulated, proved very useful to black thinkers as they struggled to comprehend the dynamics of identity and belonging constituted between the poles of geography and genealogy. For them, Jewish history in general and the idea of diaspora in particular were a useful means to regulate the conflict between the duties deriving from the place of dwelling and those different obligations, temptations, vices, and pleasures that belonged to the place of sojourn. Diaspora is an especially valuable idea because it points toward a more refined and more wieldy sense of culture than the characteristic notions of rootedness exemplified above in the words of President Mandela. It makes the spatialization of identity problematic and interrupts the ontologization of place.

DIASPORA AS A SOCIAL ECOLOGY OF
IDENTIFICATION

The idea of diaspora offers a ready alternative to the stern discipline of primordial kinship and rooted belonging. It rejects the popular image of natural nations spontaneously endowed with self-consciousness, tidily composed of uniform families: those interchangeable collections of ordered bodies that express and reproduce absolutely distinctive cultures as well as perfectly formed heterosexual pairings. As an alternative to the metaphysics of "race," nation, and bounded culture coded into the body, diaspora is a concept that problematizes the cultural and historical mechanics of belonging. It disrupts the fundamental power of territory to determine identity by breaking the simple sequence of explanatory links between place, location, and consciousness. It destroys the naive invocation of common memory as the basis of particularity in a similar fashion by drawing attention to the contingent political dynamics of commemoration.

The ancient word diaspora acquired a modern accent as a result of its unanticipated usefulness to the nationalisms and subaltern imperialisms of the late nineteenth century. It remains an enduring feature of the continuing aftershocks generated by those political projects in Palestine and elsewhere. If it can be stripped of its disciplinarian associations it might offer seeds capable of bearing fruit in struggles to comprehend the sociality of a new phase in which displacement, flight, exile, and forced migration are likely to be familiar and recurrent phenomena that transform the terms in which identity needs to be understood. Retreating from the totalizing immodesty and ambition of the word "global," diaspora is an outer-national term which contributes to the analysis of intercultural and transcultural processes and forms. It identifies a relational network, characteristically produced by forced dispersal and reluctant scattering. It is not just a word of movement, though purposive, desperate movement is integral to it. Under this sign, push factors are a dominant influence. The urgency they introduce makes diaspora more than a voguish synonym for peregrination or nomadism. As the biographies of Equiano and Wheatley suggest, life itself is at stake in the way the word connotes flight following the threat of violence rather than freely chosen experiences of displacement. Slavery, pogroms, indenture, genocide, and other unnameable terrors have all figured in the constitution of diasporas and the reproduction of diaspora consciousness in which identity is focused, less on the equalizing, pre-democratic force of sovereign territory and more on the social dynamics of remembrance and commemoration defined by a strong sense of the dangers involved in forgetting the location of origin and the tearful process of dispersal.

The term opens up a historical and experiential rift between the locations of residence and the locations of belonging. This in turn sets up a further opposition. Consciousness of diaspora affiliation stands opposed to the distinctively modern structures and modes of power orchestrated by the institutional complexity of nation-states. Diaspora identification exists outside of and sometimes in opposition to the political forms and codes of modern citizenship. The nation-state has regularly been presented as the institutional means to terminate diaspora dispersal. At one end of the communicative circuit this is to be accomplished by the assimilation of those who were out of place. At the other, a similar outcome is realized through the prospect of their return to a place of origin. The fundamental equilibrium of nature and civil society can thus be restored. In both options it is the nation-state that brings the spatial and temporal order of diaspora life to an abrupt end. Diaspora yearning and ambivalence are transformed into a simple unambiguous exile once the possibility of easy reconciliation with either the place of sojourn or the place of origin exists. Some, though not all, versions of diaspora consciousness accentuate the possibility and desirability of return. They may or may not recognize the difficulty of this gesture. The degree to which return is accessible or desired provides a valuable comparative moment in the typology and classification of diaspora histories and political movements.

"Diaspora" lacks the modernist and cosmopolitan associations of the word "exile" from which it has been carefully distinguished, particularly in the Jewish histories with which the term is most deeply intertwined.[35] We should be careful that the term "history" retains its plural status at this point because diaspora has had a variety of different resonances in Jewish cultures inside and outside of Europe, both before and after the founding of the state of Israel.

Equiano's sense of an affinity between blacks and Jews stands behind the work of many modern black thinkers of the western hemisphere who were eager to adapt the diaspora idea to their particular post-slave circumstances. Many of them developed conceptual schemes and political programs for diaspora affiliation (and its negation) long before they found a proper name for the special emotional and political logics that governed these operations. The work of Edward Wilmot Blyden in the late nineteenth century represents another important site of similar intercultural transfer. Blyden was a "returnee" to Africa from the Danish West Indies via the United States. He presented his own redemptive involvement with the free nation-state of Liberia and its educational apparatuses, along lines suggested by an interpretation of Jewish history and culture forged through a close personal and intellectual relationship with Jews and Judaism. In 1898, awed by what he described as "that marvelous movement called Zionism," he attempted to draw the attention of "thinking and enlightened Jews to the great continent of Africa—not to its northern and southern extremities only, but to its vast intertropical area" on the grounds that they would find there "religious and spiritual aspirations kindred to their own."[36]

Earlier on, in assessing the power of roots and rootedness to ground identity, we encountered invocations of organicity that forged an uncomfortable connection between the warring domains of nature and culture. They made nation and citizenship appear to be natural rather than social phenomena—spontaneous expressions of a distinctiveness that was palpable in deep inner harmony between people and their dwelling places. Diaspora is a useful means to reassess the idea of essential and absolute identity precisely because it is incompatible with that type of nationalist and raciological thinking. The word comes closely associated with the idea of sowing seed. This etymological inheritance is a disputed legacy and a mixed blessing. It demands that we attempt to evaluate the significance of the scattering process against the supposed uniformity of that which has been scattered. Diaspora posits important tensions between here and there, then and now, between seed in the bag, the packet, or the pocket and seed in the ground, the fruit, or the body. By focusing attention equally on the sameness within differentiation and the differentiation within sameness, diaspora disturbs the suggestion that political and cultural identity might be understood via the analogy of indistinguishable peas lodged in the protective pods of closed kinship and subspecies being. Is it possible to imagine how a more complex, ecologically sophisticated sense of interaction between organisms and environments might become an asset in thinking critically about identity?

Imagine a scenario in which similar—though not precisely identical —seeds take root in different places. Plants of the same species are seldom absolutely indistinguishable. Nature does not always produce interchangeable clones. Soils, nutrients, predators, pests, and pollination vary along with unpredictable weather. Seasons change. So do climates, which can be determined on a variety of scales: micro as well as macro and mezzo. Diaspora provides valuable cues and clues for the elaboration of a social ecology of cultural identity and identification that takes us far beyond the stark dualism of genealogy and geography. The pressure to associate, like the desires to remember or forget, may vary with changes in the economic and political atmosphere. Unlike the tides, the weather cannot be predicted accurately. To cap it all, the work involved in discovering origins is more difficult in some places and at some times.

If we can adopt this more difficult analytical stance, the celebrated "butterfly effect" in which tiny, almost insignificant forces can, in defiance of conventional expectations, precipitate unpredictable, larger changes in other locations becomes a commonplace happening. The seamless propagation of cultural habits and styles was rendered radically contingent at the point where geography and genealogy began to trouble each other. We are directed toward the conflictual limits of "race," ethnicity, and culture. When a diaspora talks back to a nation-state, it initiates conflict between those who agree that they are more or less what they were, but cannot agree whether the more or the less should take precedence in contemporary political and historical calculations.

The reproductive moment of diaspora raises other uncomfortable issues. In a discussion of some recent approaches to the diaspora idea and its relationship to masculinism,[37] Stefan Helmreich has identified the processes of cultural reproduction and transmission to which diaspora draws attention as being radically gender-specific. He underlines the close etymological relationship between the word diaspora and the word sperm as if their common tie to the Greek word meaning sow and scatter still corrupts the contemporary application of the concept as it were, from within. This argument can be tested and contextualized by the introduction of another family term, the word spore: the unicellular vector for supposedly "asexual" reproduction.[38] Could that alternative, gender-free linkage complicate the notion that diaspora is inscribed as a masculinist trope and cannot therefore be liberated from the quagmire of androcentrism, where it has been lodged by modern nationalisms and the religious conceptions of ethnic particularity that cheerfully coexist with them? Though still contested, diaspora lends itself to the critique of absolutist political sensibilities, especially those that have been articulated around the themes of nation, "race," and ethnicity. It seems unduly harsh to suggest that it is any more deeply contaminated by the toxins of male domination than other heuristic terms in the emergent vocabulary of transcultural critical theory. There is no reason descent through the male line should be privileged over dissent via the rhizomorphic principle.[39] Diaspora can be used to conjure up both.

Where separation, time, and distance from the point of origin or the center of sovereignty complicate the symbolism of ethnic and national reproduction, anxieties over the boundaries and limits of sameness may lead people to seek security in the sanctity of embodied difference. The new racisms that code biology in cultural terms have been alloyed with still newer variants that conscript the body into disciplinary service and encode cultural particularity in an understanding of bodily practices and attributes determined by genes. Gender differences become extremely important in nation-building activity because they are a sign of an irresistible natural hierarchy that belongs at the center of civic life. The unholy forces of nationalist biopolitics intersect on the bodies of women charged with the reproduction of absolute ethnic difference and the continuance of blood lines. The integrity of the nation becomes the integrity of its masculinity. In fact, it can be a nation only if the correct version of gender hierarchy has been established and reproduced. The family is the main device in this operation. It connects men and women, boys and girls to the larger collectivity toward which they must orient themselves if they are to acquire a Fatherland. Minister Louis Farrakhan of The Nation of Islam typified the enduring power of this variety of thinking about nation and gender in his description of the 1995 march of African-American men to Washington. He saw that event as an act of warfare in which the condition of their alternative national manhood could be gauged:

> No nation gets any respect if you go out to war and you put your women in the trenches and the men stay at home cooking. Every nation that goes to war tests the fiber of the manhood of that nation. And literally, going to Washington to seek justice for our people is like going to war.[40]

If the modern nation is to be prepared for war, reproducing the soldier citizens of the future is not a process it can leave to chance or whim. Again,
the favored institutional setting for this disciplinary and managerial activity is the family. The family is understood as nothing more than the essential building block in the construction and elevation of the nation. This
nation-building narrative runs all the way to fascism and its distinctive
myths of rebirth after periods of weakness and decadence.[41] Diaspora challenges it by valorizing sub- and supranational kinship and allowing for a
more ambivalent relationship toward national encampments.

These non-national proclivities have triggered other de-stabilizing and
subversive effects. They are amplified when the concept of diaspora is annexed for anti-essentialist accounts of identity-formation as a process and
used to host a decisive change of orientation away from the primordial
identities established alternatively by either nature or culture. By embracing diaspora, theories of identity turn instead toward contingency, in-
determinacy, and conflict. With the idea of valuing diaspora more highly
than the coercive unanimity of the nation, the concept becomes explicitly antinational. This shift is connected with transforming the familiar
unidirectional idea of diaspora as a form of catastrophic but simple
dispersal that enjoys an identifiable and reversible originary moment—
the site of trauma—into something far more complex. Diaspora can be
used to instantiate a "chaotic" model in which shifting "strange attractors"
are the only visible points of fragile stability amid social and cultural turbulence.

The importance of these nodes is misunderstood if they are identified
as fixed local phenomena. They appear unexpectedly, and where diaspora
becomes a concept, the web or network they allow us to perceive can mark
out new understandings of self, sameness, and solidarity. However, they
are not successive stages in a genealogical account of kin relations—
equivalent to branches on a single family tree. One does not beget the next
in a comforting sequence of ethnic teleology; nor are they stations on a linear journey toward the destination that a completed identity might represent. They suggest a different mode of linkage between the forms of
micropolitical agency exercised in cultures and movements of resistance
and transformation and other political processes that are visible on a different, bigger scale. Their plurality and regionality valorize something
more than a protracted condition of social mourning over the ruptures of

exile, loss, brutality, stress, and forced separation. They highlight a more indeterminate and, some would say, modernist mood in which natal alienation and cultural estrangement are capable of conferring insight and creating pleasure, as well as precipitating anxiety about the coherence of the nation and the stability of its imaginary ethnic core. Contrasting forms of political action have emerged to create new possibilities and new pleasures where dispersed people recognize the effects of spatial dislocation as rendering the issue of origin problematic. They may grow to accept the possibility that they are no longer what they once were and cannot therefore rewind the tapes of their cultural history. The diaspora idea encourages critical theory to proceed rigorously but cautiously in ways that do not privilege the modern nation-state and its institutional order over the subnational and supranational patterns of power, communication, and conflict that they work to discipline, regulate, and govern. The concept of space is itself transformed when it is seen in terms of the ex-centric communicative circuitry that has enabled dispersed populations to converse, interact, and more recently even to synchronize significant elements of their social and cultural lives.

What the African-American writer Leroi Jones once named "the changing same"[42] provides a valuable motif with which to fix this supplement to the diaspora idea. Neither the mechanistic essentialism that is too squeamish to acknowledge the possibility of difference within sameness nor the lazy alternative that animates the supposedly strategic variety of essentialism can supply keys to the untidy workings of diaspora identities. They are creolized, syncretized, hybridized, and chronically impure cultural forms, particularly if they were once rooted in the complicity of rationalized terror and racialized reason. This changing same is not some invariant essence that gets enclosed subsequently in a shape-shifting exterior with which it is casually associated. It is not the sign of an unbroken, integral inside protected by a camouflaged husk. The phrase names the problem of diaspora politics and diaspora poetics. The same is present, but how can we imagine it as something other than an essence generating the merely accidental? Iteration is the key to this process. The same is retained without needing to be reified. It is ceaselessly reprocessed. It is maintained and modified in what becomes a determinedly nontraditional tradition, for this is not tradition as closed or simple repetition. Invariably promiscuous, diaspora and the politics of commemoration it specifies challenge us to apprehend mutable forms that can redefine the idea of culture through a reconciliation with movement and complex, dynamic variation.

Today's affiliates to the tradition for which Equiano and Wheatley operate as imaginary ancestors find themselves in a very different economic, cultural, and political circuitry—a different diaspora—from the one their predecessors encountered. Live human beings are no longer a commodity, and the dispersal of blacks has extended further and deeper into Europe, where elements of the scattering process have been repeated once again by the arrival of Caribbean peoples and other formerly colonial folk in the post-1945 period. Several generations of blacks have been born in Europe whose identification with the African continent is even more attenuated and remote, particularly since the anticolonial wars are over. Both the memory of slavery and an orientation toward identity that derives from African origins are hard to maintain when the rupture of migration intervenes and stages its own trials of belonging. However, the notion of a distinctive, African-derived identity has not withered and the moral and political fruits of black life in the western hemisphere have been opened out systematically to larger and larger numbers of people in different areas.

The black musicians, dancers, and performers of the New World have disseminated these insights, styles, and pleasures through the institutional resources of the cultural industries that they have colonized and captured. These media, particularly recorded sound, have been annexed for sometimes subversive purposes of protest and affirmation. The vernacular codes and expressive cultures constituted from the forced new beginning of racial slavery have reappeared at the center of a global phenomenon that has regularly surpassed—just as Wheatley's complex poetry did long ago— innocent notions of mere entertainment. What are wrongly believed to be simple cultural commodities have been used to communicate a powerful ethical and political commentary on rights, justice, and democracy that articulates but also transcends criticism of modern racial typology and the ideologies of white supremacy. The living history of New World blacks has endowed this expressive tradition with flexibility and durability.

Bob Marley, whose recordings are still selling all over the world more than a decade after his death, provides a useful concluding example here. His enduring presence in globalized popular culture is an important reminder of the power of the technologies that ground the culture of simulation. Those same technological resources have subdued the constraints of nature and provided Marley with a virtual life after death in which his popularity can continue to grow unencumbered by any embarrassing political residues that might make him into a threatening or frightening figure. But there is more to this worldwide popularity than clever video-based immortality and the evident reconstruction of Bob Marley's image, stripped of much of its militant Ethiopianism—yet another chosen people and another promised land to set alongside those we have already considered.

Bob's life and work lend themselves to the study of postmodern diaspora identity. They help us to perceive the workings of those complex cultural circuits that have transformed a pattern of simple, one-way dispersal into a webbed network constituted through multiple points of intersection. His historic performance at the Zimbabwe independence ceremony in 1980 symbolized the partial reconnection with African origins that permeates diaspora yearning. Like so many others, he too did not go to Africa to make his home. He chose instead, as many other prominent pan-Africanists had done before and since, a more difficult cosmopolitan commitment and a different form of solidarity and identification that did not require his physical presence in that continent.

His triumph not only marks the beginning of what has come to be known as "world music" or "world beat," an increasingly significant marketing category that helps to locate the transformation and possible demise of music-led youth-culture. It was built from the seemingly universal power of a poetic and political language that reached out from its roots to find new audiences hungry for its insights. Bob became, in effect, a planetary figure. His music was pirated in Eastern Europe and became intertwined with the longing for freedom and rights across Africa, the Pacific, and Latin America. Captured into commodities, his music traveled and found new audiences and so did his band. Between 1976 and 1980 they criss-crossed the planet, performing in the United States, Canada, the United Kingdom, France, Italy, Germany, Spain, Scandinavia, Ireland, Holland, Belgium, Switzerland, Japan, Australia, New Zealand, the Ivory Coast, and Gabon. Major sales were also recorded in market areas where the band did not perform, particularly Brazil, Senegal, Ghana, Nigeria, Taiwan, and the Philippines.

Marley's global stature was founded on the hard, demanding labor of transcontinental touring as much as on the poetic qualities he invested in the language of sufferation that he made universal. In conclusion, his

transnational image invites one further round of speculation about the status of identity and the conflicting scales on which sameness, subjectivity,
and solidarity can be imagined. Connecting with him across the webs of
planetary popular culture might be thought of as an additional stage in the
nonprogressive evolution of diaspora into the digital era. Recognizing this
requires moving the focus of inquiry away from the notions of fixed identity that we have already discovered to be worn out and placing it instead
upon the processes of identification. Do people connect themselves and
their hopes with the figure of Bob Marley as a man, a Jamaican, a Caribbean, an African, or a Pan-African artist? Is he somehow all of the above
and more, a rebel voice of the poor and the underdeveloped world that
made itself audible in the core of overdeveloped social and economic life
he called Babylon? On what scale of cultural analysis do we make sense of
his reconciliation of modern and postmodern technologies with mystical
antimodern forces? How do we combine his work as an intellectual, as a
thinker, with his portrayal as a primitive, hypermasculine figure: a
not-so-noble savage shrouded in ganga smoke? Are we prepared now, so
many years after his death and mythification, to set aside the new forms of
minstrelsy obviously promoted under the constellation of his stardom and
see him as a worldly figure whose career traversed continents and whose
revolutionary political stance won adherents because of its ability to imagine the end of capitalism as readily as it imagined the end of the world?

In Bob Marley's image there is something more than domestication of
the other and the accommodation of insubordinate Third Worldism
within corporate multiculturalism. Something remains even when we dis-
miss the presentation of difference as a spectacle and a powerful marketing
device in the global business of selling records, tapes, CDs, videos, and associated merchandise. However great Bob's skills, the formal innovations
in his music must take second place behind its significance as the site of a
revolution in the structure of the global markets for these cultural commodities. The glamour of the primitive was set to work to animate his image and increase the power of his music to seduce. That modern magic
required Bob to be purified, simplified, nationalized, and particularized.
An aura of authenticity was manufactured not to validate his political aspirations or rebel status but to invest his music with a mood of carefully calculated transgression that still makes it saleable and appealing all over the
planet. Otherness was invoked and operates to make the gulf between his

memory and his remote "crossover" audiences bigger, to manage that experiential gap so that their pleasures in consuming him and his work are somehow enhanced.

It is only recently that the long-ignored figure of Bob's white father has been brought forward and offered as the key to interpreting his son's achievements and comprehending the pathological motivation to succeed that took him out of Trenchtown. In that sense, the phase in which Bob was represented as exotic and dangerous is over. We can observe a prodigal, benign, almost childlike Bob Marley being brought home into the bosom of his corporate family. All this can be recognized. But the stubborn utopia projected through Bob Marley's music and anticolonial imaginings remains something that is not de-limited by a proscriptive ethnic wrapper or racial "health-warning" in which encounters with otherness are presented as dangerous to the well-being of one's own singular identity. Music and instrumental competence have to be learned and practiced before they can be made to communicate convincingly. This should restrict their role as signs of authentic, absolute particularity. Perhaps, in the tainted but nonetheless powerful image of Bob Marley's global stardom, we can discern the power of identity based, not on some cheap, pre-given sameness, but on will, inclination, mood, and affinity. The translocal power of his dissident voice summons up these possibilities and a chosen, recognizably political kinship that is all the more valuable for its distance from the disabling assumptions of automatic solidarity based on either blood or land.

II

FASCISM, EMBODIMENT, AND REVOLUTIONARY CONSERVATISM

I propose nothing short of the liberation of the man of color from himself. We shall go very slowly, for there are two camps: the white and the black.

—FRANTZ FANON

4

The non-analysis of fascism is one of the important political facts of
the past thirty years. It enables fascism to be used as a floating
signifier, whose function is essentially that of denunciation.

—MICHEL FOUCAULT

. . . one must surely study the role of sport . . . Sport is ambiguous.
On the one hand, it can have an anti-barbaric and anti-sadistic effect by means of fair play, a spirit of chivalry, and consideration for
the weak. On the other hand, in many of its varieties and practices it
can promote aggression, brutality and sadism, above all in people
who do not expose themselves to the exertion and discipline required by sports but instead merely watch: that is those who regularly shout from the sidelines.

—ADORNO

The modern dream of organizing
the national community into a fortified camp, disciplined under martial
rules and armed against the encroachments of other, similar expansionist

units, was only one possible scenario latent in the formation and consolidation of the bourgeois nation-state. The history of struggles over the
scope and status of "race" and its relation to the ideas of nation and culture
with which it became entangled cannot afford to minimize the impact of
less militaristic, countervailing forces. Many of the illiberal, unjust, and
brutal effects of racial hierarchy have been identified and denounced. Audible minority opinions did intermittently present modern democracy as
incompatible with the stern assumptions of raciology, but those forces,
particularly in the imperial and colonial periods, were by no means always
persuasive, let alone victorious.[1]

We have seen that when faced with apparently immutable racial difference, the best cosmopolitan intentions of an enlightened standpoint
could be undermined. They were compromised by ambiguity and conflict
over where the boundaries of humanity should fall and regularly defeated
by the white supremacist thinking that rendered most enlightenment versions of reason actively complicit with the political project involved in classifying the world by means of "race" and reading the motion of history
through racialized categories.[2] Allied with a weak sense of the unity of human life, this combination would be a dubious bequest to the Enlightenment's liberal and socialist successors. Indeed, we could say that it was only
with the defeat of the Nazis and their allies in the mid-twentieth century
that the utterly respectable raciology of the previous period was pushed
briefly beyond the bounds of acceptability. Prior to that, even voices of dissent from imperial misconduct and colonial expansionism had to engage
the same anthropological ideas of "race," nation, and culture that had
applauded imperial power, directing them toward more equitable ends
against the very logic of their meshed interconnection.[3]

To be sure, the necessarily messy operation of living imperial systems
subverted the idea of nations as closed, racialized units integrated by their
perfected, particular cultures. This image of the nation, and by implication
of its colonial extensions, had been spelled out initially by figures like
Ernst Renan and Matthew Arnold. It was elaborated into a full-fledged racial science by Houston Stewart Chamberlain and his proto-fascist peers.
The persistent refusal of colonial life to conform to the tidy prescribed pattern has been confirmed by numerous studies of sexuality and empire that
reveal the transgressive failures of both colonizer and colonized to respect
the restraining obligations placed upon their conduct by the strictures of

race-thinking.[4] Even where a strong sense of cultural differences did not wholly replace biological arguments as the key to understanding the fate of newly racialized imperial nations, degeneration as a result of either torrid climates or over-exposure to alluring native difference placed European particularity and its reproductive capacities in constant jeopardy. Back home, at the other end of an increasingly taut and substantial cultural chain, the notion of an imperial mission provided the most significant yardstick against which the fitness of the nation was to be evaluated.

For these precarious yet powerful planetary systems to endure, they had to invest in the institutionalization, codification, and purification of their imperially extended national cultures. The architects and managers of this process felt that stability and continuity depended upon the organized transmission of key cultural motifs, habits, and mentalities to distant colonizers, to a new public at home who would develop a relationship to the imperial project as supporters and as potential colonizers, and, of course, to a measured but significant proportion of the colonized who had to be given a stake in the workings of manifestly brutal and exploitative arrangements. The place of imaginative literatures in this broadly educational and governmental project has recently received an extensive, even disproportionate, treatment.[5] Less sustained attention has been directed toward the less obviously purposeful ways that, during the late nineteenth century, material culture and technological developments—new objects, commodities, devices and procedures including postcards, cigarette cards, the revolution in cheap color printing and packaging—afforded exciting new communicative opportunities and cultural vehicles for an imperial phantasmagoria.[6]

Among these opportunities was an especially rich visual culture that disseminated the militaristic and patriotic imagery of empire and colony on a vast scale celebrating and creating a stimulating world of signs to which racial difference was absolutely fundamental.[7] While photography played a special role in the consolidation and popularization of the physical anthropology of race, in Britain at least, it is no exaggeration to say that it became impossible to buy a box of tea, sugar, soap, or biscuits without being confronted with the petty but nonetheless potent manifestations of a glorified imperial ideal. The seeds of what would eventually become the science of propaganda, a communicative innovation that flourished during the 1914–1918 war, were first planted during this moment. It is also highly significant that the systematic orientation and manipulation of

British public opinion toward the pleasures of imperial adventure made such an extensive contribution to the popular political currency of "race" and nation. A new set of class and status relations was being tailored according to the specifications of the imperial system. On the packaging of chocolate and tea, in museums, school textbooks, maps, magic lantern shows, exhibitions, and magazines and other ephemeral literature, patriotism and imperial nationalism were manipulated into deliberately seductive and stirring forms.[8]

This imperial phantasmagoria was underpinned by the language and logic of raciology in its post-Darwinian incarnations.[9] It was endorsed and energized by the emergence of new popular genres and forms, many of which were oriented toward the military life of the colonies. In England, the vernacular voice of Rudyard Kipling's "barrack-room ballads" and "service songs" is still a potent reminder[10] that in Africa and India an acquiescent if not always enthusiastic proletariat was invited to find convincing patriotic voice. The emergent visual culture of advertising and commodity consumption complemented these developments. It conducted the official memory of the imperial mission into the smallest crevices of everyday life. Empire had ceased to be exclusively "out there." It came home, and thus "internalized," it conditioned social and cultural life in the heart of the imperial system. The economic and ethical agency of women in earlier consumer protests over the fruits of slave labor had already shown that the morality of "race" could become an urgent private matter. Similar anxieties emerged now at the ritual and emotional center of the public culture orchestrated by a different kind of state with unprecedented resources of violence, communication, and information at its disposal. The celebrated poem "Recessional," which concluded Kipling's 1903 volume *The Five Nations,* distills the holy nationalist mood that governed the educational aspirations of this imperial propaganda. Significantly, his words were cast as a funereal injunction against forgetting:

> God of our fathers, known of old,
> Lord of our far-flung battle-line,
> Beneath whose awful Hand we hold
> Dominion over palm and pine—
> Lord God of Hosts, be with us yet,
> Lest we forget—lest we forget!

Much contemporary commentary on colonial life has been occupied by discussion of the complex mechanisms of interdependence and syncretism that inevitably characterized the social and cultural life of the colonies. However, to focus exclusively on the important mechanisms of cultural and intellectual hybridization is to overlook Kipling's key point: the primary fact that these empires were military and militarizing structures. The intermingling of cultures, sensibilities, and ideas was not only a feature of life in the colonies themselves. Related and equivalent processes in which colonial governance, moods, and mentalities impacted the life of the metropoles can also be identified. Imperial propaganda helped to reconstitute the relationship between soldiery and citizenry in a new pattern that abrogated the political codes and moral duties of the past. It reinvented the idea of military adventure as a potent source of romance, pleasure, and fantasy even while administrations of the colonies were rewriting the rules of practical soldiery. All these interrelated processes have a bearing upon the currency of "race." The central dominant question they foreshadow is the possibility of a significant relationship between the sometimes genocidal brutality of the colonies and the later Nazi genocide in Europe.

Sadly, contemporary histories of empire, war, and militarism are not always adequate to the task of addressing this important issue. When it comes to the impact of colonial history, they do not always explore the issue of racialized difference in a sustained manner or with an adequate depth and seriousness. They may not even recognize the central place of "race" as a dynamic political, historical, and economic concept during this period. The rigid enforcement of boundaries between geographically defined and divided subdisciplines complicates this problem but exacts a heavier toll in some subject areas than in others. Anthropology, for example, has had to consider its own contributions to the bridge between colonial and domestic policy and practice more wholeheartedly than other disciplines. The patient, exemplary work of George Stocking and others has placed the dynamics of colonial society squarely in the middle of the history of their subject, and it is now difficult to deny that variations in the extent and fortunes of Europe's imperial systems affected the development and institutionalization of scientific and academic knowledge in different national traditions.

The loss of German colonies after 1918 turned German racial science in a distinctive direction by reducing opportunities to study colonial peoples at a stroke. By itself, the history of German anthropology, which was closely connected to the development of racial hygiene, raises what can only be described as an interesting prima facie case for the importance of raciology as a critical link between colonial administration and the subsequent catastrophic direction of genocidal social policy under Nazism. One pivotal figure in establishing that connection was Eugen Fischer, a prominent figure in the intellectual pantheon of the Nazi academy. He was his country's most distinguished anthropologist and expert on "race-mixing" during the interwar years.[11] He is remembered now as the director of the Kaiser Wilhelm Institute for Anthropology, Genetics, and Eugenics and as the author of *The Rehoboth Bastards and the Problem of Miscegenation among Humans,* a notable contribution to the application of Mendelian genetics to human populations published in 1913. Fischer had conducted the fieldwork for his ground-breaking study in the German colony of South West Africa in 1908—one year after the defeat of the Hereros. His subject was defined through a study of the results of racial intermixture between Dutch and Hottentot populations. The impact of this work would be felt later in the racial legislation enacted under the Nazis.

From this auspicious beginning, Fischer's career, which parallels the professional odyssey of his dear friend Martin Heidegger in a number of ways (not least his role in cleansing Germany's most prestigious university of Jews), took him to the Nazi-appointed rectorship of Berlin University in 1933, and to such tasks as judging the "ideal Nordic head" in a competition organized by popular anthropological magazines. He would later employ the same scientific skills in training the SS physicians who would make camp selections in physical anthropology and racial science at the Kaiser Wilhelm Institute and in his duties as a judge in Berlin's appellate Genetic Health Court. In concert with his better-known colleague Hans Gunther and a number of other luminaries of Nazi raciology, Fischer also helped to organize the anthropological evaluation and subsequent secret sterilization of the "Rheinlandbastarde," the mongrel offspring of German women and the French colonial troops who had been placed in the Rheinland as an occupying army after 1918.[12] Significantly, Fischer did not feel inclined to take up a formal membership in the Nazi Party until 1940. Benno Müller Hill, another rigorous and distinguished historian of racial science, appended a number of conversations with figures from this strange intellectual subculture to his classic study *Murderous Science.* One of those he spoke to was Fischer's daughter, Gertrud. She denied her father's anti-semitism, disclosed the interesting information that Heidegger visited him regularly until his death, and explained that, clear-headed to the end, "he thought a great deal about the history of the white man in Africa."[13]

The deficiencies that are more typical of contemporary historical scholarship when it comes to race constitute a form of tunnel vision. Its severity can be measured in the way that an invaluable book like Daniel Pick's insightful study of the rationalization of slaughter in the modern age makes no specific mention of the imperial and colonial conflicts where the rules of the Geneva Convention were deemed not to apply, or Omer Bartov's brilliant survey of the Wehrmacht and the new type of war it fought on the Russian front fails to even ask the question of whether colonial activity might have provided precedents for the Germans' shocking conduct in that campaign.[14] If anthropologists and distinguished professors like Fischer made use of their colonial experiences in later activities inside Europe, might not the military men have done the same thing? The possibility of any linkage need not, of course, be approached exclusively in a negative mode. We might also ask whether, by the time the Nazis had seized power, there was any lingering life left in the political and religious opinion that had protested over General von Trotha's lusty but controversial attempts at the extermination of the Herero people he held in "protective custody."[15]

For the most part, the few precious studies of technology and military power in colonial settings make equally minimal attempts to reconnect their undoubted insights into the interconnection of race, nation, and culture with social life in the metropolitan centers of the imperial system.[16] Victor Kiernan's study of Europe's empires, which includes some preliminary materials in the genealogy of that important colonial innovation, the dumdum bullet, is one partial exception to this regrettable and persistent pattern.[17] Another example is provided by John Ellis's classic historical study of the impact of the machine gun.[18] Ellis cleverly integrates cultural and techno-scientific narratives. He links an account of the practical impact of this revolutionary means of industrialized killing to ideas about race, nation, and empire. His book is essential for the manner in which it explores the discrepancy between the attitudes to deploying the death-dealing power of the machine gun against the "lesser breeds without the law" in colonial wars and the very different responses to its use in European settings, where it could only violate notions of manhood and fair play that had characterized earlier phases of thinking about how manly wars should be conducted. Ellis's account stops oddly short of commenting on the point at which the boundary between the whites and the rest was crossed and the machine gun was set to work within European borders against local people who, like so many of the victims of empire before them, were deprived by raciology of their precious status as human beings, albeit of a lesser variety than the new Aryan norm.

I view the recurrent role of systematic race-thinking in legitimizing and rationalizing later instances of industrialized killing as neither a coincidence nor a simple consequence of its similar role in earlier, colonial manifestations of the same general pathology. Although the simple fact of this recurrence ought to stimulate extremely important questions, it has often failed to do so, particularly when commentators become so habituated to the presence and supposed naturalness of racial division that they are unable to appreciate its unique impact as a means of spiritual and political integration and division. What did this practical raciology contribute to the killing process? Why did the languages of legitimation rely so heavily on the race idea, and why did the combination of that idea with the language and symbols of ultranationalism provide such a powerful means to motivate and galvanize people into the resolute, action-oriented mode that fascist ideology has always prized over the weakness represented by theory and useless reflection?

"RACE" AND FASCISM

Let us turn now toward the problems presented by these difficult historical links. A consideration of fascism and its conceptual rather than its contingently political connections to the idea of "race" provides an obvious way of recognizing the power of raciology and holding it at the center of these inquiries. It might also contribute something to a strategy for reintegrating interconnected but falsely separated histories, for bridging divergent disciplines, and for approaching the apparently incommensurable moral claims which active and deliberate commemoration of these catastrophic events sets in motion.

I approach the concept of fascism with trepidation not just because it links together so many different historical and local phenomena. It has been engulfed by the way it has functioned as a term of general abuse and corrupted by the way it has been used to express a sense of evil that is frustratingly abstract but that remains hostage to fashionable contemporary fascination with obscenity, criminality, aggression, and horror. To re-engage with the idea of generic fascism is, I hope, to work toward redeeming the term from its trivialization and restoring it to a proper place in discussions of the moral and political limits of what is acceptable.[19] The urgency of that task cannot be disputed; however, my aims in this chapter are more modest. I would like only to outline an ethical economy for the multicultural present in which both fascism and the raciologies that have been intertwined with it are accorded serious if belated attention.

The connections and continuities that come into view when the reliance of fascism on raciology is fully appreciated can be disturbing.[20] Knowing exactly where fascisms begin, updating ourselves as to what they look, sound, and feel like, and exploring the inevitable continuities between the normal orders of democratic governance and their revolutionary repudiation are all extremely difficult. However, the most rigorous and sensitive comparative work on these subjects has consistently demonstrated that there is much to be gained, morally and intellectually, from striving to bring these forbidding and gnawingly uncomfortable issues back into focus. They should be essential in our attempts to rewrite the history of our species and to distill and clarify its meanings for our own postcatastrophic predicament. We retreat from these tasks only if we are not prepared to face up to the commanding power of raciology as a means to divide and abuse.

Huge volumes have been addressed to the many difficulties concerning how fascism should be defined. We are obliged to distinguish between fascism as a historical development, a political and social movement, a rare pattern of government, and a recognizable ideological and cultural formation. Following the monumental work of the great comparative historians of fascism like Roger Griffin and Stanley Payne and specialists in its intellectual lineage like George Mosse and Zeev Sternheel, I think that pursuing a generic definition of fascism is not only possible and desirable but imperative. It is necessary not least because, although some contemporary enthusiasts for fascism conveniently opt to wear Nazi uniforms, many do not announce their nihilistic and ultranationalist commitments so boldly. It is essential, as living memory of the fascist period fades, to be able to identify these new groups and their influence on the volatile lives of postindustrial polities. Just maintaining a discussion about fascism as an ongoing heuristic project has additional value in a post–cold war setting from which the West has disappeared and where a reborn Europe must confront its past.

Pondering the nature of fascism and its recurrent appeal is not just a matter of clarifying what those of us who oppose racism are against. It is a matter for antiracists and would-be liberationists, too. It obliges us to scrutinize our own political philosophies, practices, and cultural predilections where they stray close to the dangers involved in becoming enamoured of power.[21] I will discuss the special attractiveness of fascism's political techniques to some of the peoples who have been its victims in a later chapter. In the meantime, Griffin's minimal but wieldy definition of fascism provides an invaluable starting point.[22] He accentuates its populist and ultranationalist features and draws attention to the fascists' claim to offer dynamic rebirth after periods of national weakness and decadence. Other insightful commentators have placed greater emphasis on the special investment that fascist movements have made in the ideal of fraternity. The comprehensive masculinization of the public sphere and the militaristic style with which this has been accomplished in many different settings suggest a relationship to patterns of male desire that demand comparative and cross-cultural evaluation.[23] This is not to deny the roles of women as full, energetic, and knowing participants in these movements. However, the strongly masculinist character derived principally from the exultation of war as a space in which men can know themselves better and love one another legitimately in the absence of the feminine is not incidental. It is closely associated with the varieties of belligerent ultranationalism that fascists always articulate.

Although this variety of authoritarianism has relied heavily on the rational wisdom of racial science, it has also been tightly bound in to other, less respectable, varieties of race-thinking that derive from occult, mystical, and assertively irrational sources. Little attention has been devoted to the way that shared adherence to the fundamental principle of "race" stabilizes the interconnection of these quite different and potentially incompatible systems. Their convergence around the central fact of racial difference and its consequent elevation to a timeless, metaphysical value minimizes the effect of any contradictions between the different ways they understand the connections between nationality, culture, and nature, history, destiny, and fate. Race blurs these things in ways that are essential to the workings of totalitarian power. It binds the intellectual and the anti-intellectual, the scientific and the aesthetic. It provides sources of comfort, reassurance, conviction, morality, method, and ethics. A special certainty flows from the fervent belief that the order of difference underpinning natural somatic variation has a self-evident and fundamental power to determine and divide.

THE GLAMOUR OF FASCISM

We know that the attractiveness of fascism was not reversed with the defeat of Hitler's Nazis and their allies. Traces of the Nazis are omnipresent, and fleeting images of them supply flimsy moral markers in a harsh world that often appears to be devoid of political ethics. Within the dreamworld of popular culture they represent supernatural evil and stylish, brutal power constituted with a heavy, transgressive, and erotic charge.[24] Though this pattern of representation affords interesting insights into contemporary popular culture, it reveals nothing either about the history of fascisms or about the basis of any continuing or revived popularity they enjoy. Of course, not everybody who is drawn to that style is captivated by fascist ideology, enthusiastic about the historical achievements of past fascists, or motivated toward *political* support for their contemporary heirs regardless of whether the foul heritage of organized inhumanity is acknowledged or denied. Some people are doubtless engaged by the whole historic package, but my concern here is less with those who are attracted by the slippery political programs involved and more with the almost independent life of the political style with which they have been associated. This style lives on and exerts a powerful pull that can be all the more seductive in situations where the ideology is neither known nor enthused over. In such settings, it becomes possible to separate the uniforms, boots, fires, banners, columns of light, orchestrated crowds, and perfect bodies from the terminal point of their genocidal achievements.

A perennial danger must be borne carefully in mind when entering this ground. We can easily overestimate the ideological coherence and consistency of fascist doctrines which have sometimes been taken more seriously by their critics than they are by their adherents. It is too easy, for example, to read a key text like Hitler's manifesto, *Mein Kampf,* as if the blueprint it contains was applied rationally and rigorously. In 1925, it could not have been oriented precisely toward inevitable culmination in the terror and barbarity of the Nazi genocide. The theories of propaganda, information, and will spelled out in Hitler's book suggest other ways for approaching its content, purpose, direction, and racial mood. Though the tone of the book conceals it, *Mein Kampf* is as much a projection of desire as an instruction manual. The methodological demands of historiography do not in any case admit the luxury of the retrospective mechanisms that would approach it as a complete plan for what followed. In this instance, the occult commitments that still sustain much fascist thinking, particularly an irredeemable debt to the logic-defying patterns of conspiracy theory, must be recognized before considering all the usual questions of agency and contingency. We should acknowledge that the consolidation of fascist power in government displayed an unusual degree of canny opportunism and some elaborate improvisational abilities.

Approaching the cultural complexities of fascism as part of a history of our present requires recognizing that the desire to identify with Hitler's Nazis and the desire to be a fully post-Hitlerian neo-Nazi may be quite different. Though we must concede the special role of the Nazis in largely discrediting fascism as a political model, I want to suggest that the enduring appeal of Nazi and other militaristic and fascist styles remains a significant cultural phenomenon. It therefore promises a partial rehabilitation of fascist ideas and principles via the sheer attractiveness of fascist movements, of fascist *cultures.* In an area where politics and style have been made necessarily hard to distinguish, as we shall see, fascist political culture remains somehow still pending, partly because of a continuing stylistic appeal.

New swastikas appear from time to time scrawled on the walls I pass as I move through the city where I live and work. Whatever their authors intend, and their outrageous intentions may be very complex, there is no legitimate way to plead ignorance of the evils to which those symbols inevitably refer. They are recognized and accepted as signs of and about the natural and cultural hierarchies of "race." That is why Klansmen, Odinists, Ariosophists, anti-semites, and other far-flung racist aspirants gravitate toward this particular constellation of shocking modern symbols, incorporate them into their local insignia, and ink them indelibly on their bodies. Where swastikas appear, the populist forms of race-thinking and ultranationalism are never far away. These insignia are still easily recognizable as "images of the will" of the Nazi movement, perhaps more so now than they were when Hitler and his associates first creatively adapted them to that end. In spite of the fact that we know where that development led, fascist tendencies may remain alive and attractive in part because alluring fascist style exerts such a powerful hold.

Fascism's persistent presence as both a minor political option and a major cultural reference point is also a reminder that it must be considered in its positivity. In other words, affiliations to it have to be approached as rewarding and pleasurable experiences for adherents, devotees, and, more recently, mimics. This observation points readily toward social-psychological studies of authoritarian movements and personality types, but I intend to follow a different course suggested by Hitler's own emphasis on the "creative" aspects of this metapolitical sensibility.[25] It is defined by the premise that the distinctive qualities of fascist political style, particularly its enthusiastic and strategic employment of communicative technologies and cultures, have long been associated with the enhanced power of visuality. This means that the difficult task of analyzing the pleasures and passions of fascism cannot be accomplished unless we focus on the important technological innovations in the field of visual culture that were central to the rise of the fascist movements and that still help us to define the nature of their particular allure.

Though sometimes out of tune with the antimodernity of movements that were radically conservative as well as technologically sophisticated, the new, populist pattern on which these essentially aggressive movements were built owed much to the means of communication and identification that only visual cues and stimulation could supply. The French Leftist writer Daniel Guérin, whose distinguished work reveals an acute interpretative eye for many neglected dimensions of Nazi culture and solidarity, wrote pointedly of his experiences while touring Germany in the early 1930s. He is one of many writers to have drawn attention to the dynamic qualities of Hitler's "stardom": "It's a scientific, modern advertising organization that has given Hitler's party its formidable power of expansion . . . Naturally, you'll find all the heroes of the day on post-cards, and if you desire a portrait of the Führer there is a surfeit of choices."[26]

Guérin's words provide a small illustration of the bigger process whereby people became participants in an authoritarian compact as spectators with their vision focused on the omnipresent central icon of the leader/deity. We need to remember that this could be a highly active role. Simonetta Falasca-Zamponi's study of political spectacle in fascist Italy provides further support for this argument. What she calls the "mythification" of Il Duce was accomplished by the same popular-cultural means employed to exalt Hitler. Mussolini's deified image shone out from posters, cards, and badges in a comparable system of totalizing political celebrity. One could, she relates, "even find soap bars in the shape of Mussolini."[27]

Paul Virilio and Alice Yeager Kaplan are two influential scholars who have built their insights into the history of fascism on the notion that its armed and militarized political subject not only came to know itself through the new popular medium of film, but also experienced its ecstatic, collective, ultranational selfhood as though it were a film. This "specularization" of the national community's public and private lives has provided a starting point for numerous investigations into the privileged place of visuality and visualization in the constitution of the fascist polity and the fascist public sphere. This line of inquiry is encouraged in the German setting by Goebbels's grandiose speculations about the seemingly infinite potency of visual propaganda. It might be confirmed by the quality of his musings on the change of scale involved in watching his own image on the screen: "I watch myself in a lavish film that UFA [the film company] presents to me. All my speeches since 1933. Strange and gripping. How far away things appear to be."[28] That combination of bewilderment and rhapsodic pleasure in his own dynamic activities on screen might be significant. It may also be important that in this visual culture, images of power, particularly when manifest in the person of the leader, were uncoupled from the constraint of their natural dimensions. Hitler could be enormous on a cinema screen and then shrink down to the size of a poster or postcard. This elasticity of scale was an essential element in the quality of his calculated, superhuman stature.

These authoritarian movements not only transformed the significance of visual culture and public spectacle but also systematized an approach to power and communication that Walter Benjamin and others identified long ago as the "aestheticization" and "theatricalization" of politics. Benjamin counterposed that terrifying state of affairs to an alternative political possibility that he associated with the liberatory power of communism and rather hopefully designated the "politicization of art." We have been deprived of that utopian alternative by our understanding of communists' affiliation to the principle of government by terror as much as by knowledge of their parallel enthusiasm for similar heroic, monumental technologies and aesthetic codes. More disturbingly, patterns in our own political cultures, in the lives of democratic states, also appear to have been touched by aspects of a comparable aestheticizing process. Television has compounded this problem. Our politicians routinely manipulate their physical appearances with cosmetic procedures, groom their televisual images, and massage our responses to them through their command of elocution and their constant attention to the powerful communicative dynamics of bodily gesture and posture.

The application of image-building and image-maintaining techniques has created a condition in which icons severely qualify and often dominate the vivid authority of the spoken word in ways that recall the operations of fascist propaganda. The power of speech, already substantially reduced by the imperative to supply empty but memorable sound bites, has declined even further since Hitler's innovations. In the debased civic culture that results, language renounces its lucidity and its special role in the constitution and differentiation of social and political relations. Political speech succumbs to a dismal game of interminable equivocation and staged bluster. The practice of politics is first modified and then destroyed by the mentalities of marketing and advertising. Stuart Ewen's authoritative history of public relations and spin doctoring and another recent biography of Freud's nephew Edward Bernays, the pioneer of this new communicative model, have supplied much of the history that connects these contemporary activities to their totalitarian past. Political institutions, even whole nations themselves, can be condensed into visual symbols. They are being seen and therefore experienced in novel ways. Summoned by icons, even they can be sold according to the same commercial science that sells all other products. A good example is supplied by the arguments over the "re-branding" of Britain that greeted the end of Conservative rule and recurred even more strongly in discussions of the place of the British monarchy in selling the nation worldwide after the death of Princess Diana—a primary icon for both the British nation and the idea of charity itself. One message these controversies transmitted was that the meaning of nationality and the idea of national distinctiveness are now imagined to be infinitely manipulable. Anything is possible. Something as stubbornly elusive as a postcolonial British identity can supposedly be designed on the drawing board and then projected into the world with such subtle force that it springs to life irrespective of any manifest historical or political obstacles to its spontaneous production.

Whatever significance is accorded to the totalitarian prehistory of these forms of political manipulation, it would appear that a critique of the "aestheticization of politics" and an understanding of its consequences for the development of political solidarity and political identity remain an urgent question. Indeed, since Benjamin's time, many of the technological and aesthetic patterns of political communication established by the fascist movements have passed straightforwardly over into the mainstream of political life in democratic polities. The heritage of fascist rule survives inside democracy as well as outside it. Though the glamorous interplay of leader and led remains a constant source of dramatic tension and libidinal pleasure, the strategies of political advertising for which the work of Leni Riefenstahl provided an extraordinary initial template have been considerably refined during the last sixty years and live on in contemporary advertising. The body, personality, and family of the leader are not the only foci of this influential model. The theatrical and political event, the party rally in which ordinary viewers can both discover and dissolve themselves in the rapturous, ecstatic unity of the many, is another fixed point. Nor can we overlook the affective dimensions of the contemporary political icons for which the swastika supplied the modern prototype.

However distasteful and potentially immoral it may initially seem, there is something to be gained from approaching that device as akin to a corporate logo or brand name.[29] The swastika was a new kind of symbol capable of bringing order to a chaotic and threatening world by making everyone who wore it somehow of equal value. The logo, defined by the design-guru Paul Rand as "primarily a means of identification," becomes something else at this point. It is an element of social identity blended absolutely with the distinctive "product" that stands behind it. Rand continues, "Ideally, identity and product are one." Hitler's creative adaptation of the swastika springs to mind in Rand's elaboration of this approach to visual communication: "The . . . logo serves a dual purpose: it helps to establish and authenticate a new product at the same time that it combines product and logo as an integrated unit. This is possible only when each component is designed to accommodate the other; they must be simple enough to make this union possible."[30]

Attention to these creative, communicative patterns and the narrow repertoire of images which has been used to maintain them is essential if we are to comprehend the positive pleasures aroused by ultranationalism's aesthetico-political initiatives. This appreciation is not incompatible with understanding the importance of terror in the everyday functioning of these forms of political authority that extend the domain of political processes and concerns in every direction and thus merit the name totalitarian. Of course, other signal features associated with the distinctive patterns of totalitarian governmentality—the use of prisons, the spectacularization of death, the debasement of courts, and the wholesale deformation of the public sphere—have also become commonplace features of contemporary life in the many nominally democratic countries. These tendencies, though clearly alarming, are not directly relevant to the argument here. I do not wish to be seen to be repeating the old and discredited analysis which discovers fascism everywhere or tendentiously confuses the state of emergency that abbreviates and modifies democratic processes with the more extensive process that confirms their obliteration. As far as traditions of black political reflection are concerned, the temptation to denounce the brutal and distasteful but normal workings of government as fascist has been especially strong. There is real mitigation for this, and it is connected with the way that demands for civil and human rights and social justice have sometimes found themselves opposed to democratic but exclusionary state institutions reliant upon racial typology and hierarchy. Covertly conducted attempts to disrupt the political lives of dissidents and even to kill off political opponents have been a persistent temptation to governmental power.

These tendencies converge in the courageous and inspiring prison writings of George Jackson. *Blood in My Eye,* his last work before his assassination, is memorable for its attempt to combine this type of observation with a systematic theory of fascism, as well as for his exploration of the idea that America had either developed what he called a "fascist-corporativist form of the state" or produced a new, antidemocratic hybrid that drew heavily upon the patterns pioneered by earlier totalitarian regimes.[31] The book vividly communicates the urgent intellectual passion of an autodidact writing and thinking his way out of the vocabularies, paradigms, and concepts he found in Marxism, Maoism, Fanonism, and Black Power. Almost thirty years later, many of his judgments, strategies, and commentaries have been compromised. Although his utopia may seem as absurd as his rhetoric sometimes does, the direction and gravity of his inquiries into the fundamental relations between race, fascism, and capitalism in several settings remains all the more significant for having been conducted under the most difficult circumstances. There are still important problems arising from the comparative historical study of state violence and state regulation of information under various forms of government, inside and outside the overdeveloped world. The militarization of legal administration and the orientation of citizenry toward war are only two of the issues that preoccupied Jackson and that are still worth pursuing. It is only against this background that the disastrous militarization of black political cultures during the Black Power phase can be properly understood and the continuing fascination of militaria in black popular culture explained.

Because fascist movements have no governmental program other than brutal negation and the will to rule, specific political and economic objectives and policies that can characterize fascism in general are all but impossible to identify. In the rare examples where fascists have attained governmental power, their activity had to overlap substantially with the normal workings of power. Discussion of their strategic alliances with other discrepant parties, their ideological duplicities and changes of heart, for example, with regard to the workings of market capitalism, should not be feared but rather welcomed as an important means to pursue closer specification of fascist exceptionalism. Emphasizing cultural and communicative processes gives these investigations a distinctive direction, but the problems of definition reappear if we concede that features of fascist governance like the routine manipulation of public opinion, the abuse of law, and the cults of violence, youth, and the body now appear both within mainstream varieties of popular culture, in the dreamworlds of advertising and the infotainment telesector, as well as within the narrower domain of formal politics. This consolidation has taken place in the context of a technological and communicative revolution comparable to, but more extensive than, the industrial revolution that formed the backdrop to Walter Benjamin's speculations in the 1920s and 1930s. It, too, has been associated with a degree of political and economic upheaval—de-industrialization, mass poverty, high unemployment, and the displacement of populations—that has once again invited many to find in populist ultra-nationalism, racism, and authoritarianism reassurance and a variety of certainty that can answer radical doubts and anxieties over selfhood, being, and belonging.

There is a welcome opportunity here to reassess Benjamin's hopeful meditations on the place of film and photography in the counter-movement to the aestheticization of politics. His insights need to be supplemented to take contemporary cultural technologies into account. One means to extend them can be found in the arguments that the historian Benedict Anderson and his sometime associate the Thai writer Thongchai Winichakul have made respectively about the binding powers of the printed word and the technologies of cartography. These cultural technologies and institutionalized means of education and communication fostered new forms of solidarity and interconnection. Their reach and power to synchronize lives extended and transformed the imagined community that is the nation. What then, in our own time, would we say about the residual power of radio, sound, telephones, and even cinema, the dominant power of TV, film, and video, and the emergent power of digital technologies as comparable sources of solidarity, identification, and belonging? If it is too intimidating to ask how these technological complexes construct and reproduce power, we might pursue the general question through a specific example: How does "race" circulate through them and how does it impact the relations of solidarity associated with nationality and ethnicity? What forms of belonging have been nurtured by the visual cultures these systems produce and reproduce? Above all, what do their workings communicate about the persistence of "race" as a means to classify and divide human beings? With these questions in mind, I will approach the enduring legacy of fascist communicative technologies in the contemporary dreamworld of mass culture.

IMAGE, ICON, WORD, AND SOUND

In his clever critique and exposition of the fascist modernisms of Ernst Jünger and Leni Riefenstahl, Russell A. Berman identifies elements of a distinctive approach to aesthetics that he found exemplified in their work.

In particular, he describes their common commitment to a "displacement of verbal by visual representation" in which "the power of the image renders scripture obsolete." He suggests that this feature is one of the most important keys to what is specific in the way that fascism addresses its celebrants, making spectators into participants. The impact of Berman's argument increases if we recall that *Triumph of the Will* was made only seven years after the arrival of movies with sound. Indeed, Riefenstahl's dazzlingly innovative work did much to consolidate the vocabulary and grammar of film as a medium that made emotional use of integral speech and music toward poetic or symphonic ends. As we saw in Chapter 1, this issue of vision's relation to other senses and dimensions of communication, in particular its apparent triumph over written language, is an extremely significant component in the history of raciology. It is central to Riefenstahl's own story because the postwar hearings that ruled on the extent and nature of her involvement with the Nazi cause considered this very point. One of her defenses against the accusation that *Triumph of the Will* was a straightforward piece of Nazi propaganda involved the successful argument that without a political commentary to direct the thoughts of its viewers, it could not be considered anything less than an artistic and historical document.

Berman associates Riefenstahl with Jünger even though Jünger's revolutionary conservatism had been shaped by sublime battlefield experiences during the 1914–1918 war. They are connected, he suggests, through their shared belief in the philosophical and experiential priority of image over writing. Discussing the well-known opening sequence of *Triumph of the Will*, in which Hitler's plane descends through the clouds into Nuremberg to the strains of the overture from *Die Meistersinger*, Berman makes the fundamental argument elegantly:

> The point is not that Hitler lands in Nuremberg; the point is that Hitler lands in Nuremberg and is seen. "Wir wollen unsuren Führer sehen [We want to see our leader]," cries the crowd, and the film . . . defines itself as the proper medium of a fascist privileging of sight and visual representation. The will triumphs when it becomes visually evident, and it triumphs over the alternative representational option, cited at the commencement of the film, writing and an associated culture of verbal literacy.[32]

The primacy of visuality is confirmed by Riefenstahl's own reminiscences about the problems she encountered in editing her film, particularly when trying to synchronize its musical soundtrack to the revolutionary flow of images that emerged from her overworked editing machine. Her autobiography makes it clear that neither the conductor nor the composer of the film score was capable of guiding the orchestra through the variations of tempo required by the twenty-minute parade sequence she had assembled from some thirty-five thousand feet of usable rushes:

> The rapid visual changes made it impossible for the conductors and musicians to cue in on time and to adjust their playing to groups marching at different speeds. Despite hours of practice, neither the conductor nor Herr Windt (the composer) was able to synchronize the music correctly; and Herr Windt even suggested that I simply leave out the entire parade. So I myself took over the task of conducting the eighty-man orchestra. I had every frame down pat, and I knew exactly when the music should be conducted faster and when slower.[33]

The carefully intoned martial images are accorded an absolute priority over every other aspect of the total communication. Any integrity the music might have had was enthusiastically sacrificed to this higher purpose.

I want to assume that, whether Riefenstahl was fully aware of it or not, the success of the revolution in visualizing technologies and visual cultures which she pioneered changed forever the apprehension of solidarity and the synchronized collective life of national, ethnic, or racialized communities in just the way that her associates Hitler, Speer, and Goebbels had hoped that it would. This acknowledgment risks another problem, that of confining fascist aesthetics and styles exclusively to the overdeveloped and technologically richer areas of the planet. However, embracing that risk which locates the temptations of fascism as a part of the modernizing process, I would like to endorse the basic view developed by those who argue that the scale of illusion and transparency required by fascist political cultures was "possible only in the age of film, the gramophone and the loudspeaker."[34] This observation underlines that, with the sacralization and militarization of politics that characterized fascist movements, people began to experience their belonging-together according to novel principles of association mediated by technological apparatuses. Mass events produced according to the specifications chronicled so passionately by Riefenstahl offered up the ritual and the liturgy that flowed from the fundamental doctrines of race and nation. Since then, the transformation in the power of images relative to words—written and spoken—that made these developments possible has shaped forms of solidarity, identification, and belonging more generally. Pop videos and political advertising alike demonstrate that, though they may not always draw attention to it, fascist techniques and style contribute heavily to the operations of the infotainment telesector. These communicative patterns have even been transmitted into black political culture. Their connections with "race" persist and develop because they are now part of the way that popular culture is represented and sold as a planetary phenomenon.

The reduced importance of print culture as a source of connectedness, belonging, and simultaneity, and the subsequent devaluation of speech as a medium for the acquisition of common consciousness, were among the most important elements in fascism's communicative and cultural revolution. In exploring its continuing effects upon the production and renewal of political solidarity in which mechanical integration has been superseded by iconic extension and interlinkage, we will discover that the priority accorded to visuality is not yet dominant in contemporary black political culture but that it is an essential and growing part of the preconditions in which proto-fascistic, fascistic, and pseudo-fascistic forms of political culture can take root. Irrespective of whether consideration of this history is limited to demonstrably black idioms, the central problem it raises is the mediation and solicitation of solidarity by means of visual technologies and the iconic connections that dominate them.

To identify the centrality of various communicative technologies to the populist and ultranationalistic politics of fascism is not to make visualization and the scopic regulation of community the dominant aspect in every stage of its modern history. Various combinations of technology seem to have occupied that principal role at different times. The shifts from amplified speech and print, to radio and recorded sound, and then to image, icon, film, and light seem to have been precipitated as the Nazis moved closer to the assumption of government. If Hitler is to be believed, however, from the very start of their campaigns, speeches, rallies, and meetings took precedence over the limited power of the written word. It was only after 1930 that microphones and loudspeakers became standard equipment at Nazi meetings. Prior to that, the inability to hear had placed restrictions on the scale and type of political events that could be staged.[35] Barred from the airwaves, which were still regulated by the government until the summer of 1932, Goebbels's department distributed 50,000 gramophone records of Hitler's speeches during February of that year. These recordings were played from mobile vans during the presidential election that followed. Mussolini's speeches for the Empire were not released on a set of phonograph records until 1938.

Once the Nazis attained power, they were especially active in promoting the use of cheap radio sets with limited range that were ideally suited to the task of synchronizing the nation into a single audience, a "radio unity."[36] They aimed to place a radio set in every German home, and the number of radios in use exceeded six million in 1934. However great the power of a medium addressed to hearing, a sense that cannot easily be shut down or closed off, radio technology could not be depended upon for everything. Despite Nazi efforts to collectivize and socialize the listening experience, it was still largely a private affair and thus far too easy for a listener to simply switch off the set when bored or disenchanted.[37] Hitler's public speeches were certainly broadcast, reaching an audience of some 56,000,000 in 1935, but in sharp contrast to the intimate, personal techniques employed by Roosevelt and Churchill, his solitary performances in the studio were considered ineffective and lacking in the inspirational qualities which only reciprocal collaboration with an audience could supply. It was felt that the interactive possibilities produced by encountering a real crowd were essential if his speeches were to operate at the right pitch of intensity. For twelve years, from 1933 until the end of the war, he did not transmit from a studio again.[38]

Film, on the other hand, corresponded to the needs of a nation of spectators that was in the process of turning itself from an association of mere subjects into an exclusive body of noble citizens who would be "Lords of the Reich." It provided them with new ways to experience their own actions. They were looped back into an altogether new variety of visually triggered self-consciousness via the active mirror provided, above all, by the cinema screen. The national collective could discover and take pleasure in itself and its common subordination to an all-powerful leadership in equally novel ways. Collective appreciation of the content of the national culture was also transformed. Riefenstahl, Speer, and others reduced it to the ancient, sacred elements of stone, fire, and light, which they embellished with Hellenomaniacal grandeur. The idea of a national community was adapted to and by the nation's experience of seeing itself in this guise. Its particular, official histories and memories were projected in posters and political spectacles, monumental architecture, illuminated ritual, and orchestrated, geometric mass drill. The requirements of filming shaped this process directly. It was captured, preserved, distilled, and disseminated in amplified and edited forms. The real events could not measure up to the demanding requirements of the new historical record, so Riefenstahl used her custom-built editing machine to improve upon them.

I do not want to lose sight of the varying degrees of involvement with ritual, spectacle, and display that characterize the vantage points of different viewer-participants. It is important not to erase the distinction between those for whom this visual overstimulation was encountered in real time and face-to-face and others, more distantly positioned, whose identification and synchronization with the martial tempo of the source events were remote. The latter became intimate with the core in quite unprecedented, hyper-real ways involving odd camera angles, action at varying speeds, and dissolving and superimposed images. However, I am suggesting that cinema supplied the massive, dynamic conduit for a substantial cultural shift. This change lay back in the direction of seriality and mechanical solidarity but also beyond it. It formed a nonsynchronous interconnection—a national ontology—that was mediated and accomplished via the lateral and hierarchical connections that characterize iconic association and what might now be recognized as "logo-solidarity."

Militarization was and remains the center of this comprehensive process. It is the foundation for fascist style and aesthetic values in which war as both a sacred, enlightening experience and an analog for other dimensions of brutally hierarchical sociality occupies a privileged position. The presence of uniformed men is thus a recurrent and symptomatic feature of its powers, which are common to different ceremonial and ritual orders and work across the barriers erected by the ideological formalities of Left and Right. Fascist movements marked a subtle departure from the patterns of political symbolism that had been established during the French Revolution when cockades and other patriotic emblems had first carried the institutionalized forces of popular political division over into the stream of everyday life.[39] The older, modern pattern drew attention to the fundamental unity in diversity of the revolutionary nation and its citizenry, while the newer pattern of iconic interconnection emphasized the interchangeability and disposability of the collective body's individual members. In the first case, people became the same through the intermediation of emblems; in the second, which bears the deepest imprint of race-thinking, their emblems were a desperate, external proof that despite appearances to the contrary, they were always and already fundamentally and exclusively the same.

In an acute wartime review of *Mein Kampf* that includes his reflections on the psychological dynamics of Hitlerism and a warning not to underestimate the emotional appeal of its militaristic conception of politics, George Orwell noted that "whereas socialism and even capitalism in a more grudging way have said to people, 'I offer you a good time,' Hitler has said to them, 'I offer you struggle, danger and death,' and as a result a whole nation flings itself at his feet."[40] To comprehend this superficially perverse choice, which has been repeated several times in the history of less-successful fascist movements, we must appreciate that the same bonding effects were also prompted by the visible emblems and insignia of logo solidarity. Placed on or used close to the body, these signs and gestures expressed more than assent to the revolutionary transformation of social life. They were all the more potent when they were wordless and could by the use of icons alone extend martial imperatives, habits, and discipline beyond the bounds of the uniform-wearing minority.

Hitler's reflections on these communicative patterns and his plans for their application at different stages in the development of the National Socialist movement are a valuable aid to understanding the significance of these changes and the role of the media in framing and orchestrating their entrenchment. Hitler describes a progression from the early period in which the power of the spoken word was paramount in building the Nazi cause, through a phase where mass meetings were the key organizational institution, and lastly, the final stage, during which symbols and visual cues became an overriding necessity. Although this analysis is shaped by his open contempt for the herd-like masses, his words acquire new significance in our own period, where the saturation of public space by advertising has been associated with high rates of functional illiteracy. He continues:

> At most a leaflet or a poster can, by its brevity, count on getting a moment's attention from someone who thinks differently. The pic-

ture in all its forms up to the film has greater possibilities. Here a
man needs to use his brains even less; it suffices to look, or at most
to read extremely brief texts, and thus many will more readily accept
a *pictorial presentation* than *read* an *article* of any *length*. The picture
brings them in a much briefer time, I might almost say at one
stroke, the enlightenment which they obtain from written matter
only after arduous reading.[41]

This strong sense of the value of what is seen compared with what has
been read or heard is refined considerably in Hitler's later discussion of the
power of the symbols that were employed so successfully during the building of the Nazi movement. He begins the famous passages in *Mein Kampf*
where he discusses the swastika and the newly designed Nazi flag with a
reminiscence about a communist demonstration decked out in red flags
and flowers that he had witnessed in the after-shock of the 1914–1918
war. Articulating these observations as part of his crude theory of the psychological power of symbols, he continues, "A sea of red flags, red scarves,
and red flowers gave to this demonstration, in which an estimated hundred and twenty thousand persons took part, an aspect that was gigantic
from the purely external point of view. I myself could feel and understand
how easily the man of the people succumbs to the suggestive magic of a
spectacle so grandiose in effect."[42] If this passage conveys something of the
imaginative debt that National Socialism owed to its Leftist antecedents,
Hitler's attention to the psychological and symbolic dynamics involved in
consolidating his emergent power by producing "a picture of the will of
our movement" in such concentrated form seems to have surpassed anything that the communists had accomplished up to that point.

If a black swastika against a red-and-white background was a picture,
we must now ask what kind of picture it was. Hitler's absorbing exposition
of how the colors and dimensions of the new Nazi flag were chosen need
not be rehearsed here. It is secondary to the paramount insight derived
from his observation that "an effective insignia can in hundreds of thousands of cases give the first impetus toward interest in a movement." I
would extend this with another suggestion. The role of insignia, symbols,
and icons is not confined to the initial encounter that Hitler narrates. It
would appear that the use of icons could promote, maintain, and renew
"logo-solidarity" as well as initiate it. The varieties of interconnection

icons consolidate are a fundamental aspect of the manner in which the race-conscious aspirations of authoritarian irrationalism are to be realized. By drawing attention to deeper, more authentic cultural bonds, which could not be spoken or written down without diminishing them, these signs qualified the significance of what could be said or written and made some types of speech wholly unnecessary. The muting power of icons is linked ultimately to prohibitions on what can be spoken, to the silencing of the population, and to a characteristic pressure on language itself that helps to define totalitarian governance via its obligatory investment in circumlocutions, euphemisms, and codes.

An interesting example of the practical consequences of this wordless, metaphysical solidarity created by the deployment of icons can be drawn from the acrimonious debates over the extent and character of the Nazi commitments of Martin Heidegger. His depressing case still represents the most significant testing ground for debates about the significance of Nazi, ultranationalist, and other mystical raciological ideas and cognitive systems for modern philosophical thought. One of the instances in which Heidegger is accepted to have made remarks which not only supported the Nazi cause but actually tied his own philosophical concepts directly to the National Socialist project was during a meeting with Karl Löwith. The younger man was a Jewish former student and erstwhile close associate of Heidegger's who would eventually become his colleague and play a pivotal role in raising the discussion of Heidegger's Nazism during the 1940s. Löwith left a detailed account of a meeting between them that took place in Mussolini's Rome in 1936. He has claimed that on this occasion, Heidegger readily conceded that "his partisanship for National Socialism lay in the essence of his philosophy" and that "his concept of 'historicity' was the basis of his political 'engagement.'"[43] This argument, which ultimately concerns Heidegger's view of the German nation and its political, historical, and ontic character and destiny, has been developed further by many scholars, most notably Pierre Bourdieu.[44] I cite it here, in passing, because it seems to me to be connected to Heidegger's decision to display the swastika on his own person. Against the distracting and untidy heterogeneity of appearances, it may have been the metaphysical power of a resolutely invariant icon that, to adopt a very un-Heideggerian metaphor, tuned people in to the siren call of their collective, that is, racial and national, being: "being is the enduring prototype, the always identical."[45]

The eminent philosopher had taken the opportunity to bring his family to Italy on a brief tour while lecturing on Hölderlin's poetry at the German-Italian Cultural Institute, and on Europe and German Philosophy at the Kaiser Wilhelm Institute. Löwith, who was barred by virtue of being a Jew from attending the second event, was struck by the fact that Heidegger wore a swastika badge or pin on his lapel throughout this trip. Löwith was uncomfortable that his sometime mentor did not see this gesture as inappropriate when in the company of a Jew with whom he had once been close:

> The next day my wife and I made an excursion to Frascati and Tusculum with Heidegger, his wife and his two small sons, whom I often cared for when they were little. It was a radiant afternoon, and I was happy about this final get-together, despite undeniable reservations. Even on this occasion, Heidegger did not remove the party insignia from his lapel. He wore it during his entire stay in Rome, and it had obviously not occurred to him that the swastika was out of place while he was spending the day with me.[46]

Löwith's judgment that the inappropriateness of this gesture simply had not occurred to Heidegger may be too generous, but we will never know exactly what motivated the great philosopher to make this visible commitment. That may not be the most interesting issue raised by this example. I do not wish to speculate on what Heidegger's choice might communicate about him as a man, or about his status during the visit as an intellectual ambassador for his country. Instead, it is more productive to ask what this display of "partisanship" in the National Socialist cause meant as a political act after the enacting of the Nuremberg laws, a full two years after the public book-burnings of "destructive Jewish writing" on university campuses and the start of civil and legal moves against Jews. This phase of violence and active persecution had ushered in a situation in which words and signs were charged with a new significance, particularly when the processes of cultural and racial hygiene that were under way could not separate people readily along either linguistic or somatic lines. These signs and icons, whether on clothing, or marking buildings, homes, and civic institutions, delivered spectators immediately to a special place beyond the duplicity of words where fundamental historical and racial divisions could be immediately perceived. Their use made a complex and messy situation characterized by extensive assimilation and amalgamation appear quite different. With suitably historic emblems and icons in place, the German population could conform to race-thinking's simplest binary codes: for or against, in or out.

Löwith's views of Heidegger's philosophy and his report of their conversation on this occasion have been predictably and summarily dismissed by Heidegger's most assiduous apologists.[47] I prefer to argue that Heidegger's decision to display the swastika on his person is a relevant issue in its own right. It binds him directly to the practical philosophy of Hitler in an immediate way whatever interpretation one holds of the connections between his Nazism and his other philosophical commitments.

PARAMILITARY SPECTACLE, SPORT, RACE, AND THE BODY

It bears repetition that a paramilitary orientation was an integral aspect of the way political culture was recomposed during the fascist period.[48] Long before modern ultranationalism displaced its colonial antecedents, military life had placed a distinctive emphasis on regimentation as the index of perfection. Both could be gauged through the coordinated display of the male body. This spectacular political embodiment dramatized national, governmental, and racial power. Intensified by film of the right kind, and here we should recall Leni Riefenstahl's frequently voiced distaste for filmed images that did not escape the visual conventions of mere newsreel footage, it afforded an obvious means to communicate the awe-inspiring effect of spectacular events to an ever-larger viewing public that could find itself joyfully in the racialized hierarchies that were being brought to life in the Nazis' "comprehensive creative renewal."[49]

The fascist interest in the use of sports and physical training as part of their propaganda and as a critical component of their political style is surely relevant here. This is true not only because of the obvious ways that modern sporting activities have functioned as ciphers of war, fudged the relationship between entertainment and politics, and produced the most potent and enduring of racial archetypes. I will return to these points in a moment as part of a discussion of Leni Riefenstahl's *Olympiad*, but I want to raise them initially through the equally significant example provided by the contrasting figures of Joe Louis and Max Schmeling. Hitler's views of sporting activity in the volkish state were set out at some length in *Mein Kampf.* Amid his predictable enthusiasm for giving priority to the training of the body rather than the mind, a defense of boxing, which he feels has been unjustly dismissed as vulgar by his political allies, leaps off the page and exemplifies the very model of everything that volkish physical training should instill in the youth of a soon-to-be-reborn nation:

> There is no sport that so much as this one promotes the spirit of at-tack, demands lightning decisions, and trains the body in steel dex-terity . . . above all the young healthy body must learn to suffer blows. Of course this may seem wild to the eyes of our present spiri-tual fighters. But it is not a function of the folkish state to breed a colony of peaceful aesthetes and physical degenerates. Not in the re-spectable shop keeper or virtuous old maid does it see its ideal of humanity, but in the defiant embodiment of manly strength and in women who are able to bring men into the world.
>
> And so sport does not exist only to make the individual strong, agile and bold; it should also toughen him and teach him to bear hardships.[50]

These words could almost have come from the pages of *Scouting for Boys* or *Rovering to Success.* They provide a strange, distorted echo of an older im-perial ideal.[51] From them, we can also begin to deduce how in the slippage from mass sporting participation to mass spectatorship of sport, Louis and Schmeling, who have been said by no less an authority than Andrew Young to have fought the Second World War in advance, could become a new kind of racialized popular hero. Both were elevated to a fever pitch of iconic representativeness by the integral role of the media in staging their conflicts and infusing their public personalities, their stardom, and their bodies with national and raciological significance. The fights between these two punctuated the period leading up to the outbreak of war. Their intertwined lives still counterpoint the immortal theme of Aryan mastery with a different story—the transnational marketing of sport and its role in constructing planetary audiences.

Both men would later make extensive contributions to the war efforts of the nations with which their pugilistic prowess was associated— Schmeling as a paratrooper and Louis as, among other things, a co-star with Ronald Reagan in the 1943 propaganda movie *This Is the Army*. Significantly, both would also be connected to the star system of the film industry, Schmeling through his marriage to the actress Anny Ondra, an appropriately blond movie star who would regularly accompany her husband to dinner at the Goebbels residence. At the time of their first encounter, Louis, whose historic achievements would be lauded on a record by the combined talents of Richard Wright, Paul Robeson, and Count Basie in 1941, was then the most famous black man in the United States. As is well known, he was defeated by the German champion in the initial fight, which took place in June 1936 at Yankee Stadium in the Bronx just prior to the Berlin Olympic games. Schmeling's unanticipated victory contributed a lot to the expectations of Aryan physical superiority that would be dashed a few weeks later by the extraordinary physical achievements of Jesse Owens.

Schmeling had first boxed in the United States during the late 1920s. He won the heavy-weight championship in 1930 but lost it again quickly. When he returned in the mid-1930s it was both to fight Louis and to act as an emissary for the Nazi government, which was anxious about the prospect of an American boycott of the forthcoming Olympic games, which had been awarded to the city of Berlin before the Nazis had come to power. Schmeling says that he was a careful student of the films of Louis's performances in the ring. He claims that when lunching with Hitler in Munich just before the first fight, the Führer was concerned that the challenger was risking the prestige of his nation and his "race" in combat with a black man (it should be noted that this sort of sporting combat between blacks and whites was illegal in parts of the United States at the time). Schmeling's victory over Louis delighted the leaders of his country who had played down the fight in anticipation of the opposite result. It was also well received by many white Americans keen to consign Louis to mediocrity and quite prepared to embrace the racialized triumph of the "terrific Teuton" over a cocky and confident young black man who had apparently over-reached himself. Hitler and Goebbels enthused over this triumph and identified it as a powerful symbol of innate white supremacy. Schmeling himself had attained ownership of the full rights to overseas distribution of the film of the bout, which he watched in Hitler's company soon after returning to Germany. Goebbels's ministry edited together the fight footage with training-camp scenes of both boxers and images of

Schmeling's triumphant reception in Frankfurt. The resulting film, *Max Schmeling's Victory, a Germany Victory,* played to packed houses.[52]

It took some time for Louis to reestablish himself as the most attractive opponent in Schmeling's eyes. He was assisted in this task by the efforts of the Anti-Nazi League, which was alive to the symbolic political gains involved in the likely outcome of any return match and of course by the idea that, if he could defeat Louis a second time, the German would once again become a world champion. Louis, who was now twenty-four, and the second black heavy-weight champion following his defeat of Jimmy Braddock, had a long period of training in which to prepare for the second fight. It finally took place in June 1938 in a heavily politicized atmosphere that Schmeling himself identified as an imitative American response to the politicization of sport during the Third Reich. Louis described his growing sense that the whole world would be watching their second encounter:

> From what I could gather, reading the papers and listening to people talk, the whole world was looking to this fight between me and Schmeling. Germany was tearing up Europe, and we were hearing more and more about the concentration camps for the Jews. A lot of Americans had family in Europe and were afraid for their people's lives. Schmeling represented everything that Americans disliked and they wanted him beat and beat good. Now here I was, a black man. I had the burden of representing all of America. Black and white people were talking about my fights; they were talking about me as a person, too. I guess I looked good to them. White Americans—even while some of them still were lynching black people in the South—were depending on me to K.O. Germany.[53]

A summons to the White House for dinner with the President underlined the political significance of the fight and made a strong impression on Louis. Franklin Roosevelt felt the boxer's muscles and commented, "Joe, we're depending on those muscles for America."

Louis's extraordinary victory in the second fight required only two minutes and four seconds. The film of the bout was so brief that it was elongated by means of slow-motion replay. Nazi film technicians would later re-edit the fight for their own newsreels so that a postmatch claim by Schmeling's management that he had been hit by a foul blow could appear plausible.[54] Schmeling was visited in the hospital by the German ambassador Hans Heinrich Dieckhoff, who urged him to file a protest against the manner of Louis's triumph only to be told that there had been no foul and that Louis's victory was legitimate. Louis concluded his reflection on the historical and political significance of the fight with the following observation: "I even heard that when the Germans learned how badly I was beating Schmeling, they cut the radio wires to Germany. They didn't want their people to know that just a plain old nigger man was knocking the shit out of the Aryan Race."

The ramifications of Louis's victory would be important for the politics of "race" in both nations. Louis's own account of it cut against the grain of most press commentary but did not pose Germany and the United States against each other in a simplistic manner. His memoirs challenge America's moral claims by quietly drawing attention to both nations' reliance on a politics of "race." He describes, for example, the presence of the home-grown American Nazis who had turned up at his training camp to demonstrate their enthusiastic endorsements of Hitler's message of hate. In the aftermath of the fight, the *New York Times* struggled to persuade its readers that the outcome was meaningless and that "nothing had happened." But intense discussions, which had been conducted in the black press as America struggled to distinguish the Nazi politics of "race" from its own systems of segregation and disenfranchisement, were rekindled. In the *New York World Telegram*, Heywood Broun articulated an altogether different mood:

> One hundred years from now some historian may theorize . . . that the decline of Nazi prestige began with a left hook by a former unskilled automotive worker who had never studied the policies of Neville Chamberlain and had no opinion whatever in regard to the situation in Czechoslovakia . . . It was known that Schmeling regarded himself as a Nazi symbol. It is not known whether Joe Louis commonly regards himself as a representative of his race and as one under dedication to advance its prestige . . . But that may have been in his heart when he exploded the Nordic myth with a bombing glove.[55]

In Germany, opponents of Hitler's regime organized their own spontaneous celebrations of Louis's triumph. But this was not the only response to the big fight. The figure of Heidegger springs to mind once again. Sadly, we do not know what his reaction was in 1938, but three years earlier in the course of lectures later published as *Introduction to Metaphysics* he had expressed disgust at the dismal situation in which a boxer could become recognized as a national hero. The accompanying polemic against "the darkening of the world" linked this regrettable historical occurrence to a critique of the corrosive force of modern technology, a scathing view of mass rallies, and his antipathy toward other features of technological regimes, presumably including actually existing Nazism. Given that this is the text in which Heidegger not only affirms the "inner truth and greatness"[56] of the National Socialist movement but also employs the concept of "race" in a brief discussion of national spirit, beauty, body, and combat, these passages have been rather unwisely trumpeted as providing evidence of the philosopher's repudiation of the fervent Nazi views he had previously held while rector of Freiburg University. Heidegger's strong view of Hitlerism's failure to measure up to the exacting personal standards that he had set for it do not amount to a repudiation of Nazism either in general or in the ideal forms he idiosyncratically espoused. However, he may have been more right than he knew when, with an insider's wisdom, he helpfully identified these particular features of Nazi political culture as the troubling historical essence of what National Socialism had become.

LENI RIEFENSTAHL AND THE CHARISMATIC COMMUNITY

Although the history of Hitler's vocal and dramaturgical coaching and of the "Wagnerian" elements in the staging of Nazi ritual are well-trodden critical paths, they need to be recalled now, however briefly, as additional dimensions to what Hitler described as "the suggestive magic of spectacle." It is important that we do not approach the technologies of specularization as secondary or subsidiary factors, something that came afterward and simply conducted authoritarian irrationalism to a mass audience. I have already argued that the camera was directly responsible for the quality of solidarity celebrated by the fascist movements. It did not just attend the festivities arranged to mark and communicate the rebirth of the nation after its periods of weakness, decadence, and slumber. Though it may be going too far to say that these events were always enacted for the primary benefit of their remote rather than their immediate audiences, we can be confident that the spectacular festivities aimed at producing what Roger Griffin has called a "charismatic community"[57] were staged with the power and agency of the camera in mind.

In conclusion, we must return to Leni Riefenstahl and her revolutionary artistic and technological accomplishments, which raise a number of interlinked issues addressed in this chapter. The enduring power of her work confirms that it remains the ground on which the plausibility of fascist style and its associated aesthetic values will be settled. The circumstances surrounding the production of *Triumph of the Will*, her record of the sixth Nazi Congress and the second film that Riefenstahl made during the Nazi period, cannot be reconstructed in detail here. But it is important to grasp the place of *Triumph* in Riefenstahl's career path from actress to director to appreciate the erotic spell that she cast on the Nazi leadership, to understand its relation to her earlier Alpine films set against the sublime extremity of ice and snow, the natural backdrop for Nordic racial myth and heroism, and to comprehend something of the substantive technical innovations that constitute the most obvious link between this film, *Olympiad* (the film she made of the 1936 Olympic games), and the new visual culture they begin.

These fundamental issues aside, we must appreciate the extraordinary scale of the production. *Triumph of the Will* was the most expensive documentary film produced to date and involved hundreds of thousands of meters of film and dozens of highly skilled camera operators. It required countless hours at the editing machine, and its technical standards prompted a host of further professional innovations. The new palette of long shots, slow dissolves, variations in camera speed, and juxtapositions with which Riefenstahl extended the boundaries of her medium has been discussed in detail by film historians. However, none of this should obscure either the film's basic political contribution to the realignment taking place between the party, the movement, and the nation following Hitler's assassination of the populist, Brownshirt leader Ernst Rohm, or its most telling accomplishment: the orientation of the national community toward a war that Riefenstahl made appear desirable as well as inevitable. Her seductive affirmation of the historic power, cultural beauty, and civilized

strength of German mastery is the setting for Hitler's own diffident stardom, a strange combination of rage and authority with what Orwell called
the "pathetic dog-like face . . . of a man suffering under intolerable
wrongs." The film's dynamic animating energy is the love borne by the
people for their leader, communicated by Riefenstahl's rhapsodic climaxes
and the ecstatic faces in her cheering crowds. The synchronized, uniformed marchers flow past in oceanic tides while a reassuring cat snoozes
on a window ledge under the Nazi flag.

Final judgments on Riefenstahl's fascist aesthetic rest upon the question of continuity between *Triumph of the Will, Olympiad,* and, later on,
her well-received "anthropological" photographs of the Nuba people of
the Sudan. This extraordinary creative sequence and its relationship to fascist visual culture was first raised provocatively and usefully in 1972 by Susan Sontag.[58] Her devastating and acute reading of Riefenstahl's work has
retained much of its intellectual force and contributed a welcome strategic
block against both feminist and avowedly antipolitical attempts to rehabilitate the aging Nazi filmmaker. Although Sontag's essay still provides a
welcome starting point for the consideration of fascist aesthetics, it is
marked by its own time. It does not, for example, explore the issue of racial
differentiation as such or the questions of ultranationalism, symbolism,
typology, and hierarchy that follow from it. These are, nonetheless, factors
in Riefenstahl's work that have direct bearing upon her aesthetic choices
and strategies. In seeking to amend Sontag's account by taking these problems more comprehensively into consideration, we should recall that
Riefenstahl's affiliation to and support for the Nazis were accomplished
without the benefits of formal party membership. Her evident pleasure in
friendship with the senior party figures who used her elegant, white-clad
glamour to modify and project their own public personalities comes across
very strongly in her lengthy memoir and in her many other attempts to
vindicate herself. The familiar self-portrait is of a blithely nonpolitical and
essentially artistic figure undone by her rhapsodic pursuit of beauty, and
unjustly persecuted by the ignorant and the unreasonable.

The lack of party membership should stand as a warning to those
whose understanding of the cultural character of Nazism remains wedded
to these official and inadequate means of calculating complicity.[59] We can
add that Riefenstahl's complex but nonetheless intimate and enthusiastic
relationship to the Nazi cause did not require that she act the part of an

antiblack racist in any crude sense. The Negro was not a central problem of contemporary politics as far as she was concerned, and she could therefore, unlike Hitler, sincerely congratulate Jesse Owens on his historic physical achievements. Her professed enthusiasm for Africa, and the evident pleasure she took in the natural perfection she discovered in the supple, shining bodies of young Africans, offer an additional illustration of the crisis of "race" and representation outlined in my opening chapter. But even in the 1930s, her fascination with Owens's physique reveals that this fascist aesthetic was not bounded by "race" or, to put it more accurately, is not bounded by "race" in the ways that we might anticipate. But neither is her work, as some advocates of her rehabilitation would have it, redeemed by this apparent race-lessness.

We should recognize that Riefenstahl's outlook was comfortable with the notion that some blacks at least might be aristocrats of the body. But this acceptance did not mean that race-thinking had been renounced, transcended, or abandoned. Aspects of it were clearly confirmed by this phenomenon. We should also recall that, in her hands, the Olympian festival of nations staged in Berlin in 1936 was presented as a festival of beauty and strength. This is a potent combination. It betrays not just an obvious Nordicism but also older "Spartan" themes recast in the Hellenomaniacal codes that identified Greece and Germany as related parts of a single unique sensibility.[60] Her cameras linger over Owens, and that pre-sentiment of her later dalliance with the people of Nuba, whose culture and society she made over in an undiluted and belligerent savagery she clearly found exhilarating, has been repeatedly cited as offering mitigation for her attachment to the Nazi cause. Again, her superficially benign recognition of black excellence in physicality need not be any repudiation of raciological theory. In this world of overdetermined racial signs, an outstandingly good but temperamental natural athlete is exactly what we would expect a savage African to become. The notion of black beauty is a more complex issue, but even that need not be a doorway into liberation from the idea of race and its non-negotiable natural hierarchies. It, too, can cement the most destructive bonds between blackness and the body to the obvious detriment of any possible connections between blackness and the mind.

Let me be clear: it is not that recognizing the cognitive and rational capacities of blacks is necessarily more valuable than recognizing their physical attributes, though in social relations built upon a sharp and dualistic division between mind and body this is a fair question to ask. The central issue is simpler still: associating blackness with intelligence, reason, and the activities of the mind challenges the basic assumptions of raciology—in common-sense and scientific versions—whereas giving "The Negro" the gift of the devalued body does not, even if that body is to be admired. The black body can be appreciated as beautiful, powerful, and graceful in the way that a racehorse or a tiger appear beautiful, powerful, and graceful. Beauty and strength are, after all, understood by Riefenstahl as exclusively natural attributes rather than cultural achievements. They are the coincidental products of good fortune in nature's racial lottery rather than products of hard work, discipline, training, and self-denial. Their very effortlessness signifies a lower value when coded in strong, sinuous black flesh.

Riefenstahl's joyful, erotic celebration of the human body might be understood as initiating a new angle of vision. Humanity is invoked but it is a hierarchical humanity, fractured and sharply differentiated along visible racial lines. The underlying, implicit tragedy is the Aryan loss of physical power, not the African retention of it. The possibility that Riefenstahl might be a founder of the visual culture that produces and aestheticizes "race" as a meaningful category does not arise in most of what has been written about her. The obvious connections between her work and the body-portraiture of Bruce Weber or Robert Mapplethorpe, that other gifted and eccentric crypto-fascist who, like Heidegger, chose to display a swastika on his lapel, remains unexplored.[61]

Whatever Riefenstahl's connections to the Nazi cause, her films contain no overt anti-semitism, and this, when combined with her "positive" projection of the Nuba and her appreciative eye for the achievements of athletes like Owens and Kitei Son, the Korean winner of the marathon in 1936, settles the matter. She could not have traded in racism, and her celebration of the achievements of exemplary nonwhites becomes vital evidence used to support her insistent claims to be entirely nonpolitical. In this interpretation she becomes an innocent poet of the human form, a celebrant of sporting activity in general whose innovative cameras were concerned only with recording the universal endeavor of her nameless athletes outside of or beyond the claims that their nation-states might choose to make upon them.

Riefenstahl's most recent biographer, Audrey Salkeld, who has the dubious distinction of being Riefenstahl's most craven apologist, goes furthest down this road in her attempts to turn the tables on Sontag by labeling her rather than the much wronged and misunderstood Riefenstahl as the more skilled propagandist! She asserts that society has lost more than it has gained by "hobbling" Riefenstahl's extraordinary talents and claims that critics have paid insufficient attention to the ways in which Riefenstahl's art was shaped by her "being a mountaineer and nature-lover." Along the way, Salkeld accuses the cultural historian, film critic, and sociologist Siegfried Kracauer, a contemporary of Riefenstahl's who fled Germany when the Nazis came to power, of "rushing into print with the first politically-correct post-war study of German Cinema . . . (searching) zealously for the springs of Nazism." It is hard to see why Kracauer's enterprise is regarded as illegitimate and equally difficult to avoid the conclusion that it enrages Salkeld only because his path-breaking work on the connections between the romantic critique of industrial culture that Riefenstahl inherited from the Mountain Films in which she had starred points toward a more negative assessment of her later work than Salkeld's own revisionist attempts at benediction.[62]

Physical strength, sport, combat, competition, and their accompanying values may not be the core components in a generic fascist aesthetic. But the way they present the relationship between national and racial identity and physical embodiment lies at the center of what distinguished the fascist movements of the past and what remains fascistic in their influence on contemporary culture. In 1928, long before it was clear what lay ahead for Germany, and long before Riefenstahl brought its visual culture to life, Emmanuel Levinas struggled to make sense of the philosophy of Hitlerism. He drew particular attention to a feeling of identity between selves and bodies that was being constructed where the fascist movements gave the body and its pleasures back to people who had been schooled in the cultural and spiritual assumptions of Christianity and liberalism. These doctrines told them that their sense of embodiment and corporeal constraint was a stage to be passed through en route to a higher and more valuable sense of freedom associated with the ideas of the soul and the spirit. In contrast to these traditions, Levinas warned, Hitlerism finds and founds a new definition of freedom from an acceptance of being constrained by the body. The soul or spirit does not disappear, but its essence is redefined by the fact that it is chained to the body: "Man's essence no longer lies in freedom, but in a kind of bondage. To be truly oneself . . . means becoming aware of the ineluctable original chain that is unique to our bodies, and above all accepting this chaining."[63] His words provide a suitable caption for the rapturous physicality captured and projected larger-than-life by Riefenstahl's cameras as they track her straining, beautiful athletes to the limits that they must exceed if the will is, after all, to triumph. The truncated definitions of freedom that this creates will be explored in the next chapter.

5

The biological, with the notion of inevitability it entails, becomes more than an *object* of spiritual life. It becomes its heart. The mysterious urgings of the blood, the appeals of heredity and the past for which the body serves as an enigmatic vehicle, lose the character of being problems that are subject to a solution put forward by a sovereignly free Self. Not only does the Self bring in the unknown elements of these problems in order to resolve them; the Self is also constituted by these elements. Man's essence no longer lies in freedom, but in a kind of bondage. To be truly oneself does not mean taking flight once more above contingent events that always remain foreign to the Self's freedom; on the contrary, it means becoming aware of the ineluctable original chain that is unique to our bodies, and above all accepting this chaining.

—EMMANUEL LEVINAS

A crowd of men and women moiled like nightmare figures in the smoke-green haze. The juke box was dinning and it was like looking into the depths of a murky cave. And now someone moved aside and looking down along the curve of the bar past the bobbing heads and shoulders I saw the juke box, lit up like a bad dream of the Fiery Furnace, shouting Jelly, Jelly, Jelly, All night long.

—RALPH ELLISON

The specific traditions of public interaction that were originally products of the agency of slaves are being surpassed. They are, as I have already argued, declining now that postslave cultures are being recomposed around new priorities and opportunities associated with digital media, de-industrialization, and the growth of consumerism. The cultural achievements provoked by slave life provided more than the contested core of American identity: they supplied a platform for youth cultures, popular cultures, and styles of dissent far from their places of origin. Today they are fractured by the obvious divisions between north and south, by overdeveloped and underdeveloped regions of the planet that are being enforced by the globalization of commerce and power. They remain powerful but the breadth of their appeal has created new difficulties. Are they local or global forms? To whom, if anyone, do they belong?

This chapter suggests that an exploration of this large and irreversible change in the life of the Atlantic diaspora and its successor-cultures is overdue. More controversially, it employs a discussion of changing patterns in black popular culture to explore the continuing impact of fascism's cultural revolution on the contemporary world. Against that background, I would also like to view some of the ethical and political questions that have arisen when critically inclined intellectuals have been called upon to account for the enduring potency of black cultural styles. These have often been outlaw forms that challenge conventional commentators and demand an end to disinterested and contemplative varieties of criticism. However, they have posed even greater problems for politically engaged critics whose work—irrespective of the noble motives that generate it—is revealed to be inadequate where it moves too swiftly or simplistically to either condemn or celebrate. What do they have to say about the currency of biopolitical notions that bear the historic imprint of Riefenstahl and her ecstatic, racialized physicality?

An especially vivid version of these problems has taken shape where complex and morally testing vernacular forms have appeared recently and belatedly as objects of academic scrutiny. They have been manifest in scholarly discussions of hip-hop and rap, where liberation and justice are still demanded but have taken a back seat in recent years to revolutionary conservatism, misogyny, and stylized tales of sexual excess. These cultural expressions have been produced at a time when people seem less sure than they once were about what defines the cultural particularity they still need to claim. Their vernacular arts precipitate and dramatize intracommunal conflicts over the meanings and forms of identity and freedom. They project a growing lack of consensus about what the defining cultural or ethnic core of blackness should encompass. The resulting problems are multiplied by the fact that the swift and extraordinary global transformation triggered by hip-hop was wholly unanticipated. With this unforeseen planetary change on our side, black critics have displayed a special reluctance to give up the authority to expound and translate that we fought so hard to attain. However, we are still heavily dependent upon the disreputable authenticity of vernacular forms. Some critical discourses have even implied that only the vernacular can confer the medal of representativeness upon a range of other, less obviously authentic, cultural activities.

These problems of value, of judgment, and of course of class division inside the racial collective have been compounded in a time of great uncertainty about the limits of particularity and solidarity. Though it has won wide acceptance, the idea that vernacular forms embody a special "ethnic" essence has been most regularly articulated by critics who are comfortable with the absolutist definitions of culture I have criticized. In their hands, the black vernacular can become a piece of intellectual property over which they alone hold effective copyright. Their expositions of it specify the elusive qualities of racialized difference that only they can claim to be able to comprehend and to paraphrase, if not exactly to decode. The desire to monopolize the practice of these valuable transcultural skills and to engage in the opportunities for social regulation that they invite has furnished some critics with an even greater investment in the uniqueness, purity, and power of the vernacular.

But that exaggerated uniqueness has sometimes been punctured where underground phenomena appear suddenly amid the gloss of the cultural industries and their insatiable machinery of commodification. It is understandable why commentators, especially renegade academics cutting their scholarly teeth on fashionable popular material, should desire to enlist the ruthless alterity of hip-hop as part of an argument for the legitimacy of their own interpretive activity.[1] But political and ethical issues cannot be side-stepped when they do so. We are entitled to ask what pressures bear down upon the critics who broker and cheerlead for rebel cultures even as they melt down into attractively packaged pseudo-rebellion. What factors shape the way these intellectuals construct the political attributes of the lowly cultures they illuminate and pronounce upon?

These questions did not arise with quite the same force in earlier generations, for whom nihilism, violence, and misogyny were not the strong selling points they have become today. They prompt a renewed consideration of the matters of class and power that have persistently disrupted the convenient, body-coded, and biopolitical solidarities supposedly based on invariant "race" and gender identities. To put it more pointedly, in what sense might hip-hop be described as marginal or revolutionary today? Anyone asserting the continuing marginality of hip-hop should be pressed to say where he or she imagines the center might now be. I prefer to argue that hip-hop's marginality is now as official and routinized as its overblown defiance, even if the music and its matching life-style are still being presented—marketed—as outlaw forms. The music's persistent association with transgression is a raciological mystery that aches to be solved. Clues to its longevity may be furnished by delving into uncomfortable issues like hip-hop's corporate developmental association with the commercially sponsored subcultures that have been shaped around television, advertising, cartoons, and computer games[2] or by interrogating the revolutionary *conservatism* that constitutes its routine political focus but that is over-simplified, mystified, or, more usually, just ignored by its academic celebrants.

Henry Louis Gates, Jr.'s, principled defense of Luther "Luke" Campbell's 2 Live Crew against obscenity charges in the early 1990s should always be remembered as an important historical moment in which these difficult issues could be initially clarified. Almost a decade later, the bypassing of Campbell's Caribbean affiliations and his elective affinity for the other Luke Skywalker, the prince of whiteness, seem less problematic than his occasional appetite for regionally based conflictual dialogue with East and West Coast rappers; his enthusiastic involvement in the well-heeled world of celebrity golf; his reported eagerness to become involved in publishing soft-core pornographic magazines designed for black "readers"; his hosting "Peep-Show" on BET pay-per-view television; and, most interesting of all, his enthusiasm for the dubious work of the infamous English comedian Benny Hill. The idea that Hill's gurning techniques and his Brit-vernacular characters like Ernie the Milkman may have, through Campbell, contributed to the impure, hybrid multiplicity that is hip-hop should have provided a last nail in the coffin of any ethnocentric account of its origins and development.[3] Campbell told one English journalist:

> The way that I get updated on my thing is I get different girls, and I ask them what they like to do. *Playboy* been around for years, and *Penthouse.* Benny Hill been around a long time here . . . maybe I'll start going off and doing more of the Benny Hill type thing, and being more funny.[4]

Campbell's deep and sincere appreciation of Benny Hill's comic achievements reminds us that syncretism will always be an unpredictable and surprising process. It underlines the global reach of popular cultures as well as the complexity of their cross-over dynamics. Crossing, like outer-national diaspora dispersal, is no longer something that can be conceptualized as a unidirectional or reversible process. The way back is barred by Campbell and his open-minded peers. His case and subsequent commercial activities also ask us to consider how the transgressive qualities in hip-hop have led to its being identified not as one black culture among many but currently as the very *blackest* culture—the one that provides the measure on which all others can be evaluated. These valuable attributes have a complex relationship to the signs of pleasure and danger that solicit identification from the music's white affiliates and practitioners. Squeamish, "insiderist" critics do not want to face the extent to which, in a global market for these seductive products, white consumers currently support this black culture.[5] They retreat from the obvious possibility that the music's transracial popularity might be significant in political struggles against white supremacism that undoubtedly lie ahead. They have difficulties in accepting the catholic tastes of the creators of these musical forms whose loyalty to the phattest beats usually exceeds their commitment to imaginary racial purity and any rules that would specify phenotypically coded musical production.[6]

The possibility that globalization has pushed the hip-hop nation into a complex intercultural predicament is shunned even though Missy "misdemeanor" Elliott appears in ads for the GAP; Lord Tariq and Peter Gunz make anthemic, karaoke-style hip-hop out of cannibalized and recycled Steely Dan; and "No Woman No Cry" is sung-over again by Caribbean settlers in New York, belatedly becoming a hit twenty years after Bob

Marley's first version. After twenty years of hip-hop, the black American heartland has shown scant interest in the responses that Euro rap by M. C. Solaar, Nique Ta Mère, and IAM have made to its own earlier calls.

The quest for better accounts of popular-cultural syncretism and its changing political resonance in the United States and beyond demands adjustments in the way we approach the popular phenomena that are grouped together under the heading hip-hop. The first involves questioning the hold this insubordinate form itself exerts on critical writers, thanks to its quiet endorsement of their own desire that the world can be readily transformed into text—their professional faith that nothing can resist the power of written language. This is a familiar handicap that Michel Foucault stated succinctly in his famous cautioning against reducing the bloody "open hazardous reality of conflict" to the "calm Platonic form of language and dialogue."[7] It bites sharply in this area especially when the phenomenology and integrity of musical creations are dismissed in favor of the easier work of analyzing lyrics, the video images that complement them, and the de-skilled, technological features of hip-hop production.

Second, we need to pay far more patient and careful attention to the issues of gender and sexuality than critics have been inclined to do so far. These are the primary conduits of cross-over potential as well as the unstable core of spuriously naturalized racial particularity. Third, we will have to produce a better understanding of the relationship between hip-hop and the other (sub)cultural styles with which it is in creative dialogue.

In order to address these issues I will focus initially on the point where the eddies that hip-hop has produced de-stabilize and flow back into more recognizably traditional and predictable currents. I want to start by acknowledging that hip-hop has contributed something positive to the reinvigoration of rhythm and blues traditions. It has released much-needed new energy to the slow jams and the uptempo "swing" beats that—in Britain at least—have an altogether different potential for cross-over appeal to white listeners whose support they have not actively sought. I will begin and end with musical articulations of the apparently sex-obsessed culture that defines a privileged point of entry into the subaltern public sphere and affords a key to the notions of freedom that rather unexpectedly thrive there, turning racialized infrahumanity back into nonracial humanity once again.

EROS, THANATOS, AND EROS AGAIN

There is a significant moment in the old-school re-mix of R. Kelly's hit "Bump and Grind" when the singer recycles the famous hookline from the Five Stairsteps' 1969 hit "Ooh Child." Sticking closely to the melody and phrasing of the original cut, Kelly cautioned or possibly promised the women to whom his song of seduction is addressed that "things are gonna get freakier." This transformed the relatively wholesome and optimistic spirit of the original, which had comforted its listeners with the reassuring news that "things are gonna be easier." It seems that in the mid-1990s that message was no longer plausible advice to the black listening—and viewing—public.

Some six years after he first appeared, Kelly remains a gifted producer and artist whose career helps to periodize important changes in African-American and black Atlantic cultures. He has been more faithful to the profane muses of rhythm and blues than have many of his fellow practitioners of the hybrid offspring of soul and rap. His formal, almost operatic opposition of the interlocked, warring voices of an unhappy black couple on Sparkle's classic "Be Careful" comes off especially well when compared with the works of his principal competitors: Missy Elliott, Erykah Badu, and the other emerging stars of "black alternative" pop programming. In this case, however, his citation and adaptation of the earlier tune were not motivated by a desire to engage in the archaeology of living "intertextual" traditions. They worked like a stolen sample or a borrowed instrumental riff to index the interperformative relationships that constitute a counterculture. Like Sean "Puff Daddy" Combs, who has built an impressive career from similar gestures, Kelly made the past audible in the here and now but *subserviently*. Musical history was conscripted into the service of the present.[8] Unlike, say, Charlie Baltimore's contemptuous reworking of the OJays' "For the Love of Money" into shocking celebration of all that money can buy, Kelly's subversive transformation of an old tune cut in the year that he was born betrayed the oedipal impulses that are a cornerstone of this covert modern tradition. His creative gesture, which managed to be simultaneously both insubordinate and reverent, expressed, in a small way, the contraction and remodeling of the black public sphere. These processes have developed closely in step with what might be termed the narrative shrinkage of the rhythm and blues idiom: one of the more pernicious effects of the preeminence of a hip-hop culture that has been dominated by grim tales of sex, drugs, and gun play. Kelly's cool pose was entirely complicit with what bell hooks identified as the "life threatening choke hold (that) patriarchal masculinity imposes on black men."[9]

It could be argued that the explicit repudiation of social amelioration that Kelly's words contained conveyed in its small way something profound about the imploded contemporary character of black political culture, which finds it progressively difficult to find a political tone at all. However, I want to suggest something different and slightly more complex. Kelly's repudiation of progress was notable for the way it was combined with an unusually fervent endorsement of the pursuit of sexual pleasure. That combination of sorrow with anticipation and compensation was a special event. It provided a precise historical embodiment of the dismal process in which public politics became unspeakable and a body-centered biopolitics began to take hold.

R. Kelly's great popularity was one of many signs that the black body politic was regularly being represented internally and externally as an integral but "freaky" body. Wild, intense sexual activity between consenting heterosexual adults in private was the residual, transcoded trace of earlier political rebellions. The androcentric and phallocratic presentation and representation of heterosexual coupling at which Kelly has continued to excel were the sign and the limit of a different charisma and a different utopia from those that Kenny Burke and his siblings had in mind in Chicago thirty years ago when they cut the original version of "Ooh Child."[10] Their choice of the name "Stairsteps" for their pre-Jackson family quintet had suggested upward momentum, racial elevation, and communal movement toward something "brighter," something closer to the heavens, if not to the God of their Islamic faith.

I want to explore the possibility that this goal, which was identifiable thanks to its illumination amid the darkness of the white supremacism that threatened to engulf it, was named Freedom—another word that has been steadily disappearing from the political language of blacks in the West and that will be even more remote from their consciousness now that the liberation of South Africa has been officially accomplished. I mourn the disappearance of the pursuit of Freedom as an element in black vernacular culture and ask why it seems no longer appropriate or even plausible to speculate about the freedom of the subject of black politics in the overdeveloped countries. I also want to examine the effects on black politics of transposing that yearning for freedom into a different, private mode, signaled by the growing centrality of what might be called a "racialized biopolitics." Ritualized sexual play of various kinds and an erotic delight in the body supply the new means of bonding this new freedom and black life. What was once abject life becomes nothing more than one life-style among other, less exotic options.

Here the move toward biopolitics is best understood as an outgrowth of the pattern identified as "identity politics" in earlier periods by a number of writers.[11] It is a mood in which the person is defined as the body and in which certain exemplary bodies at various times during the 1990s—those of Usher, Tupac, Mike Tyson, Michael Jordan, Jada Pinkett Smith, Naomi Cambell, Lil' Kim, and Veronica Webb—could become impacted instantiations of community. This situation necessitates a different conception of freedom from those hitherto channeled into modern citizenship or developed in post-slave cultures, where bodily and spiritual freedoms were sharply differentiated and freedom was more likely to be associated with death than with life. On this historic frequency, organic intellectuals from Frederick Douglass to George Clinton suggested that the most valuable forms of freedom lay in the liberation of the mind. Dr. Funkenstein's prescription was "Free your mind and your ass will follow." The dualism was problematic, but it could be forgiven because, against the expectations of raciologists, it was the mind that came first! Racialized biopolitics operates from altogether different premises that refuse this distinction. It uses a reversal of these historic priorities to establish the limits of the authentic racial community. This is achieved almost exclusively through the visual representation of racialized bodies—engaged in characteristic activities, usually sexual or sporting—which if they do not induce immediate solidarity, certainly ground and solicit identification.

This development is problematic for several reasons. For one thing, it marks the racial community exclusively as a space of heterosexual activity and confirms the abandonment of any politics aside from the ongoing oppositional creativity of gendered self-cultivation: an activity that is endowed with almost sacred significance but undertaken in something of the same resolute spirit as working out with weights. If it survives at all, politics becomes an exclusively aesthetic concern with all the perils that implies. The racialized body, buffed, invulnerable, and arranged suggestively with a precision that will be familiar to close readers of the Marquis de Sade, whose writings anticipate this development, supplies its critical evaluative principle. Affiliates of the racialized collectivity are thereby led "to focus their attention on themselves, to decipher, recognise and acknowledge themselves as subjects of desire, bringing into play between themselves and themselves a certain relationship that allows them to discover, in desire, the truth of their being."[12]

The termination of reflections on freedom and the proliferation of signs and talk about sexuality as purposive racialized recreation have coincided. Together they point to a novel form of artistic production that goes beyond therapeutic cultures of compensation in which simple sameness supplied the rationale and the entry ticket into an aesthetic sense of racial difference for which the sculpted and inked male bodies that adorn albums by bands like Jodeci's KCi and JoJo and post-Kelly crooners like Ginuine and Usher are a notable popular signifier.[13]

These silences and carnal signs yield further insights into the changing character of the black public sphere. They represent the end of older notions of public interaction that helped to create and were themselves created by the forms of densely coded, intersubjective dialogue that nurtured racial solidarity and made the idea of an exclusive racial identity a credible, operable one. The timeworn model of black publicity derived from sacred rituals and musical utility survives vestigially in an utterly profane form. Its precious dialogic attributes retain some ethical significance even as this drains away and is replaced by morbid phenomena like the Americo-centric image of the black public sphere recast in the dimensions of an inner-city basketball court. This is an exclusively male stage for the theater of power and kinship in which sound is displaced by vision and words are generally second to physical gestures. The natural aristocracy defined by means of bodily power and grace can announce its heroic godly presence where life becomes a game of hoops.[14] A hint of the epochal significance of this location emerged in one of R. Kelly's interviews:

> Robert Kelly grew up all over the South Side of Chicago. He and his boys are into basketball, and three or four mornings a week they show up at one of their favourite courts (18th, 47th, 63rd, 67th or 115th street). "When I hit the court and people know me, it's 'Hell, naw, that's that guy that be singin.' They don't realize I'm just a reg-

ular guy. I'm anxious to prove myself. I can ball just like you do. I'll take it to the hole just like you, if not better."[15]

At present, the poetic topography of race and place centered on the basketball court has no exact equivalent in Britain's cultural landscape. Attachment to soccer still blocks this outcome in Europe, Africa, and much of Latin America, but that situation is changing rapidly. In any case, equally problematic fraternalist relations can be projected through any segregated sporting spectacle. Perhaps this is why the European fascist regimes of the 1930s turned swiftly to the combined potency of sport, politics, and propaganda and drew a "performative language" from the world of sporting activity that they endowed with a new significance.[16] In Franco's Spain, for example, sportsmen representing their country on the soccer field were subject to military discipline. The blue shirts of the Falange replaced the republican red and the fascist salute was introduced before the kick off. Suspect players and referees were purged and a censored press reported the game in the new political spirit.

These points about the relationship of identity, publicity, and masculinity can be illustrated by the popularity of black basketball movies like *Above the Rim* and Spike Lee's more recent *He Got Game.* The soundtrack CD to the former was issued in 1995 and pioneered a new approach to marketing rhythm and blues by featuring material from eighteen different artists. This format was a powerful means to increase interest in a film that promised to complete and even extend the narrative of *White Men Can't Jump* in a more gritty mode that took its reality effects from hip-hop's masculinist lexicon. The popularity of film-associated CD anthologies like the *Above the Rim* soundtrack album provided more evidence that the independent power of music was waning while the authority of the image culture on which music has become increasingly parasitic was growing steadily. It was, after all, a similar soundtrack album from Bill Duke's film *Deep Cover* that had first unleashed the curious talents of Snoop Doggy Dogg, the young rapper from Long Beach who rapidly became the most successful artist in the history of the genre and who preceded Notorious BIG and Tupac at the center of intense moral and political panics about the social consequences and causes of gangsta rap. One track from the *Above the Rim* set had featured the talents of D. J. Rogers, a.k.a. "The Message Man," easily the greatest male gospel singer of his generation. As part of a bid to revive Rogers's career, he had been induced, presumably by the record's producer, Dr. Dre, to sing "Doggie Style," a song that endorsed and even amplified Snoop's historic call to cultivate a set of distinctive sexual habits that could bring certainty, confidence, and resoluteness back to the machinery in racialized being:

> Let's do it doggie style
> I really like to ride it doggie style . . .
> baby come closer I want to undress you
> I'm gonna give it to you baby until you can take no more . . .
> you and I on the floor let's get freaky . . .
> baby don't you move you'll disturb my groove . . .
> turn over lay your head down so I can get freaky
> please let me lick you in my favorite way
> turn over baby and back up into me so let me love you down
> there's no need to worry I'm your doggy style man.

A traditional chorus of sanctified voices interposed all the appropriate antiphonal exhortations. This was more than the pursuit of sexual pleasure as compensation for the wrongs wrought in the name of white supremacy. It was more even than a dionysian, Prince-like alternative to the asceticism of stern paramilitary figures like Ice Cube, who responded to uncertainties about racial identity and solidarity with an austerity program that articulated some ancient priestly notions about the association of sexual abstention with the acquisition of knowledge and the forms of self-love necessitated by communal reconstruction.[17] It was confirmation not only that gangsta rap was having to combine and compete with an alternative, "booty rap," but that however much they tried to conceal their traditional features, both versions of that de-skilled style could still readily tap into the timeworn strengths of black church music.

The changed composition and signification of the black body politic suggested by these conflicts has been associated with a number of other social and technological shifts that cannot be explored in detail here, though they must be noted in passing. First, this transformation cannot be separated from the privatization of both cultural production and use—a long-term trend that has important implications for attempts to defend the political significance of black popular culture. The basketball-court configuration of the public sphere is again suggestive. It indicates that the vernacular forms that were once called "street culture" are in the process of deserting the streets. They are no longer seen primarily as a privileged space for the elaboration of cultural authenticity but rather as the location of conflict, violence, crime, and social pathology. This turnabout can be seen clearly in the sharp contrast between The Crusaders' late-1970s dance anthem "Street Life" and Fugee Wyclef Jean's ominous 1997 track "Street Jeopardy." The vital unfolding of racialized culture is now more likely to be imagined in discrete private, semiprivate, and private-public settings that can be found, like the basketball court, between the axes established respectively by the intimacies of the bedroom and the fortified mobile enclosure of a sports utility vehicle.

Second, the family supplies the sole institutional site for this biopolitics, and, as pointed out elsewhere, a radical localism operating under the sign "hood" projects community as the simple accumulation of family units.[18] The family remains preeminent because it narrows the horizons of any lingering aspiration toward social change. But as Jodeci made clear, its sanctity could be sacrificed when more important hedonistic objectives came into view. As one might expect, the relationship between parents and children is seen as crucial for the health and the wealth of the "race" as a whole, but the duty of parental care exists in opposition to the space of sexual intimacy. There are, in effect, two private realms rather than one. These wholesome and profane privacies must compete to be recognized as the locus in which the most intense meanings of being black can be established:

> girl where is our child?
> send it to your mother's for a while
> all my friends are gone you know I send them home
> girl I live for you so I don't give a fuck about the news
> so please turn off the T.V.
> and if you give a damn about me I wanna hear you moan
> let's be alone
> what's better than you and me? you're better than a damn
> movie
> our love is so much fun
> let's do some freaky shit and then I'll make you come . . .

The gender-neutrality of the child in this torrid narrative suggests extreme paternal indifference rather than political correctness. It is clearly significant that on this scale of excitement it is cinema that provides the benchmark. The patterned use of black music reveals a lot about the changing qualities of this subaltern public culture. The dominant place of radio in fixing the limits of the black public sphere as an interpretive community has been ceded to video in ways that compromise the power of sound and the dialogic principles on which the black vernacular was built in times past. It is interesting to note that Snoop Dog had dramatized each medium's different claims for the right to represent the culture as a whole in the snippets of humor and drama inserted between the rapped contributions to his first and best album (also entitled *Doggy Style)*.

The proliferation of jokes, sketches, and other humorous material on recent black popular music recordings does more than try to fill up the enhanced playing time made possible by the CD format. This tactic is common to notable offerings by Snoop, Wyclef, Erykah Badu, Xscape, and a host of others. It seems to be a bid to simulate and thus recover a variety of dialogical interaction that has been inhibited by the technology of production but is sought by underground users nonetheless. It may also provide carefully constructed cues to the cross-over listenership that can attune them to the signs of pleasure and danger that they desire. The proliferation of these dramatic inserts is yet another indication that the founding authority of the performance event has been undermined by the emergence of musical forms that cannot as a result of their reliance on technology be faithfully or easily translated into concert settings. The impact of problems arising from the political economy of clubs and other venues should also be noted. Faced with these changes, street culture has become many things, most notably "jeep culture." Military-style vehicles have become larger-scale equivalents of the Walkman[19]—a piece of technology named by a word that, by lacking a plural, signifies its association with the same sad process of social privatization.

While everyone else was following N.W.A. into naming their bands with mysterious sequences of initials or numbers that only initiates could decode—U.N.V., M.O.P., S.W.V., D.R.S., D.M.X, and E.O.L. are the most obvious examples—R. Kelly had called his original musical back-up team Public Announcement, a name that bypassed the urge to encrypt. It openly acknowledged a historic obligation to service the alternative, subaltern public spheres that had hosted the processes of vernacular identity formation through a variety of different communicative technologies—

print, radio, audio, video—and in a wide range of settings at various distances from the core event of real-time, face-to-face performance.

These successive communicative technologies organized space and time in different ways and solicited and fostered different kinds of identification. They created and manipulated memory in dissimilar ways and staged the corporeal and psychical enigmas of cultural identity in contrasting processes. Their political effects are various and contradictory, but the long-term tendency for music, sound, and text to take second place to images cannot be dismissed. We must ask whether scopic identification and desire differ from what might be called the alternative, "orphic" configurations organized around music and hearing. Do the latter privilege the imaginary over the symbolic? In an obvious link to the fascist history discussed in the previous chapter, the growing dominance of specularity over aurality might be thought of as contributing a special force to representations of the exemplary racial body arrested in the gaze of desiring and identifying subjects. Misrecognized, objectified, and verified, these images have become the storehouses of racial alterity now that the production of subjectivity operates through different sensory and technological mechanisms. We must be clear about what is gained and what may be lost in the contemporary displacement of sound from the epicenter of black cultural production:

> In sound, and in the consciousness termed hearing, there is in fact a break with the self complete world of vision and art. In its entirety, sound is a ringing, clanging scandal. Whereas in vision, form is wedded to content in such a way as to appease it, in sound the perceptible quality overflows so that form can no longer contain its content. A real rent is produced in the world, through which the world that is *here* prolongs a dimension that cannot be converted into vision.[20]

THE TRIALS OF FREEDOM

Contemporary studies of black vernacular culture are just as silent as the hip-hop literature about the concept of freedom and its political and metaphysical significance. This is puzzling given the complex historical connections between slavery and freedom that are evident in the forms black culture assumed, and the ways it was engaged by its producers and its users. Freedom has consistently emerged as a theme in the writing of black history, and the dialectical interrelation of freedom and slavery has been addressed, but where this has happened, freedom has usually been presented as a singular occurrence: a once-and-for-all event. It is seen as a threshold that was irrevocably crossed once slavery was formally declared to be over and populations of ex-slaves moved uneasily into the new spaces of enhanced autonomy—intimate, private, civic, and economic—that the concept helped to define.

The desire to acquire civic and economic freedoms and the pursuit of personal freedoms had been closely aligned during the period of struggles against slavery. Considerable tension between these different dynamics developed in the post-Emancipation period. The fundamental shift represented by the Jubilee was felt to require the opening of a new chapter in the narrative of black history, even where the forms of civil society in which the newly freed found themselves instituted novel unfreedoms that compounded powerlessness, immiseration, and poverty or retained and modified patterns of racialized domination from the slave period by depriving people of formal political rights.[21] Freedom was seen to be relevant primarily because it represented the termination of slavery rather than the beginning of a different sequence of struggles in which its own meanings would be established and its future limits identified. Once free status was formally won, it could appear that there was no further need to elaborate the distinctive meanings that freedom acquired among people radically estranged from the promise and practice of freedom by generations of servitude enforced by terror. The end of slavery produced several new "technical" solutions to the problems of discovering and regulating free black selves:

> After the coming of freedom there were two points upon which practically all the people on our place were agreed, and I feel that this was generally true throughout the South: that they must change their names, and that they must leave the old plantation for at least a few days or weeks in order that they might feel really sure that they were free.[22]

Only among blacks in the United States did ready access to political institutions define freedom's post-slave boundaries. Even in that exceptional situation, the limits of freedom had to be first found and then tested. Leon Litwack[23] has pointed to the significant role of marriages in symbolizing and demonstrating the free status of the freed slaves. The place of the family, the significance of domesticity, and the need to acquire clearly demarcated spaces for intimate and private activity are all important issues in the technologies of the free self that have left lingering imprints upon today's libidinal economies and erotic allegories of political desire. The relatively limited role of political institutions in establishing the history of those incomplete emancipations that did not straightforwardly deliver substantive freedom in the form of political rights is therefore something that needs to be explored carefully. If bell hooks is right, the compensatory assumption of patriarchal masculinity by ex-slaves and the masculinist and fraternalist proclivities of their descendants might be fruitfully factored into critical analysis of the development of democracy compromised by the imperatives of white supremacy.

The coercive regimes that followed modern racial slavery under the banners of freedom were, just as slavery had been, internal to Western civilization. Their histories complicate the history of democracy and the assumption of social and moral progress toward which that heroic tale is usually directed. Under the guidance of ideologues who were self-consciously developing the arts of governing, disciplining, and educating the post-slave self, the former slaves and their descendants gradually and unevenly acquired the freedoms to vote, associate, organize, and communicate. They became bearers of rights and practitioners of skills that confirmed their equal value as free people in circumstances that made liberty and equality impracticable though not unthinkable. Their descendants continue to stretch the bounds of the civility that enclosed and promoted these rights.

It would be mistaken to assume that the gap between formal, rhetorical declarations of black emancipation and the practical realization of democratic hopes defines and exhausts the politics of being free. I would like to suggest that, however important the relatively narrow understanding of freedom centered on political rights has been, it leaves untouched vast areas of thinking about freedom and the desire to be seen as free. A politics of freedom (and indeed of being free) needs to be addressed today with a special sensitivity because the meanings of freedom and the idioms through which it is apprehended have become extremely significant for interpretations of contemporary popular culture. Important work has already been undertaken in this area by the anthropologist Daniel Miller,[24] by historians of African-American religion such as Mechal Sobel[25] and Charles H. Long,[26] and in particular by Lawrence Levine, whose invaluable study *Black Culture and Black Consciousness*[27] points to important historical connections between the subcultural reproduction of gender and mythic and heroic representations of freedom. Freedom has been less of an issue in broadly sociological studies of the black vernacular: sacred and profane.[28]

Rather than delve into the forms assumed and promoted by the protean consciousness of freedom, analysts have usually investigated the impact of becoming free on the slaves and on their patterns of cultural production. Exploring the transformations wrought by Jubilee and the effects of its ritual commemoration can, however, proceed without confronting either the value of freedom itself as an element in the lives of ex-slaves or the distinctive idiomatic practices through which they strove to represent the psychological, social, and economic differences freedom made: to themselves, to their descendants, and to the slave masters and mistresses who were themselves embarking on a journey out of slavery: ceasing to be oppressors and becoming exploiters. The memory of slavery is rarely addressed though the silences and evasions around slavery that popular culture reveals make this more understandable. I have suggested that the dominance of love and loss stories in black popular musical forms embraces the condition of being in pain,[29] transcodes and interweaves the different yearnings for personal and civic freedoms, and preserves the memories of suffering and loss in a usable—irreducibly ethical—form. The incorporated memories[30] of unfreedom and terror are cultivated in commemorative practices. Song and the social rituals that surround it became a valuable means to cultivate a rapport with the presence of suffering and death. Amid the terrors of slavery, where bodily and spiritual freedoms were readily distinguished along lines suggested by Christianity—if not African cosmology—death was often understood as a welcome escape from worldly sufferings. It offered the opportunity to acquire a higher, heteronymous freedom in which the mortal body—unshackled at last—would be cast aside as the newly liberated soul soared heavenward or took its place among the ancestral pantheon. Many practices that were forged in the habitus of slavery have lingered on. But today the social memory of slavery has itself been repressed or set aside, and the tradition of dynamic remembrance it founded is being assaulted from all sides. Although the victim status that slavery confers and the survivor identity it promotes are sometimes valued highly, the memory of slavery is seen mainly as an encumbrance. It is an old skin that has to be shed before one can hope to attain an authentic life of racialized self-love.[31]

The music of R. Kelly, Snoop Dogg, S.W.V., Biggie, Tupac, and the rest registers these changes. The sharpest break between the older traditional patterns and the newer biopolitics is evident where what were once love stories have mutated into sex stories. Even when they were systematically profane, the modes of intersubjectivity described and sometimes practiced in earlier stages in the unfolding of rhythm and blues were informed by the proximity of the sacred and the definitions of spiritual love that were cultivated there. It did not, for example, take much to adapt "I Had a Talk with My God Last Night" into its profane equivalent, Mitty Collier's epochal Chess recording "I Had a Talk with My Man Last Night." Spirituality cast long shadows over the emergent forms of secular and profane creativity in which songs of passion were often simultaneously songs of protest. Aretha's "Respect" is the obvious paradigm case here.

Today, the old songs are repeated without any additional creative input. Monica's 1998 sing over of Dorothy Moore's "Misty Blue" or Sparkle's version of Minnie Riperton's "Loving You" do not attempt to add anything to the originals. The fact of citation seems to be a last, desperate attempt to prevent song from being relegated to the subordinate role of soundtrack for the expansion of the image world. The game of truth is updated and the new rules are fixed via a different, I am tempted to say postmodern, conception of mortality. The traditional cultivation of a rapport with the presence of death is recast because death is no longer felt to be a transition or a release.[32] Dr. Dre, the producer of Snoop's records, called the label that he founded with Suge Knight Death Row Records. Big Punisher calls his album *Capital Punishment*. Following the pattern established by Snoop's 1994 recording "Murder Was the Case," which imagined the experience of dying and was constructed as a mock death announcement, The Notorious BIG and Tupac both rehearsed their own departures from this mortal coil. The changed value and understanding of death that have developed amid the AIDS crisis, the drug economy, and the militarization of inner-city social life thus also contribute to the reshaping of the black public sphere and its historicity:

Daily life becomes a perpetual dress rehearsal for death. What is being rehearsed . . . is the *ephemerality* and *evanescence* of things that
humans may acquire and bonds that humans may weave. The impact of such daily rehearsal seems to be similar to one achieved by
some preventive inoculations: if taken in daily, in partly detoxicated
and thus non-deadly doses, the awesome poison seems to lose its
venom. Instead, it prompts immunity and indifference to the toxin
in the inoculated organism.[33]

It bears repetition that biopolitics specifies that the person is identified
only in terms of the body. The very best that this change precipitates is a
principled anti-Christian confrontation with the idea that life continues
after death. This refusal of religious antidotes to death is often described as
nihilism.[34] In these circumstances, the desire to be free is closely linked
with the desire to be seen to be free and with the pursuit of an individual
and embodied intensity of experience that contrasts sharply with the collective and spiritual forms of immortality esteemed in times gone by. Just
as soul and reggae were gifts to overground youth cultures in earlier periods, today these styles have become the heart of a globalized pop culture
creating an unremarked-upon intensity of potentially race-transcending
feeling in the pre-packaged, body-obsessed, and body-transcending cultures of teen consumers everywhere.

Jean Luc Nancy has emphasized that freedom is linked to a politics of
representation.[35] This relationship accumulates special significance where
"race" becomes the rationality for denying and withholding liberty and
where studied indifference to the death and suffering of others provides a
short cut to the enduring notoriety and celebrity associated with gangsterdom. This is now a social phenomenon by virtue of its antisociality. As
old certainties about the fixed limits of racial identity have lost their
power to convince, ontological security capable of answering a radically
reduced sense of the value of life has been sought in the naturalizing
power of gender difference and sex as well as in the ability to cheat death
and take life. Sex and gender are experienced—lived conflictually—at a
heightened pitch that somehow connotes "race." Gender difference and
racialized gender codes provide a special cipher for a mode of racial authenticity that is as evasive as it is desirable. In these circumstances, the
iterative representation of gender, gender conflicts, and sexualities con-

tributes confidence and stability to essentialist and absolutist notions of racial particularity. These may, like the homophobic dancehall stars of the mid-1990s, demand the death of all "batty bwoy" as the price of their reproduction over time. They may, like so many rhythm and blues artists, perform highly stylized ritual celebrations of heterosexual intimacy that suspend and transcend the everyday incoherence and dissymmetry of gender turning them into an ordered narrative of racial being and becoming. It is therefore necessary to acknowledge that the centrality of gender to black popular cultures can also be analyzed as an alternative articulation of freedom that associates autonomous agency with sexual desire and promotes the symbolic exercise of power in the special domain that sexuality provides.

In this crepuscular space, Bell Biv Devoe, a group that took the basketball tropes considerably further than anyone else, used them to provide a coy invitation to practice anal intercourse; D.R.S. (Dirty Rotten Scoundrels) issued their hapless female associates with the simple command to "strip"; and S.W.V. (Sisters with Voices) urged their partners to go "Downtown" and discover a way to their heart between their thighs:

> . . . You've been wondering how you can make it better
> baby it's easy to turn my world inside out
> your discovery will take us to another place
> baby of that there is no doubt
> I've been waiting for the special moment, anticipating all
> the things you'll do to me
> make the first step to release my emotions and take the road
> to ecstasy
> you've got to go downtown . . . to taste the sweetness will
> be enough . . .[36]

These are far from unprecedented themes in black popular culture, but their significance has lately been transformed. Other racialized discourses that would qualify and therefore contest their representative status have fallen silent as the distance between the profane vernacular and sacred and spiritual concerns has increased. The biopolitical focus terminates any conception of the mind/body dualism and ends the modernist aspirations toward racial uplift that were once figured through the language of public-political citizenship. The body, in motion on the ball court, striving against machinery in the gym, at the wheel of the sports utility vehicle, between the sheets, and finally decked out in branded finery on the mortuary slab, is now all there is. The Notorious BIG's moving and disturbing "Suicidal Thoughts" presents the decision to take one's own life as the culmination of these grim conditions.

NIHILISM AND PSEUDO-FREEDOM

As I have said, the theme of freedom remains important because it relates directly to contemporary debates about the antisocial consequences of black nihilism.[37] Influential interpretations of contemporary black politics have stressed the meaninglessness, lovelessness, and hopelessness of black metropolitan life and argued that the chronic ethical crisis from which they apparently stem generates further symptoms of black misery: the homophobia, misogyny, anti-semitism, and fundamentalist nationalisms currently being affirmed in black political cultures. The community-corroding power of this vernacular nihilism is traced to a variety of different causal mechanisms. Sometimes it is seen as a capitulation to me-ism and now-ism, the market values—individualism, ruthlessness, and indifference to others—that dominate the mainstream corporate world and its popular-cultural commodities. Alternatively, it has been interpreted as a set of "ethnic" habits peculiar to blacks. Whether it is a mechanistic response to racism and material privation or a more creative "ethnic" trait, it has been readily linked to the patterns of household organization, kinship, and community that supposedly distinguish black social life. Lastly, it is viewed as a structural feature of de-industrialized capitalism that no longer has need for the living labor of terminally broken black communities that are now marginal to the ongoing practice of flexible accumulation and may be contemptuous of the limited economic opportunities offered to them by "neo-slave" employment in a caste of servile, insecure, and underpaid domestic laborers, caregivers, cleaners, deliverers, messengers, attendants, and guards. The segmentation and casualization of employment, health, and dwelling are the foundations on which the destruction of the inner-city's civic order have come to rest.

The concept of a socially excluded underclass mediates these different accounts of black nihilism. Each of these explanations offers a tiny rational kernel in a large mystical shell, but even when taken together, they do not satisfy. The nexus of consciousness and behavior that is reduced to the pejorative term "nihilism" is associated with idiomatic representations of freedom. Its main contemporary genres and styles are property, sex, and the means of violence. From this perspective, "nihilism" ceases to be antisocial and becomes social in the obvious sense of the term: it generates community and specifies the fortified boundaries of racial particularity.

Once again, the sedimented memory of slavery provides the starting point in understanding the development of this vernacular pattern. It directs attention toward the complex symbolism of wealth and status in black popular culture. The visual culture of hip-hop pivoted briefly on the alchemical transformation of iron shackles into gold chains.[38] Racialized by Mr. T, whose bold exploits live on in the timeless world of cable TV, gold chains externalized the changing price of the (wage) slave's labor power—calculated on the basis of exchange value. The gold in the chains expressed the limits of the money economy in which they circulated but which they were also able to transcend—especially in times of crisis. The free humanity formerly bestowed by God could now be conveyed in displays of wealth that far exceeded the value of a person—of a body. The same sort of ostentation can be detected in some contemporary hip-hoppers' appetite for cars as symbols of status, wealth, and masculine power:

> Dre boasts a collection of cars: a white Chevy Blazer, a convertible 300 sec Benz, a 735 BMW, two 64s and a Nissan Pathfinder ("My moms jacked my Pathfinder, she's like my sister, she looks young. She's flossing in my shit so I guess I only have five cars.")[39]

In order to move toward a consideration of the forms that the relationship between civic and personal freedoms might take in the postliberal age, we must cultivate the ability to disentangle the ludic from the programmatic and find any threads of politics that run between them. We may appreciate that the problems displayed in these attempts to reckon with freedom were born from slavery, but the civic freedoms of the modern West that constitute the privileged object of these inquiries were not antithetical to slavery and other forms of legal and legitimate bondage.

The enduring effects of slavery are most evident in the oft-stated desires for freedom from the servitude of work and freedom from oppressive, unjust law. They can also be felt in the identification of freedom with death that marks some versions of black Christianity very deeply and defers emancipation and the possibility of redemption to a better, future world. Equipped, among other things, with the living traces of an African onto-theology, slaves in the western hemisphere neither sought nor anticipated the mode of dominating the external world that had provided Europeans with the essential preconditions for developing consciousness of freedom. The plantation system made that way of dominating nature part of the slaves' experience of unfreedom. They resisted it along with its accompanying notions of property, time, and causality. The end result of this process has been well described by Murray Bookchin:

> Domination and freedom become interchangeable terms in a common project of subjugating nature *and* humanity—each of which is used as the excuse to validate control of one by the other. The reasoning involved is strictly circular. The machine has not only run away without the driver, but the driver has become a mere part of the machine.[40]

Because it was so reliant on the institutionalization of their unfree labor, the slaves viewed the civilizing process[41] with skepticism and its ethical claims with extreme suspicion. Their hermeneutic insights grounded a vernacular culture premised on the possibility that freedom should be pursued outside of the rules, codes, and expectations of this conspicuously color-coded civilization. The transgression of those codes was itself a sign that freedom was being claimed. It presented the possibility of an (anti)politics animated by the desire to violate—a negation of unjust, oppressive, and therefore illegitimate authority. By breaking these rules in small but nonetheless ritualized ways, it was possible to deface the clean edifice of white supremacy that protected tainted, and therefore inauthentic, freedoms. Cultures of insubordination located more substantive and worthwhile freedoms in the capacity to follow moral imperatives in restricted circumstances. They were elaborated through the media of music and dance as well as through writing. Music expressed and confirmed unfreedom while evolving in complex patterns that pointed beyond misery toward reciprocity and prefigured the democracy yet to come in their antiphonic forms. Dance refined the exercise of autonomous power in the body by claiming it back from the absolute sovereignty of work. It produced the alternative "natural" hierarchy—wholly antithetical to the order required by the institutions of white supremacism—which to-day forms the basis of black sports cultures, cast superhuman Michael Jordan as an enslaved cartoon character, and has set about making so much black music into nothing more than a distracting accompaniment for the postmodern self-discipline of working out.

DOGGIN' AROUND

They may be bonded by their cartoon manifestations and by an ethnic enthusiasm for playing ball, but the superhumanity of Jordan and the heroic fraternity for which he is the muscular point man represent the polar opposite of Snoop Dogg, whose infrahumanity induced him to present himself in dog-face, as less than human. It is best to set aside the question of whether the historic oral trademark "1–8–7 on an undercover cop" that announced his arrival on the *Deep Cover* soundtrack might simply be an idiomatic restatement of some very well known modernist anxieties over the limits of existential agency, autonomy, and subjectivity in particular, about the relationship between making oneself and deliberately taking the life of another.[42]

Snoop's music and rapping remain doggedly faithful to the antiphonic forms that link New World black styles to their African antecedents. The fading public sphere is configured negatively, not nihilistically, but it is still just about as recognizable as a post-traditional transcoding of the black Christian congregation. Snoop's instructions to his audiences "If you don't give a shit like I don't give a shit wave your mother-fuckin' fingers in the air" aren't very far from the cries of the old-school rappers whose cross-over ambitions required them to curse less than he does or even from the preachers who sought similar gestures of solidarity from their congregations.[43] In any form, these gestures enforce the priority of the enunciative moment, of the saying over the said. We must also remember that in this vernacular, "dog" is a verb as well as a noun.

The sleeve of Snoop's album *Doggy Style* was printed on recycled paper. He used it to send out extra special thanks to—among other people—Golgotha Community Baptist Church (presumably where his career as a performer started as a chorister and pianist). The G side of Snoop's album begins with what is still his best-known track. Its title is formed by two foundational questions that have arisen repeatedly, like twins at the heart of the historic dialogue that demands completion of the ontological inquiries in which newly freed slaves engaged as they strove to define and clarify the boundaries of their new status as free modern individuals: "WHO AM I (WHAT'S MY NAME)?"

Snoop has wisely asserted that his work has no political significance whatsoever. When he is pressed to operate in that restricted mode, his extremely conventional opinions are a long way from anything that could reasonably be called nihilistic:

> As far as me being political, the only thing I can say is the muthafuckin' U.S. can start giving money to the 'hood, giving opportunity and starting businesses, something to make niggas not want to kill each another. Give them some kind of job and finances 'cos the killin ain't over love nor money. They are killin and jackin one another 'cos there ain't no opportunity. As long as it's black on black or black-on-brown it's cool—they don't like black on white. They send national guards like when we took off on their ass in 4.29.92, armed forces and army muthafuckas with big ass machine guns—on account of niggas stealing.[44]

The saucy cartoon on the cover of *Doggy Style* presented Snoop as a cartoon dog. It did not provide a more reliable guide to the supposed nihilism and other antisocial qualities of his work. We need to consider why a young African American would choose—at this point—to present himself to the world with the features, with the identity, of a dog.[45] How does Snoop's manipulation of the dog mask that he did not invent but which he has used so creatively facilitate his cross-over celebrity? Is he locating and testing out the limits of a de-racialized humanity or creating a new and sustainable relationship with nature within and without? Does the pussy-chasing, dog-catcher-outwitting dog persona simply seek to make a virtue out of immiseration and insult in the familiar process of semiotic inversion capable of changing curse words into words of praise, of revalorizing the word "Nigger" and making "dog" into a term of endearment? Is there a sense in which calling himself a dog expresses an accurate evaluation of the social status of young black men? What comment on the meaning of black infrahumanity does Snoop's movement between bodies —between identities—express?

A dog is not a fox, a lion, a rabbit, or a signifyin' monkey. Snoop is not a dog. His filling the mask of undifferentiated racialized otherness with quizzical canine features reveals something about the operation of white supremacy and the cultures of compensation that answer it. It can be read as a political and, I believe, a moral gesture. Choosing to be a low-down dirty dog values the infrahuman rather than the hyperhumanity promoted through body-centered biopolitics and its visual signatures in the health, sports, fitness, and leisure industries. It would be missing the main point to overemphasize that the dog is a sign for Snoop's victim status as well as for his sexual habits or that it sometimes requires the technoscientific resources of a firearm before it can interact with real, that is, white, humans on equal terms. In opting to be seen as a dog, he refuses identification with the perfected, invulnerable male body that has become the standard currency of black popular culture cementing the dangerous link between bodily health and racial purity, dissolving the boundary line between singers and athletes, and producing strange phenomena like Dennis Rodman's stardom, R. Kelly's eroticized appropriation of Michael Jordan's divine masculinity, and Shaquille O'Neal's short career as a singer and rapper. Snoop's "morphing" between the human and the canine displays those elements of identity that are not reducible to the six-foot, four-inch human frame of his sometime owner, the doggfather "Calvin Broadus." There is something left over when that somatic operation is performed. The metamorphosis requires us to confront Snoop's reflexive capacities. His stylized portrayal of a well-meaning gangsta self—protean, shape-shifting, and multiple—is probably less significant than the full, vulgar, antibourgeois force of the black vernacular that crouches somewhere behind it.[46] His low-down, dirty, animal self directs critical attention to the difficult zones where some people fall through the cracks in the Kantian moral edifice into the fiery pit of infrahumanity.

These arguments have become urgent matters in consumer-capitalist societies where things regularly assume the social characteristics of people, and people can become, to all intents and purposes, things. Levinas and Yi Fu Tuan have both reminded us that the fate and the role of animals can be quite different.[47] Though they can be agents and even bearers of rights, animals are neither things nor people.[48] To underline the point, their modern destiny has been closely connected to the development of systematic raciology. Considering this link might even contribute to the restoration of a lost humanity. Levinas has instructively recounted the story of the wandering dog Bobby, "the last Kantian in Germany," who comforted him in the Nazi camp for Jewish prisoners of war where he and his comrades had been "stripped of their human skin" and become "subhuman, a gang of apes." Snoop's interspecies shape-shifting performs a similar service. He, too, presents a case that

> one cannot entirely refuse the face of an animal. It is via the face that one understands, for example, a dog. Yet the priority here is not found in the animal but in the human face . . . The phenomenon of the face is not in its purest form in the dog. In the dog, in the animal there are other phenomena. For example, the force of nature is pure vitality. It is more this which characterises the dog. But it also has a face.[49]

The second half of *Doggy Style* commences with a bathroom scenario that gives the proceedings a traditional, "private" framing moment. It is a throwback to a previous era in the odyssey of rhythm and blues when the discourse of racial authenticity called for the removal of clothing rather than the exchange of human skin for canine fur. This little drama presents Snoop in conversation with a girlfriend. He is resenting the intrusion of the public world into their space of intimacy. Their conversation makes no mention of soul, but it is the bond between them. They stick closely to a script refined on hundreds of "turn out the lights and light a candle" soul records. However, their moves are not legitimated by references to any notion of love. The dog and the bitch belong together. They are a couple, but their association does not bring about sexual healing. There is no healing in their encounter because the power of sex is not at work here as a means of naturalizing racial difference. Nor is the unhappy union of bodily health and racial purity being celebrated. In this bathtub, cleanliness is not next to godliness, though funkiness may be. Their funky, bestial sex is not about authenticity and offers neither a moment of communal redemption nor any private means to stabilize the reconstructed racial self—male or female. Snoop's work exceeds the masculinist erasure of the sexual agency of black women that it undoubtedly contains.[50]

These images circulate in a vulgar, insubordinate public conversation about sex and intimacy, power, powerlessness, and bodily pleasure that can be reconstructed even from the fragments of antiphonal communication that have been captured in commodity form and circulated multinationally on that basis. I want to end this chapter by suggesting that the ethical and political significance of Snoop's affirmation of blackness in dog-face has one last important layer. Its simultaneous questioning of humanity and proximity can be used not only to reinterpret what passes as "nihilism" but to construct an argument about the positive value of intersubjectivity in black political cultures that are now subject-centered to the point of solipsism. In this sense, Snoop's dog may help to sniff out an escape route from the current impasse in thinking about racialized identity. Arguing against those who would deny black popular culture any philosophical and metaphysical significance, we can bring the etho-poetics in his call to "do it doggy style" into focus by inquiring why individuals should recognize themselves as subjects of freaky sexuality and asking about the premium that this talk about sex places on touch and the moral proximity of the other.

Without wanting to supply a couple of esoteric "ethnic" footnotes in the history of the desiring subject, I'd like to try to situate Snoop's dog and the chain of equivalences in which it appears somewhere in the genealogy of technologies of the free black self. The radically alienated eroticism toward which Snoop and his canine-identified peers direct our attention might perversely contribute some desirable ethical grounding to the debased black public sphere. It confirms that we need to talk more, not less, about sex. The "dual solitude" transmitted and celebrated in the popular trope of doing it doggy style was not about a naive or pastoral mutuality. It breaks with the monadological structure that has been instituted under the stern discipline of racial authenticity and proposes another mode of intimacy that might help to recreate a link between moral stances and vernacular metaphors of erotic, worldly love. A periodization of the subaltern modernity that encompasses this possibility is established in the movement from "domestic allegories of political desire"[51] to political allegories of private desire. Perhaps this conversation about sex can also rehabilitate the untimely issues of intersubjective responsibility and accountability that have been expelled from the interpretive community during the reign of ethnic absolutism and its bodily signs.

The sociality established by talk about sex culminates in an invitation to acknowledge what Zygmunt Bauman, again citing Levinas, describes as the pre-ontological space of ethics.[52] In this setting we can call it a being *for* the other or even a willful nonbeing that exists prior to the racial metaphysics that currently dominates hip-hop's revolutionary conservatism. This ethical core was central to the musical cultures of the New World as they adapted sacred patterns to secular exigencies. It was first undervalued and then sacrificed. Snoop, R. Kelly, S.W.V., Usher, Lil' Kim, Foxy Brown, and the rest of the crew are already playing their parts in its revitalization. My concern is that the revolutionary conservatism that dominates hip-hop is likely to have limited patience with them. Revolutionary conservatism's enthusiasm for the market means that the commercial achievements of these artists will be respected. However, impurity and profanity cannot be tolerated in the long run because they contribute nothing to the heroics required by racial reconstruction. Authoritarians and censors can play the authenticity card, too. Revolutionary conservatism: this formulation takes us immediately to the limits of our available political vocabulary. There is something explicitly revolutionary in the presentation of violence as the key principle of social and political interaction and perhaps also in the hatreds of democracy, academicism, decadence, tepidity, weakness, and softness in general that have been regularly rehearsed. Conservatism is signaled loud and clear in the joyless rigidity of the gender roles that are specified in an absolutist approach to both ethics and racial particularity and, above all, in a gloomy presentation of black humanity composed of limited creatures who require tradition, pedagogy, and organization. This seems to go hand in hand with a fascistic fear and contempt of the masses. Ice Cube has reported this revealing conversation with his sometime mentor Minister Louis Farrakhan:

> Mentally he told me, the people are babies. They are addicted to sex and violence. So if you've got medicine to give them, then put the medicine inside some soda so they get both and it won't be hard for them to digest.[53]

It is important to remember that the dangers deriving from the fusion of biopolitics and revolutionary conservatism are not to be found in hip-hop alone. Black popular culture represents only one factor—albeit an important and influential one—in a wider balance of forces. Yet the conflict between revolutionary conservatives and other, more democratic and emancipatory possibilities is readily visible there. Market-driven black popular culture is making politics aesthetic usually as a precondition for marketing hollow defiance. And now, it is no longer communism that responds immodestly to this grave danger by imagining that it can politicize art but rather an insurgent intellectual practice that reacts to these fascistic perils by revealing the extent to which popular art has already been politicized in unforeseen ways.

6

THE TYRANNIES OF UNANIMISM

I read every account of the Fascist movement in Germany I could lay my hands on, and from page to page I encountered and recognized familiar emotional patterns. What struck me with particular force was the Nazi preoccupation with the construction of a society in which there would exist among all people (*German* people, of course!) *one* solidarity of ideals, *one* continuous circulation of fundamental beliefs, notions, and assumptions. I am not speaking of the popular idea of regimenting people's thought; I'm speaking of the implicit, almost unconscious, or pre-conscious, assumptions and ideals upon which whole nations and races act and live.

—RICHARD WRIGHT

The narrower the scope of a community formed by collective personality, the more destructive does the experience of fraternal feeling become. Outsiders, unknowns, unlikes become creatures to be shunned; the personality traits the community shares become ever more exclusive; the very act of sharing becomes ever more centred on decisions about who can belong and who cannot . . . Fraternity has become empathy for a select group of people allied with rejection of those not within the local circle. This rejection creates demands for autonomy from the outside world, for being left alone by it rather than demanding that the outside world itself change . . . Fragmentation and division is the very logic of this fraternity, as the units of people who really belong get smaller and smaller. It is a version of fraternity which leads to fratricide.

—RICHARD SENNETT

This is an especially important period in the political lives and consciousness of the African-descended peoples of the overdeveloped countries. Their journeys through modernity have recently reached a significant staging-post as Africa's struggle against colonial domination, which defined so many political aspirations in the period after slavery, has reached its conclusion. African countries are still exploited and excluded, but the quality of their marginalization has changed. The distinctive patterns of nineteenth-century imperialism have receded. New battles over health, technology, ecology, and particularly debt have emerged to expand and adapt our understanding of colonial and possibly postcolonial political conflicts. The world's richest countries remain deeply divided over the desirability of writing off the debts held by African governments.

In this nominally postcolonial period, the desire for freedom, which was for so long the center of the modern black political imaginary, must pause and reflect seriously when confronted by the deceptively simple questions: "freedom from what?" "liberty to accomplish what?" The emancipation of South Africa from Apartheid's criminal governance, incomplete though it may be, provides a timely opportunity to reconsider the wider relationship between Africa's New World diaspora and Africa's future. This reflection involves pondering the politics of decolonization in an age without colonies, and seeking the possibility of anti-imperialist consciousness in an era without triumphant empires arranged along bold, racist, nineteenth-century lines. It confronts the historical and philosophical limits of the idea of liberation and promotes a reevaluation of those fundamental modern notions freedom and revolution.

A language of revolution may persist, but these days it is more likely to turn away from the complexities of wholesale societal transformation and promote an "inward," New Age turn. This timely orientation is something quite different from the historic process of self-possession that James

Brown famously identified during the Black Power era as a "revolution of the mind." We have seen that it involves a changed understanding of the racial self articulated exclusively through the body and its imaginary power to determine human social destiny. This revolution, if revolution it be, is a biopolitical project that not only produces new common-sense truths about "race" but, in doing so, sets mind and body in a distinctive relationship so that managing and training the latter become the key to regulating the former.

The genocide in Rwanda and the continuing conflicts in Congo, Burundi, and elsewhere are only the most notable recent events to have endowed inquiries made by diaspora blacks into the status of racial difference, solidarity, and democracy with further disquiet about the limits of *racialized* particularity. Recall here that the first people ever to be convicted of the crime of genocide were the Africans Jean-Paul Akayesu and Jean Kambamba. This should not obscure the fact that tribalism, though it has been manifestly invented rather than transmitted seamlessly from the precolonial past, and asserts itself as a supremely powerful force for "ethnic" solidarity and sectarian division, is very ambiguously placed in relation to modern ideas of "race."[1]

To complicate matters even more, the political and ideological divisions set down in earlier times are becoming blurred. The black puppet leaders of the Apartheid pseudo-state, Bophutatswana, disastrously summoned the white supremacist Afrikaner Weerstandsbeweging (AWB) to protect them, bonded across the color line in spite of their political differences by deeply fascistic investments in mythologies of masculinism, the fiction of purity, and a common hatred for the dilution of their sacred distinctiveness. Closer to home, the Strasserite ideologues who first forged a "third position" for the neo-fascist British National Front during the late 1980s presented Louis Farrakhan in their publications as "a God-send to all races and cultures," distributed leaflets in support of his Nation of Islam, and visited its #4 Mosque in Washington, D.C., in order to study its antidrug programs.

Around the same time, the National Front magazine, *Nationalism Today,* interviewed another ultranationalist African-American, Osiris Akkebala, "an elder of the Pan African International Movement (P. A. I. N)," based in Florida. He told them that his organization invested the separation of the races with a sacred significance in keeping with its status as part of the law of God, and that members opposed intermarriage between black and white because it "results in racial genocide."[2] Fraternal relations between these two ultranationalist groups appeared to be intact ten years later, when Akkebala reappeared in Britain. This time, he served as a witness for the defense in the 1998 trial of the British National Party (BNP) activist Nick Griffin, the publisher of *The Rune*, who had been charged with incitement to racial hatred. On this occasion, he told the British black newspaper *New Nation:* "We see the B. N. P. as our natural allies. We both see the necessity of preserving our distinct races."[3] The BNP may have been eager to recover its position after suggestions that it had been implicated in the murder of Stephen Lawrence. But that is not enough to explain its active support for the family of an unemployed, twenty-six-year-old Bermuda-born chef and Rastafarian, Archie O'Brien, whom BNP members joined in a demonstration outside the Home Office in September 1996. O'Brien was seeking the financial sponsorship of the British Government for his plan to emigrate and settle in Africa, preferably Ghana. Interviewed by *The Guardian,* he said that, unlike his BNP associates, he was not advocating a compulsory return to Africa for all black people. He explained: "I can't express myself here. I can only express myself in Africa, surrounded by my own people and by nature . . . It's not for everyone. You have to reach a certain level of consciousness and be able to live off the land before you go there. Black people have to be prepared before they return to Africa."[4]

These contacts contribute to a pattern of disturbing events that precipitates further anxiety about the changing nature of the claims that modern ideas about "race" can make upon a world in which racial solidarities no longer enjoy an automatic allegiance or uncontested priority over other competing collectivities based on age, religion, language, region, health, gender, or sexual preference. These worries have been rendered all the more troubling in a new geopolitical context that increasingly lacks even the possibility of imagining an alternative to capitalism, the regulating mechanisms of the market, and the vicious logic of economic rationality. It is not yet an issue of whether blacks in the overdeveloped world, who are likely to be substantially cushioned from the brute scarcity that defines the developing areas, will want to go on associating themselves with Africa. Though that outcome remains a distinct possibility in the medium term, at present it is more a matter of how tenuous, precious connections might be maintained or enhanced in the interest of economic justice, political democracy, ecological equilibrium, and ongoing battles against white supremacism and other forms of absolutism. In this climate, it becomes important to consider how the vital symbolic and cultural links between Africa and its modern diaspora might be protected. They might even be made to mean something important for the future development of both locations at a time when the material and experiential gulf between over-developed and under-developed zones of the planet is being widened by accelerated technological change and new modes of exploitation typified by punitive, interminable debt and the burgeoning trade in hazardous waste.[5]

This apprehension of a deep change in the location and significance of Africa for the political imaginary of its most recent diaspora is also being registered at a time when black communities inside the overdeveloped zones are experiencing both an unprecedented degree of internal differentiation and new levels of economic immiseration. The metropolitan areas where those populations have been concentrated can be characterized by the demise of that common lifeworld once shared by the poor and the privileged. These groups no longer cluster in integrated cross-class communities and may no longer even reside in the same physical space, let alone dwell in the same undifferentiated "culture" or experience racism in essentially the same ways. This divergence in black experience and history has fed the underlying crisis in understanding racial particularity sketched in earlier chapters. Increasingly desperate assertions of a common, invariant racial identity cannot plausibly be projected through the idea of a common culture; rather, they find alternative expression in a significant return to aspects of an older racial science. Identity, understood only as sameness, is once more lodged in and signified by special properties discernible in black bodies. Interest in the biochemical properties of melanin and in the workings of distinct racialized forms of memory have been two of the most prominent themes in this revival. The biological codes of the eighteenth century have been brought back in inverted form. Leavened with New Age and occult themes, they have been made to produce tantalizing glimpses of a redemptive and compensatory black superiority. These tropes are part of a powerful new racial poetics, but it has not been sufficient to complete a cosmetic procedure capable of concealing the scars of intracommunal division that are visible through economic lenses and confirmed by disputes surrounding the moral, behavioral, and carnal rather than corporeal attributes of blackness. Well-publicized panics over the decadence, misogyny, and nihilism of slackness, gangsta rap, booty rap, and the subversive vulgarity of the Jamaican dancehall (which now circulates in eddies far from its Caribbean ghetto sources) have provided valuable insights into the class- and gender-based pathologies of the black body politic.

The multiple controversies surrounding the conduct of the former heavyweight boxing champion and convicted rapist Mike Tyson are instructive. During the summer of 1995, to mark his release from jail, where he had served time for the rape of Desiree Washington, and well before Tyson developed his tragic taste for the raw flesh of his opponents, it was proposed that he should make a heroic "homecoming" to Harlem. The proposed public celebration would have enabled him to "declare that he intends to lead a positive life, following in the footsteps of Joe Louis and Muhammad Ali." The event, which was also set to involve a street parade and a major gala event at the Apollo Theatre, was immediately denounced by a wide range of political figures. An organization called African Americans against Violence attacked the event's complicity with "the merchandizing of violence" and its "breath-taking display of black-woman hate, greed and collective irresponsibility." This forgotten episode neatly symbolized the deepening divisions that had appeared in earlier controversies over the nihilism, cynicism, and violence of gangsta rap. The muscled and tattooed body of yet another black male athletic hero, recast here as a victim of conspiracy by unsavory antiblack forces, was placed at the center of this drama. Many of the same elements would be replayed in a major key around the figure of O. J. Simpson.

It is only a slight oversimplification to suggest that in the United States, Britain, and parts of the Caribbean, two opposed but strangely complementary definitions of black nationalism have been confronting each other. The first was putatively streetwise, working-class, and habitually gendered male. It often answered the accusation of cynical commercialism by claiming for itself the role of the war correspondent who reports vividly, but as dispassionately as possible, the unacceptable realities visible from the frontlines of the ghetto. The other formation, for whom Dr. C. Delores Tucker, the head of the National Political Congress of Black Women, provided one convenient figurehead, was assertively feminist, unselfconsciously bourgeois, undoubtedly moralistic, and clearly confident in its core belief that however much money popular forms might bring to those who peddled them, they were trafficking in the most base and destructive stereotypes, which could only be detrimental to communal interests.[6]

Where this chronic binary conflict took root, it created a new sickness that has proved resistant to the simple remedies once supplied by the sweet-tasting medicines of nationalism and essentialism. To bolster their declining effectiveness, these failing therapies must now be supplemented by an austere corrective regime centered on the regulation of personal and interpersonal conduct between men and women and, to an increasing degree, between parents and children. In both versions of this strategy, the black family is seen as the principal object of the technologies of racial self-hood that aim to rebuild black people and remake black households, training them toward a common national consciousness and a suitable gender hierarchy. Family defines the limits of the forms of political agency that are deemed integral to rebuilding the fading nation. Ominous New Age rhetoric conditions the ambitions of this Afrocentrism even as it disavows Europe and its devilry.[7]

Black feminist analysis has rightly repudiated the identification of the race's fortunes with the public integrity of its masculinities. The impact of its critiques has added substantially to uncertainty about collective particularity and the conditions in which racialized solidarity can emerge and be sustained. Political conflicts over the compatibility of black homosexuality with the favored masculinist patterning of racial identity have also underlined the absence of spontaneous or automatic solidarity and the disappearance of an ethics of care from intraracial interaction.

A cultural elite in which black intellectuals and academics have been prominent, though by no means dominant, has also appeared during this fateful period, operating as something like the vanguard of a new middle-class minority that has substantially improved its own position. Whether it is located in the engine room of the entertainment industries or is clinging by its toehold in the older, more respectable professions, this influential group enjoys a deeply conflictual response to the black poor whose fate it has escaped, but upon whom it remains dependent for its understanding of the difference that "race" makes. Its advent, at a time when the words "exclusion" and "underclass" are never very far from the lips of policy-makers and political opinion formers, points once more toward the vexed issue of that stubborn order of class differences that can be identified inside what can no longer be credibly called a single racial community.

De-industrialization ensures that the economic predicament of these divided black communities is bleak, particularly where their subaltern social world is circumscribed by a high degree of spatial segregation.[8] At the same time, elements of globalization and the centrality of black cultures to popular culture, youth cultures, advertising, cinema, and sports have never been greater. However, this enhanced visibility does not mean that the black body is imaged in postures or roles that would be chosen as a means to articulate or complement black political interests. It can be argued that novel communicative technologies and the faceless forms of appropriation they foster impact negatively upon solidarity-building tactics devised in earlier periods and refined where black subculture moved above ground during the 1960s and 1970s. Consciousness of kind and synchronized action previously mediated by print and sound have been changed and have begun to break down in the different atmosphere created by communicative and representational regimes dominated by images. The growing power of visuality tips the balance away from sound and even from print to create new forms of minstrelsy and new remote audiences hungry for the pleasures they display and orchestrate. Music and dance, so long the core of the alternative public world in which dissidence was worked into a counterculture, reluctantly yield their traditional places of authority to pseudo-performances and video-based simulations. Black culture is not just commodified but lends its special exotic allure to the marketing of an extraordinary range of commodities and services that have no connection whatever to these cultural forms or to the people who have developed them. So much for the good news.

THE LIMITS OF REVOLUTIONARY CONSERVATISM

From one angle, the following observations on the place of "revolutionary conservatism" in contemporary black political culture might be read as an extended commentary upon rapper Ice Cube's role in selling the movies *Street Fighter, Dangerous Ground,* and *Anaconda.* The first movie caught my attention because it seemed to represent a highly developed instance of multiformat marketing. Hip-hop, computer games, and cinema were suggestively cross-linked in a way that foregrounded Cube and his official marginality as much as the changed profile of a youth culture in which music was no longer the central element. It was also interesting that no contradictions were perceived between Cube's informal Nation of Islam affiliations and the variety of Hollywood mainstreaming represented by *Anaconda* and *Dangerous Ground* and his collaboration with that well-known "cave bitch" the English actress and model Elizabeth Hurley. The apparent ease with which he could move through these mainstream Hollywood projects prompted me toward a reassessment of the currency of racial marginality in youth culture's economy of rebel signs. It initiated a different kind of speculation about the compatibility of powerful revolutionary political rhetoric with the more conventional if not explicitly conservative forms of economic thinking. It is important to appreciate that Cube's assertive espousal of racial separation as both a necessary therapy and a positive politics apparently relates exclusively to the realm of *interpersonal* conduct. This convenient restriction also exempts from consideration any issues arising from the sale of his own art to the legions of young white males who are—officially at least—hip-hop's major consumers. No problems there. Transracial intimacy is not considered insurmountable in the corporate spaces that he inhabits and that are essential to the scale of his cross-over stardom. In the commercial world, just as in the dark space of the performance venue, contact across the color line can be tolerated and legitimized as an unexceptional though possibly regrettable fact of economic life. In more intimate locations it becomes much more of a problem:

> One thing I believe we need to do, we got to separate. We really have to say, "O.K. white folks. You wanna help us? You go to your community and break down the walls." When they're in there talking in the boardroom talking about us, you go correct them. Don't come here picking up trash.[9]

This strategy was summed up in another statement Ice Cube made in the same conversation: "You handle yours, we'll handle ours." In his characteristically eloquent speech, these pessimistic words are part of a precise indictment. They help to animate a discourse that identifies the treacherous role and inadequate conduct of black political leaders. It is deeply significant that the compromised actions of that reviled group are conceived along lines analogous to the improper and inadequate role of fathers in unstable black families and unsustainable households from which masculine authority has been absent. The replacement of these leaders and fathers is necessary in the process of building racial recovery. Fatherhood becomes the principal means of communal reconstruction. Its primary characteristic is not tenderness, insight, patience, love, sympathy, or care but strength—preferably the same variety that is currently lacking from the actions of those "spineless" black leaders who "took their eyes off the prize in the 70s" and, again according to Cube, committed the grave mistake of "trying to make the public schools better instead of building our own schools." This remark reveals the logic of privatization operating here. Racial identity is being privatized in exactly the same way as education should be. The motif of withdrawal—civic and interpersonal—governs this new form of segregation that is being proposed.

Cube's public relations spin reveals repeatedly that he takes pride in his own activities as a father. But fatherhood has another resonance here. It affirms the naturalness of hierarchy. Complete separation is only an issue for those who occupy the subordinate roles in this ideal scheme. The dads (who presumably will be the ones to enforce these rules) can themselves pass at will across the line of color. They move to and fro freely, as the needs of their cross-over careers dictate. They offer their subordinates and followers a fantasy of segregation while themselves consolidating its absolute opposite: a network of economic, cultural, and political relationships that is driven only by the exigencies of the market and the strictest delineation between private and public worlds. Everything is to be politicized but only for those at the bottom of the heap.

It seems to me that in order to locate this type of thinking in its sorry modernist political lineage, we require a topography that operates in more dimensions than the one defined by the outmoded opposition between Left and Right. The chain of fundamental(ist) meanings established here—strength, masculinity, fraternity, self-reliance, discipline, hierarchy—is articulated above all through and by appeals to the value of racial purity. It is not powered by its own hermeneutic capacity, but is rendered believable nonetheless thanks to a default that operates all the more effectively in the absence of any alternative interpretative language that could challenge the overwhelmingly catastrophic value placed on mixture, intercultural, and "transracial" contacts. Its triumph underscores that we lack an adequate language for comprehending mixture outside of jeopardy and catastrophe. Finding this valuable new idiom does not require merely inverting the polarity of hybridity's internal circuits so that what was previously seen in terms of loss, dilution, and weakness becomes valuable instead and offers an opportunity to celebrate the vigorous cosmopolitanism endowed in modernity by transgressive and creative contacts with different people. Perhaps, pending a more complex organicity that comprehends difference in the forms of interarticulation and unremarkable interdependence suggested by the idea of symbiosis, we might begin to comprehend what is still best named "transcultural" mixture, and the assumptions about alterity that it promotes, as phenomena without any necessary or fixed value at all. This transitional but possibly radical suggestion could also be useful when linked to a plea for what might be termed an "indifferent modernity." Under that promising sign, antiracist democracy, care, and viable notions of civic reciprocity could thrive in the absence of an obligation to possess or even completely comprehend the forms of otherness signified by that narrow band of phenotypical variations that produces racialized difference.

These modest aspirations can be connected to the idea that we should take the *scale* upon which the calculus of human difference is to be judged more carefully into account. The shift away from a Euclidean geometry (which operates within closely bounded scalar limits that are anything but natural) and its analytic Cartesian successor, which links perception to a deterministic rationalism, and toward a fractal geometry that problematizes the questions of scale and scaling in a radical fashion offers a useful analogy here. Bodily scale is certainly important, but it is not the only possible basis for calculation and interaction. Varieties of solidarity other than the local and the national assert their presence and have to be placed within an explicit hierarchy of scales with multiple patterns of determination. In Chapter 1 I argued that this attention to scale and its effects is demanded by the emergence of the human genome as a "code of codes" and the principal focus of concern with human distinctiveness. What Fanon called the "epidermalization" of difference operates only at one scale, which will not always be able to claim priority over other, less readily visible modes of differentiation and determination. The varying degrees of melanin in the body seem a poor alternative vehicle for these biosocial speculations and the radically realist epistemology through which they must work.

Biologists like Richard Lewontin and Steven Rose have reminded us that we stand on the threshold of a transformed understanding of the visible differences coded inside human bodies. The old notions of "race" are likely to look very different, less natural, and more unstable than they now do when confronted with a pattern of predispositions to health, illness, and longevity that does not obey the predictive rules of Linnean racial typology. Perhaps a new, as it were "postracial," genetic science will appear before long. It is already being prefigured in several forms, not all of which will respect a vestigial racial theory as the frontier of some enhanced eugenic ambitions. In the meantime, the complexities of separating somatic cells from germ cells and the problems involved in distinguishing "periphrastic" from fully functional genetic information can only confirm the contingent but inescapable wisdom which stipulates that human beings are more alike than unalike and asserts the overwhelming natural and biological unity of the human species where polymorphism is enhanced but not diminished once we shift to this nano-political scale.

THE FRATERNITY OF PURITY-SEEKERS

In Britain, the United States, South Africa, Bosnia, and elsewhere, politically opposed purity-seekers have been prepared to bury their differences and become partners in the dismal dance of absolutism. It is therefore important to repeat that contemporary conflicts over the status of racialized difference have taken shape in an area far beyond the grasp of simplistic distinctions between the Left and the Right, radical and conservative. I would suggest that at root, these confluences are manifestations not of *political* ideology at all but of something anterior to it that challenges the rules and assumptions of modern politics by exalting particularistic ontology and primordial kinship above the distinctive blend of solidarity and autonomy for which the word modernity has long been emblematic. However much melanin is present in their cells, these purists voice a distinctive understanding of culture, tradition, self, kinship, ethnicity, nation, and "race" that blurs the lines between views formerly located at opposite ends of the spectrum of modern political ideologies. To recognize this is not to capitulate to the old—and in my view misguided—liberal assertion that intolerant and antidemocratic extremes merge readily into one another to found an anti-ideological or pragmatic totalitarianism. This is not an organic blending of ideologies or some inevitable closing of the narrow circuits of human frailty, imagination, and evil. For politically opposed groups to discover common cause, things have to happen—meetings must be conducted, language adjusted, objectives redefined, and purpose and solidarity reconfigured.

I am asking you to venture into the unstable location where white supremacists and black nationalists, Klansmen, Nazis, neo-Nazis and ethnic absolutists, Zionists and anti-semites have been able to encounter each other as potential allies rather than sworn foes. In the words of Primo Levi, it "is a grey zone, with ill defined outlines which both separate and join the two camps of masters and servants. It possesses an incredibly complicated internal structure, and contains within itself enough to confuse our need to judge."[10] Understanding the forms of complicity that arise there is not only a matter of recognizing the possibility that enemies can, in exceptional circumstances, acquire a common political interest.[11] It involves accepting the possibility that, interests apart, they may share parallel ways of understanding the meaning of their own particularity, of responding to the idea of transgressive contact between groups and of conceptualizing ethnicity and "race" as general, even necessary, principles of human differentiation. For example, the common investment in the idea of segregation that marks many of these encounters should not then be read as some spontaneous eruption of fundamental human antipathy toward otherness. It is better understood as a negotiated political outcome that has been produced through regimes of seeing and knowing the world that have a history.

I would like to recognize the existence of these gray and ambiguous zones in order to assess the value of linking a variety of different historical and cultural phenomena that are not normally associated. The common features of the political forces that join hands secretly there are overlooked because the groups involved in this tacit contact appear, from one angle of vision, to be politically opposed. This overly narrow conceptualization of their politics can be misleading. The situation is compounded when racial, religious, or cultural differences are invoked as a reason to place similar actions or attitudes in different moral categories. For example, it has sometimes been argued that only white people can be judged racist because racism is a defining attribute of whiteness or an intrinsic property of the power it holds. Racism can only be a consequence of power and so, the argument runs, since blacks have no power—as a "race"—they cannot, by definition, be racist. The tautology passes unnoticed and the jump between individual action and societal patterning is glossed over. I would argue that it might be better to interpret these and other similar statements as a means to solicit racial identification and endorse the principle of racialized difference as a valid means to classify and divide human beings. Attempting to adjust the scale upon which human interests are calculated so that it is no longer compatible with raciology reveals disturbing patterns that demand a reassessment of where the lines between revolutionary and conservative, modern and antimodern are deemed to fall. This situation becomes even more difficult when a favored group seeks or is endowed with a special or unique ethical status because of past experiences of victimage. On these historical grounds, normal standards of judgment can be suspended as restitution or reparation for past suffering. The idea that victims of racism are immunized against the appeal of racism precisely because they have been victims, or the idea that prior victimage renders victims and their descendants exempt from normal standards of conduct and judgment, are typical of these types of argument. This kind of reasoning was reduced to nonsense in the vulgar formula that suggested racism could be defined as the simple sum of prejudice and power. The proposition that only white people could be racist became confused with the different notion that black people could not be racist. The slippage between these two interlinked propositions is a symptom that should alert us to the pernicious power of racializing categories to reassert themselves even in the moment of their supposed erasure.

The capacity to do the wrong thing is an omnipresent possibility for which modernity afforded unprecedented opportunities. Exploring the linkage between various modern forms of authoritarianism, absolutism, masculinism, belligerence, intolerance, and genocidal hatred is important now because it has become abundantly clear that the fascisms of the past have not exhausted the palette of barbarity and the syntax of evil. Those histories of suffering can be used to bring a counteranthropological, strategic universalism into view.

The revolutionary rhetoric sometimes employed in interaction between black nationalists and separatists and their white-supremacist associates is misleading. To be conservative is to be engaged in a politics of cultural conservation. It is to subscribe to a doggedly positive and always over-integrated sense of culture and/or biology as the essential reified substances of racial, national, and ethnic difference. In this view, rather than being a product of profane politics and complex history, an obvious, biologically based, and natural apprehension of "race" initiates the development of both culture and identity. The junction of those two foundational terms—"race" and "culture"—indexes something so important and yet so fragile and brittle that it is in ceaseless jeopardy and can be readily destroyed. Whether the social and psychological processes we term culture and identity are really so insubstantial cannot be debated here. The idea that priceless, essential identities are in perpetual danger from the difference outside them and that their precious purity is always at risk from the irrepressible power of heteroculture has certainly supplied the pivot for some unlikely political alliances. Those formal connections are extremely important, but the word "alliance" suggests links that are too deliberate and too self-conscious to capture the tacit convergences and common habits of mind that should be recognized as equally significant. Perhaps the retreat into the spurious certainties that were once the exclusive stock in trade of European raciological thinking itself conveys the extent to which political tactics produced in the struggle against racial slavery, for democratic political rights and beyond those rights for a measure of social autonomy and cultural recognition, have become utterly exhausted.

The Malcolm X cult was one early symptom of a process in which the recent past of the black liberation movement was recycled and reimagined as well as actively reinvented. The Nation of Islam now provides the most significant model of solidarity here. It is important precisely because, though it buys heavily into the idea of Nationhood,[12] its own ideology is based not on nationalism, notions of citizenship, or rights but on an older and more straightforwardly authoritarian form of kinship that is masculinist, intolerant, and militaristic and shares important features with other "fraternalist" and "fratriarchal" political cultures. To find the substantive reasons for this enduring pattern requires an extensive historical detour by way of Garveyism and its antecedents. It would also have to take in the neglected phenomena that Wilson Moses has called the "pseudo-militarism of the Hampton-Tuskegee traditions, where uniforms and drill practice re-emphasized the importance of a New Negro who would repudiate the legendary cultural softness of an excessively languid and aesthetic people."[13] Further clues can be drawn from the work of Frederick Douglass, who, surveying the predicament of his racial siblings in July 1848, ten years after his own escape from slavery, first asked the famous, endlessly repeated question: "What Are the Colored People Doing for Themselves?" His characteristically bold plea for more black self-activity in the cause of antislavery was delivered more in sorrow than in anger and, he tells us, was addressed primarily to "comparatively idle and indifferent" free African-American men. He measured their local failures against the energetic way in which "the oppressed of the old world were holding public meetings, putting forth addresses, passing resolutions and in various other ways making their wishes known to the world." Contrasting their indifference to their political welfare with their great enthusiasm for the grand fraternal rituals of freemasonry and odd-fellowship, and the follies of the latter with the attainment of real character, Douglass's lament is worth quoting at length:

> If we put forth a call for a National Convention, for the purpose of considering our wrongs, asserting our rights, and adopting measures for our mutual elevation and the emancipation of our enslaved fellow countrymen, we shall bring together about *fifty;* but if we call a grand celebration of odd-fellowship, or free-masonry, we shall assemble, as was the case a few days ago in New York, from *four to five thousand*—the expense of which alone would be from seventeen to twenty thousand dollars, a sum sufficient to maintain four or five efficient presses, devoted to our elevation and improvement. We should not say this of odd-fellowship and free-masonry, but that it is swallowing up the best energies of many of our best men, contenting them with the glittering follies of artificial display, and indisposing them to seek for solid and important realities. The enemies of our people see this tendency in us, and encourage it. The same persons who would puff such demonstrations in the newspapers, would mob us if we met to adopt measures for obtaining our rights. They see our weak points, and avail themselves of them to crush us. We are imitating the inferior qualities of and examples of white men, and neglecting superior ones. We do not pretend that all the members of odd-fellow societies and masonic lodges are indifferent to their rights and means of obtaining them; for we know

the fact to be otherwise. Some of the best and brightest among us are numbered with those societies; and it is on this account that we make these remarks. We desire to see these noble men expending their time, talents and strength for higher and nobler objects than any that can be attained by the weak and glittering follies of odd-fellowship and freemasonry.[14]

Some of Douglass's frustration may have been aimed at his close associate Martin Delany, an enthusiastic mason who would publish a pamphlet on the legitimacy of the movement among colored men just five years later. Delany's arguments in favor of masonic activities are notable, but he was only one of many distinguished nationalists who found the segregated fraternal milieu of Prince Hall masonry,[15] with its rituals, hierarchies, secrecy, and military associations, a suitable environment in which to advance their social and political ambitions. Unlike Douglass, he had been freeborn and was therefore untroubled by the convention that freedom was an essential precondition of masonic membership.

The history of black masonry has been carefully surveyed by a number of historians who have pondered the movement's class character, identified its military roots, and recognized the valuable space it provided for building forms of moral solidarity, formal sociality, and political ideology among its black practitioners. The masons' advocacy of the centrality of ancient Egypt to the advance of civilization has been appreciated as a source of later nationalist theologies and ideologies, but their enduring impact upon subsequent patterns of political style and organization has been curiously overlooked.[16]

Prince Hall masonry was a profound if sometimes indirect influence on the thinking of Marcus Garvey and Noble Drew Ali (the founder of the Moorish Science Temple), two fundamental figures who inspired the later work of W. D. Fard and Elijah Muhammad.[17] The institutional foundations of the fraternal movements would collapse in the 1930s amid the same economic turmoil that witnessed the birth of the Nation of Islam, but their cultural, psychological, and political impact has continued into the present and is all the more pernicious where it is unrecognized.[18] The Nation of Islam certainly made use of the Prince Hall tradition, transforming its teachings so that masonry could be seen to be based upon the truths of Islam. Thus the masonic association of so many of America's founding fathers is employed as a way to specify the world conspiracy to which they contributed.

Where the ideal of fraternity shaped a distinctive political style, it raises still more difficult cross-cultural puzzles, both genealogical and interpretative. These puzzles demand an unconventional historical understanding of fascist groups and the traditional brotherhoods that shaped their development, and require new approaches to the conspiracy theories on which they relied.[19] Fraternal and fratriarchal movements ask us fundamental questions about the power of secrecy, particularly when combined with homosocial hierarchy and ritual. Analyzing them requires a more detailed historical sociology and psychology of movement behavior than is currently available, something that can extend the preliminary agenda set long ago by Simmel's invaluable speculations in this field: "the secret society must seek to create a sort of life totality. For this reason, it builds round its sharply emphasized purposive content a system of formulas, like a body round a soul, and places both alike under the protection of secrecy, because only thus does it become a harmonious whole in which one part protects the other."[20]

The resurgence of the fraternalist Nation of Islam has been central to notable recent changes in the black political imaginary, but the quest for a mechanical, premodern form of racialized solidarity that underpins its popularity takes a number of other forms, some of which manage to be much less forbidding and obviously fascistic. Though superficially more attractive, they are still connected to the authoritarian revision of community less by their investments in the fraternal style than by the widespread belief that working on maleness is the primary means to racial restoration and national reconstruction.[21] Simmel's observations on the appeal of secret societies and the absolute but necessarily temporary protection they afford their members linked a discussion of secrecy and betrayal to a sociology of adornment. His approach alerts us to the possibility that the magical production and simulation of community by means of uniform clothing can take diverse forms. It is as likely to be accomplished these days by a pair of boots or a hat supplied by "101% black-owned" Karl Kani™ as it is by the campy, bourgeois dignity of a bow tie or the bright embellishment of a colorful Kente cloth. These days, the role of uniforms is different because adequate proof of identity is not provided by a would-be state machine to which Garveyite or even Black Power uniforms tied their wearers. The privatized uniforms of the 1990s come with the multiple blessings of the corporate world. Donning them in pursuit of solidarity is a largely self-motivated gesture of submission to or immersion in a virtual community that cannot be socially confirmed by a radically fragmented everyday world.

The same breakdown of a political culture in which the contending values of solidarity and autonomy could be held in an unstable equilibrium is also conveyed in the disaggregation of embattled, alternative public spheres and the notions of freedom that were created there, often under the ambivalent protection of the black Protestant church. These and other factors have produced the anxieties that we routinely name as a crisis of "identity." Hankering after identity and the related desire to acquire the certainty and legitimacy that its possession supposedly confers has become associated with some spectacular disavowals of modernity. These patterns mark the black populations of the overdeveloped world rather unexpectedly as full participants in some mainstream cultural currents. Today, identity and its characteristic discontents are not marginal concerns at all, but phenomena that appear at the very center of the contemporary political agenda. This drive to resolve critical problems of social solidarity via a technology of the self is not the only point where an abject minority has been bound by the same assumptions and cultural processes as those who dominate it.

UNIVERSAL FASCISM

The word fascism is a surprisingly recent and imprecise term seemingly remote from the concerns of black cultural politics. Its short, contested life has made it hard to use, and there is a strong and entirely appropriate inhibition about setting the concept to work in analyzing phenomena that are remote in space and time from the site of its original usage to describe one recent phase in Europe's barbarities.[22] I prefer to see the dispute about its character as part of what is useful about it. It draws us into a valuable confrontation with the moral and political limits of both democracy and modernity. Let us work within the flexible framework established by two contentious hypotheses. The first suggests that a generic fascism can be identified;[23] the second that, even though there are real problems about isolating its ideological and conceptual signatures, fascism does have a coherent ideological shape born, to put it crudely, in the articulation of nationalism and a form of socialism.[24] Of course, this pseudo-socialism is an anti-marxist variety, but it retains certain utopian and indeed revolutionary attributes that play with and distort the ideal of fraternity into an antidemocratic and viciously hierarchical caricature that silences the competing claims of its sibling term—"equality."

Although extreme nationalism underlines the affinity of this generic fascism with the Right, it need not be seen as their exclusive ideological property. In some of its earlier forms, this fascism suggested a third way between the twin evils of socialism and capitalism. Though I recognize the danger that contemporary critics may end up taking the ideological pretensions of fascist doctrine far more seriously than many of its adherents, I reject the suggestion that recognizing the overarching power of the will to deception and destruction relieves critics of the unpleasant task of delving into fascist morality, law, aesthetics, and science.[25] It is unavoidable and indeed useful that the concept should remain enveloped in all sorts of disputes: political, ethical, and historical. For a long time, it became a debased coinage through being employed as a vague and general term of abuse. Lines drawn around analyses of its specific historical incarnations became entangled in debates about the attributes of the fascist state, the activities of fascist movements, the quality of fascist ideologies, and their complex and shifting relation to the normal forms, rules, and institutional patterns of color-coded bourgeois democracy, especially in the United States, where raciology and eugenic social policy were loudly articulated. However, fascism is more than just a political system, and there is far more involved in defining it than undoubtedly important inquiries into the characteristics of fascist states and governments. Distinctions between fascist ideology and culture, fascist governmentality and fascist economic and political strategy are indispensable, but if a generic fascism is to appear plausible, we must also be alive to fascism in its prepolitical, cultural, and psychological aspects. Fascism remote from state power and distant from the possibility of its acquisition is different from fascism in government, being rationally practiced as a means of modern political administration. Though relatively few fascist movements have actually taken power, these different dimensions of fascist politics can become linked, particularly in situations of civil war.

The lines of descent from 1930s fascists shamelessly claimed by some contemporary neo-fascists precluded the necessity of working to define which elements of earlier incarnations were being retained by today's adherents and supporters. This has been an acute problem, not where the Nazi label was conveniently applied to their own activities by contemporary subscribers to fascist doctrine, but where post-Hitlerian nationalism, racism, anti-semitism, and other related doctrines obscured the purity of their lineage. The antiracist and anti-fascist movement in Britain was, for example, constantly challenged to demarcate where legitimate patriotism ended and callous neo-Nazism began. Whatever one may think of his politics, Alain Finkielkraut's *Remembering in Vain*[26] had the virtue of focusing with some clarity on the exceptional nature of fascist crimes against humanity and the contested reconstruction of that exceptional status in the light of French colonialism's catastrophic consequences. Because these judgments have presented substantial political problems, it is not banal to recall that the history of Nazism and of Italian fascism associates them intellectually and organizationally with other forms of nationalism, traditionalism, and authoritarianism, as well as with syndicalism, socialism, and environmentalism.[27] We need to be able to see precisely where the practitioners of racial science became enmeshed with the normal practice of eugenics and euthanasia in Europe and the United States. Similarly, without becoming overly protective or defensive, we should be prepared to acknowledge the forms of linkage (in my view neither wholly necessary nor wholly contingent) that can be shown to connect to the Nazi cause the works of important figures like Heidegger, Riefenstahl, Mies Van der Rohe, Paul de Man, Carl Gustav Jung, and a host of other profound and stimulating artists and thinkers. Each of these celebrated examples has generated an extensive literature that cannot be reconstructed here, though it may be useful to note a certain similarity in the postures assumed by those who have sought to redeem these figures and their genius from the taint of Nazism, which is understood in all these cases to be external to whatever they had to say that is enduring or valuable.

Taking these observations on board should not mean that the specificities of fascism are allowed to disappear, merging into what is familiar. If that were to happen, the normal imperfections of capitalist democracy would become indistinguishable from the exceptional governmental state for which the concept of fascism provides a vital signature. Fascism is not to be separated from normality by a question of degree. And yet, the modes of cultural expression and the practices of everyday life under the Nazi regime so tellingly reconstructed in the priceless labor of historians like George Mosse, Detlev Peukert, Gisela Bock, Jill Stephenson, Alison Owings, Peter Adam, Michael Kater, and Robert Wistrich have a very familiar look.[28] Volumes of moving testimony from other genocidal war zones demonstrate how swiftly an exceptional brutality can be triggered from the seeming stability of normal interaction. Stefan Kühl and Edward Larson[29] have provided a means to emphasize the kinship between white supremacist regimes in different places and their recruitment of eugenic racial science into social policy. Recognizing the complexity of these interconnections, we must work harder to find fascism's characteristic features in philosophy, aesthetics, and cultural criticism as well. This vigilance should not just be directed toward the possibility that past forms may recur but should also recognize the danger that fascism is still somehow pending—a possibility that remains inherent in all attempts to organize social life according to orderly modern, raciological principles. It is inappropriate, then, to seek a final extrahistorical formula for fascism that would enable us to devise a simple test for its presence or absence. To desire a device of that type is also to trivialize the complexity and mutability of these unsavory political phenomena that we cannot reduce to being either modernity's repudiation or its fulfillment, reason's betrayal or its immoral affirmation.

Events in Latin America and Indo-China as well as in Southern Africa and the Middle East testify that Hitlerism did not exhaust the forms that fascism can take. Emmanuel Levinas pointed long ago to the difference between the philosophy of Hitlerism and the philosophy of the Hitlerians. We would do well to reflect on similar distinctions and employ their correlates in all considerations of the contemporary phenomena that we want to identify as wholly fascist or, with even greater difficulty, as tendentially fascistic. There are additional obstacles in trying to determine exactly what the status of the unspeakable past should be in defining the meaning of the concept today. Irreconcilable memories of fascism are articulated and projected by fascists and their opponents. This appears in gross form where the scholarship of the Holocaust "negationists" faces the testimony of survivors, their families, and other moral advocates, but there are numerous other, less dramatic instances of the same sort of conflict. To seek to open and utilize debates over what counts as fascist is not to downplay the importance of knowing with as much detail as possible what really happened in the past. It is to recognize that both easy exceptionalism and simplistic notions of repetition offer unsatisfactory ways of facing the enduring power of fascisms and racisms: scientific, pseudo-scientific, and antiscientifically cultural. This line of inquiry might also play a role in cultivating the special skills necessary to recognize and oppose fascism when it appears without the convenience of an identifying label and in inhospitable circumstances far outside the overdeveloped countries where we might be most attuned to the possibility of its reappearance. This endeavor has been made urgent not only by the intermittent denial of fascist crimes against humanity but more controversially by the emergence of respectable forms of nationalism and patriotism that have been able to accommodate "strong" versions of ethnicity and invite comparison with fascist discourses but that bid for a legitimate place in official political institutions.

The categories that have emerged from detailed historical analyses of fascist movements become somewhat fudged in the transition to more general and abstract thinking. Perhaps it is better not to attempt to pronounce finally upon the balance between reason and occultism outside of any particular historical example or to try to make general estimations from material relating to concrete issues like the place of racist ideologies in any particular fascist "polity."

Emphasis on the genocidal processes in which fascisms have culminated should not diminish our sensitivity to the proto-fascist potentials secreted inside familiar everyday patterns of government, justice, thought, and action. The notions of absolute ethnicity that have created a sense of culture as something organic that can be grown or husbanded by the state and owned as a form of property by individual subjects are an interesting example of this possibility. They suggest that members of the dominant social group in a racialized social hierarchy do not have to imagine themselves to be superior; they need only assert unbridgeable difference to awaken the possibility of a fascistic solidarity.

I recognize that while there are still plenty of openly active, self-confessed fascists around, this degree of reflexivity may be seen as a luxury that antiracist politics cannot afford. It may be criticized as a dangerous distraction because its speculative tone could divert attention away from their actions and toward more problematic areas where the label will be unproductively contested. There will also be a risk of diluting opposition to fascistic political activity by finding fascism and its preconditions everywhere, but this need not be the case. By confining the term and restricting it to those cases in which unbroken continuity with past fascisms can be established, we may also minimize contemporary dangers and diminish our sense of what antiracist and antifascist action might mean as a future-oriented politics rather than an essentially defensive operation against violence and terror.

Those of us tied by affinity as well as kinship to histories of suffering and victimage have an additional responsibility not to betray our capacity to imagine democracy and justice in indivisible, nonsectarian forms. Perhaps because of what we have witnessed or chosen to commemorate we have a special obligation to be vigilant and alert to the possibility that barbarity can appear anywhere, at any time, not only where economic rationality or the logic of capital dictates it as the preferred outcome. These qualifications ensure that histories of suffering are not reduced to the private experience of their victims. Mourning is only one of many practices of memory, and it involves more than remembering. Bolstered by the cautious, strategic universalism toward which the history of fascism inclines us, diverse stories of suffering can be recognized as belonging to anyone who dares to possess them and in good faith employ them as interpretative devices through which we may clarify the limits of our selves, the basis of our solidarities, and perhaps pronounce upon the value of our values.

Whether or not you agree with the attempt to apply the concept of fascism to these different phenomena, ask yourself this: What, in the face of the proliferating chronicles of human barbarity, would it mean to seek to contrive a pastoral and permanently innocent ethnic or racial identity? What is at stake in the desire to find an entirely pure mode of particularized being, and to make it the anchor for a unique culture that is not just historically or contingently divorced from the practice of evil but permanently fortified against that very possibility by its essential constitution? Perhaps the desire for that fiction of particularity is an especially problematic feature of contemporary black politics but one that supplies ironic confirmation of its distinctively modern lineage. It seeks to shield its supposed beneficiaries from the effects of the complex moral choices that define human experience and to insulate them from the responsibility to act well and choose wisely: favoring negotiation over violence and the will to justice over the will to dominate. It would usher black politics into a desert, a flattened moral landscape bereft of difficult choices where cynicism would rule effortlessly in the guise of naturalized morality. Secreted inside that exaltation of biologically grounded innocence and its over-identification with moral legitimation is a promise that the political agenda set by the innocent will, at some future point, be emancipated from moral constraints. The institution of innocent identity makes the difficult work of judgment and negotiation irrelevant. Fascism will flourish where that innocence is inflated by the romances of "race," nation, and ethnic brotherhood.

BLACK FASCISTS?

Writing in 1938, in "A History of Negro Revolt," a political and theoretical coda to *The Black Jacobins,* C. L. R. James had the following to say about Marcus Garvey:

> All the things that Hitler was to do so well later, Garvey was doing in 1920 and 1921. He organized storm troopers, who marched, uniformed in his parades, and kept order and gave colour to his meetings.[30]

James revised the tone of this prewar evaluation in later work, but these words summon up not the least of the many historiographical controversies buried in the analysis of the Garveyite movement. Did Garvey's ideology of fundamental race consciousness incline him toward a version of the generic fascism sketched above, or was his sympathy for the activities of the European dictators won by their practical achievements and his similar enthusiasm for the career of powerful, heroic figures like Napoleon? What matters more than these undecideable though absorbing inquiries is a consideration of whether Garvey's militaristic movement, with its exhortation to manhood and repeatedly stated desire to "purify and standardize" the race, can be understood as a family member to the other, similar movements of that period and whether the variety of authoritarian leadership that Garvey practiced was akin to the type that was being developed by fascists in Italy and Germany. James was only one of the many political commentators to have compared Marcus Garvey and the United Negro Improvement Association (UNIA) to the fascists. To draw attention to this is not to undermine any of the extraordinary and important achievements of the Garvey movement. It is, however, to entertain the possibility of a profound kinship between the UNIA and the fascist political movements of the period in which it grew. These affinities can be approached via the idea of a common political style that usefully shades simplistic distinctions between ideology on the one hand and organizational techniques and strategies on the other. According to the historian J. A. Rogers, in a 1937 interview quoted in what has become a celebrated passage from the second volume of *The World's Great Men of Color*, Garvey himself compared his organization's activities to those of Hitler and Mussolini:

> We were the first Fascists. We had disciplined men, women and children in training for the liberation of Africa. The black masses saw that in this extreme nationalism lay their only hope and readily supported it. Mussolini copied fascism from me but the Negro reactionaries sabotaged it.[31]

Robert A. Hill, a perceptive commentator on Garvey,[32] has offered an especially valuable exposition of his authoritarian political philosophy and its explicitly antidemocratic and Spartan conceptions of law, self, nationality, and duty. Hill describes Garvey's identification with fascism as "naive" but notes that it was able to merge with Garvey's explicit anti-semitism, something Hill does not minimize. The point at issue here is not whether Garvey's claims to have been an inspiration to Mussolini and Hitler are true but rather what it means for us today that Garvey, "the master propagandist," may have believed them to be so. Though it takes us into even more perilous territory, it seems worthwhile to attempt to situate Garvey's own account of his project in relation to his early associations with the Ku Klux Klan and other white supremacist ideologues, something that did not draw unequivocal support from members of the UNIA. The symbolic summit of these connections was a two-hour meeting between Garvey and Edward Clarke, the Klan's second in command, that took place in Atlanta in June 1922. However, before that, Garvey had spoken favorably of the organization's having "lynched race pride into the Negroes"[33] and applauded its segregationism. These positions went hand in hand with support for the activities of other individual segregationists and white supremacist organizations in the North and the South:

In our desire to achieve greatness as a race, we are liberal enough to extend to others a similar right . . . All races should be pure in morals and in outlook, and for that we, as Negroes, admire the leaders and members of the Anglo-saxon clubs. They are honest and honorable in their desire to purify and preserve the white race even as we are determined to purify and standardize our race.[34]

Purify and standardize: Garvey is saying that racial purity and standardization have to be fashioned. The combined, deadly weight of racial difference, subordination, and oppression is insufficient to generate them spontaneously. The martial technologies of racial becoming—drill, uniforms, medals, titles, massed display—have to be set to work to generate these qualities that are not immediately present. Garvey's views were framed and sanctioned by a version of nationalism figured through the familiar masculinist values of conquest and military prowess:

This is a white man's country. He found it, he conquered it and we can't blame him because he wants to keep it. I'm not vexed with the white man of the South for Jim Crowing me because I am black. I never built any street cars or railroads. The white man built them for their own convenience. And if I don't want to ride where he's willing to let me then I'd better walk.

It has been suggested that these arguments may have been produced to aid Garvey's long-term strategy for building the UNIA in the Southern states. Tony Martin, another distinguished historian of the UNIA and Garvey biographer, who is more sympathetic than Hill to the call for separatist politics, has described the Garvey movement's relationship with the Klan and other white supremacist and segregationist individuals and organizations during this period as a symbiotic one. Dismissing as "simplistic" any understanding of these connections that sees them as an alliance based solidly on a common desire for racial purity, enthusiasm for emigration, and hostility to integration, Martin notes the emergence of areas of "common concern" between these political constituencies and quotes with approval Garvey's own defense of the contacts between the two organizations. Martin ends his extremely valuable historical study of Garvey and his organization with Garvey's telling description of that famous encounter with the Klan leader: "I was speaking to a man who was brutally a white man, and I was speaking to him as a man who was brutally a Negro."

This suggestive moment of transracial symmetry pivots on two recurrent attributes of what I feel can be justifiably named fascism: brutalism and masculinism. Some version of a shared and appropriately gendered humanity is ironically confirmed by their presence even as the a priori significance of racial codes is being asserted. Garvey's implied superiority is communicated only by the way that he monopolizes the role of speaker in the encounter.

Another troubling example from the same interwar period can be built around Zora Neale Hurston's anthropological trips to Haiti in 1936 and 1937. Hurston explains that she was captivated not only by a well-dressed Haitian colonel who was "the number one man in the military forces in Haiti" but also by his authoritarian and populist plans to reintroduce something like slavery into the country:

> He is a tall, and slender black man around forty with the most beautiful hands and feet that I have ever beheld on a man. He is truly loved and honored by the three thousand men under him ... There is no doubt that the military love their chief ... Anyway, there is Colonel Calixe with his long tapering fingers and his beautiful slender feet, very honest and conscientious and doing a beautiful job of keeping order in Haiti ... he is a man of arms and wishes no other job than the one he has. In fact we have a standing joke between us that when I become president of Haiti, he is going to be my chief of the army and I am going to allow him to establish state farms in all the departments ... a thing he has long wanted to do in order to eliminate the beggars from the streets of Port Au Prince, and provide food for the hospitals, jails and other state institutions ... He is pathetically eager to clear the streets of Haiti of beggars and petty thieves ... what a beautifully polished Sam Brown belt on his perfect figure and what lovely, gold looking buckles on his belt![35]

There is something about a man in uniform! Hurston is clearly swept up in the erotic charge attached to the charismatic figure of this man of destiny. Her extraordinary enthusiasm is also an important moment in which some of the psychoanalytic issues involved in being invited to identify with the would-be dictator might also be noted. Her suggestion that he is an object of love for his subordinates is, for example, striking. What variety of love is this that blends the heterosexual and homosexual and delicately flavors the blend with fear and coercion? The colonel's conspicuous physical attributes symbolize the innocence of his political inclinations. The combination of bodily perfection and a firm political hand on the beggars and thieves is not, of course, enough to damn him as a fascist, but the resonance is a strong one, and it is significant that Hurston also articulates a contempt for the moribund political system that, in her view, fetters Haitian progress. This view is shared with the young Caribbean men of action who captivated her.

In numerous settings, fascism has involved precisely this idea that political solutions can be imposed upon the mass of people by an elite group. Its populist character is thus circumscribed and directed. Its primary political goal is defined by a restless exaltation to act toward the institution of a national community. The process of national becoming must of course be perpetually deferred because on the day that it dawns, much of the distinctiveness of fascist politics will be lost. Superficially at least, Malcolm X's repudiation of the Nation of Islam's later contacts with the Klan presents even more fissile material than the Garvey and Hurston cases. Malcolm has himself been represented as a charismatic and authoritarian leader, but he differs sharply from Garvey in that he repudiated the links with the Klan and the Nazis that were a central part of his complete break from the Nation of Islam. Though Malcolm's comprehension of these contacts is couched in terms of a conspiracy theory, his open contempt for the immoral outcome they represent comes across very strongly:

> I know for a fact that there is a conspiracy between, among the Muslims and the Lincoln Rockwell Nazis and also the Ku Klux Klan. There is a conspiracy . . . Well, the Ku Klux Klan made a deal with Elijah Muhammad in 1960 in the home of Jeremiah X, the minister in Atlanta at that time, in the presence of the minister in Philadelphia. They were trying to make a deal with him to make available to Elijah Muhammad a county-size tract of land in Georgia or South Carolina where Elijah Muhammad could then induce Negroes to migrate and make it appear that his program of a segregated state or separated state was feasible. And to what extent these negotiations finally developed, I do not know. Because I was not involved in them

beyond the period of December 1960. But I do know that after that, Jeremiah, who was the minister throughout the South, could roam the entire South and the Klan not bother him in any way shape or form, nor would they bother any of the Black Muslims from then on. Nor would the Black Muslims bother the Klan.[36]

Just as in the case of Ice Cube, it would seem that practical implementation of that longed-for separation essential to racial rebirth actually requires, indeed legitimates, transgressive contact with the forbidden Other in a strange but entirely predictable act of fraternalist mirroring. The segregationists and purifiers who are located on both sides of the fatal boundary between "races" claim monopoly of the useful capacity to handle those contacts with the enemy that would be damaging to everybody else. The enemy who announces himself to be your enemy ceases to be an enemy. He becomes an ally, and a more authentic and treacherous foe is produced in the form of the enemy who tells you he can be your ally in the coalitional struggles that can bring about justice and rights for all. The Nazi and the Klansman are preferable because they are open and honest about their racialized beliefs. You know where you are with a Klansman.

Perhaps, recognizing the problems in seeking to apply the label fascist to the Klan, we should consider what justifies an association between an openly Nazi organization and a spiritual movement dedicated to the emancipation, uplift, and protection of Africans abroad. It is, of course, the acquisition of sovereign territory: a national homeland, a piece of ground, that legitimates these aspirations. Garvey's oldest son, Marcus Garvey, Jr., put this point with a brutal and disarming clarity in a 1974 anthology organized as a tribute to his father:

> African National Socialism postulates that the children of the Black God of Africa have a date with destiny. We shall recreate the glories of ancient Egypt, Ethiopia and Nubia. It is natural that the children of mother Africa scattered in the great diaspora will cleave together once more. It seems certain that the world will one day be faced with the black cry for an African "Anschluss" and the resolute demand for African "Lebensraum."[37]

The idea that fascism involved making politics aesthetic also raises the question of its exceptional status and relationship to the normal business of the bourgeois nation-state in which politics has had to become aesthetic to hold the attention of people sensitized to the accelerated communicative pace of advertising. The recent bloody histories of authoritarian regimes in Iran, Greece, Latin America, Indo-China, and Africa all suggest that fascism is not productively grasped as Europe's own private and internal drama. Though it is neither the flipside of a Europe-centered modernity nor something eternal and evil, outside of history and secular morality altogether, it does have something to do with the pathologies of modern development that Rousseau called "the fatal ingenuities of civilized man." The capacity to perpetrate evil is not itself modern, but the metaphysics of modernity brought a special tone to it. The scale and power of the nation-state condition it. We have to deal, not only with the old dangers of occultism and irrationality, but with the new evils represented by the rational application of irrationality. There is a utopian element here, too, and it is signaled in the antidemocratic but nonetheless modern value of fraternity and projected through the desire for a simpler world premised on racial sameness and racial certainties. Homogeneity and hypersimilarity become the principles of a hierarchical, authoritarian, and antimodern bonding. Solidarity is simulated in silent, spectacular rituals that must remain voiceless in order to mask the differentiation within the totality. The modern impulse to recreate and perfect the world is trivialized by being reduced to a narrowly racial project. We must concede today that making politics aesthetic has become harder to distinguish from Walter Benjamin's alternative—the politicization of art—and that both possibilities exist together, embedded in the more benign but decidedly volatile forms of authoritarian populism to which we have grown accustomed in the overdeveloped countries.

It bears repeating that a susceptibility to the appeal of authoritarian irrationalism has become part of what it means to be a modern person. It is bound to the dreams of enlightenment and autonomy as an ever-present alternative. To recognize that blacks are not after all a permanently innocent people, forever immune to this dismal allure, is, perversely, to embrace our status as modern folk who can think and act for ourselves.

III

BLACK TO THE FUTURE

Humanity is waiting for something other than blind imitation of
the past. If we want to advance a step further, if we want to turn
over a new leaf and really set a new man afoot, we must begin to
turn mankind away from the long and desolate night of violence.
May it not be that the new man the world needs is the non-violent
man?

—MARTIN LUTHER KING, JR.

7

"ALL ABOUT THE BENJAMINS": MULTICULTURAL BLACKNESS —CORPORATE, COMMERCIAL, AND OPPOSITIONAL

O my body, make of me always a man who asks questions!

—FRANTZ FANON

If you wore a pair of size 34 jeans, you were buying a size 40 just 'cause we don't want our jeans fitting up in our crotches. They ain't designed for black people. Black people got certain physiques— black men and black women. Those other companies design with a preppy kind of customer in mind, not black people. That is where I come into the picture. People see black people as trendsetters, they see what we're on and they wanna be onto the same thing, figuring it's gonna be the next big thing. They try to take things away from us every time. Slang we come up with ends up on T-shirts. We ain't making no T-shirts.

—KARL KANI

The period in which genomic raciology articulated nano-politics also involved bitter conflicts over the civic and commercial status of cultural differences. Multiculturalism was attacked by the advocates of absolute homogeneity but invoked against them by their opponents: the apostles of an equally absolute diversity. The actions of both groups left the deterministic speculations of resurgent sociobiology bypassed and unanswered. Formerly radical forces were distracted by the calculus of particularity that projects cultural identity not as relation but as the simple product of either sameness or difference. As we saw in the previous chapter, to make matters worse, the absolutists on both sides of the color line developed a set of shared assumptions about what culture is and about the nature of its hold on "races."

Multiculturalism has equally uneasy relationships with the contending vocabularies of liberal pluralism and post-Marxian speculation. Both have struggled to employ it in their different attempts to revive the practice of politics and adapt it to new circumstances. Multiculturalism has been turned into a businessperson's handbook by Cable Network News (CNN) and abused by conservatives as a new form of racism.[1] It may not have been adequately politicized, but with the demise of mass marketing it has certainly become a dominant commercial consideration. Its corporate life has been fueled by the fact that in the era of targeted precision marketing, the appeal of black faces and styles need no longer be restricted to black consumers. These profound changes have stimulated demands for exotica and authentic inside information that have been met enthusiastically by a new contingent of cultural brokers: a hip vanguard in the business of difference.

In December 1996 Spike Lee, who has been the figurehead for much of this activity, announced an unprecedented commercial collaboration with the Madison Avenue advertising giant DDB Needham, a unit of the Omnicom Group that handles prestigious consumer brands like McDonald's and Budweiser. His close association with the firm led rapidly to the formation of a new advertising agency called Spike/DDB, with Lee, the 51 percent majority shareholder, in the combined role of "president and creative director." This novel corporate marriage was itself historic, and not only because DDB recognized Spike's own position as a brand of popular culture by referring to him as an "icon" in the statement that heralded the new venture. The new company placed a respectable corporate imprimatur on the realization that the American "urban consumer" (you know who they mean) now fixes *planetary* patterns for selling and using some highly profitable products. This shows that the culture industry is prepared to make substantial investments in blackness provided that it yields a user-friendly, house-trained, and marketable "reading" or translation of the stubborn vernacular that can no longer be called a counterculture.

According to the *International Herald Tribune,* after six months in business, the new company had "accumulated a robust roster of accounts with billings estimated at $35 million.[2] Lee, who had directed commercials for Levis, AT&T, Snapple, and Nike well before this venture, insisted that his agency is not specifically targeting African Americans but is pitching its clients' products more broadly at the younger, trend-setting, sports- and fashion-conscious consumers who compose the "urban market." The needs of African-American or indeed black Atlantic political cultures can only look parochial when contrasted with these glittering post-traditional possibilities. Budweiser's owners, the brewing conglomerate Anheuser-Busch, returned Lee's favor by sponsoring a promotional tour and advance screenings for Lee's 1996 Million Man March feature *Get on the Bus.*

Diverse political interests have tried without success to claim the prize of multiculturalism exclusively for themselves, but that overloaded, pivotal concept does not refer to some readily identifiable philosophical or political stance. Its meaning is still being determined in a wide-ranging, conflictual, and, at present, open process. These conflicts have encompassed the questions of cultural integrity and cultural value but moved beyond them, releasing a political energy that can deliver us right to the heart of contemporary thinking about cosmopolitan democracy.

The tempo of these hostilities has been dictated by controversies over the idea of nationality, the changing character of nation-states, and the forms of sameness they can demand from their heterocultural citizenry. In turn, these conflicts have produced anxiety over the difficulties involved in maintaining cultural and biological purity in answer to the corrosive effects of differentiation manifested, above all, in the presence of postcolonial peoples—always out of place—at the hub of the old imperial networks. Underlying all these fears is one further question: whether today's inescapable encounters with difference might be understood as having any sort of positive value.

Other elements of the large political and ethical agenda for which the discourses of multiculturalism provide a timely index have also been revealed by the sheer intensity of discussions conducted around the rational, moral, and aesthetic heritage of Western civilization. This has been symbolized by the desperate plight of the educational system, where multiculturalism has acquired a strong institutional dialect, and in the evolving role of imperial public institutions like the museum in collecting, rationalizing, displaying, and reproducing both culture and civilization.[3] Multiculturalism has been developed quite differently in these different areas of policy and politics. It has appeared in publicly insurgent and privately transgressive modes and is still being engaged variously: to address fears about the canon of Western thought; to evaluate the contemporary authority of scientific endeavor and aesthetic value; and to illuminate the crisis of the humanities in which crossing intellectual boundaries and questioning where borderlines have been placed (between cultures and scholarly disciplines) have suggested promising routes toward new forms of knowledge. Most fundamentally, in a time of planetarization and accelerated technological development, when the politics and significance of location, presence, and proximity are being actively recomposed and rethought, multiculturalism has been deployed to interrogate the significance of nationality as a principle of social cohesion and to criticize unthinking attempts to maintain Europe as the innocent and privileged center of history's great unfolding. Lastly, multiculturalism might also be understood as a sign marking the end of Europe's hegemony in the world of ideas. It no longer enjoys a special monopoly of access to scientific, ethical, or aesthetic modernities.

The stubborn imprecision of multiculturalism has only enhanced the concept's capacity both to name the special forms of jeopardy that endanger the nation today and, on the other side, to help in defining emergent, utopian alternatives to the congruency of bleached-out culture with the fading borders of the nation-state. Uncoupled from its associations with unbridgeable, absolute difference and reconfigured with a wider sense of the unevenly developed power of subnational (local) and supranational relations, multiculturalism can force nationalisms and biosocial explanations of race and ethnicity into more defensive postures. Their legitimacy, the scale upon which they comprehend solidarity, and their foreclosure of human agency are all being questioned in the name of the cosmopolitan consciousness constituted where the historic link between cultures and nations is broken. The very recurrence of the term "multiculturalism" in so many discrepant settings connects them and suggests that they may be presenting the various symptoms of a common, social transformation.

With the addition of that fateful prefix "multi," layer upon layer of conflict was spun around the central concept of culture. It has emerged from that cocoon as a master signifier: as powerful today as justice, right, freedom, and reason must have been long ago. Thus there is more to multiculturalism than its role as a special sign used to display and articulate the manifold pressures acting on the nation-state from within and without. I want to approach it here, not as a clearly delineated goal or a reified state to which one can be finally committed, but as an ethical and even aesthetic principle routed through the distinctive historical experiences of modernity we have already noted and confirmed by the special promise and syncretic dynamism of contemporary metropolitan life. Perhaps we can consider what it would mean to embrace rather than flee from multiculturalism's political implications. That accommodation with politics need not involve the betrayal of creativity and artistic autonomy.

Although it is seldom openly acknowledged, for most of us in Europe these telling arguments over culture and difference and the relationship of nationality to power and history revive the fading after-images of the colonial and imperial past. The residual significance of these outlines on the retina of the national imagination is signaled by too many sullen responses to the supposedly disruptive presence of postcolonial peoples at the conflict-ridden core of metropolitan social life. For critics and other brave souls prepared to navigate the roughest waters of contemporary cultural politics, that half-forgotten imperial history is still present and potent, though it remains latent, mostly unseen, like a big rock beneath the surface of the sea. The traces of imperial modernity—its contested social memory—may be apprehended only intermittently, but they can still produce volatile material even if these days it is still cultural differences rather than the straightforward biological inferiority of those (post)colonial peoples that create alarm and define the threat they represent to brittle monoculture.

Reinvented as much as nostalgically remembered, the filtered imperial past gets invested with a new power to soothe.[4] It supplies comfort against the shock of Empire's loss and the realization of national decline. Across Europe, memories of imperial greatness are one potent and neglected element in the resurgent appeal of newly confident neo-fascisms as well as the populist and nationalist strategies devised by worried governments to outflank their electoral appeal. They are also powerfully active in the anthropological, nineteenth-century definitions of humanity that still supply the ground upon which judgments of truth, beauty, and goodness are routinely made.[5] The enduring effects of this legacy are urgent issues for critics. The predicament of Salman Rushdie amply demonstrates that it is art and culture rather than science and reason that have supplied the best for cultur-ally oriented racism and confirmed its vision of absolutely incompatible ways of life. We must ask whether the production and reception of art might now contribute something valuable to a provocatively postanthropological understanding of both culture and humanity. Vernacular forms of artistic practice have already disrupted the stable standpoints from which pro-nouncements on these important matters are made. The image world of corporate multiculture seems poised to do something similar.

IT'S IN THE MIX: CULTURE, POSTANTHROPOLOGY

Avowedly postmodernist thinkers stay closest to the modernist project where they have questioned the figure of Man and identified its role as an integral trope in the modern ideologies of inhumanity that appeared dur-ing the colonial and imperial periods. This image of Man has been de-nounced by some of them as a transposition of the duplicity that bonded rationality with terror. The problematic relationship between modernity and barbarism, progress and catastrophe that was elaborated in the Nazi period has become paradigmatic. At present it would be inappropriate and indeed impossible to announce a final verdict on its significance. In the places where it is systematically remembered, the quest for the wholesome finality of another new beginning is an immoral one, and there are many important political and ethical questions at stake in how that period of au-thoritarian irrationalism and rational authoritarianism should be com-memorated. I want to suggest two things: that acknowledgments of the uniqueness of that catastrophe should not become prescriptive, and that recognizing its special character should not mean that we expel it from history and thereby cut its significant ties to modes of government and so-cial discipline that are routinely considered normal and comprehensible if not exactly benign. Adorno's rigorous speculations about the forms of ar-tistic creation that might be appropriate after Auschwitz remain a valuable source of further insights. Similar concerns can be voiced in a different key today, not only when we remember those horrors in a fashion that shows the immorality in seeking to place them exclusively behind us, but when we appreciate the continuing vitality of fascisms that seek to harness the national principle in the service of absolute ethnicity and its occult faiths.

Today's racialized political conflicts remain deeply connected to the mentalities that produced fascisms and the moral and economic logics that sanctioned them. The glittering careers of Jean-Marie Le Pen and Bruno Mégret are only the most obvious reminders that this is more than a British disease. In many countries, hostile responses to cultural, linguistic, and religious differentiation and fascistic enthusiasms for purity lie dormant within the most benign patriotic rhetoric and the glamour of national sameness it promotes. These difficulties arise from present conditions, and the nature and meaning of any links to past horrors are elusive. I want to suggest that some formidable moral and political challenges reside in the responses of European societies to contemporary racism and anti-semitism and that disputes over cultural value and the ethnic integrity of national cultures are central to them. These problems are posed by fortress Europe's official multinationalism and by its indifferent and intolerant attitudes to the presence of refugees, asylum seekers, and other "immigrants," many of whom turn out not to be immigrants at all, but rather settler-citizens who have enjoyed intimate and long-standing relationships to the history and culture of their unhomely homelands.

A suitably complex account of Europe's successive encounters with evil, ignorant, and primitive peoples generates neither a sequence of discrete episodes in some totalizing narrative of unreason nor the conclusive proof that heroic liberal, democratic, and humane values will always, inevitably, triumph over "dark" forces. Assessing the status of difference in Europe and for Europe generates important deliberations over what its supranational order will become. Current attempts to recreate Christendom in the teeth of antimodern Islamic fundamentalism have also given pride of place to culture. It is the essential medium in which the crusades of tolerance against its swarthy foes are now registered. The bodies of women provide the stage on which its dramas are enacted.[6] Evaluation of art and culture has provided one important opportunity in which the meaning, not of different cultures, but of cultural heterogeneity itself, is being tested out and worked through.

Some of the most useful questions so far identified in these conversations are the following: Can we improve upon the idea that culture exists exclusively in localized national and ethnic units—separate but equal in aesthetic value and human worth? What significance do we accord to the histories of imperialism and white supremacy that are so extensively entangled with the development of modern aesthetics, its storehouses, collections, and museums and the anthropological assumptions that governed their consolidation? How, if we can reject the over-simple diagnoses of this situation offered by ethnic absolutism, might we begin to frame a trans- or cross-cultural criticism? What role does expressive cultural creativity play in mediating or even transcending racialized or ethnically coded differences? What recognition do we give to the forms of non-national and cross-cultural practice that are already spontaneously under way in popular-cultural or disreputable forms, many of which have supplied important resources to the transnational social movement against racism?

We have already encountered how these questions were being addressed when the military struggles to liberate Africa from colonial rule were still in train. Frantz Fanon reformulated them in a different but nonetheless recognizable voice. His famous words bear repetition:

> It is a question of the third world starting a new history of Man, a history which will have regard to the sometimes prodigious theses which Europe has put forward, but which will also not forget Europe's crimes, of which the most horrible was committed in the heart of man, and consisted of the pathological tearing apart of his functions and the crumbling away of his unity . . . For Europe, for ourselves and for humanity, comrades we must work out new concepts, and try to set afoot a new man.[7]

Leaving aside for a moment the important issue of whether multiculturalism could be one of these valuable new concepts, we must reckon with the fact that Fanon comprehended this obligation via a binary code almost as pernicious as the manichean dualism that he sought to supplant. Recall that his overly stern liberationist perspective was an organic product of wars against Nazism and colonialism. It sprang from militarized social life in the colonial city. There, he noted that the zones inhabited respectively by colonizer and colonized were mutually opposed but that their opposition could not be reconciled "in the service of a higher unity."[8] For him, the distinctive political order and spatial rules that configured colonial segregation would be elaborated in the Apartheid system. They allocated people to two great camps—close but nonsynchronous worlds—that encountered each other only rarely. Fanon tells us that contact between them was mediated exclusively by the functional brutality of the police and the military, who enjoyed an essentially permissive relationship to colonial government through the flexibility of colonial law.

Today, in Europe at least, there is less justification for this stark dualistic diagnosis. The erstwhile barbarians are within the gates and may not live in a formally segregated ghetto or enclave. The frontiers of cultural difference can no longer be made congruent with national borders. The cities do not belong exclusively to the colonizers and their kin. Isolated areas in which elements of colonial social life persist and thrive can be identified, but these urban worlds draw their vitality and much of their appeal from varieties of cultural crossing—mixing and moving—that demand the proximity if not the presence of the Other. More than that, the cultures of the natives, not just their labor, can now be bought and sold as commodities. Their exotic achievements are venerated and displayed (though not always as authentic art) and the fruits of alterity have acquired an immediate value, even where the company of the people who harvested them is not itself desired. We have seen that selected elements of their culture are actively projected into the lives of the dominant group by cultural industries that make great profits from that operation.

No less than in Fanon's time, the occasional conflict between these groups is not something that can be resolved prematurely, neatly, or dialectically. It should certainly not be displaced onto a higher level or conjured away via the invocation of a more exalted unity. And yet, the expressive cultures that have grown up in these polyglot urban spaces—transnational and translational vernacular cultures—supply and celebrate a variety of interconnection that not only acknowledges interdependency but, at its insubordinate and carnivalesque best, has been known to project an immediacy, a rebel solidarity, and a fragile, universal humanity powerful enough to make race and ethnicity suddenly meaningless.

This worthwhile message was signaled long ago by Rock against Racism and the mongrel social movement that created its surrogates in various countries.[9] More than twenty years since it first appeared, that movement still moves, but more quietly and in de-centered, less formal patterns. Its effects are still conveyed in the underground club and rave scenes, in illegal radio broadcasting, and in the alternative public spheres that surround these initiatives. The most visible parts of this counterculture are still youth-based and assertively metropolitan in character, but the whole movement cannot be reduced to those attributes. A profound incompatibility with the pervasive moods of colonial and imperial nostalgia is more important in defining the forms of symbolic treason it promotes and the cosmopolitan and democratic possibilities they bring into being. A new style of dissidence is being reproduced in which discrepant forms combine, conflict, and mutate in promiscuous, chaotic patterns which require that the politics of influence, adaptation, and assimilation be rethought. Who, after all, is now being assimilated into what? The implications of this complex cultural amalgamation are repressed, and any political significance it may hold are routinely denied by spokespeople for all parties to this joyous transaction. This still-emergent means of living with and through difference is domesticated, truncated, and tamed in the multicultural initiatives of companies like Benneton, Coke, Swatch, and McDonald's. Brokered by Spike DDB and their peers, the glamour of difference sells well.

Comprehending the conspicuous successes of privatized multicultural commerce requires a revised genealogy of what used to be called "youth cultures,"[10] ideally one that can link analysis of these contemporary political phenomena with older issues like anxiety about the degenerative influence of black music on Europe's youth in the 1930s and 1940s. A different understanding of the place of "race" in Europe is waiting to be constructed from exciting material like Richard Wright's rich speculations about the aftershock of fascism. He linked the growth of interest in black culture to the immediate moral and political climate:

> To the degree that millions of Europe's whites were terrorized and driven by Nazism, to that degree did they embrace the Negro's music and his literary expression. Here was a development that white America did not foresee or understand. Hence, the Negro became to a large measure for Europe the one and only human aspect of an otherwise brutally industrialized continent.[11]

The main problem that we face in making sense of these and more recent developments is the lack of a means of adequately describing, let alone theorizing, intermixture, fusion, and syncretism without suggesting the existence of anterior "uncontaminated" purities. These would be the stable, sanctified conditions that supposedly preceded the mixing process and to which presumably it might one day be possible to return. Whether the process of mixture is presented as fatal or redemptive, we must be prepared to give up the illusion that cultural and ethnic purity has ever existed, let alone provided a foundation for civil society. The absence of an adequate conceptual and critical language is underlined and complicated by the absurd charge that attempts to employ the concept of hybridity are completely undone by the active residues of that term's articulation within the technical vocabularies of nineteenth-century racial science.

The density of today's mixed and always impure forms demands new organic and technological analogies. Its poetics is already alive and at large. Notions of mixing are being celebrated that owe nothing to the world of biology and everything to the skillful work of black hands on phonograph turntables released from one role as passive reproductive apparatuses and made productive through the act of doubling, which fostered a new creativity and ushered in a sense of infinite musical time. The problematic of origins appeared at an important point in the story of modernist racial and cultural typologies. Although it becomes irrelevant where the old dead skins of ethnic and racial particularity have been shed, it cannot be repeated too often that deconstructing "races" is not the same thing as doing away with racisms.

It is not so much that the multiple origins of these dense, compound forms are unknowable but rather that the obligation to discover them that was once so urgent appears now to be pointless and is disconnected from their legitimation and from their enjoyment. We do know where hip-hop, reggae, soul, and house originated and can identify the historical, technological, and cultural resources from which they were constituted, yet this information does not help either to place them or to assess their contemporary consequences. The modernist obsession with origins can be left behind as itinerant cultures are propagated by unforeseen means and proceed by unknown routes to unanticipated destinations. Traveling itself contributes to a sense of multiplicity for which utopian—technically placeless—patterns of cultural use constituted around popular music provide the most pertinent example. Chaotic cultural dissemination in more and more elaborate circuits itself enjoys a complicated relationship to the technologies that have conquered distance, compressed time, and solicited novel forms of identification between the creators of cultural forms, moods, and styles and various groups of users who may dwell far from the location in which an object or event was initially conceived. This art is dispatched in provisional and unfinished forms that anticipate further input and flow in a communicative economy in which creative recycling rather than immoral disposability is the regulative norm.

With its biblical force somewhat diluted, the idea of diaspora can be useful again here. It complements the antiphonic balancing of the hidden public sphere formed around making and using black music. Diaspora allows for a complex conception of sameness and for versions of solidarity that do not need to repress the differences within a dispersed group in order to maximize the differences between one "essential" community and others. Diaspora's discomfort with carelessly overintegrated notions of culture and its rather fissured sense of particularity can also be made to fit with the best moods of politicized postmodernism. Identity conceived diasporically resists reification in petrified forms even if they are indubitably authentic. The tensions around origin and essence that the diaspora brings into view allow us to perceive that identity should not be fossilized in keeping with the holy spirit of ethnic absolutism. Identity, too, becomes a noun of process. Its openness provides a timely alternative to the clockwork solidarity based on outmoded notions of "race" and disputed ideas of national belonging.[12]

The history of these subaltern political cultures' tangled associations with the rise and gradual globalization of the cultural industries is also germane. The corporate multiculturalism noted above has simulated their celebrations of difference and set a tame version of their patterns of cultural disaggregation to work as part of its marketing operations. These vernacular cultures have an ambivalent relationship with the corporate world and often articulate an open hostility toward it. The citation and simulation of these cultures do not reproduce their extensive ethical investment in face-to-face, body-to-body, real-time interaction. The distinctive privilege accorded to the process of performance and its rituals is already under pressure from the de-skilling of instrumental competences. Digital technology has precipitated a different notion of authorship and promoted a sense of culture that cannot be confined to legal and habitual codes that imagine it to be individual property.

This loosening of proprietary claims has also given the advertisers and iconizers an additional license to plunder and appropriate the vigor of racialized countercultures. The solidarity of proximity yields to the faceless intersubjectivity of communicative technologies like the Internet. The marketing of sports and sports-oriented commodities and the forms of heroism these operations require become a vitalist counterpart to the sedentary practice of staring into a screen. These are the perilous conditions in which investments in otherness emerge as a new vehicle for alternative values supposedly unsullied by capitalism, techno-science, and commerce.

Some of Europe's oldest romances with primitives and noble savages are being rekindled. What is euphemistically called "world music" supplies this moment with a timely soundtrack. We can appreciate the hunger for cultural forms that stand outside the immorality and corruption of the overdeveloped world, but imprisoning the primitive other in a fantasy of innocence can only be catastrophic for all parties involved. This danger is compounded when the interests of the romantic consumers begin to converge with those of people inside the minority communities who want to enforce another definition of invariant (and therefore authentic) ethnicity for their own dubious disciplinary reasons. Linguistic, traditional, and local particularities may all be in danger from the leveling effects of corporate multiculturalism, but in responding to that threat we do not have to choose between fetishizing and therefore capitulating to unchanging difference and its simple evacuation or erasure. There is a greater danger when absolutism is blindly endorsed by cultural institutions that fall back on an ossified sense of ethnic difference as a means to rationalize their own practices and judgments in a parody of pluralism which perversely endorses segregation.

In our period Fanon, whose work yields so many precious insights, becomes less than helpful precisely because his thinking remains bound to a dualistic logic we must now abjure in asking what the analysis of culture and the development of cultural politics (and policy) might contribute to the new humanism he called for thirty years ago. It is not now, or rather not only, a matter of the Third World's initiating a new, less triumphalist humanism that can be its own special gift to civilization, but a matter of building upon the narratives and poetics of cultural intermixture already alive inside Europe's postcolonial popular cultures in order to see how those polar positions have already been rendered redundant.

I am suggesting that in considering the status of difference we work to adopt a more future-oriented stance and that we make the most of our historic opportunity to rethink the whole question of how value is assigned to cultural forms and ethnic differences. In doing so we can encourage the unlooked-for contingencies of racialized value. This should be done, not so that we can say with an affected pseudo-toleration that everything is some-how suddenly as good as everything else, but so that we can speak with confidence from somewhere in particular and develop not only our transla-tion skills but the difficult language of comparative (not homologizing) judgment. This program is premised upon the idea that any discoveries we might make could transform our understanding of the cultures from which we imagine ourselves to speak, as well as the cultures we struggle—always imperfectly—to judge.

THE NEGRO IS ONLY BIOLOGICAL

Class divisions inside black communities have been highlighted by the emergence of postmodern consumer culture. However, rather than accept the economic and social logic of this historic change, ethnic absolutism has joined with nostalgic nationalisms and argued that "race" remains the pri-mary mode of division in all contemporary circumstances, that a unitary black culture is still essentially intact, and that an identifiable pattern of bodily experiences and attributes can serve to connect blacks regardless of their wealth or their health, their gender, religion, location, or political and ideological habits.

These doubtful propositions are entirely compatible with the cultural emphasis developed by corporate multiculture and the targeted ethnomarketing that requires global brands to communicate with con-sumers in a number of different tongues simultaneously. They have been severely tested by recent changes in the traditional, performance-centered expressive culture of the black Atlantic, where, against the expectations of both bio- and cultural-nationalists, class- and gender-specific responses to the loss of essential connectedness have been persistently evident. That vernacular culture can be used to examine the battle between fashionable and sometimes fascistic views that see the body as a cipher of absolute dif-ference and another perspective in which the body emerges bearing ironic confirmation of the essential similarity of species being. Until the color of skin has no more significance than the color of eyes, there *will* be war. Hostilities are being conducted on both sides of the color line.

We should follow Fanon here, too. There is more to say about the body, the patterns of solidarity and identification established by the body-world, and the processes of political anatomy, epidermalization, and nano-politics that occur there. We must remember, first of all, that the black body seldom speaks for itself. Some people will always see a scar on tortured flesh. Others prefer to perceive the more pleasing outlines of a chokeberry tree. Toni Morrison's *Beloved*, from which that striking image is taken, seems to me to suggest that, even if forgetting incorporated memories is impossibly difficult, the decision to set aside the claims of the flesh and break their special compact with past trauma need not always be unethical or illegitimate. Second, we should question the ways in which the body has emerged as an anchor in the stormy tides of identity politics. In Chapter 5 we saw that the body has become the means by which both individual freedom and racial solidarity are bound to life itself. These black bodies are no longer to be supervised by the souls that were once imagined to outlive them. There are no souls here; they have been banished by the fatal affirmation of carnal and corporeal vitality celebrated by Tupac, Biggie, and company. The enthusiasm with which this was undertaken recalls Fanon's disturbing observation about the importance of fantasies of bodily potency and activity in the motionless, manichean colonial setting—white supremacism's world of statues:

> The first thing the native learns is to stay in his place, and not to go beyond certain limits. This is why his dreams are always of muscular prowess; his dreams are of action and of aggression. I dream I am jumping, swimming, running, climbing; I dream that I burst out laughing, that I span a river in one stride, or that I am followed by a flood of motor cars that never catch up with me . . . the native never stops achieving his freedom from nine in the morning until six in the evening.[13]

Spike DDB and other corporate traffickers in black culture have become rich from ensuring that these are no longer *only* the natives' dreams. Similar corporeal schema have been solicited, projected, and mediated by new technological means and by cultural industries that substantially exceed the power of the radio, which captured Fanon's attention as a means of conducting revolutionary sensibilities into the counterpublic sphere of anticolonial Algeria. The successors to Fanon's leaping male native are visible everywhere in the image world of corporate multiculture. Their exceptional physical prowess lends its magical qualities to the sale of commodities like cosmetics, sports shoes, and clothing, all of which promote complex forms of mimicry, intimacy, and perhaps even solidarity across the line of color. You *will* believe a man can fly.

We do not know if Fanon had encountered Leni Riefenstahl's *Olympiad,* but his clinical research and his metropolitan wanderings led him to appreciate the significance of Joe Louis and Jesse Owens[14] (who was, incidentally, also one of the first athletes to appear in advertisements for Coca-Cola). Fanon's early presentiment of what would be a big historic change remains instructive and was all the more impressive for being made so long before the industrialization and commodification of health and fitness in which blacks have been so prominent:

> There is one expression that through time has become singularly eroticised: the black athlete. There is something in the mere idea, one young woman confided to me, that makes the heart skip a beat.[15]

Images of black vitality have provided the brightest flowers in the garlands of postmodernity, so bionationalists who see the body as supplying belated confirmation of racialized hierarchy have been especially eager to lay claim to it. Their bids have appeared in various forms, as arguments for substantive racial difference and even for black superiority. In either guise, they always operate in conjunction with the genetic and biological determinisms that are now being voiced, not only by the Bell Curve ideologues with their mechanistic biosocial science, but in comparably pernicious versions by a range of opinion from within the black communities themselves. I do not share John Hoberman's positive openness to the idea of biomedical racial differences, but his detailed critical enumeration of the damage done to black political interests in the United States by the racialized romance of sporting prowess is extremely valuable.[16] Common-sense debates over the meaning of black athletic achievement have mobilized new scientific theories and timeworn myths in equal measure. Aspects of scientific raciology and primitivism have been recycled and reworked in patterns that have proved attractive in the cultures of compensation with which many blacks answer their poverty and misery.

Pseudo-scientific, New Age, and occultist presentations of the pigment melanin as a dermal and nano-political measure of superior black physicality provide an interesting example of this popular tendency.[17] Published by independent presses and distributed through underground networks, this reversion to mystical, pre-Boasian accounts of racial difference enjoyed a considerable revival during the 1990s. A cautious and still nominally scientific version of these arguments has been offered by T. Owens Moore, a professor at Howard University, in *The Science of Melanin: Dispelling the Myths*.[18] His downbeat, New Age approach links these explosive themes to an anodyne discussion of the vitamin and mineral supplements recommended by "African-centered nutritionists" and marketed as PROMELANIN 2000 by Khem Sci Nutrition, Inc. The moral and political flavor of the melanist project emerges from the work of autodidacts like Carol Barnes, who is typically unconstrained by any scholarly protocol:

> What makes BLACK CULTURE? Why do BLACK HUMANS express themselves uniquely and differently from non-BLACK human species? Why do we . . . DANCE—SING—DRESS— WALK/RUN—COOK—LAUGH/CRY—PLAY THE GAME OF FOOTBALL/BASKETBALL—THINK—WORK ETC. . . . differently from other races? If you compare BLACK CULTURES around the world, you will become pleasantly aware that BLACK HUMANS are not different! From one end of the globe to the other end of the globe, you will find black humans are EXPRESSIVE—COLORFUL—CREATIVE—INDUSTRIOUS—GENEROUS —COCKY . . . just like your neighbor across the street or across town. All "Industries" created and designed by the BLACK HUMAN (and from his culture) will be "RICH" in essence and depth! Even when the BLACK HUMAN is poor, the resources he has to work with may be limited but the produce that he produces will be well prepared and EXPRESSIVE!
>
> The driving force behind this trait in the BLACK HUMAN is the chemical MELANIN![19]

I puzzled for a long time over these curious sentences, which in the images of neighborhood and community seem to articulate yearning for a lost scale of sociality as readily as they convey a taste for the vain alchemy of hypersimilarity and absolute invariance. Work is notably present in this segregated utopia from which biology has expelled all difference. This is a utopia that adds veracity to the oldest of racist stereotypes and reenergizes a worn-out Victorianism. Barnes's tropes of "humanism" are striking, too.

It is less surprising that the masculine prowess of the ball court and other popular representations of sporting excellence supply him with a key figure: they create the climate in which black superiority appears plausible. At last we can know *why* white men can't jump. But this is not the transcendence of race—washed away by the force of fraternal bonding—as it was in the film of that name. It is partly a reconciliation with older patterns for reifying race through the icons of black physicality. Most modern techniques for organizing the relationship between body and soul are renounced in the gleeful reduction of the black body to its biochemically programmed, natural physical superiority. These "expressive, colorful, creative, industrious, generous, cocky" racial selves are nothing but their bodies. "The negro is only biological," said Fanon. This is not a matter of black identity being chained to the body, for that would introduce the possibility of separation—of breaking the chains.

And yet even among the most ardent "melanists," the technologies of the racialized self make an inevitable appearance. Even under this iron law of racial biology, people have to be induced into the approved identity. They have to be taught how to recover and remember the potency of melanin in their organs and trained so that they can listen once again for the ways in which their bodies—conceived nano-politically and broken down here into the units of their cells—call out to them and to each other the siren song of collective (never individual) racial memory. An article in the British-based Afrocentric magazine *The Alarm* cautioned its readers:

> The rate at which one loses touch with Melanin's powerful influence on the spiritual self is directly related to the amount of European socialisation and "education" received . . . the avenues to our Melanin centres are partially blocked by our adoption of western diets, environmental pollution, and ways of thinking. Since Melanin acts like an antenna or highly tuned receiver, it will resonate in sympathy with whatever is going on in your environment. So if you surround yourself with negative forces (in your family, workplace, social life, or bad food you consume), they will alter physiologically and neurologically that which acts to preserve your Melanin.[20]

The article from which the above quote has been extracted discussed the role of melanin in transmitting messages from sound sources, especially low bass frequencies. In a similar mode, Owens Moore proposed this oddly antiquated program of melanist cultural research:

Today the drum is used in all forms of Black music. Rap music, in particular, is an African phenomena that deserves research. Rapping to music is no easy task and requires advanced brain functioning. Moving rhythmically, staying on beat, thinking, creating and remembering words is a skill mastered by very few outside the black community. The subcortical brain structures in the basal ganglia that are responsible for movement and the intercommunication between the two hemispheres, must function at a higher level of brain functioning in order to produce a musical form such as rap. Studies using the electroencephalograph could be conducted to measure the brain activity of skilled versus non-skilled rappers.[21]

With these sad proposals in mind, we can approach the planetary circuitry of black vernacular culture once again through the useful figure of R. Kelly. The shaven-headed crooner is also to be remembered because he built his career at the intersection of the emergent youth cultures based on sports and computing and those still residually based on music and dance. At that crossroads, Kelly celebrated the eloquence of the black body with his song "Your Body's Calling." Its characteristic affirmation of the freaky body's communicative powers should be a reminder that EXPRESSIVE black flesh can be made to speak in various tongues. Bob Marley's Rasta prophecy that there will be war until the color of skin is of no more significance than the color of eyes springs to mind again here, too, and not just because its recognizably anticolonial humanism continues to find new favor with peoples all over the globe. We are entitled to ask whether the dwindling idiom of Jamaican eschatology Bob favored was any less dynamically physical than the privatized sports-utility culture for which R. Kelly has been the best spokesman. Unlike the integral body favored by the disreputable female freaks and wholesome male athletes who seem to have supplied Kelly's inspiration in equal measure, Bob's powerful phrase sets the body against itself in pursuing the project of stripping white supremacism of its rationality. For him, the black body was neither whole nor integral. It could not speak with one voice. Eyes and skin, body components of equivalent communicative potential in the era before mandatory tattoos, transmitted opposed messages about the material truths of race and their social signification. That contested process of signification was identified as the principal issue.

The biopolitical impulse to present the body as a cipher of solidarity is common to a wider range of black political thought than these quirky examples suggest. It connects the out-and-out occultism of those who believe that melanin guarantees black superiority to the less obviously biologistic writings of more respectable scholarly folks who might even oppose some of the political positions adopted at the meeting point of eighteenth-century racial science and Americocentric millennial nationalism. The body and its semiosis have come to host a battle royal in which these different interests fight for the pleasure of annexing soma's special communicative powers in their contending representational regimes.

There is another, more mystical vogue for theories of racial particularity centered on the idea of common attributes coded into black flesh. We are often urged to discover those codes by undertaking what a fashion spread from the Los Angeles–based magazine *Image* (empowering the man of color) described as "the internal journey" in a photo-tableau that presented a selection of classy menswear modeled in a simulated African environment. A few pages later, the full import of this implosion was made explicit in an image that had also been reproduced on the cover of the magazine (see Fig. 1). Michael Gunn's poetry and photograph made the dimensions of this empowerment clear. It was patriotic, religious, masculinist, and exclusively oriented toward the past. It nonetheless affords real insights into the cultural condition of black America in the period between the police assault on Rodney King and the Nation of Islam's Million Man March. Gunn's words resonated very strongly in one of those periods in African-American political culture when the integrity of the "race" as a whole was being defined exclusively as the integrity of its menfolk. Their lowly status was identified as the result of a race-specific mode of masculinity that had been damaged by the operations of white supremacy through slavery and since. Black masculinity once again became the focus of restorative and compensatory activities that bore upon the race's capacity to act in pursuit of its own wider interests. This involved a political project that was understood along nationalist lines and which therefore depended all the more crucially on the minor nation's revolutionary power to reproduce itself in appropriately manly forms. Masculinity was both the necessary catalyst and the prized outcome of that reproductive process.

Michael Gunn's powerful representation of the ways African Americans suffer was used as the cover of *Image*.

The manhood of African Americans had to be renewed and repaired if their political fortunes were to be improved.

An elaborate literature of self-help, self-analysis, and self-worth has grown up around the idea that black masculinity can, in atoning for its failures and thereby redeeming itself, transform the plight of those who have undergone procedures of symbolic castration that deny them access to the personal and political benefits of authentic maleness. Without this intervention, long after slavery and Jim Crowism have been dismantled, black men would be doomed to remain mere boys in a world dominated and manipulated by the fratriarchy of real men whose superior status is conveyed in their common whiteness. Trapped among the tragic shadows cast by dead and larger-than-life heroes more likely to be drawn from the worlds of sports and entertainment than from the arena of official politics, the crisis of black life was plausibly and persistently but mistakenly apprehended as a crisis of black masculinity. On one side stood the wretched but peculiarly heroic figures of men like O. J. Simpson, Tupac Shakur, and Mayor Marion Barry, while on the other the well-intentioned demand for positive role models was being raised. Calls for gender-segregated education and the re-institutionalization of father-centered parenting could be heard amid a new fraternalist discourse on the multiple pathologies of matrifocal social life. Gunn's image was captioned with these lines:

> My country tis of thee
> This is what 400 years has done to me.
> I'm the man you brought here by force.
> I'm the man who worked your fields.
> I'm the man who fought wars I didn't even create.
> I'm the man who cleaned toilets I couldn't even use.
> Notice I don't desecrate the flag
> I hold it up trying to hold on to the idea of the "American
>   Dream"
> But the marks on my body give proof of my existence here.[22]

A more sophisticated version of some of these themes appeared during the same period in another polite neonationalist polemic contributed by the respected poet and academic Elizabeth Alexander to the catalogue of an exhibition entitled "Black Male: Representations of Masculinity in Contemporary American Art," held initially at New York's Whitney Museum.[23] In an extraordinary convergence with melanist concerns, she made the idea that American blacks shared a common, embodied social memory the central theme of her polemic against "anti-essentialist, post-identity discourses." Surveying the cases of Rodney King, Emmett Till, and Frederick Douglass according to an approach laid out by the distinguished literary critic Hortense Spillers, Alexander identified a "text carried in the flesh" composed of "ancestral" memories of terror. The traditional symbolic potency of mere blood was being recognized as insufficient. Somehow, this hidden "text" endowed black flesh with special cognitive capacities. It fixed the limits of the racial collectivity as a whole and allowed Alexander, avowedly operating beyond "the biological reductions of 'race' and the artifactual constraints of 'culture,'" to "talk about 'my people.'" At that moment, the people constituted an entirely undifferentiated political and historical subject that could be roused from its routine anaesthetized state by watching George Holliday's eighty-one-second videotape of Rodney King being beaten. The people's reaction was not the result of a righteous moral, political, or civic anger at this all-too-familiar injustice but derived instead from shared racial memory.

Alexander did not have an opportunity to discuss the body of the late Eazy E, but it can supply another contested exhibit for the bleak landscape of this dark continent. As with the more recent mourning triggered by the loss of those immortal figures Biggie and Tupac, the discomforting work of remembering Eric Wright, the originator of gangsta rap, provides an interesting supplement to Alexander's procession of respectable heroes. I don't know how many times Eric watched that historic videotape, but the melanin and race memory in his gangsta cells didn't stop him from supporting the claims of Officer Theodore J. Briseno—one of Rodney King's assailants. Unlike the melanists, Alexander does not explore the issue of how that common memory might be forgotten or which social mechanisms bear upon its repression and erasure.

Browsing through the June 1995 edition of *The Source* that commemorated Eazy's life and contributions to black vernacular culture raised for me the difficult problem of what can distinguish the memory work organized around his life and death from the social and cultural processes to which Alexander had drawn attention. Couldn't the "story-telling tradition" of which she was clearly proud be amended to include his complex narrative of individualism, indifference, and self-destruction and the resulting contest over the contemporary and future meanings of blackness that it indexed? Wasn't the narrating of Eazy's life and the forms of antiphony that it instantiated more significant than the damaged thirty-one-year-old male body at its center? Frank Williams's observation that "there was no politically correct shit with N. W. A. nor overt messages of Black empowerment, which dominated hip-hop at the time. It was straight up drinking, getting women and unloading your gat on some bustas"[24] gives some clues about the problems of slotting Eazy/Eric into a pantheon like Alexander's. In another echo of the melanist perspective, her argument presented the black body in itself. It is a whole repository of meaning, a conductor of racial memory that refused to be differentiated by class or gender, wealth, or health. The body was the final, special, ultimate, absolute truth of black identity that Alexander named the "bottom line." All those problematic intraracial divisions opened up by Eazy's death from AIDS to his celebrity, uncomfortable questions like poverty, politics, and power, could be conjured away at a single stroke. Racial politics became a matter of intertextuality as the Rodney King tape intersected with the memory tape carried in those black cells.[25] Gender, privilege, hierarchy, wealth and health; none of them mattered anymore. The body will take care of everything when solidarity is triggered into action by the sight of all that battered black male flesh.

Flesh that has been damaged by disease is less alluring, more uncanny in its impact than flesh marked by violence. For all its obvious complicity with the corporate pimping of black culture, at least *The Source* made the social work of commemoration complex and difficult. Though the masculinism and fraternalism integral to cross-over sales blocked most of its radical pretensions, the magazine used Eazy's death to produce a discussion over precisely how he should be mourned and remembered and what forms of solidarity might arise from that social activity. The following are some of the responses to those questions supplied by luminaries of the hip-hop nation:

Guru: Eazy E should be remembered as an entrepreneur.

Method Man: I feel like it's bad because he went the way he went, but it can be good if it gets the message out to the rest of us that this disease can hit home. There are a lot of brothers out there playing Russian roulette with their dick.

Masta Ace: I bought his first record a few months ago. When I listen to it now, certain lines have a whole new

meaning. When I hear him say, "It's about fuckin'
this bitch or that bitch . . ." it means something totally different now . . . I think one trend you'll see is
lots of rappers are gonna start getting married.[26]

I wonder what Dr. Fanon would have made of these strange postures?
Looking at them through the colonial frame, would he have identified the
comforting unanimist scenario advocated by critics like Alexander as a
fantasy of the more privileged groups, of a guilty elite somewhat akin to
that produced in colonial settings in the form of the native petite bourgeoisie? Surely he would have noted that the longed-for, racialized unity
was only perceptible, only plausible, from afar? As a medical practitioner
he might have been sensitive to the change of scale evident in the shift
away from the epidermal signification of difference toward the qualities of
differentiation projected nano-politically onto the cells themselves.

Alexander's epigraph was taken from the work of Saul Schanberg, a
medical researcher at Duke University who had been quoted in *Natural
Health* magazine. This citation communicates her leveling impulse perfectly in the claim that "memory resides nowhere, and in every cell." Regrettably, the suggestion was not clarified in Alexander's piece. Schanberg
presumably meant that it was shared by every cell in a single body, whereas
Alexander's essay suggests that every cell in the black body politic enjoys
the same recollective faculty. This tidy homology between cells and racial
subjects breaks down when we appreciate that cells are not interchangeable, even in one body, and further that the differences between cells taken
from different people, even those with similar phenotypes, may be telling,
particularly in the era of AIDS. Perhaps these small but decisive differences point toward a different conception of the significance of phenotypes in relation to genotypes and beyond that to the redundancy of
eighteenth-century racial typologies?

CLASS AND GUILT, THE OTHER G THAANG

Contemplating these attempts to resolve the crises of racial sameness and
solidarity by appealing to the power of the body drew me into a more be-
nevolent attitude toward the subversive profanity of black vernacular culture. Eazy E, Snoop, Willie D, Biggie, Lil' Kim, and their insubordinate

peers adopted a deliberately vulgar and disorderly stance that resisted discipline and pushed all the time toward the border zones where those stubborn divisions of region, class, sex, and gender reassert themselves and
refuse to be translated into invariant, epidermal, cellular, or nano-political
inscriptions. The boyz and girlz from the hood will not be drafted into the
program of racial recovery and uplift that has been proposed by their bet-
ters in the bourgeoisie. In contrast to the transcendent essentialism of
hypersimilar cells and interchangeable racial memories, the gangsta consciousness they celebrate is fiercely territorial. The form of solidarity it fa-
vors, if solidarity is recognized at all, is spatialized. The gs locate and
adhere to the lived boundaries of their community. This agenda assumes
an absolute minimum of a priori racial unity. It prompts our understanding of what solidarity adds up to in a dog-eat-dog world. MC Eiht, beside
whom Snoop and Eazy E sound tender and tame, has put it like this:

> Muthafuckas is successful now, right now. Everybody in this
> muthafucka got the mentality we don't give a fuck about what no-
> body say. Nigga gonna make his money, he gonna live like he
> wanna live. When that day come if a nigga got to die, that's the day.
> For the community—it always seems to me that eveytime a nigga
> get to a certain level he got to come back to the community and he
> got to put community centers etc. That justifies him saying, "Okay,
> I love the community and I'ma do something for where I'm from." I
> ain't dead, muthafucka. That's me. When I was in the muthafuckin
> neighborhood, I ran with the niggas. Niggas didn't put no money in
> my pocket, niggas wasn't givin' me no dope. Niggas wasn't doing
> shit for me except sayin', "He the homie." So for my community,
> I'ma make the music that my niggas like but I ain't gonna sit up
> here and go build me a child center over here and build me this over
> there 'cause that's fuckin bullshit. I'm in this shit for me . . . I ain't
> no political muthafucka. I ain't talkin about muthafuckin' stop the
> violence. I ain't talkin about the Black movement 'cause that shit
> ain't going on in the hood. Ain't no muthfucka comin' up with no
> bean pies standin' on my corner.[27]

Here the ghetto-centric individualism of the poor appears to have defeated
the convenient bioessentialism of the elite. You *choose* to be a gangsta and
you can renounce the affiliation at any time. Eiht states the consequences

of this changed orientation clearly when he derides the black voices raised against gangsta rap in these terms: "Them color-coated ass—I don't even call them Black, they ain't Niggas to me."[28]

Equally deep divisions have been revealed in bitter intraracial conflicts arising from vernacular discourse on sex. The body figures here, too. But again, it is not presented whole, as an organic vehicle for some common racial memory. Like the dog and the bitch whose nihilistic bonds were celebrated most powerfully by Biggie, the gangsta is driven by instinct—a form of memory not susceptible to regulation. You may recall that Snoop laments the fact that he cannot help chasing that cat. Nature is not the friend, guide, or ally that it appears to be in the discourse of the pseudo-scientists. It is a curse, another indefinitely suspended sentence. Just as it was in the Marley song, the body is fragmented, zoned. Different areas need to be worked in different ways. Moving far beyond Bob's innocent distinction between eyes and skin, the gs prize particular parts of the body. Selected zones are affirmed and celebrated because the space over which power can be exercised just keeps on shrinking and because they are closer to the disguised animal dimensions of vitality than to the purified, automatic body favored by melanists and memory merchants.

Here we are obliged to consider the way the black Atlantic has responded to the summons that Blackstreet and others have eulogized as a "booti call." The reevaluation of the booti/butt/batty is another element in the same desperate quest to center black particularity in the body. But it is not only a restatement of the traditional hedonism articulated in previous vulgar reclamations of the black body from the troubled worlds of work and labor or its celebration as a locus of resistance, pleasure, and desire. This is something more potent that reorders the hierarchy of body zones and organs in a pattern that moves decisively beyond the old oscillations between sex and violence that James Baldwin identified as alternate fillings for the shell of black cultural expression. bell hooks and Carolyn Cooper have pointed out that in different locations, the vernacular butt cult revalorizes the abject bodies of black women, but butt lore has another significance. The authoritarian aspect of the nationalist movements we have discussed requires us to recognize their obvious attempts to manage and contain the disruptive possibilities that emanate from homoerotic desire, introjected and otherwise. The anal penetration that is simultaneously affirmed and disavowed in hip-hop's injunctions to "grab your ankles baby" has no single fixed or eternal meaning. It acquires a variety of different accents in specific discursive settings. It is, after all, the fundamentalists who have made deviation from compulsory heterosexuality into a betrayal of racial authenticity. DJ Shabba Ranks, whose pronouncements in the area of sexual morality went beyond homophobia into a more complicated realm of ambivalence, shows how taboos regulating sexual practice have come to specify the limits of the racial collectivity: "I don't care what they want to say about me, so long as no one can say that I suck a pussy or fuck a batty."[29] The scar/chokeberry tree point can be made again here in order to underline the mutability and multiaccentuality of the black body.

In this vernacular, blackness has not been written into or even onto the body, for the body is not stable or still long enough to permit that act of inscription. It is not what the body is or carries inside it that counts but rather what the body does in its immediate relationship to other bodies. A mind-body dualism is not being covertly reinstated through appeals to memory over which a guilty, privileged "colonial" elite can preside. Blackness emerges as more behavioral, dare I say cultural? It can be announced by indicative sexual habits and other bodily gestures. Under some circumstances, it can even be acquired in simple economic processes. Identity as sameness and solidarity is definitely not being essentialized here. Items can be purchased that lend an eloquent uniformity to the mute body on a temporary, accidental basis. This is not an internal journey after all but a journey to the mall, preferably undertaken in an appropriately ostentatious form of private transportation.

Style and fashion offer something of the same forms of mechanical solidarity conferred by the uniform of the bourgeois male, which works a different racial magic for the Nation of Islam. In both cases, the unclothed body is not considered sufficient to confer either authenticity or identity. Clothing, objects, things, and commodities provide the only entry ticket into stylish solidarities powerful enough to foster the novel forms of nationality found in collectivities like the Gangsta Nation, the Hip hop Nation, and, of course, the Nation of Islam. This is not nihilism, for there is an axiology here—the axiology of the market. So much, then, for *cultural* difference. The African-American clothes designer Carl Williams, who sells his designs under the trademark Karl Kani, which has been tattooed into his upper-right arm, has told us that "appearance is everything," and he should know. His name is a question to which his clothing and accessories answer yes.[30]

Inside the black communities, old certainties about the fixed limits of racial identity have lost their power to convince or even make sense of the extreme divisions produced by de-industrialization. An ontological security capable of answering a radically reduced sense of the value of black life has been sought in the naturalizing powers of the body: clothed and unclothed, fragmented or whole. The old compensatory themes that answered black powerlessness—sex and gender—have been changed by the rise of body-centered nano-politics. The freaky program of sexual play and recreation celebrated by artists like Usher and R. Kelly appears as an alternative to the mechanical solidarity of "race," whether this is articulated through the austerity of the nation and its surrogates or through the fantasy of masculine hypersimilarity projected through the culture of black sporting excellence and the heroism cultivated there by marketing men and women.

Sex is more disorderly and unstable than the conventional images of black vitality that have become complicit with the core of white supremacism. Shabba's case reveals exactly how sex has to be trained, domesticated, diverted, and technologized into appropriate channels in order to ground the family and thus the nation. The body emerges in the double role of actor and contested object. It is being claimed by various regimes of representation and desire that create distinct forms of identification and usher in widely differing political possibilities that are not so conveniently arranged as to be mutually exclusive. Fashion spills over into the sports cult, which bleeds into the dreams of chemically programmed black superiority. Items of clothing are trafficked between the public, cross-over world and its hidden black counterparts. The discourses playing on, coding, and materializing black flesh promise power but can readily revert to simple racist type, especially where excessive physicality banishes cognitive capacities and wanton, equally excessive sexuality supposedly defines us outside the official syntax of gender. These dangers are not confined to the effect they may have on white spectators but can also be felt when blacks begin to live, not with, but through them and the doubtful forms of empowerment they can offer.

We need to follow the signposts of corporate multiculturalism and open up the interface between sports, music, video, and the sale of black culture to ever larger audiences far removed from the locations in which those cultures were first made. These are often, though not always, audiences whose enthusiasm for the fruits of alterity and the glamour of difference, especially when offered in appropriately gendered form, may not be matched by any equivalent enthusiasm for the people who produce the culture in the first place. The same obsession with masculine activity, power, and vitality that appears as an imaginary resolution of the crisis of black solidarity where the political community is reduced to the dimensions of a basketball court is also right at the center of selling black cultures, styles, and creativity simultaneously to a "cross-over" audience and an audience of insiders. Magazines like *Vibe* and *The Source,* in some cases serviced by prominent black commentators, have been at the forefront of this cross-over operation. A glance at the *Vibe* pages on the Internet will attest that these are not parochial matters. Imaginary blackness is being projected outward, facelessly, as the means to orchestrate a truly global market in leisure products and as the centerpiece of a new, corporately directed version of youth culture centered not on music and its antediluvian rituals but upon visuality, icons, and images. Retreating into the certainties of essential black embodiment will not deal with the cataclysmic consequences of this shift. Corporate multiculture is giving the black body a makeover. We are witnessing a series of struggles over the meaning of that body, which intermittently emerges as a signifier of prestige, autonomy, transgression, and power in a supranational economy of signs that is not reducible to the old-style logics of white supremacism.

Faced with that struggle and with de-industrialization, the proliferation of intracommunal divisions based upon wealth and money, sexuality and gender, the black elite may find it expedient to fall back on exceptionalist narratives and essential identities. It may even reconstruct them through a variety of political languages: melanin, memory, authoritarian nationhood, and Afrocentrism, or some combination of them all. I understand those responses, but I wonder how much they are about a privileged group mystifying its own increasing remoteness from the lives of most black people, whose priorities, habits, and tastes can no longer be considered self-legitimating indicators of racial integrity. The body is being used to restore that fading integrity in ways that abrogate the historic responsibility of intellectuals (not academics) to make it communicate the precious, fragile, and contingent truths of black sociality. In the face of reborn biopowers, is it possible to articulate an alternative, postanthropological understanding of culture that has anything like the same explanatory power?

FOR THE RECORD

Theories about culture are implicated in the divided world they strive to explain. There are too many well-fortified zones bounded by deference to the authoritarian claims that origins can make, where purity is prized and mixture and mutability arouse fear and distrust. But there are also precious moments when concern with the mechanisms of cultural transmission and translation must become a priority, when the promiscuous antidiscipline associated with complex cultural dynamics rewrites the rules of criticism and appreciation in novel, emphatically postanthropological codes. These periods direct attention away from the issue of origins and toward the vectors of traveling modern culture. They conjure up the problem of culture's routine and irreverent translocation. This is incompatible with the arcane desires of the butterfly-collectors who prefer their cultures integral and like their differences to remain absolute. Though their occasional appetite for national liberation and other schemes for ethnic conservation sometimes disguises it, they are Conservatives in the most precise and technical sense of that term.[31] Their increasing influence certainly offers no protection against the resurgent power of raciological thinking with which it has often been covertly complicit. For that reason alone, their arguments need to be answered in an assertive cosmopolitical mode that concedes nothing to either the primordialization or the reification of culture.

Of course the perils of globalization have unleashed some potent versions of national and ethnic absolutism.[32] They have been made all the more desperate and volatile by the destructive power of processes that flatten out cultural and linguistic variation into the blander, more homogenous formations in which elements of consumerism can take hold. Their fantasy of armored particularity reaches out from its starting points in the overdeveloped world. It links rational raciology not just to xenophobia and nativism but to new hostilities and anxieties conditioned by forms of jeopardy that have taken shape more recently. We must recognize the special spell cast by the glamour of purity and identify the varieties of fear and hatred that have been directed, not so much at the strange and the different, but with a new intensity at those whose difference or strangeness persistently eludes capture by the social and political categories available to make sense of it.

The anthropological tribunes of these complacent and ethnocentric conservatisms come well equipped with culturalist alibis for the refusal of political concerns. I wish to speak against them from a location where the old game of cultural authenticity is harder to indulge in and the profane components from which selves are composed are inescapably diverse. There is no purity around here, and the anxious desire for it is deeply distrusted as scarcely more than a dubious source of the cheapest political legitimacy.

For almost thirty years, I have been gripped by a passionate obsession with listening to music, most of it produced in parts of the planet far from the corner that I inhabit. Its distant sources were not part of the pleasure it afforded me. Whether they came to London from Cali or California, Trenchtown or Malaco, Mississippi, those tunes had to travel. Trafficking in them constituted an intricate circulatory network that overlapped with but was not dominated by the distributive systems of brash, indifferent overground commerce. In pleading against the charge of trivial consumerism, I would say that if that half-hidden web was remembered and reconstructed, it could usefully complicate our historical sense of cold war capitalism, its cultural industries, and the dissidence they unwittingly formed and disseminated. My experience with these objects is part of living through the final commodification of the extraordinary cultural creativity born from the slave populations of the New World. I have watched their oppositional imaginings first colonized and then vanquished by the leveling values of the market that was once, but is no longer, stimulated by commerce in live human beings. Any lingering countervalues are seen today as a pseudo-transgressive adjunct to the official business of selling all sorts of things: shoes, clothes, perfume, sugared drinks. In a sense, the black vernacular cultures of the late twentieth century were the death rattle of a dissident counterpower rooted, not so long ago, in the marginal modernity of racial slavery from which it had a conspicuous exit velocity. For a spell, plastic discs stuck with colored paper—"records"—furnished unlikely and unanticipated vectors for a restless, traveling sensibility. They became part of outer-national culture-making, and their history extends arguments about the role of communicative technologies in augmenting and mediating forms of social and political solidarity beyond the imagined communities achieved via the almost magical agencies of print and cartography.

It is worth remembering that world of sound now that it has almost departed—dispatched by the forces of rampant iconization. The slaves' aural bequest to the future was also notable for its interestingly dissonant relationship to the processes of its own commodification. This can be defined by a pattern of conflict that reveals much about the incapacity of capitalism to reconfigure the world instantly according to the rhythm of its own insatiable appetites. Even in the fixed and frozen forms demanded by the industrialization of culture, dissident, transcendent music was produced and dispatched radically unfinished. Its openness anticipated the involvement of remote audiences. They were keen to make supplementary, but nonetheless essential, creative input into the social use rather than the privatized consumption of a culture that could be only partially objectified. Two warring aspects of the social life of these special objects became entangled. The cultural life of recorded sound was not reducible to the simple economic relations in which it was enmeshed. Indeed, a whole tradition grew up around the idea that this music had a value beyond money, beyond the profits it made for those who sold it without regard to its ethical attributes, thinking, mistakenly, that they had its full measure.

As this historic period draws to a close and even its best residual features fall prey to the culture of simulation and iconization that impacts corrosively upon memory, time, and place, I am very conscious of having been shaped by a translocal, transcultural movement constructed on the "post-Bandung" planetary scale revealed by the movement of these loaded commodities. I call them "loaded" to underline the historic supplement they carry in addition to either their use or their exchange values. To the children of postcolonial settlers, a utopian black culture that had traveled west to east and south to north underscored the truths of a history of migration that was emotionally and politically close at hand but not always spoken. Perhaps, like slavery, it enclosed a trauma that resisted being turned into speech or writing? Of necessity, it founded new communicative media, used new vectors, and inhabited new hosts.

Alert to the special relationship that this sub-subculture had established between art and artifact, I amassed recordings on vinyl and immersed myself in the ephemeral and disreputable scenes that surrounded them. I could and probably should have paused at the point at which the printed and illustrated cardboard in which the music was clothed became almost as interesting to me as the sounds inscribed on the ridged surface of the plastic inside its seductive covers. Instead, I pressed forward, keen to comprehend the overall architecture of the non-national, cultural, and political formation to which these products became integral by refusing their official status as disposable and transient. The older, ethically charged communicative pattern they consolidated was born from the hidden public spaces of black Protestantism and then systematically adapted. It has been gradually crushed by new commodities, technologies, and desires. It is now being replaced by a culture of simulation that changes the value of blackness in the globalized businesses of information, entertainment, and telecommunication. The supercession of the analog by the digital is an appropriate symbol and symptom of these developments. Blackness as abjection gives way steadily to blackness as vitality, eternal youth, and immortal dynamism. The ideal body of the black male athlete or model now supplies a ubiquitous key signature for this strange theme. An exemplary black physicality, mute and heroic, has been conscripted into service to build a militarized and nationalized version of planetary popular culture in which the world of sports counts for more than the supple, subtle public relationships improvised around the gestalt of song and dance.

The transnational black movement with which I was affiliated was choreographed against the backdrop provided by the liberatory anticolonial violence of cold war politics. Solidarity with those important struggles provided a perverse training for emergent postmodern sensibilities. That movement discovered a bridge between the overdeveloped world and the colonies. It announced the resulting political claims through the language of rights and justice. Even when we reassured ourselves that we were dealing with human rather than civil rights, the tension around this debt to modernity was plainly evident. Civil rights derived from sovereign states and artful government, whereas human rights sought legitimation from other, more usually moral and spiritual, sources. They were the rights that the hybrid, populist art of Bob Marley and Peter Tosh assured us were worth standing up for. The new technologies of the free black self caught the postcolonial wind and were blown hither and thither, finding unexpected but nonetheless fertile resting places far from the territories where monocrop plantations had once been. They created and communicated an anti- and transnational ecology of belonging. They fed a vernacular anticapitalism and, most important, nourished a body of distinctive critical ideas regarding the place of "race" in relation to the goal of democracy and the workings of history from which Africa and Africans had been excluded by the unsentimental law to which Hegel gave such memorable expression when geography became the natural amphitheater in which the drama of History was to be played: "at this point we leave Africa, not to mention it again."[33]

These observations are intended to underline that the theories of inter- and multiculture that are currently available do not assist in capturing half of the stories we need to consider. It is probably uncontroversial to suggest that globalization needs a longer and more careful periodization than it has received so far. However, it also needs to be made part of reckoning with modernity on a planetary, rather than a parochial, Europe-centered scale. This latter task requires the specification of imperial and colonial modernities and conquest and plantation modernities. The issue of travel is frequently assigned to the margins of settlement that provide the premise of cultural life. It is made into the property of marginal people: migrants and refugees. To be sure, the idea that culture can travel has recently found a receptive audience, particularly among the international class in the overdeveloped countries. This de-territorialization yields insights, but there is always the suggestion that they have been too cheaply bought, too easily accomplished. Culture loses its adhesive qualities, and the romanticization of displacement is a persistent danger. It can combine disastrously with a willful forgetfulness about the constitutive, brutal force of imperial and colonial power. Unless we are careful, our reforms of the durable Hegelian scheme end up by fitting culture into the cracks between the fortified aggregations of encamped nation-states that previously provided its primary repositories.

There is more to do in order to disabuse ourselves of the illusions that follow from a sedentary understanding of culture-making.[34] We do not have to be content with the halfway house provided by the idea of plural cultures. A theory of relational cultures and of culture as relation represents a more worthwhile resting place. That possibility is currently blocked by banal invocations of hybridity in which everything becomes equally and continuously intermixed, blended into an impossibly even consistency. In opposing that unhelpful sense of cultural process, we must acknowledge and confront the eloquent arguments that have been made about the inescapability of ethnocentrism, about the necessity of being culture-bound. They assert a clean and logical split between particular "ethnic" attachments, which are seen as both inevitable and desirable, and the vicious forces that take shape under the banners of "race." If these two essentially dissimilar phenomena are linked, we are told, it is only by contingency. A long and authoritative pedigree descending from Levi Strauss is claimed for these arguments that routinely conceal their own political orientation behind a sham sophistication that marks the true connoisseurship of difference.[35] The desire for a rooted cosmopolitanism is opposed to a trivial and merely political distaste for racism. The same motive is professed as the source of principled objections to the encroachments of empty postmodernism and banal cultural studies.

In conclusion, I want to address the pessimism of the influential position from which Richard Rorty has reduced our options to a tense choice between privileging the group to which we belong and pretending an "impossible tolerance" for the rebarbative practices of others to whom one does not have to justify one's beliefs.[36] It should not need to be said that one is not necessarily affiliated with some single, overarching group that is always able to claim a special and fundamental allegiance that wipes out all other contending claims. It is more important to appreciate that different groups are constituted on different bases that correspond to the various frequencies of address that play upon us and constitute our always incomplete identities in an unstable field. Against a priori ethnocentricity, I would argue that raciologies and nationalisms promote and may even produce certain quite specific types of collectivity, characteristically those that are hierarchical, authoritarian, patriarchal, and phobic about alterity. The failure to engage with nationalisms as a historically specific power that connects the pathologies of contemporary racist movements with the history of European raciology and ethnic absolutism is a weakness. The related refusal to engage with the specific qualities of raciological discourses, the solidarities and modes of belonging that they promote, and the forms of kinship they both construct and project, compounds the problem. The mild and worthy "ethnocentrisms" that we are told we cannot and must not do without, are everywhere shown to be eagerly compatible with the palingenetic forms of populist ultranationalism that represent the mythic core of a generic fascist minimum.[37]

The pious counterposition of good or unavoidable ethnocentrism against regrettable but exceptional racism is an empty charade favored by those who evade and mystify the moral and political responsibilities that fall to critical commentators in this most difficult of areas. Are we to accept that culture can be racialized and nationalized? The choices are clear. Are ethnic groups overwhelmingly national and "racial"? And on what scale is group solidarity to be practiced and recognized: room, street, neighborhood, city, region, state; blood kin, species kin, planetary kin? Even if we were to accept the unitary, fundamentalist form of belonging to an "ethnos" outlined by Rorty and turned into catechism by his less sophisticated disciples, there is nothing to suggest that the boundaries around that version of monadic collectivity must inevitably coincide with the arbitrary political borders of contemporary "ethnic" groups. Belonging-together can make just as much sense either below or above that fateful threshold, and politics, sent packing by raciology, needs to be reactivated, not closed down. This dispute over the status of culture and its claims upon individuals entails a further quarrel with the way politics itself is to be understood.

Against the fashion that would reassign these sibling concepts—politics and culture—to separate and contradictory domains, I want to join them, or more accurately, to relish the fact that they are already inescapably joined both by the idea of politicized art and by the currently unfashionable notion of a politics of everyday life. Politics is still frequently conceived as though it, too, existed exclusively within the confines of closed national borders that are aligned precisely with those of sovereign governmental authorities. This idea can still hold, even when the official goal of multi*culturalism* arrives to force a degree of reconceptualization in the way political pluralism is understood. In that case, the nation emerges as an organic receptacle for several discrete, impermeable, and ultimately incompatible formations. These days, each one is usually understood as a market, entire in itself.

Estrangement from the nation-state has been consolidated by a contemporary mood in which the commitment to nationality as an overriding, ethically charged or ethnic community has become harder to sustain. The political technologies that solicited national belonging are very different now from what they were in the age of industrialized culture. And yet the dream of naturally national cultures is still alive in the midst of a phantasmagoria of invented traditions that does not allow the tidy separation of civic (good) and ethnic (bad) nationalisms. The resurgence of spectacular commercial sport at the core of the "infotainment telesector" is the most telling feature of its renewed power.

We have entered what is, by Hegelian standards, a condition of post-History in which Africa and its contemporary fate are able to emerge as significant political and moral issues. The histories of imperial modernity that will follow this long-overdue adjustment offer a timely alternative to Europe-centeredness with its overly innocent notions doggedly centered on the fantasy of progress without catastrophe. In grudging response to this new predicament, the nation-state is still being defended as the least-bad version of governmental practice. It is still presented as the only available arrangement for organizing the essential task of administering justice and orchestrating long-term projects toward cultural recognition and economic redistribution. In my view this is an overly defensive, unimaginative, and unnecessarily pessimistic response. It finds nothing worthwhile in the history that links modern commerce to the formation and development of race-thinking or in the extraordinary record of translocal movements from antislavery and feminism to Médicins sans Frontières. Symptomatically, it concedes no influence to the power of feral art or of other patterns of culture, solidarity, and affinity that have worked, rather like my precious records, in wider orbits and founded translocal circuits, unpredicted and underappreciated. A postanthropological understanding of the human condition is only the most basic prize awaiting the re-animation of political culture simultaneously on subnational and supranational scales.

8

"RACE," COSMOPOLITANISM, AND CATASTROPHE

The question of why people love what is like themselves and hate
what is different is rarely asked seriously enough.

—ADORNO

The present war of our enemies is a struggle against the foundations
of all European nations. A flyer sent out by political gangsters who
lets down his bombs on the most beautiful cultural places of Europe
does not know what he does, he has not the slightest idea of what
culture is altogether. And when the USA lately goes so far as to put
Negroes on its bombers, this shows how that country, once founded
by Europeans, has fallen.

—ALFRED ROSENBERG

"Whenever I hear the word cul-
ture, I reach for my gun." Recalling these famous words, uttered not so
long ago by an infamous Nazi, ought to inhibit the academic fluency with
which the word "culture" is currently being tossed about. His words are
cited here in order to communicate an important invitation: they ask us to
comprehend the fragile nature of the political environments that support
the cultures of dissidence that have been constituted by contemporary opposition to raciological codes and hierarchies. Reflecting on the horrible
context in which those words were first uttered and thinking about the

deadly pattern of institutions that fitted around them can help us identify the very different ways in which dissenters from racial observance still inhabit a beleaguered niche.

The widespread conflict between neo-fascism and its democratic opponents has regularly been manifested as a struggle over culture and its relationship to fundamental values. One of the principal architects of Sarajevo's destruction was Nikola Koljevic, the vice-president of the Bosnian Serbs and the author of eight books on Shakespeare. He is said to have had the city's National Library specifically targeted for bombardment because it was a symbol of the cultural hybridity and intermixture that he hated. Similar anxieties over the corrosive effects of cultural mixture are routine on the ultra-Right. Cultural conflict has, for example, been evident in recent battles in France centered on local government authorities controlled by the neo-fascist Front Nationale. There, the ultra-Right is pursuing a crusade against the subversive and unworthy culture of the Left, immigrants, and other groups it regards as alien or unpatriotic. The Front's vision of proper, purified French culture has committed it to the censorship of school and other public libraries. Its ultranationalist utopia has been defined against the outrageous activities of dissidents like the hip-hop group Nique Ta Mère, banned from rapping in November 1996 by a magistrate in Toulon, and the cinema manager in Vitrolles, near Marseilles, fired for refusing to withdraw films depicting homosexuality. Also in Vitrolles, the Front had unacceptable modern sculpture removed to the local rubbish dump.

Culture and its institutions not only furnish the index against which national decline and rebirth are to be measured, but also provide the primary battleground on which the fascists seek to establish their moral authority. The historian Saul Friedländer has pointed out the importance of the cultural struggles that characterized the early stages of anti-semitic violence in Nazi Germany. The cultural domain, he wrote, "was the first from which Jews (and 'leftists') were massively expelled."[1] It would trivialize the history that followed these conflicts over culture to suggest that they led inexorably and irreversibly to the gates of the death factory. However, conflicts over cultural values, hierarchies, institutions, and relations can still function as a crude barometer for changing levels of political pressure. Their recent history in neo-fascist France and elsewhere suggests that we now need a more complex picture of these cultural battles than the one in which a self-proclaimed and therefore easily identifiable Nazi reaches for a firearm in order to extinguish culture, to kill its bearers and advocates.

Following the contours of earlier varieties of ultranationalist thinking, the first Nazis claimed culture for themselves. Their raciology made the Aryan and the German its historic custodians. They selected and judged culture. They estimated which races were capable of cultural development and pronounced the apparent culture of the Jew to be nothing but a sham.[2] Their extensive anthropological competencies gave them the confidence to calculate what culture to promote and which of its degenerate forms to suppress and destroy.[3] The need to combat the resurgent fascisms of our own time is a reminder that we must always be alive to the preeminent place of "race" in making and legitimating these cultural and political judgments.

Long before the Nazis, the civic language of culture had been intermingled with the ideas of "race" and national character. Their interconnection provided a principle of differentiation that had competed with the alternative models proffered by late-nineteenth-century political biologies. After 1945, the effects of the Nazi genocide made respectable academic opinion shy and cautious about openly invoking the idea of racial difference in purely biological terms. In those conditions, the concept of culture supplied an alternative descriptive vocabulary and a more acceptable political idiom with which to address and simplify the geographical, historical, and phenotypical variations that distinguished racialized inequality. Reworked and rethought in line with the older imperatives of pragmatic anthropological reason, this version of culture supplemented and then supplanted the raciology that had been discredited by the wholesale implementation of industrialized race-hygiene.[4] In these new circumstances, culturalist theories of racial difference, which had been present for a long time but were muted by the conspicuous successes of political biology, could once more take wing. The varieties of violence and brutality that they sanctioned were no less barbarous than genocidal expressions of biopolitics had been. It bears repetition that "race" provided the common denominator for all these operations; however, its primary but ambivalent associations with culture have not always been recognized, let alone subjected to the careful analysis they merit.[5]

The contested status of the concept of culture has, of course, been well understood by commentators from a variety of political positions. More than a century of explicit debate over the cultural dimensions of power, national government, and class antagonism has not obscured the fact that culture retains another set of meanings that underpin but also resist the political conflicts that emerged with its pluralization, racialization, and ethnification. In English at least, though strongly inflected by class and its hierarchies, the concept helped to signpost the wholesome and attractive alternatives to anarchy, barbarization, nihilism, and anomie. It suggested not the mechanistic application of inhuman, modern reason but the organic growth of social life inside stable territorial boundaries. It can still bring to mind the promotion of mutuality and creativity in an imaginative regime that reaches toward the realization of collective truth, beauty, and right. Nonetheless, as Robert Young has shown, even that culture's energy and history were identified as products of a great racial dialectic between contending instincts of Hebraism and Hellenism.[6]

In Chapter 2 we saw this distinctly modern and imperial understanding of culture being nationalized and particularized in the sovereign, imperial space of "encamped" nationalities. We have traced some of its transnational circuitry and considered some of the communicative connections—both negative and positive—that it established. We now need to turn in a different direction. Our concern with moral and political humanisms, albeit with the rare and delicate varieties that can only be found in the very jaws of catastrophe, requires us to consider what happens when the idea of culture is usefully and constructively deployed at a different level of abstraction. There, it need no longer be hierarchical, race friendly, or ethnic, and it allows more obviously ethical and aesthetic problems to reemerge in the consolidation of democratic and cosmopolitan formations that are not only humanist but also hybrid, impure, and profane.

With these concerns to the fore, this lengthy chapter begins with an unapologetic reminder of how deeply culture has been associated with "race" and then moves toward a related issue: not the role of "race" and raciology in the destruction of culture but the prospective significance of cosmopolitan culture in the eventual erasure of "race." The acknowledgment of anxious Nazi antipathy toward culture with which I opened the chapter should not therefore be misunderstood. The reconfiguration of culture according to the racialized patterns demanded by totalitarian government yields an extremely complicated history that has significant implications for the way the relationship between normal and exceptional regimes is still to be understood.

Although elements of fascist culture, style, art, and governance are residually present both inside and outside contemporary democracy, the emergency that fed them in earlier periods has faded away. Today's emergency is no longer an acute, exceptional condition or critical phase that exists for a limited duration before things revert to their more stable, normal state. This emergency is a chronic, routine condition to which we are increasingly habituated. Our national governments with their supranational struggles against terrorism, fundamentalism, and disorder, and our routinely transnational mediascapes, have obliged us to accept the place of the exceptional alongside and within the normal. These two conditions can coexist readily in a world where cosmopolitan and itinerant cultures are besieged and sometimes engulfed by nationalisms and ethnic absolutism. As civility, as everyday creativity, and as hope, those cultures are pitted against the system of formal politics and its numbing representational codes. Their democratic aspirations are opposed by the dehumanizing values of multicultural commerce and the abjection of the postindustrial urban life with which they are intertwined. In these conditions, culture is assailed by political movements and technological forces that work toward the erasure of ethical considerations and the deadening of aesthetic sensibilities. The resurgent power of racist and racializing language—including modern anti-semitisms, ultranationalisms, and their sibling discourses —constitutes a strong link between the perils of our dangerous time and the enduring effects of past horrors that continue to haunt us.

MODERNISM'S NEGATIVE LOYALTY TO MODERNITY

Modernist artistic practice grew up where modernity's countercultures had taken root. It was enhanced by the fact that it was destined to be perpetually impure and was thus, by the ethnocentric standards of nationalist cultural criticism, chronically illegitimate. The Nazis denounced its degenerate expressions of a disgusting "halfness," but, loyal to art only, modernism reveled in the transgressive potential endowed in it by its hybrid constitution. It was reconstituted and redefined once the link between progress and evolution was seen to have been broken, above all by the cataclysm of the 1914–1918 war. That modernist culture has appeared as a profane force quite capable of cutting through the knots of immiseration, consolation, and resistance that characterized equally modern unfreedoms. Its expressive and creative forms, which playfully but wisely announce that they have no right to exist but stubbornly refuse to die away, have borne witness to the fragile human truths of the catastrophic modernity that I have employed in this essay to connect the colony and the metropolis.

Transforming the practice of cultural criticism so that it can correspond to this new object requires a considerable change of perspective. Among other things, it asks that we become more sensitive to the existence of modernity's ethnic and racialized countercultures and more attentive to the systemic conditions in which they have been able to reproduce if not exactly to thrive. Face to face with the precarious, endangered condition of cultural values, these adjustments need not mean that critiques of modernity lose their bite. Writing from the icy core of the cold war, the black Atlantic expatriate Richard Wright outlined a "negative loyalty"[7] to modernity that he felt could be made compatible with the difficult, urgent work of maintaining a sense of Western culture's irreducible antinomy— its dialectic of enlightenment—and, even more important, of making that apprehension politically and ethically useful in the development of agonistic, raceless democracy. Following these pointers, we can aspire to forms of democracy capable of resisting racialization and its distinctive hierarchies and of answering the powerful appeal of nationalisms with a cosmopolitan utopia. Wright articulated this goal through questions directed at his postwar peers who were struggling with the practical tasks involved in fighting colonialism and in building postcolonial institutions in the newly independent, formerly colonized countries:

> How can the spirit of the Enlightenment and the Reformation be extended now to all men? How can this accidental boon be made global in its effect? That is the task that history now imposes upon us. Can a way be found purged of racism and profits, to meld the rational areas and rational personnel of Europe with those of Asia and Africa?[8]

Wright's intellectual and political journey describes a complex species of dissidence that arose after 1945 in Europe and its colonies. An understanding of tainted modern culture's foundational relationship to racialized violence and terror was central to the culture of dissent it created. His insights, which were common to many among the Bandung generation—the postcolonial elite charged with applying the moral and political lessons to be learned from victory over the Nazis to the processes of decolonization and desegregation—had been nurtured by further disturbing realizations. Racial science, racialized reason, and the enforcement of their boundaries around official human status were not straightforward or simple aberrations from more noble or consistent standards.[9] More equitable and inclusive definitions of humanity could not be summoned into being by positive declaration. This was especially true where worthy goals such as liberty and equality had been debased in the unjust racialized surrogates promoted by the workings of empire and colony. If the extent of the bitter process first identified by Wright and his peers has now been fully appreciated, something more is called for than a routine defense of the same moral and cultural values that shone all the more brightly when confronted by the barbarities that might once have been mistaken for their simple negation. We can shed the convenient fantasy that civilization and barbarism stand opposed to each other in a tidy zero-sum arrangement or conflict only in the comforting pattern of a dialectical antagonism that promises resolution.

As shown in Chapter 2, much of the special authority associated with the term "culture" in modern Europe was worn away by the stresses of maintaining colonial civilization. The bloody histories on which that observation is grounded have had to acknowledge the power of raciology. They have repeatedly communicated the complicities of civilization with barbarity, rationality with terror, and reason with unreason. However finely grained they may be, local histories of Europe's failures are not sufficient sources of insight into these translocal matters. They struggle to strike a balance between two standpoints. On one side, there is the need for a meticulous fidelity to uncomfortable historical truths, which can sometimes feel parochial. On the other, there are bigger, bolder claims made through abstractions that may be born from the highest motives and directed toward the emergence of a misanthropic universalism but that sometimes sound hollow. Although the former remains an essential aspect of demands for justice, it inevitably truncates the almost alchemical power of racial discourses to transform one element of each unhappy pairing into the other. The latter redeem themselves through their cosmopolitan intent and an ability to answer the prescriptive force of absolute particularity, especially when it is articulated in the language of ethnic and therefore cultural incommensurability.

The tension between these two emphases appears in the shadow of a further, more shocking realization. It represents a profound source of shame and discomfort for all would-be practitioners of Wright's negative loyalty. At the cost of oversimplification, let me recall another argument that has been touched upon in earlier chapters. Ancient, prescientific racial myths, fears, and typologies were mobilized around the modern racial sciences of the nineteenth century. Bound together with the languages of enlightenment, progress, order, and social health, this combination afforded moral and practical sanction for genocidal racisms long before goals of this type were openly voiced as governmental objectives in Europe itself.[10] This argument merits repetition because even now, the philosophical and historical complexity of this process persistently slips through critical fingers. It evades reputable methods and repels the gaze of inquiries premised upon the legibility of evil and the transparency of the irrational. Appreciating the substantive power of raciology can make the previously incomprehensible appear suddenly obvious.

This partially explains why "race" remains an uncomfortable problem for the humanities. Of course, the task of explicating it is too frequently assigned to blacks, Jews, and other Others as if it were our special intellectual property or some exclusive "ethnic" responsibility associated with histories of suffering. The humanities are still dominated by particular liberal and, I would suggest, sometimes ethnocentric assumptions about what counts as knowledge and where the renunciation of particularity fits into the pursuit of truth. This is a problem not just for Jews or blacks, but for anyone who rejects the idea that the unmarked place from which academic protocols oblige us to speak extracts no price for the loan of its authority. Now that irrefutable accusations of "political correctness" have made too many good people uncomfortable and defensive about professional standards and their compatibility with serious interdisciplinary work, "race" has attained the status of an open secret. The word summons up a catalogue of intellectual and political puzzles that is intermittently displayed (sometimes prominently) and yet systematically overlooked, forgotten, and ignored in embarrassed silence lest the charges stick, and contemplative, disinterested scholarship capitulates to the noisy demands of ill-disciplined diversity and insurgent multiculturalism.

The history of the relationship between racial typologies, cultural difference, and mass killing is extensive enough to provide a license for these continuing investigations into "the fatal ingenuity" of civilized man. That history confounds the bold lines we would like to place between the industrial and preindustrial, the primitive and modern. In this zone, the Nazi's words about reaching for his gun can serve a vital mnemonic function. They help us to comprehend the ethnocidal energy released in the conjunction of raciology and culture. They can be used as a means to recollect how the stakes of life and death were made intrinsic to the deployment of that overloaded word "culture."

WITNESSING CATASTROPHE

The tension between local histories and cosmopolitan abstractions has also been resolved in the histories of travel and traveling that have contributed to the cosmopolitan ideal since Montaigne.[11] The translocal experiences of the elite black intellectuals who arrived in interwar Europe to claim the cultural prizes represented by an education in the colonial mother country have already been employed to update and refine this very possibility. I have drawn attention to their complexity and the distinctive, humanistic tones audible in their insiders' critiques of Western modernity. Their grasp of its unprecedented opportunities and their frustration at the damage done to it by raciology were profound. I have also argued that the theories of culture, right, and justice that they salvaged and bravely offered to the decolonizing, cold war world had been shaped by their observations of fascism's consolidation prior to the outbreak of conflict and by their experiences in the war against it. In particular, their exploration of connections between the abominations perpetrated by Hitlerism and those wrought by the colonial order from which they had both suffered and benefited would generate authoritative moral resources. Nowhere are these more powerful and articulate than in Senghor's poem "Tyaroye," a concentrated expression of his outrage against the 1944 French massacre of Senegalese colonial soldiers who had returned from four years of incarceration by the Nazis.[12]

A similar sensibility would be used later by other leaders of the Bandung generation to indict the ruthless logic of capitalist economic development and the failures of complacent and stubbornly color-coded liberal traditions of understanding politics. That argument can be complicated and extended here by making another detour en route to the destination favored by these thinkers: a credible, postanthropological, and resolutely nonracial humanism. It involves considering the normative and ethical character of a distinctive cosmopolitan culture manifest in the lives and experiences of wartime black Atlantic itinerants and their successors: workers as well as students. These may have been fugitives from the United States seeking both culture and liberation from Jim Crow; soldiers in pursuit of the citizenship and recognition they imagined they could find only by staking their lives on the battlefield in defense of their countries; or numerous other postwar travelers, some of whom were drawn into extremely complex relations of affiliation with Europe and its cultures through their participation in cleaning up after the conflict with Hitler. All these groups encountered aspects of fascism. Their reflections and commentaries on its preconditions, its characteristics, and its consequences led them in interesting directions that can have a bearing upon the constitution of European identities today and Europe's multicultural future tomorrow. In necessarily simplified form, their story begins not with the Second World War but with the cultural and historical rupture represented by the First.

The extensive deployment of colonial troops in the 1914–1918 war is as well known as its pivotal significance for black Americans. The latter is usually assumed to reside in the large-scale internal migration northward that accompanied American involvement and in the marked changes in the political atmosphere that greeted the returning troops.[13] Against the assumption that the conflict in Europe was remote from African-American concerns, some influential commentators immediately identified the moral and historical importance of the war with Germany. In his 1918 volume *Africa and the War,* Benjamin Brawley argued that "the great war of our day is to determine the future of the Negro in the World,"[14] and in a notorious editorial for *The Crisis,* Du Bois, who had lived in Germany for a significant period of time, proudly traced his own European ancestry to French and Huguenot rather than Anglo-Saxon sources. Although he had long recognized the imperialist character of the war, he spelled out the opportunities that it nonetheless might bring to advance the desperate position of his community. In what was a substantial change of political orientation for the magazine, which has sometimes been cited as evidence of Du Bois's weakness and vanity,[15] he argued that black Americans' participation in the conflict had to be wholehearted even if they had no obvious or immediate interest in it:

> This is the crisis of the world. For all the long years to come men will point to the year 1918 as the great Day of Decision, the day when the world decided whether it would submit to military despotism and an endless armed peace—if peace it could be called—or whether they would put down the menace of German militarism and inaugurate the United States of The World.
>
> We of the colored race have no ordinary interest in the outcome. That which the Germans represent today spells death to the aspirations of Negroes and all darker races for equality, freedom and democracy. Let us not hesitate. Let us, while this war lasts, forget our special grievances and close ranks with our fellow citizens and the allied nations that are fighting for democracy. We make no ordinary sacrifice, but we make it gladly and willingly with our eyes lifted to the hills.[16]

Du Bois may well have penned these words with a commission in the U.S. army intelligence corps in mind, but his substitution of "the world" for "America" is telling. It directs us toward the tension between his local, parochial, and more cosmopolitan commitments. Apart from the obvious idea that a preparedness to sacrifice life in pursuit of national interests was a means to bring the utterly subversive idea of black citizenship to belated life, his words also convey the more significant realization that democracy was not divisible. There are some significant changes of conceptual and imaginative scale here. First, the struggles of black Americans were boldly translated into issues for the world as a whole. Second, Du Bois articulated a transnational dimension to African-American politics that is closely associated with his increasingly Pan-African outlook. This was made urgent in the aftermath of the war by the proposal that Germany's newly liberated African colonies should become the nucleus of a new African homeland. This sensitivity would flourish in the four Pan-African congresses held between 1919 and 1927, three of which occurred on European soil, and it was entirely congruent with Marcus Garvey's parallel arguments in favor of what he called "international racial adjustment" for the Negro.[17]

Du Bois arrived in France in December 1918 to investigate the wartime treatment of black soldiers on behalf of the National Association for the Advancement of Colored People (NAACP) and also to gather materials that could be used to write a history of the war. Only a small proportion of African-American troops had attained combat roles, and the majority of them were poorly treated by the U.S. army. The achievements of a few, particularly of the four regiments of the 93rd division who, in one of the war's strangest developments, fought bravely under the French flag, provide the best starting point from which to consider the large historical and cultural shifts precipitated by the passage of the American Negro into the life and mind of Europe. It was not only that the black soldiers who had fought in France brought back militant knowledge of how narrow and specific the American regime of racial stratification had become, but that they were also exposed to a variety of timely political and cultural influences, including Bolshevik communism and nationalism. The unprecedentedly bloody summer of antiblack violence that greeted their return to the United States charged these discoveries with a new significance as they faced a revival of the Klan in what John Hope Franklin has called "the greatest period of interracial strife the nation had ever witnessed."[18] This political turbulence was matched by changes in the cultural life of Europe.

The difference between these Western blacks and the other colonial soldiers had been fully appreciated. Setting aside the effects on military thinking of their successes in combat, and of the conflicts between European and American authorities about the consequences of race-mixture that would recur in the war against Hitler, it is significant that the military was the most important means through which attractive and exciting aspects of black American culture were first introduced into the heart of Europe. The appeal of African-American military bands began an elaborate process whereby European popular cultures would eventually be revolutionized. The famous 369th infantry was noted for both the excellence of its music and its battlefield exploits during a period of 191 days in combat, longer than any other regiment in the Allied Expeditionary Force.[19] Under the overall direction of Lieutenant James Reese Europe,[20] the regimental band was also guided by its drum major, Noble Sissle, who had made a study of the effects of the band's interpretations of ragtime on French audiences:

> We have quite an interesting time playing our homeland tunes for the amusement of every nationality under the sun . . . When our country was dance mad a few years ago, we quite agreed with the popular Broadway song composer who wrote: "Syncopation rules the nation, you can't get away from it." But if you could see the effect our good old "jazz" melodies have on the people of every race and creed you would change the word "Nation" quoted above to "World" . . . I sometimes think if the Kaiser ever heard a good syncopated melody he would not take himself so seriously.
>
> If France was well supplied with American bands playing their lively tunes, I'm sure it would help a good deal in bringing home entertainment to our boys, and at the same time make the heart of sorrow-stricken France beat a deal lighter.[21]

The interwar period saw a steady flow of remarkable African-American performers, singers, and musicians pass through the breach these bands had consolidated and transform the musical, theatrical, and artistic life of Europe's capital cities. After spells in London and Paris, Sam Wooding's "Chocolate Kiddies" revue, which featured an eleven-piece band playing material scored by Duke Ellington, opened at the Berlin Admiralspalast in May 1925.[22] Josephine Baker had worked with Sissle in the United States and would herself eventually capture the rapturous attention of Berlin. A few months later, on the back of the Kiddies' popular triumph, she arrived in Paris, where Louis Armstrong had already performed, to star in *La Révue Nègre*.[23] By the time of the 1929 stock market crash, when well-heeled African Americans were setting out to see Europe in unprecedented numbers, European demand for authentic black entertainment had increased so much that travel-seasoned artists were having to pass themselves off as fresh talent plucked from the nightclubs of Harlem and Chicago.[24]

The growing number of black Americans working and traveling in Europe may have been a factor in the great interest that African Americans took in the German situation prior to the Nazi assumption of power. Marcus Garvey's brief visit to the country in 1928 had left him impressed with German thoroughness and discipline, as well as with the Germans' inclinations toward self-reliance.[25] The political and economic situation in Germany, especially with regard to "race," was followed very closely by African-American publications all over the United States. In the first few years of the twentieth century, violence against Jews in Russia and Eastern Europe had triggered sympathetic and comparative assessments in the black press; their treatment had been of considerable interest to the black reading public. As the Nazi movement became more prominent, their victimization by means of "race" was once again a major point of interest.

The increasing visibility of black anti-semitism in the United States was another important factor behind the attention that was directed toward racial problems in Europe. This development was of such concern that under the direction of Ralph Bunche, the Sociology Department at Howard University launched a research project into the attitudes and responses of the African-American community toward anti-semitism that were revealed in its independent press and print media. Guided by Bunche's observation that "no people in the world today is immune from the contagion of racial stereotypes and race hatred," the researcher Lunabelle Wedlock examined the contents of major African-American publications and their coverage of European events for seven years, from 1933 to 1940.

Wedlock's detailed study was published in 1942.[26] It is a rather repetitive and patchy document that presents very loose and elastic definitions of anti-semitic thought. Nevertheless, it offers an invaluable survey of how black Americans saw the plight of European Jews. After a general historical argument about the role of independent publishing in the constitution of what we would now call a "public sphere" and some remarks about the effects of the Depression on relations between "two disadvantaged minorities," Wedlock mapped out the points of debate and comparison that were being identified between the histories of the two groups. She attempted a rough periodization of black Americans' changing consciousness of Nazism as both a political philosophy and a mode of racial government that invited comparison with conditions in the United States and constructed a political geography of the black anti-semitism that she described as "a dangerous luxury for Negroes." This "false racial creed and prejudice" was, she argued, "centered principally in the larger cities of the East" and strongly associated with the life of the Negro middle class, placed "in the ironical position of sympathizing, in at least one respect, with Nazism."

Wedlock communicates her frustration with the reluctance of the African-American community to comprehend its situation "as international." This is second only to her concern that "prejudice and group chauvinism continue to divide Negroes and Jews." Interestingly, she identifies knowledge of the Jewish situation in Germany as itself a factor in the high expectations that blacks have of the Jews with whom they come into contact: "they seem to expect more sympathy and help from Jews than from any other group, because of the German-Jewish situation."

In establishing the intermittent pulse of interest in the Jewish predicament, Wedlock reveals that some Negro papers, particularly the *Washington Tribune,* had discussed the possibility of a massacre of Germany's Jews as early as March 1933. According to Wedlock, the levels of newspaper commentary and reporting on these topics rose and fell. The peaks of interest followed major symbolic events like Jesse Owens's Olympic triumph, the fights between Louis and Schmeling, and the exclusion of Marian Anderson from Constitution Hall by the Daughters of the American Revolution (DAR) and the Columbia Board of Education in 1939. On that occasion, it was pointed out that "the noted Negro contralto" had previously been received by both Hitler and Mussolini, who appeared, in this respect at least, to be ahead of the American bigots. Wedlock's book repeatedly reveals the extensive nature of comparative arguments about the relative experiences of disenfranchisement and violence that both groups were undergoing. These were sometimes accompanied then, as they are now, by speculations about the "cultural kinship" of these two communities.

Of more practical and immediate significance were assessments of the segregation of black and white athletes inside the United States occasioned by the Olympics. The idea that Hitler had snubbed Jesse Owens in his moment of glory raised the tempo of a wide-ranging discussion that encompassed the power of the Constitution to inhibit discrimination, the legality and illegality of prejudice in both regimes, and the idea that "Georgia fears the Negro will lower the level of Anglo-Saxon civilization; [while] Hitler fears the Jews will raise it too high." Another way in which Nazi Germany was thought comparable to contemporary America was glimpsed by Wedlock in the way that black newspapers reported the "Jew-baiting" activities of Sufi Abdul Hamid, a self-styled "Black Hitler" based in New York whose campaigning ended abruptly when he was killed in a 1938 plane crash. Harlem's black Jews were reported in 1934 to be pledging funds for a worldwide anti-Nazi drive.

Papers such as the *Philadelphia Tribune,* the *Brown American,* and the *Amsterdam News* included a number of articles about Negroes living "in terror" in Germany and about the Nazi view of blacks. They revealed, for example, detailed knowledge of Nazi plans to sterilize the "bastard" black children of the Rhineland and the Ruhr and raised acute questions about the way the Nazis saw the French colonial troops who had fathered them. Two 1934 headlines drawn from the *Norfolk Journal and Guide*—"Hitler, the Modern Simon Legree" and "Hitler: The German Ku Klux"—seem to have typified the tone of much of this coverage. There was discussion of whether it was appropriate that African-American residents in Germany were being registered as Africans and of the treatment that black American travelers were likely to encounter. Nazi responses to "the evils of Jazz" were also noted with alarm and a degree of relief when, for example, the same paper quoted a German report that shifted the blame for jazz from blacks to Jews under the headline "Nazis 'Clear' Us of Jazz; Blame Jews."[27]

ADORNO, LOCKE, AND THE ARGUMENT OVER JAZZ

European analysts of fascism's ascendancy had also noted the prominence of black culture in general and of jazz in particular in the pre-fascist culture of the Weimar period. The intrusion of blackness into Europe was not something these commentators were prepared to celebrate uncritically. The Nazis and many of their opponents could agree that the strange ability of black American culture to be simultaneously ultramodern and ultraprimitive provided proof of its decadence and the dangers it presented to the body politic. From this point of view, its popularity among Europeans debased and corrupted not only their proper art and culture, but their racial selfhood, which was invaded and diseased by the jazz "bacillus." The cosmopolitan enthusiasm for what would soon become known as "Nigger Jew Jazz"[28] had unlikely consequences. The stern political solutions to these chronic conditions, offered by fascists peddling militaristic fantasies of national rebirth, began to look attractive.[29]

In his notorious attempts to unravel the puzzles that jazz presented to the dialectician, Adorno, who had famously greeted the first Nazi controls on "Negerjazz" with enthusiasm, unearthed what he saw as a deep bond between jazz and fascism. He dismissed the music in part because of its historic links with the military bands that had reawakened Europe. These martial connections led him to assert that "jazz can easily be adapted for use by fascism. In Italy it is especially well-liked, as is Cubism and artisanry."[30] When combined with a volkish but only pseudo-democratic element and other formal and stylistic attributes that were regressive, this military inheritance made jazz and fascism part of the same regrettable sociocultural turn. They were twin aspects of a debasement of experience into "mechanical soullessness or . . . licentious decadence."[31] Rather than entertain the possibility that jazz was helping to define and practice new freedoms, Adorno saw it as the pernicious dissemination of an alienated and destructive pattern that had first been established in the music-making of slaves, when the lament of unfreedom was first combined with its oppressed confirmation.[32] For him Josephine Baker was not the personification of expressionism.

Whereas Adorno saw and feared the pseudo-democracy staged in jazz, contemporary black critics, struggling to balance modernism against primitivism in ways that enhanced their own agency, were inclined to see a more authentic liberatory moment. Writing in the *New Negro*, J. A. Rogers had suggested that a truly democratic spirit resided in the music's "mocking disregard for formality." In America the music celebrated a new spirit of joy and spontaneity that, he continued, "may itself play the role of reformer." Rogers's important insight had certainly been bought at the price of accepting a view of jazz as an exotic and primitive force "re-charging the batteries of civilization" with much-needed new vigor. Today, it may be more useful to read those elements of his argument as an inessential, decorative concession to the temper of the times that does not compromise his central thesis:

> . . . in spite of its present vices and vulgarizations, its sex informalities, its morally anarchic spirit, jazz has a popular mission to perform. Joy, after all, has a physical basis. Those who laugh and dance and sing are better off even in their vices than those who do not.[33]

Voices on all sides of the dispute about the value and meaning of interwar black music in relation to nascent fascism appear to have accepted the proposition that even if music was not itself a means of democratic restoration and rebirth, it could provide a useful gauge from which the developmental progress of the race might be read. It was here that music began to be imagined as a creative model for the visual arts and a technical blueprint for novelists and poets.

The great sage Alain Locke, fresh from three years as a Rhodes scholar in Oxford and two more in Berlin, adopted this approach in his careful exposition of the state of music-making published in 1936. Locke understood jazz in tripartite terms as "part Negro, part American, [and] part modern." He recognized the fundamental role that James Europe's band—which he described as "the musical wonder of the decade"—had played in bringing the music to a wider public. He juggled the racial origins and character of jazz against the cosmopolitan and modernist qualities that emerged when Negro forms mixed with input from whites and Jews in a "great interracial collaboration": "today's jazz is a cosmopolitan affair, an amalgam of modern tempo and mood . . . jazz is basically Negro, then, although fortunately, also human enough to be universal in appeal and expressiveness."[34] What matters, he continued, "is the artistic quality of the product and neither the quantity of the distribution nor the color of the artist. The common enemy is the ever-present danger of commercialization which, until quite recently, has borne with ever-increasing blight upon the healthy growth of this music."[35]

Like Adorno, Locke was alert to the dangers in the commercialization and commodification of the music. Again like him, in good Hegelian style, he tried to comprehend the meaning of jazz's emergence as "the dominant recreational vogue" in its historical context, a stage he repeatedly described as "hectic and neurotic." He argued that the "vogue of jazz should be regarded as the symptom of a profound cultural unrest and change" which would "be an important factor in interpreting the subtle spirit of our time."[36]

Locke did not identify fascism explicitly as another element of this cultural flux, preferring instead to emphasize the way that jazz opposed both Protestantism and the monotonies of machine-ridden civilization. He acknowledged the explanatory power of the dominant theories of jazz, which saw it as a means of emotional escape on the one hand and a means of emotional rejuvenation on the other. However, jazz was not only a subtle combination of narcotic and stimulant in the way that these influential theories suggest. Identifying the fact that serious forms of jazz had moved far beyond their role as "the Negro's desperate antidote and cure for sorrow" and become "the characteristic musical speech of the modern age," Locke raised the possibility that this joyous music could be a "cultural anti-toxin, working against the most morbid symptoms of the very disease of which it itself was a by-product." Again, like Adorno, he recognized the fundamental significance of "the erotic side of jazz," which had "a direct relationship to the freer sexuality of this age."[37]

A fragmentary counterhistory of artistic modernism is waiting to be distilled from these suggestive observations, but Locke leaves the possibility of "direct connections" between "jazz and the crises of modern civilisation" frustratingly open. His insights help to establish more than merely contingent connections between black and white cultures and histories, between the culture of New World blacks and the fate of Jews in Europe bonded together by Nazi racial-hygiene under the abusive sign of rootless cosmopolitanism. However, they stop short of showing how blacks bore active witness to the catastrophic circumstances to be found at the terminal point of Europe's racial typology.

ETHICS AND METHODS

Equally unsettling cross-cultural stories can be spun around the heroic black figures who may be thought of as having dished out small but significant symbolic defeats to the Nazis: Josephine Baker, Jesse Owens, and Joe Louis. Michael Kater has done more than anyone else to collect and analyze the mind-boggling tales of the presence of jazz and its local offshoots in the cultural life of Nazi Germany, and to trace the music even into the workings of the concentration camps.[38] These connections and reflections can, of course, be dismissed, along the very lines suggested by Adorno's critical comments, as nothing more than instances of the interconnected nature of alienated and reified cultural life after the industrialization of cultural production. From that perspective, they would reveal only the transnational reach of black American culture and display some of the dynamic resources it supplied to the life of prewar and wartime Europe. But that is all. I take a different view which sees important opportunities in this crossing of cultures. These histories of rootless cosmopolitanism become a catalyst for the multiculture of the future.

Historical work by Kater, Detlev Peukert,[39] and others has unearthed powerful accounts of that musical subculture's centrality to oppositional consciousness among young people especially. It is extraordinary that the Nazi regime had such an extensive battle to co-opt and recuperate these modern styles for their own purposes. Assessing this layer of additional connections, transcultural conversations, and unexpected stylistic convergences should include an extended consideration of the visibility of blacks in Nazi art, propaganda, and popular culture and of the place of "race" in what has tentatively been called "fascist aesthetics," but that task is beyond the scope of this book.[40]

The innovative and enduring cinematographic revolution initiated by Leni Riefenstahl and briefly examined in Chapter 4 will doubtless be central to those considerations. One must think also not just of Goebbels's attempts to manufacture racially acceptable surrogates for jazz but of his desire to produce grand Nazi entertainment that could provide a cinematic equivalent to *Gone with the Wind*. The 1941 epic *Ohm Krüger* was, for example, set in South Africa against the background of the Boer war. In *Quax in Afrika* and *Congo Express,* colonialism provided an appropriate vehicle for the same powerful pleasures and fantasies. Like the better-known orientalist reverie of Josef Von Baky's *Münchhausen,*[41] these productions had the unforeseen effect of helping a significant number of Afro-Germans and African-American prisoners of war survive the hardships of wartime through work as film extras.[42] Goebbels's biographer Ralf Georg Reuth tells us that though Goebbels castigated *Gone with the Wind* in public, it was "among the Hollywood films . . . that entranced him the most."[43] Exactly what it was that caught his eye and engaged his emotions will also have to be considered in more detail than is possible here. Suffice to say that there is in this example further preliminary evidence both for seeing the colonial staging of these epics as important and for appreciating the significance of a racializing background against which the world-historic conflict between English and German nations could be appreciated with increased clarity. To put it another way, what did the African setting and presence of blacks contribute to the intonation of these fascist images?

Recognizing but also retreating from the dizzying scope of these big questions, I would like to consider the possibility that there is another, possibly more fundamental, variety of linkage to be explored between what need no longer be regarded as discrepant histories assigned unproblematically to their various ethnic practitioners. This more conceptual connection appears to have been generated by the distinctive political logic of racial typology and differentiation that underlies the contingent cultural connections mentioned above. It made the cultureless Jews responsible for the black music that was, Hollywood aside, their most pernicious cultural weapon in the secret struggle for world domination. This linkage is best approached as a simple product of the conspiratorial antilogic that operated in Nazi raciology. The childlike Negro produced music and dance but was not equipped to comprehend or exploit their seductive primitive power as a means to distract, ensnare, and ultimately destroy the unsuspecting Aryan, who was in turn made vulnerable to this infection only through the devious machinations of international Jewry. Where the degenerative power of black music was unleashed on unsuspecting and vulnerable Aryan youth, antiblack racism and anti-semitism were readily reconciled in practical politics. They were bound together theoretically by varieties of reductionism, determinism, and mechanism that involved the coding of biology as culture and the coding of culture as biology. These different forms of raciology have been distinguished more recently as the old racism and the new, but it is important to remember that for much of the period with which we are concerned they formed what George Stocking has called an "ethnographic gestalt" in which "physical type was perceptually unseparated" from other signs of difference.[44]

Whether biology or culture claimed ultimate precedence, an underlying logic expressed through racial ontologies and the marginalization of ethical matters that is their signature provided important legitimation for brutality, terror, and historically mandated ethnocide of the different and the inferior. It is necessary constantly to test the specific capacity of these *racializing* discourses. They can be compared, not only with the language of some fundamentalist and sectarian religions, but with the exterministic ambitions represented by class-based desires to kill which occur elsewhere in the history of European totalitarianism. It is also worthwhile to reflect upon the specific lines within which appeals to racial and ethnic solidarity and belonging were operative. The brutalities perpetrated in conjunction with what might be called "a poetics of blood," via the enduring regime of power and representation that Fanon called "epidermalization" and conducted more recently through the emergent nano-political discourse of "race" (recast contemporarily in terms of genes and information), all demand that this possibility be considered.

The specific force of *modern* racist discourse can be registered in places and times seemingly remote from the illustrations that have made Western Europe the sole point of entry into critical considerations of fascism. Two different examples suffice to underline this point. The first is drawn from the history of Croatian nationalism, in which, under the leadership of Ante Pavelic, descent from heroic Aryan sources became a linchpin of murderous aspirations that merit the name fascistic. The second arises from the charnel houses of Rwanda. There, the Hamitic hypothesis as to the origins of "racial" differences between Bahutu and Batutsi that was introduced by missionaries and consolidated by colonial administrators has been identified as an important element in the constitution of a genocidal mentality. In both instances, the narrativity of absolute identity emerges as a central problem. Wherever the mythic forces of racial and ethnic difference appear, powerful solidarities emerge along with distinctive forms of legitimacy.[45] At the most basic—I am tempted to say human—level, we must also note the ways in which the techniques of soldiery that the military psychologist Lieutenant Colonel Dave Grossman has aptly called "killology" acknowledge the role that an enhanced sensitivity to "ethnic" and "racial" difference has played in removing the fundamental inhibition against killing:

> It is so much easier to kill someone if they look distinctly different from you. If your propaganda machine can convince your soldiers that their opponents are not really human but are "inferior forms of life," then their natural resistance to killing their own species will be reduced. Often the enemy's humanity is reduced by referring to him as a "gook," "Kraut" or "Nip." In Vietnam this process was assisted by a body-count mentality, in which we referred to and thought of the enemy as numbers. One Vietnam vet told me that this permitted him to think that killing the NVA and VC was like "stepping on ants."[46]

Primo Levi, who was also occupied by the role of numbers in the process of dehumanization, considered elements of this problem from a different point of view in a section of *The Drowned and the Saved* in which he discovers the real utility of the apparently useless violence he witnessed as an Auschwitz inmate. That brutality was useful above all as a means of producing solidarity between its perpetrators. It enabled them to behave more freely, unencumbered by the moral, religious, emotional, and psychological factors that would have disrupted their operations if they had accorded their victims a human status comparable to the one they had bestowed upon themselves. Colonel Grossman's discussion of what he calls "killing empowerment" suggests that, in this at least, the Nazis' grand program of racial murder does not appear to have been exceptional.[47]

It is a small step further to entertain the possibility that racializing language and associated action can solicit the very feelings and solidarities that are usually assumed to precede them. These programs of action are racializing regimes—structures of feeling and doing—that produce "races" in hierarchical arrangements by making "race" meaningful and keeping it as an obvious, natural, and seemingly spontaneous feature of ordered social life. The quality of order becomes all the more precious and relevant in situations of extremity. The hierarchy, authority, and absolution that order can provide facilitate the process in which men and women become capable of killing other human beings. This complex pattern involves reciprocal interaction between raciology and its consequences. We must therefore be prepared to confront the agency of violence—and indeed, of blood itself—as a means of *producing* the very "racial" differences that do not exist in advance of so many gory and brutal attempts to bring them about.

The distinct order of "racial" differentiation is marked by its unique label, by the peculiar slippage between "real relations" and "phenomenal forms" to which it always corresponds, and by a special (a)moral and (anti)political stance. It has involved not only confining "nonwhite" people to the status of animals or things, but also reducing European people to the intermediate status of that lowly order of being somewhere between human and animal that can be abused without the intrusions of bad conscience.

Today, in circumstances that manage somehow to prohibit as well as demand an insurgent cultural politics, our choices are more complex than those suggested by Goebbels's apocryphal statement cited in this chapter's opening sentence. A conveniently labeled, original fascism, bent on the obliteration of culture and the destruction of its advocates and silent custodians, does not stand boldly and assertively opposed to an innocent, integral, anti-fascist consciousness that summons culture and civilization to its side in the battle against evil. The seeds of European fascism have been carried far and wide in what Primo Levi called "the silent Nazi diaspora." We should note that fascism's complex lineage has been complicated further by the widespread mimicry of its political style by various regimes, which though they may be ultranationalist, violent, or conservative in character, do not share the anticonservative, antiliberal, populist, fraternalist, and revolutionary orientation of fascism proper. Fascism's technologies of self and solidarity have proved as influential and attractive as the appeal of any of its systematic ideological features.[48] Perhaps this is how fascisms have been able to speak repeatedly in the name of culture and become eloquent about the racial, national, and ethnic hierarchies constructed by the idea of absolute cultural difference along national lines. In a sense, then, fascism can be said to have acquired or even become a culture in its own right. This operation has taken place within the boundaries constituted by what Deleuze and Guattari refer to—in their celebrated warning that the seductions of fascism spare no one—as its "molecular, focal points."

BLACK COSMOPOLITANS FACE TO FACE WITH FASCISM

Baker, Fanon, and Senghor are probably the best known of many blacks who opposed fascism in battle and in the resistance. There are other, little-known and largely unremembered people who joined the opposition to Hitler, passed their lives in camps and detention centers of various kinds, or who survived quietly and retreated back into the strange ambiguities of their existence as black Europeans. Among those who should be brought to mind here are Hilarius "Lari" Gilges, who was beaten to death by Nazis in Dusseldorf in 1933 and is one of the few black victims of Hitler to have a public memorial of any kind. The Belgian activist Johnny Vosté was a member of the resistance movement. He was arrested in 1942 and not only survived Dachau but helped some of his comrades to do so as well. Another was Johnny William, a Frenchman originally from the Ivory Coast who was deported to the Neuengamme camp complex near Hamburg, where he survived, he believes, thanks to the warmth provided by the Walther armaments factory, where he was set to work as forced labor. He has testified that there were five or six other black inmates of the camp who, initially at least, benefited from the reputation for physical prowess established in the minds of their captors by Jesse Owens's triumph in 1936.[49]

As the earlier discussion of Senghor suggests, material on the life of the large camps set up by the Germans for colonial prisoners of war is rather sketchy. However, a small but extremely useful literature chronicles the contradictory and sometimes bizarre experience of black prisoners of war at the hands of Nazis who were unsure of exactly where blacks fitted into the racial scheme of things. Though he rather peremptorily dismisses Johnny Vosté as a "male mulatto who claimed to be at Dachau" without documents to verify his case, Robert W. Kesting, an archivist at the United States Holocaust Memorial Museum in Washington, D.C., has assembled a useful if brief collection of material drawn mostly from the files of postwar investigators into war crimes.[50] His preliminary research confirms that there is evidence from right across the European theater of both colonial and African-American soldiers and Air Force personnel being summarily killed and mutilated in abuse of the terms of international treaties that govern the treatment of POWs. There is also material suggesting that the Nazis were inconsistent if not exactly confused about how to deal with the blacks they captured in combat. Horrible tales of battlefield butchery and raciologically inspired violence are matched by other accounts in which black prisoners admit that they encountered a measure of consideration that acknowledged their humanity or were treated reasonably on the basis of a racial hierarchy that specified their status as less than fully human and therefore unworthy of ill treatment in the same way as livestock or pets.

Britain's Royal Air Force (RAF) recruited a significant number of black personnel via the Air Ministry Overseas Recruitment Scheme. One Guyanese RAF officer, Cy Grant, was captured after being shot down near Arnhem in 1943 and spent the next two years in a POW camp. He has reported that "the only racism that I encountered [there] was from an American . . . a corporal or something like that who happened to be in this holding camp. And he called me a nigger one or two times, but I got nothing from the Germans. They didn't single me out for any special treatment."[51] Ransford Boi, a seaman in the British merchant fleet, was captured off the coast of Liberia in December 1939 and transferred to the camp at Sandbostel between Bremen and Hanover. He spent two years there before moving to another unnamed internment camp where there were about thirty other black inmates. The regime was relaxed enough for him to have a number of unlikely picaresque adventures.[52] Although these fragments should not be accorded a disproportionate significance, they should be allowed to assume an appropriate place in accounts of the practical complexities of Nazi raciology in the context of war. More obliquely, this type of material might also be used to point toward a different kind of narrative: the prehistory of a multicultural Europe.

Though formed culturally and intellectually by pressures and institutions quite different from those influencing these offspring of the colonies, the African-American soldiers who eventually arrived at the gates of the Nazi concentration camps as part of the victorious military forces have also testified that their understanding of the racial order to which they had been subject in their unhomely homelands was transformed by exposure to the sheer scale of the camps' rationally pursued horrors. The sense of basic human shame that they shared with their white fellows was complicated in their case by the knowledge that they too in milder everyday ways had been victims of raciology and its trademark brutalities. Much of the work of cleaning up at Dachau and Buchenwald was undertaken by the 183rd battalion of combat engineers.[53] Their presence in that lowly role traditionally assigned to the Negro opens the door to consideration of the experiences of black soldiers who had taken combat roles against the Nazi army.

The presence of these black soldiers at the liberation of one camp was noted by Benjamin Bender, an inmate of Buchenwald searching for his brother amid the chaos of the camp's last hours:

> The ground adjacent to the gatehouse was covered with bodies. Many had torn blankets over their heads. These inmates had refused to join the final death-march to Dachau; some were wounded, some were dead. The scene was gruesome . . . At the side of the road jeeps and half tracks were parked . . . The huge roll call square was full of American soldiers, General Patton's best, tall black men, six footers, with colourful scarves around their necks. I had never seen black men before. They were unreal to me. The soldiers were trying to help, carrying inmates on stretchers, some dead, some dying and stretching out their hands saying, "Brother, I'm dying, give me your hand." The soldiers were in shock, crying like babies. They gave them their hands. Some inmates were just sitting stupefied.[54]

Samuel Pisar, a Dachau inmate, gave an account of his own "liberation" to the *Washington Post* in May 1995. Hiding in a barn after escaping from a death march, he spied an unfamiliar tank on the road nearby:

> The tank resumed its cautious advance . . . Automatically I looked for the hateful swastika, but there was none. Instead I saw an unfamiliar emblem—a five-pointed white star.
>
> In an instant the unimaginable flooded my mind and my soul. After four years in the pit of the inferno, I, convict no. B-1713 also known as Samuel Pisar, son of a loving family that had been wiped off the earth, have actually survived to behold the glorious insignia of the United States Army.
>
> My skull seemed to burst. With a wild roar I stormed outside and darted toward the wondrous vision. I was still running, waving my arms, when suddenly the hatch of the armoured vehicle opened, and a black face, shielded by helmet and goggles, emerged, swearing at me unintelligibly . . . Pistol in hand, he jumped to the ground to examine me more closely . . . To signal that I was a friend, and in need of help, I fell at his feet, summoned the few English words my mother used to sigh while dreaming of our deliverance, and yelled: "God Bless America!" With an unmistakable gesture the tall American motioned me to get up, and lifted me through the hatch into the womb of freedom.[55]

Elie Wiesel and Israel Lau are two well-known former prisoners who have mentioned the presence of black soldiers in similar moments drawn from their own lives. Yale University's Fortunoff Archive of videotaped testimony by Holocaust survivors contains a number of additional examples in which inmates recount being liberated by black American troops or describe encountering them soon after fleeing from the camps.[56] As with Benjamin Bender, these meetings were often made memorable precisely because they were the first occasions on which a black person had been beheld.

These encounters are powerful reminders of the arbitrariness of racial divisions, the absurdity and pettiness of racial typologies, and the mortal dangers that have always attended their institutionalization. Their eloquent testimony to the unity and sameness of the human species and the morality of intersubjective recognition is all the more valuable for being offered innocently from the twentieth-century core of radical evil. How-

ever, these very unsettling qualities have made them disturbing and extremely difficult to handle in a racially coded world whose stubborn
assumptions these cosmopolitan histories de-stabilize. The implicit demand that the minor differences identified as racial amount to nothing
when seen in the aura of the horrors that "race" has brought to life is currently impossible to satisfy.

In the United States, the contemporary significance of these grim tales
has been disputed and diluted by the controversy that still surrounds the
ground-breaking documentary film *Liberators* made by Nina Rosenblum
and Bill Miles and shown on public television in the United States and on
Channel 4 in Britain during the early 1990s. As part of a wide-ranging
commentary on the place of African Americans in the military and on the
relationship between their struggles against fascism and America's own
failure to fulfill the human and civil rights of its black citizens during the
same period, the film brought together former camp inmates and black
veterans to commemorate and explore the historical, moral, and political
import of their first encounters at the shameful camp gates. The local text
of this was their courageous attempt to change the terms in which the poor
relations between blacks and Jews were being conducted at that point, especially in the New York area.

In order to understand the storm of criticism that enveloped the film
after the initial enthusiasm that greeted its appearance, it is important to
appreciate that the term "Liberator" has acquired a specific technical
definition in this context. To be worthy of it, soldiers had to have arrived
at a camp within forty-eight hours of its being opened to the eyes of the
incredulous world. The official military records relating to the movement
of the black soldiers and their tanks are missing, inconclusive, and contradictory, but nobody disputes that the African-American soldiers arrived at
Mathausen and its Gunskirchen subcamp within the specified time-frame
or that they were seen in Dachau and Buchenwald at some point close to
the moment of liberation, though not necessarily within the required
forty-eight-hour period. With both photographic evidence and survivor
testimony to support its case, the film made the same "Liberator" claims
for black soldiers at Dachau and Buchenwald: more famous camps that
were more prestigious in the economy of official Holocaust memory. It is
far more interesting that the film, which received a major public endorsement from Rev. Jesse Jackson, appears to have offered a profound chal-

lenge to the state of the relationship between blacks and Jews in the United States. Its sense of the indivisibility of racism and of the importance of blacks' bearing witness to the Nazi genocide violated a popular view that sees this history as the property of particular groups and interests for whom it serves important functions of legitimation and solidarity. Denunciations of the film as a lie and a distorted example of politically correct rewriting of history followed. It was identified and repudiated for its revisionism and its role in marking out a "new line on the Jews" for the radical and controversial Jackson.

If the central claims made in the film, namely, that African Americans were bravely involved in the war against Hitlerism and the opening of its death factories and other camps, are not deniable, then the haggling over the key status of "Liberator" seems misplaced. To the outsider, it seems to be an odd byproduct of the mysterious process whereby military honors were restrictively awarded to particular units and selected commanders. In a situation where blacks were actively denied the share of national recognition proportional to their battlefield heroism, it is no surprise that any role they may have had in these events has been obscured. The quarrel over timing and positioning also looks trivial when considered alongside the undenied presence of blacks and other nonwhite Americans in these struggles. This is a historical fact that has been insufficiently appreciated and contextualized. It is part not only of the history of blacks and Jews in New York but of the history of Europe in the next century. The details of these encounters certainly do matter; they are a bulwark against attempts to deny that the Nazi genocide took place. Patchy and incomplete records from the chaos of war should not become a cloak for contemporary political battles that serve only to reify and entrench spurious racial differences.

THE STONE FACE

In drawing together the implications of this long argument, we are left with the question of how these cosmopolitan, translocal histories of extremity and human mutuality might be used. What place, if any, should they be accorded in contemporary arguments over "race" and in conflicts over the direction and character of European culture and civilization? These issues were of particular concern not only to the African-American and colonial troops who had participated in the war but also to those who arrived in Europe immediately after formal hostilities were concluded. The African-American novelist and writer William Gardner Smith had been part of the occupying forces in Germany and opted to make his home in Paris after the war. His work provides an especially interesting response to these moral and political challenges—not because his novels manifest the greatest literary qualities but because, with an exemplary bravery, they dare to approach complex and important questions that have a direct bearing upon the problems of identity, belonging, and nonraciological justice that concern us today.

Smith's first novel, *The Last of the Conquerors*, was published in 1948 when he was just twenty-two years old. It traced the fortunes of a contingent of black GIs in Germany in the immediate aftermath of the war. Smith explores a range of contrasting positions and experiences as these young black men survey the wreckage of the Nazi regime and watch the Germans begin to rebuild their lives. The soldiers contemplate and discuss the prospect of their own, in some cases reluctant, return to the United States. They are a diverse group, and any unified sense of racial community is fractured by their regional backgrounds and loyalties. The Southern and Northern blacks are culturally and educationally different. Even the racism deeply institutionalized in army life is insufficient to unite them.

The book shows that America's oppressive relations between black and white were not modified to accommodate the experiences of men who had been prepared to risk their lives for their country in combat abroad but who were still denied basic human and civil rights in the land of their birth. The black troops confront an army hierarchy that is eager to purge its ranks of the black soldiers whose combat role was sanctioned only reluctantly but who became pivotal to allied military successes.

Amid the chaos of postwar privation, the black market, and the emergent cold war, Smith presents the U.S. authorities as agitated about the relationships between black troops and white German women. This transgressive contact constitutes a central theme in the novel. Even more perhaps than they were in Britain,[57] African-American soldiers in Germany were abused and criminalized by their commanders and military police for "fraternizing" with local girls and women. Wherever Jim Crow attitudes and Southern chivalry were widely articulated, the women were also treated harshly by the occupying military authorities. This is the strange background against which Smith's soldiers contemplate the meaning of racial differences and debate the relationship between the Nazi genocide legitimated by raciology and their own experiences of color-coded racism inside and outside the military, at home and abroad.

Smith's protagonists—patriotically inclined Randy, sensible Homo, the wise professor, hot-headed Murdoch, and Hayes Dawkins, a quiet typist from Philadelphia who acts as the author's principal voice—all accept the crushing centrality of "race" to their lives but do not share unified views of either America or Germany. The difficult task of making sense of Nazism and its aftermath divides them even more sharply. Some of the battle-hardened veterans are inclined to take what they see as the official army line and identify all Germans with Hitlerism, whereas others, including Dawkins, gradually evolve toward a more complex and disturbing position that sees antiblack racism as fundamentally linked to anti-semitism. They learn this not just from realizing that the Nazis were also concerned with the fate of their Negro inferiors but from grasping a harsh lesson taught by the vicious anti-semitism of their white countrymen. In a relaxed after-hours drinking session, one apparently liberal white captain acknowledges the effects of antiblack racism in the United States and its army. He defends American democracy and makes a subtle plea for the re-education of the German nation before expressing his appreciation for the work that the Nazis accomplished toward the goal of eliminating the Jews:

> "Men, I forgot. There was one good feature about Hitler and the Nazis."
>
> We waited for the one feature.
>
> "They got rid of the Jews."
>
> A bolt of tenseness landed in the room. You could not see or hear it, but you could *feel* it land. The German girls especially were struck . . .
>
> "Only thing. Only good thing they did . . . We ought to do that in the States."
>
> How do you stop a captain from talking?
>
> "Jews take all the money," the Captain said. "Take all the stores and banks. Greedy. Want everything. Don't leave anything for people. Did it in Germany and Hitler was smart. Got rid of them. Doin' it now in the States. Take the country over and the Ameri-

cans ain't got nothing to say about it. Let the Jews run their country."[58]

This unsettling insight into the operations of race-thinking places the black characters' moral and political orientation under great strain. It is particularly pronounced once the double standards that allow the U.S. government to attack Nazi conduct while itself practicing a different but nonetheless brutally institutionalized form of racism have been elaborated. Smith conjures up a complicated, morally demanding world in which American anti-semites and other racists could fight European fascism sincerely under the banners of their own imperfect democracy without questioning their own raciology in any way.

It may be worth repeating that these comparisons between the two differently racialized regimes in Germany and America had been routinely made by black Americans before the Nazi genocide was launched. The passage of discriminatory laws curtailing Jewish rights and opportunities prompted extensive discussion of the wrongs sanctioned under the two opposing systems. Smith's black GIs discuss all of this at some length. They also resolve these problems practically in their close relationships with various Germans whose post-Nazi views of America and its racial hierarchy are ambivalent, in their chronic conflict with their white officers, and, most important, in their regular friction with the military police who seek to regulate the soldiers' public conduct in line with the racist prescriptions of Senator Bilbo of Mississippi and the Southern members of the U.S. General Staff.

The specificity of this historical moment has been captured by various autobiographical writers[59] but has not been adequately explored by historians. This was the important phase in which the American authorities first sensed their country's international vulnerability to criticism of its domestic racial hierarchy. It is significant that apprehension of the full extent of the Nazi genocide had refined that indictment of color-coded U.S. democracy. This mood has also been captured in the wartime reminiscences of African-American soldiers, some of whom have pursued their government in order to win public recognition of their contribution to the war effort, in combat and in support of it.[60]

Smith's Americans have all fought against Hitler, but they divide into those who endorse his aims and those who disdain them. His Germans must also be recognized as a differentiated group. The question of their collective responsibility for the Nazi genocide is raised early on in the narrative:

> "You know," Randy said, "I can't believe this. Two years ago I'd a shot the son of a bitch that said I'd ever be sittin' in a club drinking a toast with Hitler's children."
>
> It was like an electric shock, the word Hitler. I could feel the girl next to me stiffen . . . Randy laughed . . . "You're all the same. All of you. The same people we're sittin' with tonight is the ones that burned people in camps and punched the Jews in the nose."

Smith has Randy's attack on the Germans answered by an equally angry young German woman who reapplies his blanket condemnation of her country in a different example provided by the American setting:

> "How can you talk? What about the white Americans? In your country you may not even walk down the street with a white woman. The white Americans hang you from trees if you do." She was smiling with the corner of her mouth.
>
> "Where d' you hear that junk?" Randy shouted. The red came through even his dark skin.[61]

Sexual and emotional intimacy between black men and white women is offered as more than a primary symbol of the differences between Europe and America. It is also the main source of conflict between the black soldiers and the army to which they belong. Smith dramatizes the ways in which these young black men are made to reflect not just upon the meaning of their own blackness but, through the circuits of military travel, on the nature of democracy itself. Like the value of love and the possible significance of common humanity that sexual desire brings into focus, this is understood more clearly when it is seen against the backdrop provided by fascism's demise. Relaxing on a sandy beach watching the water at Wannsee with his new German girlfriend, Ilse Mueller, Hayes Dawkins meditates on precisely these topics:

> I had lain on the beach many times, but never before with a white girl. A white girl. Here, away from the thought of differences for a while, it was odd how quickly I forgot it. It had lost importance.

Everyone was blue or green or red. No one stared as we lay on the beach together, our skins contrasting but our hearts beating identically and both with noses in the center of our faces. Odd it seemed to me, that here, in the land of hate, I should find this one all-important phase of democracy. And suddenly I felt bitter.[62]

Ilse teaches Hayes elegant German, *Hochdeutsch* not *Blatt Deutsch!* She also introduces him to her aunt and uncle and brings him into their home, where he charms them with welcome gifts of cigarettes. As time flows past, the young black soldiers bond around talk of sports, politics, girls, and the omnipresent music of the American Forces Network. Hayes reveals that he has become as familiar with Berlin as he had been with Philadelphia and New York. In the afterglow of Perry Como singing "Prisoner of Love"—one of several key moments in which music and the sentiments it releases play a special role in the narrative—he listens to Murdoch explain his reluctance to leave Europe and return to the United States. This encounter is worth quoting at length: "Listen, Hayes, I can't leave this place. I can't. I don't want to go back there again. I swear I don't. I don't ever want to go back." Murdoch, a combat veteran who has been pretending that he comes from Chicago, reveals that he hails from Georgia, where the best he can hope for is hard physical labor as a ditch-digger. He continues:

You ain't been away from all that s—— as long as I have. You in't got the feelin' of being free. I like this goddam country, you know that? . . . It's the first place I was ever treated like a goddam man. You know what I learned here? I learned how to do all them goddam fancy dances, and now I know what it is like to walk into any place, *any* place, without worrying about whether they serve colored. You ain't been here long enough to feel like I do. You know what the hell I learned? That a nigger ain't no different from nobody else. I had to come over here to learn that. I hadda come over here and let the Nazis teach me that. They don't teach that stuff back in the land of the free . . . Maybe you think it's these goddam chicks here. They can all go to hell far as I care. I just feel like a *man*. I feel like ain't nobody turning up their nose at me because of my skin. If I wanted to, I could buy any house here. I can act like everybody else. I feel like a man. You know that? Just like a man.[63]

Murdoch reluctantly makes his way back to a miserable life in Georgia, but another disenchanted member of the group, Homo, chooses differently when he is ordered to return to the United States and heads for a life of exile in the Russian sector. He has been encouraged in that course of action after a meeting with Russian soldiers who are surprisingly familiar with the details of the race question in the United States: they are knowledgeable about the Scottsboro Boys case and well versed in the history of the Philadelphia P.T.C. strike. He accepts that he may not fare any better materially in the Communist bloc, but explains that there are other, less tangible benefits in following this difficult course.[64]

The pregenocidal aggression of the Germans toward the Jews is repeatedly compared to the Jim Crow system, its informal Northern approximations, and the white supremacist violence meted out in Europe by the military police. Though Smith does not make the point forcefully, this convergence suggests that genocidal possibilities may be latent or dormant within the forms of everyday racial brutality and hatred that operate at lower thresholds. Hayes is shocked to discover that there are other blacks—of colonial and mixed descent—still to be found in Berlin who have lived through the Nazi period. He also encounters Sonny, the beautiful four-year-old son of an African-American soldier and a German woman who is being brought up by Ilse's German friends.

Hayes and his companions are suddenly ordered to a new posting in Bremburg. Hayes is mortified at the prospect of being forced apart from Ilse and sad to lose the camaraderie of his Berlin barracks and the cosmopolitan vigor of the city and its nightlife. He finds the quality of daily life quite different in the new, more segregated environment, where racism is viciously and openly expressed and the white police, military and civilian, seek to enforce a strict, almost formal line between black soldiers and the local population. This change is apparently part of the way the army is managing its own racial tensions in the postwar phase. Bremburg is known colloquially as "nigger hell" and offers a number of formal and informal inducements to black troops to leave Europe and army life. Men are court-martialed for missing bed checks and receive punishments if they contract a venereal disease. A lot of ingenious effort goes into containing the black soldiers and keeping them confined as much as possible to the immediate area of the base:

> They got nearly every colored soldier in Germany right around here in the Bremburg area. Seems like they decided to pick this one spot to put nearly all of the boots . . . It's a slick system. Now when they want to make orders strictly for colored troops they just have the group commander give an order for all his troops. That way it affects only the Negroes but they don't have to mention race. It's a slick system all right . . . All the Officers are crackers.[65]

The local German girls are ingenious in circumventing these regulations. Ilse, whose love for Hayes has induced her to be equally resourceful, manages to defeat the rules that regulate ration cards, PX supplies, and civilian movement between sectors to follow him to Bremburg. In the course of seeking somewhere for her to live, Hayes meets Kurt Schneider, a young blond and blue-eyed German veteran who has recently returned from being interned as a prisoner of war in the United States, first at Fort Leonard Wood in Missouri and then at Camp Lee in Virginia.[66] Schneider's first-hand observation of race relations in the South lends his verdict on America an especially pungent flavor. It seems that he, too, has benefited from the special political magic that transforms "ethnic" Europeans into American whites once they arrive on American soil:

> "In America they do almost the same thing with your people—the black Americans—as the Nazis did here to the Jews. When I was at Camp Lee in Virginia I had to go to town sometimes with other prisoners to work, and sometimes a black soldier would come to guard us. At time to eat the soldiers would take us to a restaurant. But you know what? We could eat in the restaurant, but the soldiers could not. Because they were black. The prisoners could eat but they would not serve the guards. Back in the camp the German soldiers always laughed about that. It was very funny . . . You know what you need in America?"
>
> I was waiting.
>
> "A Hitler."
>
> He looked at me with smiling eyes . . .

"You need a Hitler," he said. "Someone who is strong enough to make sure everyone is treated alike. Hitler would have made sure."

"Like he did with the Jews?"

"He would not have done it to the Negroes."

"Did you read *Mein Kampf*?"

"No," he said.

"You should. You'd find out what he thinks of the Negroes."[67]

This is Smith's second acknowledgment of Hitler's commentaries upon Negroes. It precedes an interesting scene in which the reunited lovers attend the local movie house. There the racialized lighting techniques and coon-show conventions of the short opening movie attract their critical attention and are identified as part of a process that is inducting uncertain European audiences into the racial codes of the American entertainment industry. Later on at home, Hayes's "softer" American masculinity attracts a certain amount of comment from the German women who are not used to seeing any man eagerly doing his share of the dishes. The young couple's happiness is interrupted when, as a result of being seen in public with Hayes, Ilse is arrested by racist military police and charged punitively with being a prostitute. Hayes is threatened and abused when he goes to inquire about her fate. He fights with the MPs, who have succeeded in making links with the German Polizei and drawing them into the American-made net of their white supremacist thinking. It is two weeks before the couple see each other again, but they are able to reconstitute some of their joy in each other before the pressure on Hayes to quit the army and return to the United States increases.

Meanwhile, Steve, a fellow soldier who assists Hayes with the paperwork in the company's office, is awaiting court-martial for his failure to obey a direct order issued spitefully by the sergeant, who is determined to make the soldier's life as miserable as possible. This charge is welcomed by their superiors as a convenient device to force one more unwanted black out of the army as well as a means to settle an old score. It backfires catastrophically after Steve is sentenced to six months' detention. He turns a weapon against his persecutors and flees down the autobahn. The ensuing circumstances lead the captain, who has survived Steve's murderous onslaught, to try to force Hayes out in turn. Hayes can escape being court-martialed on the trumped-up charge of having missed a bed check only if he is prepared to say that he has opted to leave the army voluntarily. Faced with this coercion, Hayes leaves resentfully, pondering the multiple ironies involved in having had to travel to Germany in order to discover democracy. He has assured his German friends that, against their expectations, he will come back.

Smith's later novel *The Stone Face* (1962) shares and extends many of the concerns of his first book. Here, too, the protagonist is a displaced and dislocated African American who has chosen European exile, this time in Paris. More significantly, the book extends and modifies Smith's attempts to consider the consequences of race-thinking comparatively and transnationally. Once again, the Nazi genocide is present. This time it is also played off against the very different brutality involved in American conflicts between black and white. Smith's characters dwell in the shadows cast by this monumental event, and it becomes the essential context in which important ethical and political calculations can be made. This time, however, a third history overdetermines and mediates the relationship between the world-historic processes that have shaped his principal characters and brought them together: the war surrounding French decolonization in North Africa. *The Stone Face* attempts to answer how the racism of the de-colonizing process connects with these other racialized systems. It draws attention to the cold war setting in which questions of racial difference emerge as central and acknowledged aspects of geopolitics.

Smith's protagonist in this novel is Simeon Brown, another smart young African American who has fled Philadelphia to work as a journalist in France. He is one-eyed, having been deprived of his sight through a sadistic and malicious assault carried out by a gang of young whites who captured him while he was crossing their turf. Simeon views his blinding as an exchange rather than a loss. Diminished sight has endowed him with other kinds of strength. He has gained strength, wisdom, respect, manhood, and self-discipline as a result of being maimed. His disability of sight is a key element in his capacity to connect with Maria, a lithe Jewish woman from Poland who has survived the Nazi camps and emerged damaged but determined to use her beautiful body and graceful movement to build a career as an actress.

Simeon's partial sight is also associated with his desire to be an artist. He moves through the conflicts and jealousies that characterize the subculture of the expatriate Americans—black and white. The black colony on the Left Bank becomes an important source of sustenance where he can delight in the language and cultural play of his homeland. He makes new friends among the artists, musicians, and writers. The tension between members of this group has been sharpened by the cold war, but Simeon revels in the cosmopolitan atmosphere, the sexual freedom, and the absence of the color hierarchy and antiblack racism he has left behind in the United States. He also takes delight in the revolutionary political heritage of the French:

> He liked the faces of the ordinary French people—not the shop keepers, not the politicians, not the intellectuals, not the officials or the police, but the bus drivers, the street cleaners, the news vendors, the workers at Les Halles, the trainmen . . . He read into their eyes dim memories of the French Revolution, the Commune, the Resistance. These Things were not forgotten, they were still in the French people and through them in Simeon.[68]

It is not long before he realizes that this wonderful heritage has its limits. Racism is not, after all, absent from Paris; it just takes different forms. Though his own life is less constrained than it has ever been, brutal mechanisms that he encountered before reappear in the anticolonial racism that the French practice against the Arabs.

Apart from the jottings that bring him a minimal income, Simeon is working on a painting. It depicts a strikingly cold and inhuman face that he explains is a portrait of the man he left his homeland to avoid having to kill. Though various characters describe the unpredictable, liberatory effects of Parisian life, Simeon encounters white racists from the Southern states who have not been transformed by the gay, multicultural atmosphere. Considerably refining the technique used in his first book, Smith intersperses the Parisian scenes with flashbacks taken from Simeon's earlier life on the rough streets of Philadelphia and from his parents' miserable lives under the Jim Crow system and its Northern equivalents. Scenes in which Simeon is blinded, beaten by racist police, and attacked by a group of racist sailors on shore-leave precede tales of his father's intimidation on a segregated bus and his mother's being deprived of her chance to vote by the white woman for whom she works as a domestic servant.

In each episode, the most brutal perpetrator of racial violence seems to wear the same awful expression. Simeon perceives their features as being molded into the same inhuman and instantly recognizable face. This ghastly hallucination is the stone face that gives the book its title, and it is the frightful aspect of the stone face that Simeon is trying to capture in his half-finished painting. The face is first introduced to the reader when Simeon is blinded by his teenage tormentors: "The face shone. It grew brighter, a satanic star, burning with hatred and evil. Simeon shut his eyes against it. His legs gave way but the boys held him up. The world reeled."[69]

But rather than being the signature of American racism, this face is also familiar to Maria. It reminds her of the painful things she is working to forget. She gradually reveals that she saw something like it while being sexually abused as a nine-year-old child in a Nazi camp.

It is after one of his horrible encounters with violent whites that Simeon decides to leave his homeland. He carries a pistol in order to protect himself and fears that if he does not leave he will kill in self-defense. His parochial American understanding of race begins to shift when he is caught up in a conflict between Algerians and the police. The Algerians, who are disgusted by his lack of sympathy and insight into their struggles, taunt him for being a white man. One of them has served as part of the Free French forces and visited the United States while on duty with the navy. He berates Simeon for his limited vision and failure to appreciate the connections between what blacks suffer in American cities and what Algerians have to contend with in Paris. He tells Simeon:

> We're the niggers here! Know what the French call us—*bicot, melon, raton, nor'af.* That means *nigger* in French. Ain't you scared we might rob you? Ain't you appalled by our unpressed clothes, our body odor? No, but seriously, I want to ask you a serious question—would you let your daughter marry one of us?[70]

Not all black Americans in Paris are as prepared to open up their definition of who counts as a nigger. Simeon's friend Babe is a "race man" and former NAACP official, but he has convinced himself that the official French definition of the conflict with the Algerians is correct. He warns Simeon against seeing the situations of the two groups as connected in any way. "Forget it, man. Algerians are white people. They feel like white people when they're with Negroes, don't make no mistake about it. A black man's got enough trouble in the world without going about defending white people."[71] Simeon's dreams, by contrast, are haunted by the wise, troubling words of an old bearded black man: "Son, wherever racism exists, wherever oppression exists, anybody who lives complacently in its shadows is guilty and damned forever."[72]

This ancestral injunction is still on Simeon's mind when the first part of the novel closes with his realization that anti-Arab sentiment is precisely equivalent to the antiblack racism he endured in the American context. As the implications of this insight dawn on Simeon, Maria begins to share more of her own story of life in the camps. This deepens his understanding of the corrosive power of race-thinking, but it is far more than a cheap means to add moral gravity to Simeon's American tale. She recounts her forced parting from her parents in a camp selection carried out by her German abuser. Simeon accepts her tale of suffering as compatible with rather than equivalent to the tradition of oppression that has induced him to flee. Her reaction to his patient and sympathetic response is more complex. It is not past suffering that makes them able to communicate, to understand each other. It is their parallel struggles with murderous feelings of revenge that provide the basis for their reciprocal understanding and animate their mutual desire:

> Simeon was silent. He held her tight, feeling more close to her than ever. Perhaps they could understand each other after all. He watched the smoke from their cigarettes curl upwards to the ceiling. Maria kissed his shoulder and said, "You understand, Simeon, I do not tell you this for pity. Millions of people lived the same. But this is part of me, you must understand it to understand me. For years after the war, I dreamed of nothing except that camp, that line-up, the faces of my parents and the face of that commander. For years I dreamed I could torture and kill that man. For years, I could not sleep unless there was a knife under my pillow."[73]

As Maria and Simeon grow closer and more comfortable with each other, he is befriended by Ahmed, an Algerian radical. He visits the Algerian quarter, which he likens to Harlem. He recognizes many patterns in social and cultural behavior there that he had previously understood to be specific to black Americans. Simeon makes nothing of the fact that Algeria is on the African continent. He patiently explains that Africa is remote in space and time from the everyday life of black Americans.[74] He is also very clear that the Arabs are not Negroes. Smith has Simeon discover a deep kinship born from the condition of racialized oppression. This solidarity is confirmed when he recognizes the Algerians' beleaguered community as home. The Algerians are routinely interned in camps that are not dedicated to killing but nonetheless recall those of the Nazis:

> There are two right near Paris, and the others are in the Midwest and South. I thought everybody knew. Algerians disappear everyday, and later you learn they're in such and such a camp. They're not so agreeable, these camps. No gas chambers, of course, but the guards and officials are not gentle. It's worse in Algeria. There torture has been developed into a high art.[75]

When one of the Arabs asks Simeon how it feels to be living as a black man in a white country, his reply shows how much he has absorbed from his intimacy with Maria: "Like a man without a country. Like the wandering Jew." These words, which anticipate Babe's verdict on his own life as a "wandering Negro," are the cue for a raid by the police.

The perception that racial differences do not obstruct the significant continuities in human feeling and the realization that racisms assume various forms do not lead Smith to be naive either about the enduring character of racial divisions or about the tactics that are appropriate to bring racism to an end. Simeon replies to the perplexity of a sympathetic white hipster with these words: "any member of the privileged group in a racist society is considered guilty. Every white South African is guilty. Every Frenchman is guilty in the eyes of Algerians. Every white American is guilty. The guilt can end only when racism ends."[76] This overly neat scheme is disrupted by the force of anti-semitism that surfaces when Simeon's Algerian buddies try to express sympathy with Maria, who feels that she has been overcharged by a shopkeeper who has sold her an irresistibly beautiful bracelet:

> "Probably some dirty Jew sold it to you."
> The words exploded full in their faces. Maria jerked her head up as though she had been slapped. Lou's mouth dropped slightly open, Betty's eyes widened in surprise and pain . . . Simeon was stunned. Those words from one of the Algerians? Abruptly a whole

mental and psychological structure he had built up since the first day he talked to Hossein seemed to collapse.

Maria's face was white with anger; all frivolity had gone.

"I am a dirty Jew," she said.[77]

This pivotal scene marks the emergence of Maria as a complex, developed, and articulate character rather than a fleeting cipher for Smith's transcendence of his reluctant American parochialism. We see Simeon struggling with the disquieting possibility that anybody could be racist before Maria steps in and refutes simplistic accounts of the history and development of anti-semitism. She confronts Hossein—the political ideologue in the group of Arabs—with the fundamental question about the source of his loathing for Jews and asks him to rationalize it. He reveals that he hates Jews even more than he detests the French and the colonialists. Smith refuses closure in the bitter conversation that ensues. How, asks Simeon as he recalls and reflects on the anti-semitism he heard as a child in Philadelphia, do you argue with blind prejudice? The Algerians leave, the watching white despairs, while Simeon and Maria, who does not like to discuss big moral questions because it makes her ill, are more closely bonded than before. She is troubled by his drift toward political solidarity with the Arabs and his inclination to immerse himself in complications, causes, and political problems. She interprets this behavior psychologically as a refusal to accept the happiness that Parisian life has brought him. Simeon, who refuses "psychoanalysis and orgone boxes," counters this by arguing that the peaceful, settled life to which she aspires "might not be possible for a Negro if he thinks and feels."

Maria's experiences have also left her reluctant to declare love for Simeon. Her existential anxieties are multiplied by immediate concern over eye surgery that she must have in order to recover her failing sight. Simeon reads about the progress of de-segregation struggles in the South while waiting for the operation that will be a watershed in Maria's life. His empty eye-socket aches and he is haunted by photographs from Little Rock glimpsed in the French media. The expatriates debate the situation in the Congo at great length while Simeon waits five days to discover whether Maria's operation has been successful or whether she will lose her sight. After a positive outcome, the lovers head off for a lengthy holiday in Corsica, where Simeon muses at the image of a Negro's head on the province's flag.

The positive outcome of her eye operation increases Maria's energy and ambition. She is now determined to make her name as an actress. A party to celebrate the wedding of Babe and his Swedish girlfriend Marika comes to an abrupt end when the guests learn of the murder of Patrice Lumumba. Simeon senses the destructive impact wrought on life in Paris by the demise of French colonial power. His Algerian friend Ahmed gives up his studies to take up arms in the Front de Libération Nationale (FLN). The slow poison being released by the demise of the French empire is manifest in the growth of ultra-Right nationalism and chauvinism. Simeon notes with distaste a change in the way that the policing of the city is carried out. He compares French indifference to the fate of the Algerians to the way the German citizenry turned away from the plight of the Jews, but protectively cocooned inside the life of peace that he and Maria have improvised, Simeon can do nothing to interrupt the ugly moods from which French postcolonial consciousness is born.

One lonely evening, Simeon hears the distant sound of an Organisation Armée Secrète (OAS) bomb being detonated and wanders out into the street, only to catch a glimpse of Maria flirting with a film director, Vidal, who is determined to make her a star. Maria leaves to shoot a film and embark on a path that will lead her eventually to Hollywood, while Ahmed reenters Simeon's life. Through Ahmed he meets two Moslem women, Latifah and Djamila, who are veterans of the Algerian liberation movement. They recount the state of the conflict and challenge Simeon's assumptions about the religious aspects of the movement and in particular the subordinate position allocated to women. A massive demonstration of solidarity is called for October 1961.[78] The demonstration is put down with terrible violence by the Parisian police, and Simeon watches as the bodies of dead Arabs are dumped into the Seine. Ahmed's corpse lies sprawled in the street, and more than two hundred others are pulled from the river in the days following this massacre.

This tragedy forces Simeon apart from the rest of the expatriate community, which is more content than he to go on living a fantasy, "like foam floating on the sea of French society."[79] On a quay near Pont Neuf he spies a police officer swinging his club over an Algerian woman and her baby. In an instant, he recognizes the characteristic grimace of the stone face "twisted with the joy of destruction . . . red dots of excitement on [the policeman's] deathly pale skin." He attacks the officer, is himself hit over the head from behind, loses consciousness, and wakes up in a sports stadium surrounded by thousands of keening Algerians awaiting punishment and deportation:

> Simeon lay on his back and closed his eye tight against the pain. What would happen to him? He did not care. For the first time in a long while he felt reasonably at peace with his conscience. Had his attack on the policeman been a deliberate act of courage, or the result of momentary fury and hallucination? That didn't matter; what mattered was that he had struck back at the face . . . the face of the French cop . . . the face of the Nazi torturer at Buchenwald and Dachau, the face of the hysterical mob at Little Rock, the face of the Afrikaner bigot and the Portugese butcher in Angola, and, yes, the black faces of Lumumba's murderers—they were all the same face. Wherever this face was found, it was his enemy; and whoever feared, or suffered from or fought against this face was his brother.[80]

The Sûreté officer who releases Simeon makes a pithy little speech before he sends him on his way. There is no racism in France; it's not like the United States. We like Negroes here; we can understand why you prefer to live in this country. After this episode, Simeon resolves to leave Paris. But before he can decide where to go, he has one final encounter with Maria on the Champs Elysées. She tells him that she is going to America at last. Her new lover and mentor, Vidal, watches as they hold each other, musing that in America, Maria will have to learn not to embrace black men in the street. Simeon walks off to book his own return passage to the land of his birth. He destroys his picture of the face on the eve of sailing: "He did not need the image; the reality had penetrated. He slashed the canvas and threw the strips away."[81]

Smith was either unable or unprepared to follow the logic of his own insight to its obvious conclusion, namely, that the face of racial hatred could be fought when and wherever it appeared. Simeon's final decision to fight the face back in America rather than in Paris or Algeria means that he has accepted that he belongs there rather than elsewhere. This choice is neither illuminated nor justified and becomes an explicit if unconvincing repudiation of the cosmopolitan alternative involved in taking responsibility for the struggle against injustice in its immediate manifestations. This is capitulation to the demands of a narrow version of cultural kinship that

Smith's universalizing argument appeared to have transcended. Simeon's return seems an overly hasty way to conclude a narrative that has lost its difficult rhythm in a simpler polarized scheme that sets ethnic authenticity, activism, and good conscience against the freedom, healing, and pleasure that Europe offered to fugitive blacks. This can still be an honorable choice, but it does not measure up to the best historical examples yielded by the actual black Atlantic itinerants whose lives might be used today to affirm other, more timely and rewarding choices.

The painter Josef Nassy, born in Dutch Guiana in 1904, is one figure whose creative achievements might be considered in this light. Nassy, black and of Jewish ancestry, moved to New York, where his father's business interests were centered, at the age of fifteen. He attended high school in Brooklyn and eventually studied industrial electrical engineering at the Pratt Institute before traveling to Europe in 1929 as a U.S. citizen to take up work in the film industry: installing the new technology of sound reproduction in movie theaters. Settled eventually in Brussels and married to a Belgian woman, Rosine Van Aershot, Nassy gave up his technical work in 1939 and took up portraiture as an alternative. He was detained as an enemy alien by the Nazis in April 1942 and taken to Beverloo, a Wehrmacht transit camp in Leopoldsburg. In November of the same year he was transferred to the Laufen and Tittmoning camps for civilian detainees in the Bavarian Alps close to the Austrian border, where he would reside—with a number of other black prisoners—until their liberation in May 1945 by the U.S. Third Army. Supplied with art materials through the good offices of the YMCA, and under the "patronage" of the camp commandant, Nassy gave art lessons to other prisoners and recorded the life of the camps in which he was detained on over two hundred canvases. Nassy's portraits and other studies of camp life overwhelmingly rendered in brown, gray, beige, and black are striking expressions of the tedium, loneliness, and facelessness of detention. This body of work is now held as a single collection at the Severin Wunderman Museum in Irvine, California. While her husband was incarcerated, Madame Nassy hid three Jewish families in their house.

Nassy was not the only Guyanese itinerant whose artistic imagination bore witness to the inhumanity of the Nazis. His contemporary, my distant cousin Rudolph Dunbar, born the grandson of slaves three years later, was another cosmopolitan young man whose creative, in this case musical, ambitions drew him to Europe. After some years spent studying at the Juilliard School in New York and surreptitiously playing jazz in that city, he arrived in London by way of Leipzig and Paris, where he studied philosophy, musical composition, and conducting, and also furthered his command of the clarinet, his principal instrument.

In addition to his musical accomplishments, Dunbar published an influential technical treatise on the clarinet and contributed regularly to the British music publication *Melody Maker*. His journalistic ambitions led him to the role of war correspondent for the Associated Negro Press during the war, a position he used to attack the segregationist policies of the U.S military and to defend the bravery and integrity of African-American soldiers on the battlefield. Four months after the end of the war, in September 1945, still wearing his war correspondent's uniform, Dunbar conducted the Berlin Philharmonic Orchestra in a Victory Concert for some "3,500 German civilians and a sprinkling of allied servicemen"[82] held in the American sector. The program that night included music by Tchaikovsky and Von Weber as well as William Grant Still's Afro-American symphony.

The Russian and American authorities had been supportive of the proposal that somebody previously regarded as a racial inferior, whose earlier efforts on the podium at London's Albert Hall had been derided by the Nazis as a symptom of England's cultural decline, would be an appropriate choice to lead an event that celebrated the overthrow of Hitlerism. The British authorities, however, saw things differently and did what they could to obstruct the concert. Commenting on Dunbar's conducting, one elderly German in the audience was reportedly overheard remarking to his companion, "And I had thought they were a decadent race." Similar scenes were repeated in Paris a month later, when Dunbar conducted the Pasdoloup Symphony Orchestra in a benefit concert for war orphans held at the Palace Chaillot. The program that night was made up entirely of Grant Still's compositions.

The extraordinary stories of these black detainees, anti-fascists, veterans, liberators, and military travelers are not just welcome opportunities to recall the agency of blacks in the world-historic struggle against Hitlerism. Though that act of recovery is itself an important gesture for Europe, they have acquired another, less transient significance. They are a valuable means to place black people and their battles against raciology and its codes in the same moral and political world that encompasses the righteous sufferings of the Jews and the industrialized genocide that attended the implementation of racial-hygiene. In addition, these stories can now be part of making the "strategic" universalism toward which my argument has been moving. They promote an understanding of the vital links between racism and fascism that should be seen as part of contemporary political conflict rather than as relics which express the essential, unchanging meaning of Nazism.

9

"THIRD STONE FROM THE SUN": PLANETARY HUMANISM AND STRATEGIC UNIVERSALISM

No doubt the life of the less civilised peoples of the world, the savages and barbarians, is more wild, rough and cruel than ours is on the whole, but the difference between us and them does not lie altogether in this . . . savage and barbarous tribes often more or less fairly represent stages of culture through which our ancestors passed long ago, and their customs and laws often explain to us in ways we should otherwise have hardly guessed, the sense and reason of our own.

—E. B. TYLOR

If we now ask whether the human species can be considered a good or a bad race (it can be called a *race* only when one thinks of it as a species of rational beings on earth, compared to those rational beings on other planets, sprung as a multitude of creatures from one demiurge), then I must confess that there is not much to boast about. Nevertheless, anyone who considers human behaviour not only in ancient history, but also in recent history will often be tempted to coincide with Timon's misanthropic judgement, but far more often and more to the point, he will coincide with Momus, and find foolishness rather than evil the most striking characteristic of our species. But, since foolishness combined with traces of evil . . . cannot be ignored in the moral physiognomy of our species, it is

obvious that . . . everyone in our race finds it advisable to be on his
guard . . . This behaviour betrays the tendency of our species to be
evil-minded toward one another.

—KANT

My exploration of belonging and
its multiple ecologies, particularly the racial ontology of sovereign territory
and the cultivation of bounded, "encamped" national cultures, has been
necessarily concerned with the symbolic organization of space, place, and
political community. Kant, who did so much to endow this scholarly domain with intellectual coherence, spoke for a whole tradition of modern raciological reflection organized between the disciplinary axes of
anthropology and geography when, in some infelicitous "epidermalizing"
phrases, he matched the physical and social characteristics of the people he called "Negroes" to the climatic conditions in which European voy-
agers pursuing the "merry dance of death and trade" had first discovered
them:

> The superabundance of the iron particles, which are present in all
> human blood, and which are precipitated in the reticular substance
> through evaporation of the acids of phosphorus (which make all
> Negroes stink) cause the blackness that shines through the
> superficial skin . . . The oil of the skin which weakens the nutrient
> mucus that is requisite for hair growth, has permitted hardly even
> the production of a woolly covering for the head. Besides all this,
> damp heat promotes strong growth in animals in general; in short,
> the Negro is produced, well suited to his climate; that is strong,
> fleshy, supple, but in the midst of the bountiful provision of his
> motherland lazy, soft and dawdling.[1]

The massive relocation of populations involved in the globalization of
commerce, the enslavement of Africans, and the conquest of the New
World disrupted the natural patterns so beloved of this enlightened mechanical materialism. As they did so, the forces of nature gave way to those
of history. But for Kant, writing in the last quarter of the eighteenth cen-

tury, geography remained fundamental. It provided the basis on which human history could unfold:

> Which came first, history or geography? The latter is the foundation of the former, because occurrences have to refer to something. History is in never relenting process, but things change as well and result at times in a totally different geography. Geography is therefore the substratum.[2]

Later raciological theories followed the precepts of the Darwinian revolution and proceeded from altogether different premises far more in tune with high modernism's fascination with time and temporality. Darwin's own work had been facilitated by the conception of time he discovered in the work of the geologist Sir Charles Lyell. Transformed by the very substance of the earth, time itself could now provide the medium for comparing populations and comprehending and expressing their differences. Races were not merely to be distinguished on the basis of their various climatic origins and adaptive environmental differences; they were to be ranked in a hierarchy deriving from their relative positions on the temporal evolutionary ladder. Bernard McGrane has summed up this shift:

> *Beyond* Europe was henceforth *before* Europe. Nineteenth-century anthropology, from this perspective, existed then as the axis whereby differences residing in geographical space were turned and turned until they became differences residing in developmental, historical time, i.e., the axis whereby the simultaneity of geographical space was transformed into the successive linearity of evolutionary time.[3]

McGrane's argument is powerful, though a little too neat when applied to the transformations of raciology in the imperial period. We need to remember not only that Gobineau produced his *Essay on the Inequality of Human Races* without the benefit of Darwin's insights but that the most inhumanly brutal and sustained raciology emerged, not from speculative anthropological theory, but amid the practice of racial terror as a form of political administration in Europe's colonial empires.[4] Imperial power ensured that the theater of history was no longer to be confined to the temperate zone.

Gobineau's influential inquiries into the historical chemistry that governed the laws of decay, the problem of decadence, and the perils of intermixture linked his anxieties over the racial order and the limited duration of human civilization to a new argument that would become a staple in all succeeding versions of fascist ideology. His theory constituted the primal politics of "race" beyond the grasp of governmental superficialities and located it between the elemental poles of degeneration and regeneration. The destruction entailed by the overriding theoretical and political commitment to regenerate amounted to the instantiation of a new time in which the newly purified nation could once more become itself. Although this revolution has sometimes been identified with the institution of a transformed relationship with divine power, the extraterrestrial authority on which it depends is by no means always Christian in character.

Yearning to be free, that is, to be free of "race" and racism, has provided enduring foundations for the resolutely utopian aspirations to which a racially coded world gave rise among the subordinated, immiserated, and colonized. The breakdown of Christian theodicy which had already been transformed by the enduring potency of African spirituality should also be recognized as a significant part of our investigation into the social bases of black authoritarianism. Black Christianity was certainly future-oriented, but its sense of the future was bounded by its eschatology. Its utopia was not of this sorrowful world and required the supercession of modern, that is, of racialized and racializing, time. The worlding of that utopia, particularly by Marcus Garvey and other diaspora advocates of organized African fundamentalism, necessitated the inauguration of a new era of national development in which, as we have seen, the example of fascist political cultures was powerfully attractive. Common enthusiasm for ritual, pomp, and sacralization of the political sphere led Garvey repeatedly to claim kinship with Hitler and Mussolini and to describe himself as their inspiration.

The Nation of Islam's anti-Christian eschatology provides one relevant example of a far larger pattern whereby fascist ideology has also been deeply connected to a range of occult beliefs that associate racialized accounts of human origins and evolution with cyclical and catastrophic theories of time. In these schemes, which have a lengthy pedigree in African-American letters, divine power can be mirrored and amplified by powerful technologies that quietly contradict the archaic and organic models of family, kinship, and community that are also in play.[5] Under the leadership of both Elijah Muhammad and Louis Farrakhan, the Nation of Islam (NOI) linked the biblical account of Ezekiel's vision of a destructive wheel to contemporary reports of UFOs.[6] In the movement's key text, *Message to the Blackman in America,* first published in 1965, Elijah Muhammad conjured up an image of the end of the world. It was seen not only in terms of the high technological achievements exemplified at that point in the "space race" with the Russians, but through the weapons of mass destruction, which recalled the explosions that had brought the 1939–1945 war to its conclusion:

> The present wheel shaped plane known as the Mother of Planes, is one-half mile by a half mile and is the largest mechanical man-made object in the sky. It is a small human planet made for the purpose of destroying the present world of the enemies of Allah. The cost to build such a plane is staggering! The finest brains were used to build it. It is capable of staying in outer space six to twelve months at a time without coming into the earth's gravity. It carried fifteen hundred bombing planes with most deadliest explosives—the type used in bringing up mountains on the earth. The very same method is to be used in the destruction of the world.
>
> . . . The small circular-made planes called flying saucers, which are so much talked of being seen, could be from this Mother Plane. This is only one of the things in store for the white man's evil world.[7]

This terrifying vision, in which the earth to which blacks have been unjustly bound is destroyed as they move skyward toward a better, heavenly home, recalls nothing so much as the apocalyptic and equally racialized predictions offered by comparably eccentric occult figures like Helena Blavatsky and Carl Jung, who still remain largely unacknowledged as influences on the development of the NOI and its theology.[8] These racial visionaries respectively glimpsed the military destruction of entire cities and the earth-shattering carnage of the 1914–1918 war. Blavatsky's work may well have found its way into the consciousness of the young Elijah Poole (Muhammad) through the mystic influence of Sun Ra, the great musician and student of esoterica who had been his contemporary in Chicago and who had, like him, refused to be drafted into the U.S. army during World War Two. Blavatsky's teachings had a significant impact on American society during the late nineteenth century. She was widely read in African-American communities and contributed much to the arcane lore of several early versions of black nationalism that changed the racial polarity of her ariosophy and bent it toward the goal of black rather than white supremacism.[9] Elements taken from her theories of "race" still circulate in the more conspiratorial contemporary accounts of the agency of extraterrestrials in human history.

For the NOI, the historic appearance of these powerful spacecraft communicates more than the liberation involved in departure from this morally compromised planet. It portends the last days of earth and presages the "new rulership" of blacks over mankind. It signals not the end of racial divisions but rather their deeper entrenchment in a new theocratic order. When he took the helm of the NOI, Farrakhan positioned himself substantially beyond Elijah Muhammad's prophecy by claiming to have traveled in a UFO.[10] He reported that in September 1985 he made a flight from Mexico City to Washington, D.C., by these means and that during the trip he was reunited with Elijah Muhammad, who had died ten years earlier.

It is interesting that Farrakhan's memory of these events disappeared immediately afterward but was fortuitously restored to him two days later by a divinely inspired earthquake. This experience of being unable to account for one's time appears in many accounts of contact with extraterrestrials, UFOs, and other manifestations of alien intelligence. The fact of its persistent recurrence suggests that it might be usefully interpreted as a symptom of the way that these disturbing encounters demand adjustments to understanding where the present ends and the future commences.

Many writers have identified problems arising from the ways twentieth-century fascist movements organized their temporal sensibilities: how they manifested struggles over the proper relation between past and future, tradition and modernity, and how they inadvertently expressed the inability of different social groups to live simultaneously in the same undifferentiated present. Roger Griffin has made these movements' concern with national rebirth a vivid and essential part of his valuable generic definition of their activities. His emphasis on the special theoretical investment that fascists have always made in the "vision of a radically new beginning which follows a period of destruction or perceived dissolution"[11] points toward the fascists' great faith in the restorative revolutionary transformation of human history. Fascists affirm that social life can be turned back into the harsh but essentially natural cycles that govern the production of racially stratified humanity in strongly gendered and intergenerational forms. Their racially oriented, secular, palingenetic myths do not always, Griffin argues, derive from the religious notions that share many of the same eschatological sensitivities.

Somewhere behind Griffin we might usefully locate the figure of the philosopher Ernst Bloch. He struggled in an especially hostile environment with the idea that comprehending the positive cultural dynamics involved in the Nazi movement meant reading its romantic and mystical anticapitalism not as a nihilistic but rather as a utopian phenomenon that had been appropriated from unlikely sources. According to him, the joyful irrationalism of the Hitlerites and similar groups had to be understood—much like Levinas had diagnosed it in his attempts to link Nazism with the pleasures of being in the body—as a symptom of abiding fulfillment. This perspective implied a bitter indictment of the failures of the anti-fascist democratic cultures, which afforded their adherents no fantastic imaginings of comparable power. Applying Bloch's insights to more recent manifestations of the desire for unanimistic solidarity, rigid natural hierarchy, and authoritarian kinship that have appeared in the history of the black Atlantic should not involve the morally indefensible task of sifting its revolutionary conservatism for a few redemptive fragments that could excuse its bad political choices as effects of oppression or subalternity. We need to understand the appeal of armored utopia and the association between that response and long histories of terror and suffering. As Griffin's generic definition of fascism suggests, this understanding must take the idea of racial rebirth that marks out new time as its point of departure.

We have seen that the authoritarian and proto-fascist formations of twentieth-century black political culture have often been animated by an intense desire to recover the lost glories of the African past. The desire to restore that departed greatness has not always been matched by an equivalent enthusiasm to remedy the plight of Africa in the present. But the idea of an unsullied and original African civilization has sometimes given life to a complex archaism so powerful that it can oppose capitalism while remaining utterly alien to democracy. Romantic and sentimental distaste for the racial capitalism that, at an earlier point, had made blacks themselves into commodities, is a profound factor that influences the moral conditions in which black political cultures take shape. However, it has not always led easily into sustained criticism of market mechanisms themselves. On the contrary, black economic development along capitalist lines has been repeatedly identified as a substantial component in the uplift of the race as a whole and as the key to its transition to authentic national status in a world of modern nation-states. Even commerce can become a sign that the new era is under way.

These conflicts over the morality that will regulate communal reconstruction are minor aspects of another battle in "race" politics over what counts as authentic civilization. Is it to be genuine, sustainable mutuality that can only be practiced on a limited scale? Or restless development that opens a doorway to the perils of ultramodern, hi-tech barbarity? Terms like "savage" and "barbarian" that have cropped up in this discussion of extremity and misanthropic humanism are still traded to and fro as pejoratives. The racial economy in which they circulate reveals enduring connections between moral, cultural, and temporal characteristics. Their continuing power, like the temporal disturbances associated with the revolutionary, authoritarian, and fascistic movements we have encountered, means that we cannot evade a concluding engagement with the racial politics of temporality. This politics must be seen, as it were, from two sides: where it has been invoked by white supremacism as a principle of exclusion and social discipline and where it has been broken by raciology's victims as a means of resistance and affirmation. This difficult exercise is also necessary because my own desire to see the end of raciology means that I, too, have invoked the unknowable future against the unforgiving present. In doing this, I urge a fundamental change of mood upon what used to be called "antiracism." It has been asked in an explicitly utopian spirit to terminate its ambivalent relationship to the idea of "race" in the interest of a heterocultural, postanthropological, and cosmopolitan yet-to-come.

Becoming oriented toward the idea of a cosmopolitan future, even as it recedes, involves a variety of political work around racial discourse and racial division that is very different from what has been practiced in recent periods. In the past, these activities were dominated by the need to counter nationalistic and strongly cultural forms of racism. Bolstered by raciology, this exclusionary pattern denied blacks the possibility of belonging and forced us instead to demonstrate continually a substantial historical presence in the life of the modern national communities to which racial slavery had initially obliged us to belong. We had to show how "race" could be articulated together with other dimensions of power and to demonstrate the formative force of imperial and colonial relations in shaping metropolitan social life. There is no room to be complacent, for we can easily slip back toward this old agenda. However, this book's conclusion begins with the idea that a critical theory of raciology is now in a position to make a different inventory of political tasks around "race" and to undertake them in a new spirit. Corrective or compensatory inclusion in modernity should no longer supply the dominant theme.

The temporal adjustment that warrants this sharp turn away from African antiquity and toward our planet's future is a difficult and delicate affair, especially if we recognize the possibility that the contested colonial and imperial past has not entirely released its grip upon us. I suggest that, in moving into a new stage of reflection and aspiration that tallies with our novel circumstances as we leave the century of the color line behind, we need self-consciously to become more future-oriented. We need to look toward the future and to find political languages in which it can be discussed. There is absolutely no question of choosing now to try and forget what it took so long to remember, or of simply setting the past and its traumas aside. The recognition of past sufferings and their projection in public sites of memory and commemoration provide an important ethical alternative to the pursuit of financial compensation within the juridical and fiscal orders of discrete nation-states. Changes in communication and infomatics mean that the past's claims are qualitatively different now. For good or ill, they are weaker than they were, and the ebbing away of the brutal colonial relations that gave such a distinctive meaning to "race" is draining them further. This historic transformation is another aspect of the contemporary crisis of raciology that was sketched at the start of this essay. It is one more compelling sign that "race" is not what it was. And yet, unsettled claims deriving from past injustices are still alive, as, for example, where the remnants of the Herero people seek economic redress for the genocide wrought upon them by General Von Trotha and his associates, or the surviving descendants of the Nazis' slave laborers launch courtroom battles for reparation against the multinational companies that they were compelled to serve on pain of death.[12]

Making raciology appear anachronistic—placing it squarely in the past—now requires careful judgment as to what histories of our heterocultural present and our cosmopolitan future should entail. This work may be best undertaken in the indiscreetly anti-Marxist spirit established by that prototypical black-European Frantz Fanon in the closing pages of his first book, *Black Skin, White Masks*. There, in the first flush of his youthful enthusiasm for existentialism, he turned the full force of a still innocent anger equally against colonial white supremacy and what we now recognize as its black nationalist shadows. Writing as though he were struggling to reassure himself as much as to direct the thoughts of the readers who had managed to complete his book's exacting course, he produced these memorable sentences: "I am not a prisoner of history. I should not seek there for the meaning of my destiny . . . I do not have the right to allow myself to be mired in what the past has determined . . . The body of history does not determine a single one of my actions."[13]

Fanon presented this imaginative supercession of history as the self-conscious initiation of a cycle of freedom for black populations still dwelling in the aftershock of slavery, their founding trauma. For his peers—modern blacks who were in but never comfortably of the color-coded West—claiming a more authentic Being than the racialized order of modernity had allowed necessitated accepting but also turning away from the past. Whether it was read primarily as heroic, noble, wise, and regal or abject, brutalized, de-humanized, and enchained, their transnational and intercultural history had now to be set aside. Its claims upon the present had been rendered illegitimate by the demands of autonomy and self-possession. What Fanon called the "disalienation of humanity," in particular its liberation from division by means of "race" and the repudiation of white supremacy that must precede it, required this decisive change of orientation. The ethical and political adjustments it involved could not proceed without a change in the consciousness of time and significant adjustments to the threshold of contemporaneity.

Having at last buried the primitive status that tied the Negro to both infrahumanity and prehistory, blacks must be able to be secure, even if not exactly comfortable, in the present. According to Fanon, the capacity to address the future, both as politically abstract and as personally concrete, was a precondition for health and healing, for recovery from the alienating and corrupting antisociality of "race." His words provide the framework within which I want to draw together the closing strands of this book. I have approached the contemporary questions of racial science, multiculturalism, absolutism, and nano-politics in a utopian spirit with the communicative model provided by diaspora interculture in mind. Before I enlist the raceless future in the service of my own willfully dislocated argument, I am bound to acknowledge the history of black appeals to the future and must now look toward the vernacular formations where these themes constantly cross one another.

Music and musicians have generated especially important resources that have facilitated the difficult procedures of temporal readjustment. It is important to acknowledge their tradition of longing for a temporality that fosters the capacity to see the individual life-course as well as the synchronized movement of contingent life-worlds. That tradition has repeatedly announced secularized faith in the fact that a change *is* gonna come. This aspiration can be understood best as an even more demanding version of Fanon's already formidable appeal. Taking it seriously today means understanding that extraterrestriality, futurology, and fictions of techno-science have been articulated in the everyday rhythms and forms of what might be termed "the mainstream" of black vernacular expression. It must also reckon with the appeals that black artists, musicians, critics, and writers have made to the future—particularly in historical circumstances where *any* future had been made hard for them to imagine. This enterprise affords a belated means to confront the fact that by making necessity absolute, denying the future and the right to be future-oriented became an integral part of the way white supremacism functioned during and after the slave system.

The usurpation of the future by blacks involved them in struggles to throw off the shackles of the primitive and to win the right to address the future. This idiom did not come easily to political cultures dominated by the hermeneutics of memory. Black Christianity had been rooted in the belief that the only habitable future lay in another, better world beyond this valley of dry bones. That heavenly future was the negation and redemption of present suffering. Concern with the future was equally remote from those possessing the more readily secularized, vindicationist outlooks. Their futures were limited by and oriented toward the idea of redress and the possibility of a reconciliation with the technological and educational possibilities that had been denied by racial hierarchy. The nationalist polymath Martin Delany provides a good example here. His visionary project of futuristic black economic and political development involved the construction of a sublime technological feat, a huge railway right across the African continent. This compelling vision of resourceful-ness, progress, and racial uplift was crucial in establishing the "national po-sition" of African Americans, but it involved barely more than just catching up with what whites had already accomplished in other parts of the world. Delany's dream of modernizing Africa and providing the eco-nomic and technological infrastructure necessary to overthrow slavery in the same grand gesture exemplifies this double bind:

> [The railway] terminating on the Atlantic ocean West; . . . would make the GREAT THOROUGHFARE for all trade with the East Indies and Eastern Coast of Africa, and the Continent of America. All the world would pass through Africa on this railroad, which would yield a revenue infinitely greater than any other investment in the world.[14]

Notwithstanding the hi-tech apocalypse taught to Delany's followers by Elijah Muhammad, schemes of this sort have been very few and far be-tween. The militant vindicationist nationalism in which both men stand has been characteristically preoccupied with the need to prove and estab-lish the properly historical character of blackness as part of important cam-paigns to bring Africa and its subject peoples fully into the racially exclusive modern History to which Hegel had given such enduring and lu-cid expression. We should note that in the same writings on the philoso-phy of history that had consigned Africa to a condition of permanent historylessness, Hegel identified America as the land of the future, a spe-cial place where the burden of world history would reveal itself, "the land of desire for all those who are weary of the historical lumber-room of old Europe."[15] Remembering that provocative teleological sequence should compound our caution. It prompts us to ask how much contemporary reflection on the problems created by concern about the boundaries of self and community is really a consequence of the globalization of the Ameri-can popular cultures that currently define so much of our anxious, postcatastrophic modernity.

We are dealing, as we saw in Chapters 5 and 7, with a formation in which harsh racial codes have enjoyed a special constitutive role. To put it another way, much of this interest in disseminated black cultures—signs of blackness—may derive ultimately from the frustration of advertisers with the obvious limitations of an eternal consumer present and their ambition to deliver us into the tense states represented by the shoppers' conditional and the material future-perfect. The more skeptical, less commercially minded perspective ventured here requires us to question all time-frames, time-lines, and time-scales. It asks, in particular, that we try to be alert to the politics of temporalization and closely tuned in to the ebbs and flows, the eddies and currents, that have energized the protean black cultural creativity that has excited and provoked this essay. It might also suggest that we should not overintegrate the phenomena we want to investigate lest we underplay their contradictory and uneven character or minimize their restless, shifting qualities.

BLACK TO THE FUTURE

To comprehend the history of blackness's appeals to the future and how that history might contribute to the cultural dynamism and moral confidence of a cosmopolitan and hospitable Europe, we need to appreciate the different resonances and articulations regarding the future that have been voiced in various—emergent, dominant, and residual—phases of the process of dissent from raciology. Science, the master cipher of a future with boundless promise, has not always been an ally of the political movements involved in disaggregating modern race-thinking. Some disenchantment with science and an appreciation of the fine lines that rational raciology drew between its respectable and its pseudo varieties have been essential parts of the critique of modernity offered by the history of the black Atlantic. Distinguished African-American scientists like Benjamin Banneker and Lewis Henry Latimer have been iconized to facilitate the celebration of their achievements during black history month, but the life of complex twentieth-century personalities like Ernest Everett Just, the marine biologist who fled Howard University for Europe and was himself briefly interned by the Nazis, remains little known.[16] All these figures must currently take second place behind popular "afrocentric" assertions that the great discoveries of Western science and technology were known to ancient Africa, stolen from their ancient sources, and then assigned by white supremacist historians to the Greeks.

This position usefully interrogates the racial politics of scientific prestige and raises the issue of how European Hellenomania impacted upon the history of science, but it effectively closes off the possibility of any specific or critical engagement with science as a practice. It makes the conspiracies that covered up the theft into a principal issue. This counternarrative of progress is accompanied by a degree of temporal disturbance. It says in effect: "We were ahead of you on the ascending escalator of civilization until you displaced us by illegitimate means." These depressing cycles contribute to the climate in which authoritarian and antiliberal passions can take command of the political imagination. The well-known story of the Dogon people's unexpected and surprising knowledge of the star Sirius B, drawn—we should remember—entirely from the colonial ethnography of Marcel Griaule and Germaine Dieterlen, has been deployed by "Africa-centered" writers not only to disrupt and confound the old polarization primitive/modern, but also to demonstrate a compensatory superiority of Africans and African scientific knowledge. Meanwhile, Africa itself is shut out of the contemporary technological revolution.

Discrepancies between the different levels in the hierarchy of racialized cultures have often been identified as processes of temporal disjunction. Richard Wright expressed this point when he posed a fundamental question bearing upon the self-consciousness of black intellectuals and answered it thus:

> My point of view is a Western one, but a Western one that conflicts at several vital points with the present, dominant outlook of the West. Am I ahead or behind the West? My personal judgment is that I'm ahead. And I do not say that boastfully; such a judgment is implied by the very nature of the Western values that I hold dear.[17]

Putting aside the issue of how the supposed hypermodernity of twentieth-century black music might have contributed to the believability of Wright's assertion, addressing the implications of his standpoint takes us a long way from the exulting in black exotica or kitsch that has sometimes accompanied fascination with the African-American musical avant-garde in places where the stakes of race politics are not as high as they are in the United States. Today, what matters more than whether blacks were then ahead or behind is the degree to which those dissenting sentiments were out of step with the strict, military tempo of the cold war world. Reading Wright against the grain, I would contend that being out of step in precisely this way provided some critical and analytical opportunities and that its value needs to be recalled now that so many people are prepared to fall eagerly into line with the different tempo of a planetarized market capitalism that has been consolidated over the debris of the iron curtain.

To be against racism, against white supremacism, was once to be bonded to the future. This no longer seems to be the case. Wright's words also underline that we can listen profitably to the futurology evident in black popular cultures and interpret their comments on science and technology as having some bearing upon ethical and even political matters. Another note of caution must be sounded as soon as this interpretative problem is introduced. Claims about the complex integrity of everyday life, like the moral and the conceptual problems that arise from well-intentioned critics' finding political consciousness either everywhere or nowhere, are qualified here by the serious obligation to approach the fashionable workings and doings of modern black culture unfashionably. This means seeing them as fallout from a social movement—a liberation movement—if not as an even more direct part of that movement itself. We must identify the various political moments of this vernacular futurology and recognize that even as it fades out, the movement that produced them has created a degree of temporal disturbance. This has been registered self-consciously in the notion of a compound diaspora identity where time, historicity, and historicality have been doubly politicized: first by resistance to white supremacy and then by the uncomfortable acceptance that we are no longer what we once were and cannot rewind the tapes of our complex cultural life to a single knowable point of origin. As shown in Chapter 3, this difficult alternative yields a nonreversible diaspora that can be understood as web, multiplicity, and communicative network. It requires a change of scale in the way that both history and tradition are to be conceptualized.

The deliberately oracular, ethically charged, but still playful works of complex futuristic figures like Sun Ra and George Clinton have recently begun to draw favorable attention. Greg Tate has performed the invaluable service of connecting some of Clinton's work directly to the visual imagination of Leni Riefenstahl by soliciting the information that her photographs of the Nuba had inspired him.[18] It is especially important that we do not see the activities of these prominent techno-tricksters as the sole manifestations of a subtradition that survives exclusively in the ludic experiments of an avant-garde minority within a minority. Their significance is broader and deeper than that, not least because, by being articulated in the multiple historic settings constituted by black Atlantic populist modernism (a style that enforces its own syncopated temporal codes), their passion for the future calls the whole avant-garde idea into question.

These examples draw attention to the special status once enjoyed by music in the black vernacular cultures I have invoked. So far, celebrants and critics of those cultures have had to consider the power of meaningful sound before they could move toward the different and perhaps less demanding tasks involved in analyzing the visualization of the extraterrestrial and the futuristic in racialized forms. Now that iconization supplies the dominant communicative logic, sound is giving up its primary place in favor of visual communication, and dance is in danger of becoming an overly purposive subdivision of the fitness industry, we must tread even more carefully. The cultural terms within which the trials of racial identification are conducted have been transformed. Seeing and hearing the future need not add up to the same thing.

One more welcome effect of Wright's speculations is that they send historians of vernacular culture back to reexamine overlooked albums recorded by deliberately futuristic popular artists of the cold war 1970s: Dexter Wansell, Masterfleet, Stargard, Earth, Wind and Fire, the Undisputed Truth. This period of intense musical creativity arose between the demise of Black Power and the rise of popular Pan-Africanism triggered by Bob Marley. It was dominated by the desire to find a new political and ethical code in which the contradictory demands for blackness on one side and postracial utopia on the other could be articulated together under the bright signs of progress, modernity, and style. We see this aspiration differently when we appreciate that around the time George Clinton's mothership connection took to the heavens, the trumpeter Donald Byrd was already stepping into tomorrow, the jazz organist Charles Earland had announced the possibility of leaving this planet, and the hypermodern, hi-tech sound of synthesizers conjured the possibility that complete black mastery of techno-science would soon follow. Immediately afterward, Wansell's futuristic funk music—buoyed by technological refinements in analog sound synthesis and sequencing—had challenged diasporic dance floors by presciently affirming the possibility of "Life on Mars."

We must always remember that Wright, like Fanon, wrote as a prototypical black European. When he typed those words, he was looking back anxiously over his shoulder toward the idiosyncratic racial conflicts in his land of origin. His decision to be ahead rather than behind the rest of the West can still help to make intelligible the more deliberately opaque activities of figures like Ra, Clinton, and Slim Gaillard, another ex-centric musician whose hip interplanetary talking in tongues has been rather neglected. Wright's words might also help to unlock some of the puzzles presented by "Answers in Progress," Amiri Baraka's memorable short story that describes the visit of blue aliens to this planet in pursuit of Art Blakey records. Wright's choice of merely territorial exile as the first step toward his nonracial utopia might shed interesting light on the creative thinking that Duke Ellington revealed in "Ballet of the Flying Saucers" and, even more interestingly, in his brief 1957 essay "The Race for Space."[19] There, Ellington claimed membership in the American national community, and in the icy cold war climate that would eventually crush Wright, Fanon, and so many of their peers, he argued not only that America's modern jazz culture was "a good barometer" of its unique modern freedoms, but that the country's inability to match the technological achievements of its Russian rivals was a result of the fettering effect of race-consciousness on American creativity and American hope:

> It seems to me that the problem of America's inability so far to go ahead of or at least keep abreast of Russia in the race for space can be traced directly to this racial problem which has been given top priority not only throughout the country but by Washington itself. They're spending so much time trying to figure whether the potential Negro vote is worth making the South mad by opening white schools to Negro kids, by dropping the color bar in restaurants, railroad and bus stations, in white collar jobs and in political appointments that those in charge of the missile and nuclear programs don't know which way to go.[20]

The assumption of linear or evolutionary time and tidy teleological sequences in which progress is defined and evaluated by the tasks involved in eliminating racism has had profound consequences for black artists. In different ways all these examples deployed the hypermodernity of extraterrestrial activity (by humans and others) as a means to conduct an encoded interrogation of the dubious territorial ethics associated with white supremacism and its outmoded racial partiality. All except Elijah Muhammad and his legions agreed that race-thinking belongs in and to the past.

This is a good point to recall that American television's first interracial kiss was between William Shatner and Nichelle Nichols, more normally found working together on the bridge of Gene Roddenbury's *Starship Enterprise*. In her autobiography, Nichols described what happened after that historic episode was screened: "We received one of the largest batches of fan mail ever, all of it positive, with many addressed to me from girls wondering how it felt to kiss Captain Kirk, and many to him from guys wondering the same thing about me."[21] Though they had been forced by aliens into this unnatural embrace, the image of these nonlovers focused the widely shared sense of race consciousness as earthbound and anachronistic. It endorsed the inevitable conclusion: because race consciousness is so manifestly arcane, its victims and others who perceive the open secret of its residual status *must* be closer to advanced interplanetary travelers than they are to its deluded earthly practitioners. This is why Baraka's space travelers wanted the hippest jazz music and why, more recently, something as dangerously "old-timey" as Slim Whitman's white-bread country music could still prove fatal to the mean-spirited alien invaders in Tim Burton's film *Mars Attacks*. There is a clear implication that Burton's postmodern Martians are as comfortable with hip-hop and its profane offshoots as are the rest of the inhabitants of this decadent planet.

The universal currency of black culture was also emphasized by *Space Jam,* the popular 1997 children's movie in which Michael Jordan was kidnapped and enslaved by ruthless but incompetent aliens looking to provide an ever-more-exciting program of entertainment in their pan-galactic theme park. In that film Jordan was superhumanly athletic but also diminished in size so that he could function easily in the same world as the Warner Brothers' "Looney Tunes" cartoon characters who were his fellow slaves and buddies. Though the Jordan character was clearly not a child, he enters a child's world in an interesting way—as a toy—thereby fulfilling both the advertising agency's desire to draw in younger and younger consumers and the enduring racial codes that allow a black hero to be both more and slightly less than a man without ever acquiring the stable adult humanity that demands recognition.

Each of these examples merits extended consideration for the way that it shrugs off the label "primitive" and suggests the backwardness and the tragic, self-defeating absurdity of America's racial order. However, there is something else at work here. These images of science, space, and interplanetary contact also reveal important break points in the apprehension and comprehension of *power* by African Americans. They convey the gradual realization that black freedom struggles inside and outside colonial space had acquired geopolitical, planetary significance. The cold war setting of Wright's observations is especially significant for bringing home this point. The power of the American government could no longer be adequately understood as merely a national phenomenon. The 1939–1945 war, the Berlin blockade, and the worldwide activities of the CIA and other covert agencies had shown that Uncle Sam was more ambitious than that. These were the conditions in which the issue of "race" gradually became central to debates over the ethical fitness of American democracy as it moved toward a mature imperial phase. Black vernacular culture came to appreciate this painfully through the deaths of so many leaders of the Bandung generation who had distinguished and endangered themselves by making the global points we now take for granted.

The optimistic cold war commentaries on race and space which, like Ellington's, still aspire to conscripting science into the service of democracy, have a character quite different from that of later material in which techno-science is judged to be entirely complicit with the order of white supremacy. The later pattern turns away from a disproportionate concern with the future to address a desperate present in which extreme contrasts between rich and poor underscore the depth of racial divisions and their power to corrupt America's democratic promise. At this point, the future has arrived. That well-known *Star Trek* fan Dr. Martin Luther King, Jr., was among the first to voice an important argument that would be repeated many times in the years following his death:

> Today the exploration of space is engaging not only our enthusiasm but our patriotism. Developing it as a global race we have intensified its inherent drama and brought its adventure into every living room, nursery, shop and office. No such fervor or exhilaration attends the war on poverty. There is impatience with its problems, indifference towards its progress and hostility towards its errors.

Without denying the value of scientific endeavor, there is a striking absurdity in committing billions to reach the moon where no people live, while only a fraction of that amount is appropriated to service the densely populated slums. If these strange views persist, in a few years we can be assured that when we set a man on the moon, with an adequate telescope he will be able to see the slums on earth with their intensified congestion, decay and turbulence. On what scale of values is this a program of progress?[22]

There is a pronounced contrast between Wright's and Ellington's attempts to press the future into the service of black liberation and King's sense, only a few years later, that the gap between social and technological achievements was now so deep that it called the very idea of social and economic progress into question. Understanding the difference between these positions can contribute to the construction of a lineage for the discourses of futurology and extraterrestriality that are once again at the core of vernacular cultural practices. This genealogy will also require us to confront the translocal glamour and attractiveness of African-American culture, as well as the appearance of representative modern icons and timely indicative pursuits: exemplary bodies, characteristic musics, and typical sports. These prized attributes communicate an acceleration of the present and the enhancing of its pleasures. They have featured in the industrialization and eventual globalization of communicative and entertainment media. Nichelle Nichols has explained that King was very clear about the significance of her presence on the bridge of the *Enterprise* for African-American freedom struggles:

I turned . . . and found myself gazing upon the face of Dr. Martin Luther King, Jr. I was stunned . . . The man introduced us. Imagine my surprise when the first words Dr. King uttered were, "Yes, I am that fan, and I wanted to tell you how important your role is." He began speaking of how he and his children watched Star Trek faithfully and how much they adored Uhura.[23]

On the planetary stage, America's stubborn and parochial commitment to the idea of racial hierarchy made its democratic pretensions begin to appear absurd. Its racial order could only be contradicted by the emergent world of placeless consumer culture, where aspects of the blackness it reviled were increasingly revered as a timely supplement to some enhanced marketing opportunities. This was not the familiar situation in which an appetite for black cultures is completely divorced from an equivalent enthusiasm for the black people who produce them. I would suggest that the moment in which the cold war began to give way to what has succeeded it can be marked by the way that racially representative African-American people effectively *became* the strange, hyperhuman hybrid of ultramodern and ultraprimitive that their distinctive culture had long signaled in Europe. As they traveled further and further away from their culture's New World wellsprings, they increasingly personified some of its most appealing attributes to an adoring, translocal public. Their bodies communicated health, vitality, strength, and an absolutely racialized power capable of reconciling the primitive with the modern, the postcontemporary.

This project is now a virtual operation that can proceed without its agents' having to leave their dwelling places. To put it another way, the development of vernacular futurology has been connected to the realization that the old blackness—too narrowly understood—as American abjection must yield to a new awareness of blackness as a prestigious sign, in particular as a signifier of bodily health and fitness, of human, indeed superhuman, vitality, grace, and animal potency. This provides the horizon against which the primal scenes of privatized postmodernity are staged.

The codes of the cultural complex we call infotainment have negotiated and encompassed the aesthetico-political forces deriving from cultural technologies pioneered under European fascism. To comprehend the seductive force of these images of mankind and its orderly techno-scientific future, we have to reconstruct the confluence of these two dream worlds of mass culture where they play upon and solicit identification with superhuman black bodies, male and female. These representational systems combined and mutated into a single phantasmagoria far more powerful than anything that Fanon had first glimpsed in the 1940s and 1950s under bright enamel signs marked with the legendary, chilling words "Sho' good eatin'" and struggled to name in those sections of *Black Skin, White Masks* where—thinking of Jesse Owens and Joe Louis—he discussed the processes whereby the active physicality of the Negro symbolizes not nature but the biological.

The most obvious political consequences of this shift saw spectacle, ritual, and aesthetically textured political drama not only being served up on an unprecedented global scale but also being articulated deliberately as a means to promote the forms of solidarity, interconnection, and unquestioning unanimity that characterize the impossible ideal of homogenous nationality in a world of encamped nation-states. The celebrated sequence of superhuman black physicality that descends from Jack Johnson and Owens through Louis and Muhammad Ali to Michael Jordan and even Mike Tyson must also be appreciated as an integral part of this substantial cultural change. Their contested corporeality supplied a decisive element in understanding how the techniques and technologies of selfhood, identity, and solidarity born from nationalism and refined by the governmental and scopic regimes of Nazism have been recycled almost unrecognized in the visual workings of contemporary commerce. They now supply the everyday substance of selling sportswear, shoes, and other commodities. They provide an attractive human counterpoint to the anonymity of the corporate logo which promotes precisely those forms of solidarity that Nazi emblems first sought to impose upon a disorderly world.

It is the athletic perfection of the black male body that specifies the future here. These dynamic postmodern values reduce the experience of sporting activity to the ideal of being a winner. They are far removed from the ancient notions of honor, beauty, discipline, and competition previously associated with sport. The distance between them was sharply illustrated in the concluding game of the 1998 World Cup tournament in France when Ronaldo, at that time the most expensive and therefore apparently the best soccer player on the planet, was supposedly coerced into participating in the final, decisive contest after suffering an epileptic seizure. The Brazilian team's commercial sponsorship by the Nike Corporation, to which his iconic presence was deemed central, required him in sickness as in health to assume his place in front of the cameras. For that descendant of slaves, the future suddenly began to look a lot like the past.

In numerous ways, the assertion of radical alterity by blacks and the associated invocation of forces beyond this world have become integral to a post-traditional critique of the raciology and raciality to which Riefenstahl's work is such a subtle and enduring monument. Barred from ordinary humanity and offered the equally unsatisfactory roles of semi-deity, janitor, or pet, artists seek, like Sun Ra, another mode of recognition in the most alien identity they can imagine. The momentum they acquire in moving from the infrahuman to the superhuman finally carries them beyond the human altogether. You will believe a man can fly. That critique is still lived and enjoyed as both counterculture and counterpower, formulated at the junction point—the crossroads—of diaspora dwelling and diaspora estrangement.

BLACK NO MORE

These uncomfortable issues provided the promising setting for the first "science fiction" novel penned by a black Atlantic writer. This was George Schuyler's "Black No More," a satirical commentary on the age of the Harlem Renaissance first published in 1931. There are no space aliens or space travel in his futuristic novella. Instead, his story concerns the effects on America of the invention of a machine for turning black people into whites. As one might anticipate, the electrical and chemical technologies to accomplish this shocking transformation have been brought back to the United States from Germany by the machine's devious and cosmopolitan inventor, Dr. Junius Crookman. It is especially significant for our ethical purposes that the protagonist's first major action after undergoing his change of race is to enlist in the ranks of a vicious white supremacist organization, the Knights of Nordica. Once again, science, technology, and progress expand the field of immorality. They multiply available opportunities for doing the wrong thing. Schuyler, a political conservative who was actively anti-communist, argues misanthropically that blacks and whites are absolutely alike in their moral incapacities. His imaginary future offers no respite from that eternal cycle, only its intensification.

The tropes of extraterrestriality have recently reappeared in the era of globalized cultures and economic relations where blackness has acquired the premium I have described. This time, however, those tropes are not associated with the idea of scientific or any other variety of progress. They have been manifested in a less positive incarnation as a potent element in the articulation of what could be called a "New Age fundamentalism" with disturbing patterns of authoritarian irrationalism. Needless to say, this cipher of chronic powerlessness is not a mixture that defers to the supposedly unbreachable boundaries of color and phenotype.

In the 1970s, what we can call the liberationist invocations of African archaism and techno-scientific modernity were held in an unstable but useful equilibrium. The music, the discourse, and the visual culture of groups like Earth, Wind and Fire presented it clearly. Strange as it seems, they strove to be both nationalist and internationalist. The tension between those two commitments was resolved into a universalistic appeal to spirituality on the one hand and to shared human characteristics on the other. The latter, symbolized above all by the endlessly differing but always similar patterning of the human face, was unexpectedly but happily revealed through explicit contrast with the extraterrestrial. The music framed these possibilities by creating spaces of pleasure and discovery. The years between Billy Preston's clavinet extravaganza "Outta Space" and Afrika Bambaataa's "Planet Rock" saw dance floors filled not just by Clinton's well-known work but by innumerable *Star Wars* spin-offs and ephemeral requests for ET to phone home.

Twenty years later, mainstream American culture seems to have discovered the value of this insight, but as far as black culture is concerned, the delicate balance of the 1970s and early 1980s has now been lost. Some degree of antimodern sentiment is an understandable element in the invented traditions of a community constituted from the awareness that progress and catastrophe could not be separated in its own recent history, but both sides of the equation of identity—black archaism and black hypermodernity—appear to have got out of control. The quest for an uncontaminated space, outside the workings of a compromised and undemocratic system, from which critical commentary could be conducted and more fruitful developmental possibilities identified has been all but abandoned. People no longer play with the possibility of departure from this planet in the same spirit with which their predecessors had entertained the idea of return to Africa. Africa was a more welcoming place in the period of anticolonial wars than it appears to be today, locked as it is in postcolonial privation. The slaves' traditional desire to escape has had to be qualified. Flight is now either an internal journey or a trip to the marketplace. Today's overdisciplined enthusiasts for African antiquity seek to enlist the other-worldly powers held by space travelers or others armed with extraterrestrial insight for more mystical and more profane purposes. The aliens represent not hope and escape but basic human frustration at the growing power of the earthly governments with which they are in league and everyday rage against the transnational Illuminati who are even now plotting the subordination of racially divided humanity.

In the earlier period, the Nation of Islam theology involving space-ships was safely satirized by George Clinton and his crew of well-dressed clones. Today authoritarian irrationalism can be said to have triumphed over the subversive carnivalization to which Dr. Funkenstein had sub-jected it. From the Stephen Lawrence inquiry in London to the streets of Jasper, Texas, the humorless, military style of stern, uniformed black men confirms the unsavory lineage of their political outlook. Their discipline is applauded by spectators as if it could be separated from their other photo-genic attributes. We must ask how that glamorous, earthly militarism can readily co-exist with their enthusiastic interest in aliens, spaceships, and redemption engineered from above. There is one small clue to this in the way that science is presented in their teachings. In this subculture, science has consistently escaped criticism thanks to its capacity to negate the im-age of the stupid, ignorant, childish "Negro." There is a trace of this failing in the tale of the rebel scientist Yacub, who is credited by the Nation of Is-lam with the unnatural invention of the white devil race. He was damned not for the varieties of science he practiced but for their illegitimate inspi-ration and their catastrophic outcome. On another level, his activities, though evil, might be thought of as confirming the enterprise and genius of his race as a whole. In this version of the Frankenstein story, Yacub was to be derided for his disobedience, his hubris, and his failure to conform to the demands of piety and intergenerational authority, not for the patho-logical immorality of his scientific compulsions. The growth of the NOI, its offshoots, and the power of its fellow travelers still involves the circula-tion of these futuristic stories, which are not peripheral to the appeal of their tough program for racial regeneration. Its current popularity is only one sign that today, democratic black politics is faced by a resurgence of occultism. The archaic, tradition-inventing inclinations of revolutionary conservatism are being modified, updated, and partly replaced by heavy doses of an irrationalist techno-scientific fantasy that communicates new depths of black powerlessness and immiseration. The gnostic work of Richard King is close to the pinnacle of these depressing developments:

> Blackness, the universal solvent of all, was seen as the one reality
> from which life's loom spun. All colors, all vibratory energies were
> but a shade of black. Black was the color of the night sky, primeval
> ocean, outer space, birthplace and womb of the planets, stars and

galaxies of the universe; black holes were found at the center of our own galaxy and countless other galaxies. Black was the color of carbon, the key atom found in all living matter. Carbon atoms linked together to form black melanin, the first chemical that could capture light and reproduce itself. The chemical key to life and the brain itself was found to be centred around black neuromelanin. Inner vision, intuition, creative genius, and spiritual illumination were all found to depend upon the pineal gland blood; born chemical messengers that controlled skin color and opened the hidden door to the darkness of the collective unconscious mind, allowing the ancient priest-scientist to visualize knowledge from the mind's timeless collective unconscious memory-banks.[24]

In seeking to understand how this resurgence has been possible and in order to clarify its authoritarian character, I was drawn via advertisements in the NOI's newspaper *Final Call* to the book *Behold a Pale Horse*, produced and published in 1991 by the militia theoretician William Cooper.[25] Cooper is an Oklahoman who claims "Cherokee blood." He accentuates the "constitutional" character of his political crusade for truth and introduces the fact that he has a Chinese wife in order to prove that white supremacy is not part of his system of belief. Cooper appears to have won a substantial black readership on the basis of these strategies. His book's opening chapter is entitled "Silent Weapons for Quiet Wars." This, he tells us, is the name of an important secret document purportedly discovered in a government photocopier purchased at a surplus sale. The same phrase has already been borrowed by the uniformed hip-hop group Killarmy, a militaristic offshoot of the Wu Tang Clan, who employed it in turn as the title for their 1997 CD.

Cooper has set down an elaborate conspiracy theory that encompasses the Kennedy assassination, the doings of the secret world government, the coming ice age, and a variety of other covert activities associated with the Illuminati's declaration of war upon the people of America. His elaborate and irrefutable explanations mine old seams of the American "paranoid style." If it has been noticed at all, his book has been noted so far mainly because it includes a reprint of large parts of the text of the notorious anti-semitic pamphlet *Protocols of the Elders of Zion*. In Cooper's text, the chapter containing those excerpts is prefaced by a note from the author warning his readers that "any reference to 'Jews' should be replaced by the word 'Illuminati' and the word 'goyim' should be replaced with the word 'cattle.'" Less noteworthy has been the fact that the book's lurid cover styles Cooper as "the world's leading expert on UFOs." He seems undecided whether the aliens are a real threat or whether the Illuminati have manufactured them as a means to force humanity into the unwanted unification that follows from answering their alien power with earth's best military resources.

An elaborate conspiracy in which aliens and spaceships figure prominently as adjuncts to cosmopolitan power and as proof of governmental perfidy is an essential part of the lingua franca which bonds the Nation of Islam and its fringe culture to the outlook and actions of the authoritarian and fraternal organizations that speak in the name of militarized whiteness. Phantasmic fraternal bonding across the color line is not only a result of the way that some ultranationalist groups strategically play "race" down. Cooper's "multiculturalism" suggests that antiblack racism may have actually become significantly less important in their ideological makeup, falling behind anti-elite, antigovernment concerns in which blacks, too, can be allowed a measure of victimage—for example, as childlike targets of the government-run trade in hard drugs or as victims of the HIV that was introduced into their communities as part of a genocidal scheme to rid the planet of the black race.

Black and white representatives of this fundamentalism may disagree on the iconic status of General Colin Powell, who appears to be a key player in the constitution of the New World Order, but they converge more deeply in the value they place upon fraternity, violence, and war. While the Illuminati are prepared mockingly to allow women into their armies, the older martial culture that opposes their illicit ambitions allows real men to bond with one another in a primal love that can only grow where women have been excluded. This militaristic repertoire knows no color or culture lines.

Members of Khallid Muhammad's Military Fruit of Islam demonstrated their armed strength in the aftermath of James Byrd's brutal murder in Jasper, Texas. Gathered just a few feet away from the white Klansmen who had come to the town on a similar political errand, men who share the same anxieties about "race" purity and degeneration, and who might in other circumstances actually be allies, they made the politi-

cal implications of their antipolitical stance plain when they resolved a familiar list of grievances into the ancient demands for money and sovereign
territory. The possibility that political rights could be part of resolving
these racialized conflicts was explicitly repudiated. As their commander,
General Omar Al-Tariq, explained:

> There will never be peace in this country until the black man is sep-
> arated and given land of his own. I am not interested in civil rights.
> We want reparations, and to go to our own land. And if you do not
> realize this, there will come a time when we, the black man, will
> take the lives of Caucasian men, women and babies. We will kill
> you, all of you. You will see the black man explode and we are close
> to that—the day is upon you.[26]

From this quote we can see that the question of actual elite contact and
technological collaboration with aliens is an important but ultimately secondary issue. Far more significant is the way that governmental secrecy
around UFOs emerges as an extremely potent signifier for the general duplicity and corruption of a wholly illegitimate political order. Cooper began the dangerous trail that led him toward the workings of the secret
world government while serving in Vietnam, where the presence of UFOs
and their reported participation in the combat seem to have been a regular
event. His persistent invocation of his status as a war veteran proves more
than his patriotic credentials. It establishes the depth of the betrayal being
perpetrated by the U.S. government and provides another, bigger clue as
to the power of color-blind irrationalism and militarism. The imaginary
threat represented by aliens, their menacing technologies, and their secret
collaboration with duplicitous governments have become a means to generate and legitimize paramilitary responses. Extraterrestrials place human
life in jeopardy. The only fitting answer to their awesome power is war.
The alien menace is above all an opportunity to instigate the martial rules
that can repudiate all political processes and replace them with a natural
hierarchy. This would be modified in practice only by a belligerent fraternal respect.

While living unhappily in California, Adorno wrote a celebrated and
contentious essay entitled "Stars down to Earth." It commented bitterly on
the horoscope column then being published in the *Los Angeles Times*. His
contrary observations on the relationship between other-worldliness and

the development of authoritarian irrationalism have become once again interesting in the contemporary context. Though Adorno denied that his small study of the column could be generalized, he tried to identify the varieties of disenchantment and opacity that foster the need to believe that the sublime power of the stars and planets guides all human agency. He names the hypostatization of science, the desperate desire to break the constricting spell of what exists, and the yearning to find a short-cut out of the gloom into something better, something beyond this world. We have seen that all these tendencies are alive in the contemporary obsession with aliens, spaceships, and government conspiracies. They, too, operate best in what he called a climate of "disillusioned agnosticism." Here, no less than in his essay on the astrology column, facts, albeit shrouded from sight by the secret actions of government, are the principal, inescapable issue.

If it seems that this chapter has been in danger of becoming mesmerized by marginalia, Adorno's comments demonstrate the obligation to address overground, everyday versions of the same occult themes: "institutionalized, objectified and, to a large extent, socialized." These themes have been articulated most clearly and obviously in successful movies like *Independence Day* and *Men in Black*, where the ur-narratives of heterosexual coupling and familial reconstruction have been momentarily displaced by other urgent concerns. The bourgeois family is now apparently lost in space and there is, I suppose, some small measure of progress involved in the world's being sold an alternative image of planetary salvation wrought not by Buck Rodgers or Dan Dare but through the irrepressible American stereotypes incarnated in Jeff Goldblum's cerebral intelligence and Will Smith's adolescent physicality. But corporate multiculturalism has its limits. Though the mechanisms of the connection remain unclear, the proliferation of films in which men bond transethnically in the face of the greater dangers represented by aliens, invasions, comets, and threatened planetary conquests does affirm something of the radical powerlessness produced by a chronic inability to reduce the salience of racial divisions in social, economic, and cultural life. This trend is itself open to being read as an outcome of the dismal shifts that have nourished the growth of militarism and ethnic absolutism.

There is, however, another, more hopeful way for those who dwell in the shadow of fascist modernism to interpret the way Hollywood has recently placed these extraterrestrial motifs in the foreground. Product placement considerations aside, it is impossible to overlook the fact that this crop of movies expresses real and widespread hunger for a world that is undivided by the petty differences we retain and inflate by calling them racial. These films seek to celebrate how the desire to retain those outmoded principles of differentiation recedes when it confronts more substantive varieties of otherness and forms of life that are truly other-worldly. In this, the global dream-factory seems at last to have caught up with the best content of more mainstream currents of black political thought. Our challenge should now be to bring even more powerful visions of planetary humanity from the future into the present and to reconnect them with democratic and cosmopolitan traditions that have been all but expunged from today's black political imaginary.

NOTES
ACKNOWLEDGMENTS
INDEX

NOTES

1. THE CRISIS OF "RACE" AND RACIOLOGY

1. C. Peter Ripley et al., eds., *The Black Abolitionist Papers* (University of North Carolina Press, 1985), 4 vols.
2. "The fact that the development of computer technology, with its demands on information theory, has occurred contemporaneously with the growth of molecular biology has not merely provided the physical technology, in instrumentation and computing power, without which the dramatic advances of the decades since the 1960s would not have been possible. It has also given the organising metaphors within which the data was analysed and the theories created." Steven Rose, *Lifelines* (Penguin, 1997), p. 120.
3. Frantz Fanon, *Black Skin, White Masks*, trans. Charles Lam (Markman, Pluto Press, 1986 [1952]), p. 60.
4. Martin Luther King, Jr., *Where Do We Go from Here: Chaos or Community?* (Harper and Row, 1967), p. 53.
5. "Recent tests at the US Army Research Institute of Environmental Medicine in Massachusetts showed that 78% of women who underwent similar training qualified for 'very heavy' military jobs." Hugh McManners, "Army Sets Out to Build a Better Breed of Woman," *Sunday Times*, March 17, 1996.
6. African Rights, *Rwanda Not So Innocent: When Women Become Killers* (1975).
7. Carole Pateman, *The Disorder of Women* (Stanford University Press, 1989), esp. chapter 2.
8. Richard Rorty, "Cruelty and Solidarity," in *Contingency, Irony and Solidarity* (Cambridge University Press, 1989).
9. Beverley Merz, "Whose Cells Are They, Anyway?" *American Medical News* (March 23–30, 1990), pp. 7–8; "Modern Times: The Way of All Flesh," BBC 2 Television, March 19, 1997.

10. Jeremy Rifkin, *The Bio-Tech Century: Harnessing the Gene and Re-Making the World* (Tarcher Putnam, 1998).
11. Ilya Prigogine, *The End of Certainty: Time, Chaos and the New Laws of Nature* (Free Press, 1997), p. 29.
12. Richard Dyer, *White* (Routledge, 1997), chapter 3.
13. Fanon, *Black Skin, White Masks*, p. 161.
14. "Bodily fitness as the supreme goal, meant to be pursued, yet never reached, by means of self-coercion, is bound to be forever shot through with anxiety seeking an outlet, but generating a constantly growing demand for ever new yet untested outlets. I propose that this product of the 'privatisation' of the body and of the agencies of social production of the body is the 'primal scene' of postmodern ambivalence. It lends postmodern culture its unheard-of energy, an inner compulsion to be on the move. It is also a crucial cause, perhaps the prime cause, of its inbuilt tendency to instant ageing." Zygmunt Bauman, *Life in Fragments* (Polity Press, 1995), p. 119.
15. Donna Haraway, *Modest_Witness@Second_Millennium.FemaleMan©_Meets OncoMouse™: Feminism and Technoscience* (Routledge, 1997) p. 262.
16. "The glances of the other fixed me there, in the sense in which a chemical solution is fixed by a dye." Fanon, *Black Skin, White Masks*, p. 109.
17. *The Voice*, issue 724 (October 15, 1996).
18. Howard Jones, *Mutiny on the Amistad* (Oxford University Press, 1987).
19. Stephen Buckley, "Heritage Battle Rages at Slavery's Sacred Sites," *Guardian* (August 1, 1995).
20. "The trouble with the NPFL is that, in battle, they may capture a street corner, but then they go for a beer, and when they come back they're surprised to find that they've lost it again," Lemuel Potty told reporters in Monrovia. "They're rubbish, but at least they're better than their rivals the Krahn. They go into battle wearing women's wigs, necklaces and rubber overcoats." Potty, a National Patriotic Front of Liberia (NPFL) sympathizer who owned a nightclub in the Mamba Point district, was describing the civil war raging in his country which has so far killed over 150,000 people. "I'm not saying that the war isn't going full pelt. There are quite a few dead people lying around in the streets, but actually the gunmen are far more interested in looting luxury goods than killing each other. Shops selling trainers were the first to be looted, but they also like robbing tailors' shops. The NPFL wear brightly coloured sailors' life vests, or T shirts they've looted from the Save The Children Fund. Their basic look is ghetto rap musician. You can always spot them because they all wear blue berets, stolen from the Army and Navy store, but the Krahn are more flamboyant. One Krahn fighter dresses in wellington boots and a woman's head scarf, and calls himself Lieutenant Colonel Double Trouble. They do the real fighting in the countryside. When they come to Monrovia they don't really come to fight. They come to shop." *Eastern Express*, April 24, 1996.

21. Michael Chege, the director of African Studies at the University of Florida, has repeatedly drawn attention to the role of elite academics in formulating the genocidal doctrines implemented in Rwanda. See Tim Cornwell's "Rwandan Scholars Conspired," *Times Higher Education Supplement* (February 28, 1997). The suicide of Nikola Koljevic, prolific Shakespearean scholar, ideologue of "ethnic cleansing," and prime architect of the destruction of Sarajevo, raises similar issues in a different setting. See Janine di Giovanni's article "The Cleanser" in *Guardian Weekend* (March 1, 1997).

22. As I write, only two men, Jean-Paul Akayesu and Jean Kambanda, have been found guilty for their roles in the mass killing.

23. Kader Asmal et al., *Reconciliation through Truth: A Reckoning with Apartheid's Criminal Governance* (James Currey, 1997). See also Patrick J. Furlong, *Between Crown and Swastika: The Impact of the Radical Right on the Afrikaner Nationalist Movement in the Fascist Era* (Wesleyan, New England, 1991); and Carlos Santiago Nino, *Radical Evil on Trial* (Yale University Press, 1996).

24. June Goodwin and Ben Schiff, *Heart of Whiteness: Afrikaners Face Black Rule in the New South Africa* (Scribner, 1995), p. 177.

25. Jonathan Steele, "National Effrontery," *Guardian* (May 24, 1997).

26. Gérard Prunier, *The Rwanda Crisis: History of Genocide* (Columbia University Press, 1995), pp. 103–106.

27. Marek Kohn's *The Race Gallery: The Return of Racial Science* (Cape, 1995) and John Hoberman's *Darwin's Athletes: How Sport Has Damaged Black America and Preserved the Myth of Race* (Houghton Mifflin, 1997) are two important books that against much of the momentum of their own arguments remain determined to hold on to the idea of racial science.

28. Martin Thom, *Republics, Nations and Tribes* (Verso, 1995).

29. Guntram Henrik Herb, *Under the Map of Germany: Nationalism and Propaganda, 1918–1945* (Routledge, 1997); Jeremy Black, *Maps and History* (Yale University Press, 1997), especially chapter 4.

30. Mahmood Mamdani, *Citizen and Subject* (Princeton University Press, 1997).

31. Martin Barker, *The New Racism* (Junction Books, 1980).

32. Steven Rose, *Lifelines: Biology, Freedom, Determinism* (Penguin Books, 1997).

33. Londa Schiebinger, *Nature's Body: Gender in the Making of Modern Science* (Beacon Press, 1993).

34. Martin Kemp, "Temples of the Body and Temples of the Cosmos: Vision and Visualization in the Vesalian and Copernican Revolutions," in Brian S. Baigrie, ed., *Picturing Knowledge: Historical and Philosophical Problems Concerning the Use of Art in Science* (University of Toronto Press, 1996), pp. 40–85.

35. Jonathan Crary, *Techniques of the Observer: On Vision and Modernity in the Nineteenth Century* (MIT Press, 1992).

36. Alex Potts, *Flesh and the Ideal: Winckelmann and the Origins of Art History* (Yale University Press, 1994), esp. sections IV and V.

37. Howard Kaye points out that Haeckl's *Welträtsel,* a treatise of "national socialism in support of racial community," sold more than 300,000 copies between 1900 and 1914. Howard Kaye, *The Social Meaning of Modern Biology* (Yale University Press, 1986), p. 38.

38. Mechtild Rössler, "'Area Research' and 'Spatial Planning' from the Weimar Republic to the German Federal Republic: Creating a Society with a Spatial Order under National Socialism," in Monika Renneberg and Mark Walker, eds., *Science, Technology and National Socialism* (Cambridge University Press, 1994), pp. 126–138.

39. Sven Holdar, "The Ideal State and the Power of Geography: The Life-Work of Rudolf Kjellén," *Political Geography* 11 (1992), pp. 307–323; Herb, *Under the Map of Germany.*

40. Anna Bramwell, *The History of Ecology in the Twentieth Century* (Yale University Press, 1989), p. 50.

41. Richard Lewontin, *The Doctrine of DNA: Biology as Ideology* (Penguin Books, 1991), pp. 63–64.

42. Fanon, *Black Skin, White Masks,* p. 110.

43. Jonathan Crary, *Techniques of the Observer: On Vision and Modernity in the Nineteenth Century* (MIT Press, 1992), p. 16.

44. Michel Foucault, *The Order of Things* (Tavistock, 1970), p. 132.

45. Hegel's discussion of phrenology and physiognomy affords some insight into the troubling coexistence of these different perceptual and observational regimes.

46. "Alle Bewohner der heibesten Zonen sind ausnehmend trÑge. Bey einigen wird diese Faulheit noch etwas durch die Regierung und Zwang gemÑbigt." Kant, *Physische Geographie,* 1802, quoted by Christian M. Neugebauer, "The Racism of Kant and Hegel," in H. Odera Oruka, ed., *Sage Philosophy: Indigenous Thinkers and Modern Debate on African Philosophy* (Brill, 1990).

47. Fanon, *Black Skin, White Masks,* p. 111.

48. G. Wolstenhome, ed., *Man and His Future* (Little, Brown, 1963), pp. 275–276, 294–295.

49. Sir William Macpherson of Cluny, "A Report into the Death of Stephen Lawrence" (Her Majesty's Stationery Office, 1999).

2. MODERNITY AND INFRAHUMANITY

1. Janice E. Thomson, *Mercenaries, Pirates, and Sovereigns: State Building and Extra-Territorial Violence in Early Modern Europe* (Princeton University Press, 1994).

2. William E. Connolly, "Democracy and Territoriality," in Marjorie Ringrose and Adam J. Lerner, eds., *Reimagining the Nation* (Open University Press, 1993).

3. Peter Hulme, *Colonial Encounters* (Methuen, 1986).

4. Daniel Defoe, *Robinson Crusoe* (Penguin, 1985), p. 232.

5. Anthony Pagden, *Lords of All the World: Ideologies of Empire in Spain, Britain and France c1500–c1800* (Yale University Press, 1995).

6. Ian Watt, *Myths of Modern Individuality: Faust, Don Quixote, Don Juan and Robinson Crusoe* (Cambridge University Press, 1996).

7. Josef Chytry, *The Aesthetic State: A Quest in Modern German Thought* (University of California Press, 1989); Earl W. Count, *This Is Race: An Anthology Selected from the International Literature on the Races of Man* (Schuman, 1950); Christian Neugebauer, "The Racism of Kant And Hegel," in *Sage Philosophy: Indigenous Thinkers and Modern Debate on African Philosophy*, ed. H. Odera Oruka (Brill, 1990).

8. George Mosse, *Toward the Final Solution: A History of European Racism* (Wisconsin University Press, 1985), esp. chapter 2.

9. Robert Bernasconi, "Hegel at the Court of the Ashanti," in Stuart Barnett, ed., *Hegel after Derrida* (Routledge, 1998).

10. G. W. F. Hegel, *The Philosophy of History*, trans. J. Sibree (Dover Books, 1956), p. 96.

11. This term is taken from Thongchai Winichakul's *Siam Mapped: A History of the Geo-Body of a Nation* (University of Hawaii Press, 1994).

12. Mary Louise Pratt, *Imperial Eyes: Travel Writing and Transculturation* (Routledge, 1992).

13. Winthrop Jordan, *White Over Black* (Norton, 1977); Ivan Hannaford, *Race: The History of an Idea in the West* (Johns Hopkins, 1996).

14. I have in mind the work of Eric Voegelin, Martin Bernal, and Ivan Hannaford.

15. Eric Voegelin, "The Growth of the Race Idea," *Review of Politics* (July 1940), p. 284.

16. Ronald A. T. Judy, *(Dis)forming the American Canon: African-Arabic Slave Narratives and the Vernacular* (University of Minnesota Press, 1993), chapter 4, section 3, "Kant and the Critique of Pure Negro."

17. I. Kant, *Observations on the Feeling of the Beautiful and the Sublime*, trans. John T. Goldthwait (University of California Press, 1960).

18. I. Kant, *Anthropology from a Pragmatic Point of View*, trans. Victor Lyle Dowdell (Southern Illinois University Press, 1978).

19. Kant, *Observations*, p. 111.

20. Emily Hobhouse, *Report on a Visit to the Camps* (London, 1901); *Report of Dame Millicent Fawcett's Committee of Ladies* (Cmnd. Cd 893); Louis Perez, Jr., *Cuba Between the Empires, 1878–1902* (University of Pittsburgh Press, 1983), and *Lords of the Mountain: Social Banditry and Protest in Cuba, 1878–1918* (University of Pittsburgh Press, 1989). I am grateful to Peter Fraser for the Cuban material.

21. Berel Lang, *Act and Idea in the Nazi Genocide* (Chicago University Press, 1990), chapter 7, p. 189.

22. Ibid., p. 179.

23. I. Kant, *Anthropology from a Pragmatic Point of View*, trans. Victor Lyle Dowdell (Southern Illinois University Press, 1978), p. 230.

24. Hannah Arendt, *Eichmann in Jerusalem* (Penguin, 1965), p. 136.

25. Aimé Césaire, *Discourse on Colonialism* (Monthly Review Press, 1972), p. 15.

26. Claude LeFort, *The Political Forms of Modern Society* (Polity, 1986).

27. Houston Stewart Chamberlain, *The Foundations of the Nineteenth Century*, trans. John Lees (John Lane, 1912). See also Martin Woodroffe, "Racial Theories of History and Politics: The Example of Houston Stewart Chamberlain," in Paul Kennedy and Anthony Nicholls, eds., *Nationalist and Racialist Movements in Britain and Germany before 1914* (Macmillan, 1981); and Hannaford, *Race*, pp. 348–356.

28. Chamberlain, *The Foundations of the Nineteenth Century*, p. 261.

29. Paul Connerton, *The Tragedy of Enlightenment* (Cambridge University Press, 1983), p. 110.

30. Hegel, *The Philosophy of History*, p. 93.

31. Mark Cocker, *Rivers of Blood, Rivers of Gold: Europe's Conflict with Tribal Peoples* (Cape, 1998); Gerhard Pool, *Samuel Maharero* (Gamsberg/Macmillan, 1991).

32. Catrine Clay and Michael Leapman, *Master Race: The Lebensborn Experiment in Nazi Germany* (Corgi, 1995).

33. Michel Foucault, *History of Sexuality*, trans. Robert Hurley, vol. 1 (Random House, 1978), p. 149.

34. Hugh A. MacDougall, *Racial Myth in English History: Trojans, Teutons, and Anglo-Saxons* (University Press of New England, 1982).

35. Wilfried van der Will, "The Body and the Body Politic as Symptom and Metaphor in the Transition of German Culture to National Socialism," in Brandon Taylor and Wilfried van der Will, eds., *The Nazification of Art* (Winchester Press, 1990).

36. Michael Lowy, *Redemption and Utopia*, trans. Hope Heaney (Athlone Press, 1992).

37. Frantz Fanon, *Wretched of the Earth*, trans. Constance Farrington (Grove Press, 1963), pp. 254–255 (emphasis added).

38. Julian Young, *Heidegger, Philosophy, Nazism* (Cambridge University Press, 1997), p. 36.

39. Primo Levi, *The Drowned and the Saved*, trans. Raymond Rosenthal (Summit Books, 1988), chapter 2; Richard Rorty, *Objectivity, Relativism and Truth* (Cambridge University Press, 1991), pp. 205–206.

40. Jon Bridgman, *The Revolt of the Hereros* (University of California Press, 1981).

41. May Optiz et al., eds., *Showing Our Colors: Afro-German Women Speak Out*, trans. Anne V. Adams (University of Massachusetts Press, 1992) pp. 1–56.

42. Sandra Adell, *Double Consciousness, Double Bind* (University of Illinois Press, 1973), pp. 29–55.

43. Woodruff D. Smith, *The German Colonial Empire* (University of North Carolina Press, 1978); Hermann J. Hiery and John M. Mackenzie, eds., *European Impact and Pacific Influence: British and German Colonial Policy in the Pacific Islands and the Indigenous Response* (I. B. Tauris, 1997); W. O. Henderson, *The German Colonial Empire, 1884–1919* (Cass, 1993).

44. Max Weinreich, *Hitler's Professors: The Part of Scholarship in Germany's Crimes against the Jewish People* (Yiddish Scientific Institute, 1946), esp. p. 39 and p. 177.

45. Frantz Fanon, *Toward the African Revolution: Political Essays*, trans. Haakon Chevalier (Grove Press, 1967), p. 23.

46. Claude Lefort, *The Political Forms of Modern Society: Bureaucracy, Democracy, Totalitarianism*, ed. John B. Thompson (Polity Press, 1986), p. 298.

47. Chetan Bhatt, *Liberation and Purity: Race, New Religious Movements and the Ethics of Post-Modernity* (University College London Press, 1997).

48. Levi, *The Drowned and the Saved*, p. 51.

49. John Swan, "The Final Solution in South West Africa," *MHQ: The Quarterly Journal of Military History* 3(4), pp. 36–55; A. F. Calvert, *South West Africa during the German Occupation* (T. Werner Laurie, 1915); I. Goldblatt, *History of South Africa* (Juta and Co., 1971); L. H. Gann and P. Duignan, *The Rulers of German Africa, 1887–1914* (Stanford University Press, 1977); Everlyn Nicodemus, "Carrying the Sun on Our Backs," in *Andrea Robbins and Max Becher*, ed. M. Catherine de Zegher (The Kanaal Art Foundation, 1994).

50. T. W. Adorno, *"Commitment" Notes on Literature 2*, trans. Shierry Weber Nicholson (Columbia University Press, 1992), pp. 88–89.

51. Stuart Hampshire, *Innocence and Experience* (Harvard University Press, 1989), pp. 66–72.

52. Mahmood Mamdani, *Imperialism and Fascism in Uganda* (Heinemann, 1983), esp. Part 2.

53. Jean Améry, *At the Mind's Limits: Contemplations by a Survivor on Auschwitz and Its Realities*, trans. Sidney and Stella P. Rosenfeld (Indiana University Press, 1980), p. 4.

54. Ibid., p. 91.

55. Léopold Sédar Senghor, "Le Message de Goethe Aux Nègres Nouveaux," *Liberté 1 Négritude et Humanisme du Seuil*, 1964, pp. 84–86. My translation.

56. This incident drawn from correspondence with Pompidou is quoted by

Jacques Louis Hymans in *An Intellectual Biography of Léopold Sédar Senghor* (University of Edinburgh Press, 1971), p. 112.

3. IDENTITY, BELONGING, AND THE CRITIQUE OF PURE SAMENESS

1. Mark Leonard, *Britain™* (Demos, 1997).
2. Judith Butler, "Collected and Fractured," in *Identities,* ed. Kwame Anthony Appiah and Henry Louis Gates, Jr. (University of Chicago Press, 1995).
3. J.-J. Rousseau, "Considerations on the Government of Poland," in *Rousseau Political Writings,* trans. and ed. Frederick Watkins (Nelson and Sons, 1953), pp. 163–164.
4. *The Blackshirt* (November 24–30, 1933), p. 5; quoted in John Harvey, *Men in Black* (Chicago University Press, 1995), p. 242.
5. Leonard Thompson, *The Political Mythology of Apartheid* (Yale University Press, 1985), p. 39.
6. African Rights, *Rwanda Death, Despair and Defiance* (London, 1994), pp. 347–354. See also Sander L. Gilman, *The Jew's Body* (Routledge, 1991), especially chap. 7, "The Jewish Nose: Are Jews White or The History of the Nose Job."
7. Arthur Malu-Malu and Thierry Oberle, *Sunday Times,* August 30, 1998.
8. William Greider, *One World, Ready or Not: The Manic Logic of Global Capitalism* (Simon and Schuster, 1997); Jerry Mander and Edward Goldsmith, eds., *The Case against the Global Economy and for a Turn toward the Local* (Sierra Books, 1996); Benjamin R. Barber, *Jihad vs. McWorld: How the Planet Is Both Falling Apart and Coming Together and What This Means for Democracy* (Random House, 1995).
9. Jean-Marie Guéhenno, *The End of the Nation State* (University of Minnesota Press, 1995).
10. Zygmunt Bauman, *Freedom* (Open University Press, 1988).
11. Charles Taylor, *Sources of the Self* (Harvard University Press, 1989); William Connolly, *Identity/Difference* (Cornell University Press, 1991).
12. Chris Hables Gray, ed., *The Cyborg Handbook* (Routledge, 1995).
13. Amy Harmon, "Racial Divide Found on Information Highway," *New York Times,* April 10, 1998.
14. Sherry Turkle, *Life on the Screen: Identity in the Age of the Internet* (Simon and Schuster, 1995), p. 10.
15. Debbora Battaglia, "Problematizing the Self: A Thematic Introduction," in D. Battaglia, ed., *Rhetorics of Self-Making* (University of California Press, 1995), p. 2.

16. Benedict Anderson, *Imagined Communities: Reflections on the Origin and Spread of Nationalism* (Verso, 1983).

17. President Mandela's inaugural speech was reprinted in *The Independent*, May 11, 1995, p. 12.

18. Martin Luther King, Jr., *Where Do We Go from Here: Chaos or Community?* (Harper and Row, 1967), p. 124.

19. Donald G. McNeil, Jr., "Africans Seek Redress for German Genocide," *New York Times*, June 1, 1998.

20. James Baldwin, *Evidence of Things Not Seen* (Henry Holt and Co., 1985), p. 78.

21. Peter Hulme, *Colonial Encounters* (Methuen, 1986); Anthony Pagden, *European Encounters in the New World: From Renaissance to Romanticism* (Yale, 1993); Richard C. Trexler, *Sex and Conquest* (Cornell University Press, 1995).

22. Charles Taylor, "Understanding and Ethnocentricity," in *Philosophy and the Human Sciences, Philosophical Papers 2* (Cambridge University Press, 1985).

23. James Walvin, *An African's Life: The Life and Times of Olaudah Equiano, 1745–1797* (Cassell, 1999); Ola Larsmo, *Maroonberget* (Bonniers, 1996).

24. Peter Fryer, *Staying Power: The History of Black People in Britain* (Pluto Press, 1984).

25. Mary Louise Pratt, *Imperial Eyes: Travel and Transculturation* (Routledge, 1992).

26. Orlando Patterson, *Slavery and Social Death: A Comparative Study* (Harvard University Press, 1982).

27. Adam Potkay, "Introduction" to Adam Potkay and Sandra Burr, eds., *Black Atlantic Writers of the Eighteenth Century* (St. Martin's Press, 1995), p. 9.

28. "On the Death of the Rev. Mr. George Whitefield. 1770," lines 20–23 and 34–37; John C. Shields, ed., *The Collected Works of Phillis Wheatley* (Oxford University Press, 1988), p. 23.

29. Daniel Boyarin has explored elements of the history of this idea in his extraordinary study *A Radical Jew: Paul and the Politics of Identity* (University of California Press, 1995).

30. Olaudah Equiano, *The Interesting Narrative of the Life of Olaudah Equiano*, 2 vols. (Pall Mall, 1969), vol. 2., p. 195.

31. Ibid., p. 182.

32. Marcus Rediker, *Between the Devil and the Deep Blue Sea: Merchant Seamen, Pirates and the Anglo-American Maritime World, 1700–1750* (Cambridge University Press, 1987); Janice E. Thomson, *Mercenaries, Pirates, and Sovereigns* (Princeton University Press, 1994); E. E. Rice, ed., *The Sea and History* (Sutton Publishing, 1996), esp. chap. 5; N. A. M. Rodger, "Sea Power and Empire: 1688–1793," in P. J. Marshall, ed., *The Oxford History of The British Empire, Volume Two: The Eighteenth Century* (Oxford, 1998).

33. Edith R. Sanders, "The Hamitic Hypothesis; Its Origin and Functions in Time Perspective," *Journal of African History*, X, 4 (1969), pp. 521–532.

34. Equiano, *The Interesting Narrative*, pp. 38–40. For a ground-breaking discussion of these formulations see Adam Potkay, "Introduction" to *Black Atlantic Writers of the Eighteenth Century*.

35. Elliott P. Skinner, "The Dialectic between Diasporas and Homelands," in Joseph E. Harris, ed., *Global Dimensions of the African Diaspora* (Howard University Press, 1982).

36. Edward Wilmot Blyden, *On the Jewish Question* (Lionel Hart and Co., 1898), p. 23.

37. Stefan Helmreich, "Kinship, Nation, and Paul Gilroy's Concept of Diaspora," *Diaspora* 2, 2 (1993), pp. 243–249.

38. Londa Scheibinger, *Nature's Body* (Beacon Press, 1993).

39. "To be rhizomorphous is to produce stems and filaments that seem to be roots, or better yet connect with them by penetrating the trunk, but put them to new uses. We're tired of trees. We should stop believing in trees, roots and radicles. They've made us suffer too much. All of arborescent culture is founded on them, from biology to linguistics." Gilles Deleuze and Felix Guattari, "Rhizome," in *A Thousand Plateaus* (University of Minnesota Press, 1988), p. 15.

40. Louis Farrakhan, "A Call to March," *Emerge*, vol. 7, no. 1 (October 1995), p. 66.

41. Roger Griffin, *The Nature of Fascism* (Routledge, 1993).

42. Leroi Jones, *Black Music* (Quill, 1967), pp. 180–211.

4. HITLER WORE KHAKIS

1. Douglas A. Lorimer, *Colour, Class and the Victorians: English Attitudes to the Negro in the Mid-Nineteenth Century* (Leicester University Press, 1978), esp. chapters 7 and 9.

2. Leon Poliakov, *The Aryan Myth: A History of Racist and Nationalist Ideas in Europe*, trans. Edmund Howard (Chatto and Windus, 1974); Ivan Hannaford, *Race: The History of an Idea in the West* (Johns Hopkins, 1996); Eric Voegelin, "The Growth of the Race Idea," *Review of Politics* (July, 1940), pp. 283–317; Peter Hulme, "The Hidden Hand of Nature," in *The Enlightenment and Its Shadows*, ed. Hulme and L. Jordanova (Routledge, 1991).

3. George W. Stocking, Jr., ed., *Volksgeist as Method and Ethic* (Wisconsin University Press, 1996).

4. Ronald Hyam, *Empire and Sexuality: The British Experience* (University of Manchester Press, 1990); K. Ballhatchet, *Race, Sex and Class under the Raj*

(Weidenfeld and Nicholson, 1980); Fernando Henriques, *Children of Caliban* (Secker, 1974); Ann Laura Stoler, "Carnal Knowledge and Imperial Power: Gender, Race and Morality in Colonial Asia," in Micaela di Leonardo, ed., *Gender at the Crossroads of Knowledge* (University of California Press, 1991); Christopher Lane, *The Ruling Passion* (Duke University Press, 1995); Anton Gill, *Ruling Passions* (BBC Books, 1995).

5. The path-breaking work of Edward Said has spawned a host of inferior imitations in which critical insight is not matched by grounded ethical and political sensibilities.

6. Annie Combes, *The Reinvention of Africa* (Yale University Press, 1994); James R. Ryan, *Picturing the Empire: Photography and the Visualization of the British Empire* (Reaktion Books, 1997).

7. John M. MacKenzie, *Propaganda and Empire* (University of Manchester Press, 1984); J. W. M. Hichberger, *Images of the Army: The Military in British Art, 1815–1914* (University of Manchester Press, 1988).

8. Sophie D. Coe and Michael D. Coe, *The True History of Chocolate* (Thames and Hudson, 1996), p. 244.

9. Greta Jones, *Social Darwinism and English Thought: The Interaction between Biological and Social Theory* (Harvester Press, 1980).

10. Rudyard Kipling, *The Seven Seas* (Methuen, 1897). These patterns are not confined to Britain. The German novels dealing with the suppression of the Herero uprising in South West Africa are also a good example; see Gustav Frenssen, *Peter Moors Fahrt nach Südwest: Ein Feldugs-bericht* (Thousand, Berlin, 1936 [1907]); and Hans Grimm's *Sudafrikanische Novellen* (Frankfurt/Main, 1913). In the French setting, the novels of Ernest Psichari, the grandson of Renan, provide a good comparative example. All these and many similar works are discussed by Hugh Ridley in *Images of Imperial Rule* (Croom Helm, 1983).

11. Max Weinreich, *Hitler's Professors: The Part of Scholarship in Germany's Crimes against The Jewish People* (Yiddish Scientific Institute, 1946).

12. More detailed information on Fischer can be found in the path-breaking and inspiring work of Max Weinreich and of those scholars who have followed in his footsteps: Paul Weindling, Sheila Faith Weiss, and especially Robert Proctor. See Proctor's extraordinary essay "From Anthropologie to Rassenkunde in the German Anthropological Tradition," in George W. Stocking, ed., *Bones, Bodies, Behaviour: Essays on Biological Anthropology* (University of Wisconsin Press, 1988); and his book *Racial Hygiene: Medicine under the Nazis* (Harvard University Press, 1988); Paul Weindling, *Health, Race and German Politics between National Unification and Nazism, 1870–1945* (Cambridge University Press, 1988); Sheila Faith Weiss, "The Race-Hygiene Movement in Germany," *Osiris* (2nd series), 3 (1987), pp. 193–236.

See also Rosemarie K. Lester, "Blacks in Germany and German Blacks: A Little Known Aspect of Black History," in Reinhold Grimm and Jost Hermand, eds., *Blacks and German Culture* (University of Wisconsin Press, 1986); and Reiner Pommerin, *Sterilisierung der Rheinlande bastarde: Das Schiksal einer farbigen deutschen Minderheit, 1918–1937* (Droste, 1979).

13. Benno Müller Hill, *Murderous Science* (Oxford University Press, 1988).

14. Daniel Pick, *War Machine: The Rationalization of Slaughter in the Modern Age* (Yale University Press, 1993); Omer Bartov, *Hitler's Army: Soldiers, Nazis and War in the Third Reich* (Oxford University Press, 1992).

15. W. O. Henderson, *The German Colonial Empire* (Cass, 1993), pp. 74–114.

16. Daniel R. Headrick, *The Tools of Empire* (Oxford University Press, 1980); Michael Adas, *Machines as the Measure of Men* (Cornell University Press, 1989).

17. Victor Kiernan, *European Empires from Conquest to Collapse, 1815–1960* (Leicester University Press, 1982).

18. John Ellis, *The Social History of the Machine Gun* (Pimlico, 1993).

19. Umberto Eco, "Ur-Fascism," *New York Review of Books*, June 22, 1995.

20. Stefan Kühl, *The Nazi Connection: Eugenics, American Racism and German National Socialism* (Oxford University Press, 1994); Edward J. Larson, *Sex, Race and Science: Eugenics in the Deep South* (Johns Hopkins University Press, 1995); Marouf A. Hasian, Jr., *The Rhetoric of Eugenics in Anglo-American Thought* (University of Georgia Press, 1995), esp. chapter 3.

21. Michel Foucault, preface to Gilles Deleuze and Felix Guattari, *Anti-Oedipus: Capitalism and Schizophrenia* (Viking, 1977), p. xiv.

22. Roger Griffin, *The Nature of Fascism* (Routledge, 1993).

23. Klaus Theweleit, *Male Fantasies,* trans. Stephen Conway, Erica Carter, and Chris Turner, 2 vols. (Polity Press, 1987 and 1989).

24. James Brown, the editor of the British edition of the magazine *GQ,* published by Condé Nast, was dismissed from his post in February 1999 for describing the Nazi general Rommel as "stylish in the face of true adversity" and placing him on the publication's list of the "sharpest men of the 20th century." *Guardian,* February 19, 1999.

25. "In midsummer of 1920 the new flag came before the public for the first time . . . it had the effect of a burning torch . . . *And a symbol it really is!* Not only the unique colors, which all of us so passionately love and which once won so much honor for the German people, attest our veneration for the past; they were also the best embodiment of our movement's will. As National Socialists, we see our program in our flag. In *red* we see the social idea of the movement, in *white* the nationalistic idea, in the *swastika* the mission and struggle for the victory of the Aryan man, and, by the same token, the victory of the idea of creative work, which as such always has been and always will be

anti-Semitic." *Mein Kampf,* trans. Ralph Manheim (Houghton Mifflin, 1971), p. 497.

26. Daniel Guérin, *The Brown Plague,* trans. Robert Schwarzwald (Duke University Press), pp. 97–98.

27. Henri Béraud, *Ce Que J'ai vu à Rome* (Les Editions de France, 1929), quoted by Simonetta Falasca-Zamponi, *Fascist Spectacle* (University of California Press, 1997), p. 80. See also Emilio Gentile, *The Sacralization of Politics in Fascist Italy,* trans. Keith Botsford (Harvard University Press, 1996).

28. Quoted by Eric Rentschler, *The Ministry of Illusion: Nazi Cinema and Its Afterlife* (Harvard University Press, 1996), p. 215.

29. Malcolm Quinn, *The Swastika* (Routledge, 1995).

30. Paul Rand, *From Lascaux to Brooklyn* (Yale University Press, 1996), pp. 83–91.

31. George Jackson, *Blood in My Eye* (Jonathan Cape, 1972).

32. Russell A. Berman, *Modern Culture and Critical Theory: Art, Politics, and the Legacy of the Frankfurt School* (Wisconsin University Press, 1989), p. 100.

33. Leni Riefenstahl, *The Sieve of Time* (Quartet Books, 1992), p. 165.

34. Rey Chow, "Fascist Longings in Our Midst," *Ariel,* vol. 26, no. 1 (January 1995), p. 38.

35. Z. A. Zeman, *Nazi Propaganda* (Oxford University Press, 1964), p. 34.

36. Wolfgang Sachs points out that the success in mass production of radios provided an important precedent for the mass production of the automobiles that would bring another new sense of freedom into the lives of Germans. He quotes a speech of Hitler's from the *Völikischer Beobachter,* March 9, 1934: "Just a few months ago German industry, through the manufacture of a new people's radio, succeeded in delivering to the market and selling an enormous number of receivers. I wish now to place before the German motor-vehicle industry the significant task of designing an auto-mobile that necessarily comes to attract buyers numbering in millions." *For the Love of the Automobile,* trans. Don Reneau (University of California Press, 1992), p. 59.

37. Horst J. P. Bergmeier and Rainer E. Lotz, *Hitler's Airwaves: The Inside Story of Nazi Radio Broadcasting and Propaganda Swing* (Yale University Press, 1997).

38. David Welch, *The Third Reich: Politics and Propaganda* (Routledge, 1993), p. 34.

39. Lynn Hunt, *Politics, Culture and Class in the French Revolution* (Routledge, 1984), pp. 57–58.

40. George Orwell, *The Collected Essays,* vol. 2, ed. Sonia Orwell and Ian Angus (Penguin, 1968).

41. Hitler, *Mein Kampf,* p. 470. The source of these ideas may be the work of Ernst Jünger. See Berman, *Modern Cultural and Critical Theory,* pp. 99–118.

42. Ibid., p. 492.

43. Karl Löwith, "My Last Meeting with Heidegger in Rome 1936," in R. Wolin, ed., *The Heidegger Controversy: A Critical Reader* (MIT Press, 1993), pp. 140–144.

44. Pierre Bourdieu, *The Political Ontology of Martin Heidegger*, trans. Peter Collier (Polity Press, 1991).

45. Martin Heidegger, *Introduction to Metaphysics*, trans. Ralph Manheim (Yale University Press, 1959), p. 202.

46. Löwith, "My Last Meeting with Heidegger in Rome 1936," pp. 140–144.

47. Karl Löwith, *Martin Heidegger and European Nihilism*, ed. Richard Wolin, trans. Gary Steiner (Columbia University Press, 1995). In his recent book *Heidegger, Philosophy, Nazism* (Cambridge University Press, 1997), the philosopher Julian Young describes Löwith's report of the meeting as "relatively weak evidence" but does not view Heidegger's wearing the Nazi emblem as itself a significant communicative gesture (p. 214).

48. Scott Hughes Myerly, *British Military Spectacle: From the Napoleonic Wars through the Crimea* (Harvard University Press, 1996), chapter 1, "The Spectacular Image."

49. These words are Hitler's from page 533 of *Mein Kampf.* George Mosse has done more than anyone to provide elements of the history of these developments in his books *The Nationalization of the Masses: Political Symbolism and Mass Movements in Germany from the Napoleonic Wars through the Third Reich* (Cornell University Press, 1975), and *Masses and Man: Nationalist and Fascist Perceptions of Reality* (Wayne State University Press, 1987).

50. Hitler, *Mein Kampf,* p. 410.

51. Baden Powell's endorsement of boxing as manly exercise can be found in the section "Games to Develop Strength" in chapter 6 of *Scouting for Boys* (C. Arthur Pearson Ltd., 1941 [1908]). See also Ulf Hedetoft, "War, Racism, Soccer," in Flemming Røgilds, ed., *Every Cloud Has a Silver Lining* (Akademisc Forlag, 1986), and J. A. Mangan and James Walvin, eds., *Manliness and Morality: Middle-Class Masculinity in Britain and America, 1800–1946* (University of Manchester, 1987).

52. Chris Mead, *Joe Louis: A Biography* (Scribners/Robson Books, 1986), p. 100.

53. Joe Louis, with Edna Rust and Art Rust, *My Life* (Ecco, 1997 [1978]), p. 137.

54. The best brief account of the fights and the atmosphere around them is in Mead's *Joe Louis: A Biography,* pp. 92–159; see also Joe Louis Barrow, Jr., and Barbara Munder, *Joe Louis: The Brown Bomber* (Weidenfeld Paperbacks, 1988); Richard Bak, *Joe Louis: The Great Black Hope* (Taylor Publishing, 1996); and Joe Louis, *My Life.* Much of Mead's material on Schmeling is taken from the fighter's autobiography, *Errinnerungen* (Verslager Ullstein GMBH, 1977).

55. As quoted by Mead, *Joe Louis*, p. 159.

56. Heidegger, *Introduction to Metaphysics*, p. 199.

57. The quote is taken from Griffin's essay in Günter Berghaus, ed., *Fascism and Theatre: Comparative Studies on the Aesthetics and Politics of Performance in Europe, 1925–1945* (Berghahn Books, 1996). There is an important dispute on this point among those who have debated Riefenstahl's work. Paul Virilio quotes Riefenstahl herself as saying that the party congress filmed in *Triumph of the Will* "was organized in the manner of a theatrical performance, not only as a popular rally, but also to provide the material for a propaganda film . . . everything was decided by reference to the camera." He cites the source of these remarks as Hinter den Kulissen des Reichs-Parteitag-Films. Virilio, *War and Cinema: The Logistics of Perception* (Verso, 1989). Riefenstahl's contemporary defenders are alert to the dangers of conceding this point. Audrey Salkeld, Riefenstahl's most comprehensive apologist, has issued an outright denial: "the pageantry cannot be said to have been staged for the cameras." Audrey Salkeld, *A Portrait of Leni Riefenstahl* (Jonathan Cape, 1996), p. 133.

58. Susan Sontag, "Fascinating Fascism," in *Under the Sign of Saturn* (Farrar, Strauss and Giroux, 1984).

59. Ernst Hanfstangl, *Hitler: The Missing Years* (Eyre and Spottiswood, 1956).

60. Suzanne L. Marchand, *Down from Olympus: Archaeology and Philhellenism in Germany, 1750–1970* (Princeton University Press, 1996).

61. Patricia Morrisroe, *Mapplethorpe* (Random House, 1995), states "He had recently begun sporting a swastika pin on his jacket . . . [and] Mapplethorpe toyed with the idea of creating a whole line of 'Nazi jewelry,' and the swastika became another amulet in his fetishistic necklaces" (p. 103).

62. Salkeld, *A Portrait of Leni Riefenstahl*.

63. Emmanuel Levinas, "Reflections on the Philosophy of Hitlerism," trans. Sean Hand, *Critical Inquiry*, 17 (Autumn 1990), p. 69.

5. "After the Love Has Gone"

1. Mid-1990s work by the African-American academics Tricia Rose and Michael Eric Dyson shares this quality in spite of their obvious political differences. See Tricia Rose, *Black Noise: Rap Music and Black Culture in Contemporary America* (Wesleyan University Press, 1994); and Michael Eric Dyson, *Reflecting Black: African American Cultural Criticism* (University of Minnesota Press, 1993).

2. "PaRappa the Rapper," a Sony Playstation game, was one of several products aimed at bridging these markets.

3. Paul D. Miller, "Booty Makes Bank," *The Source*, 77 (February 1996).

4. Luther "Luke Skywalker" Campbell interview by Joseph Gallivan in *The Independent*, January 13, 1994, p. 26.

5. Tricia Rose's assertions that hip-hop is reducible to a core of invariant and exclusively African-American "black practices" that permanently resist both commodification and white appropriation typifies this mode of denial. See Rose, *Black Noise*, pp. 7 and 80–84 passim.

6. A good example of this is the use of Leiber and Stoller's "I Keep Forgettin'" as recorded by Michael MacDonald in the track "Regulate" by Nate Dogg and Warren G. This can also be found on the Deathrow/Atlantic Records soundtrack album to *Above the Rim*.

7. Michel Foucault, "Truth and Power," in *Power Knowledge: Selected Interviews and Other Writings, 1972–1977*, ed. Colin Gordon (Pantheon, 1980), p. 115.

8. This type of citation does not take the form of parody or pastiche. Its intentions are disciplinary, and it is best understood as a creative ordering that does not always serve progressive impulses. It does not play with the gap between then and now but rather uses it to assert a spurious continuity that adds legitimacy and gravity to the contemporary. Another example of the shifting political resonance between these different periods in popular politics is provided by the way the group Arrested Development borrowed parts of Sly and the Family Stone's "Everyday People" and changed it into "People Everyday." The earlier song was an affirmation of pluralism that pivoted on the chorus:

> There is a blue one who can't accept the green one
> For living with a fat one trying to be a skinny one
> And different strokes for different folks . . .
> I am no better and neither are you
> We are the same whatever we do
> You love me—you hate me you know me and then
> You can't figure out the bag I'm in
> I am everyday people.

The decisive line of antagonism between different "races" that the earlier song located and then erased is moved in the later one and is seen to operate within the racial group around the disrespectful drunken conduct of "brothers" toward the singer's "black queen."

9. bell hooks, "Reconstructing Black Masculinity," in *Black Looks: Race and Representation* (South End Press, 1993), p. 113.

10. "I know this might sound funny coming out of my mouth but I do try to be different, I try to hit on a romantic sexual level, leaving just a touch to the imagination," R. Kelly interviewed in *Pride* (May/June 1994), p. 35.

11. An insightful version of this is outlined by June Jordan in "Waiting for a Taxi," in *Technical Difficulties: African-American Notes on the State of the Union* (Pantheon, 1992).

12. Michel Foucault, *The Use of Pleasure* (Viking, 1986), p. 5.

13. See also Michael Jordan, *Rare Air: Michael on Michael,* ed. Mark Vancil (HarperCollins, 1993).

14. George L. Mosse, *Nationalism and Sexuality: Middle-Class Morality and Sexual Norms in Modern Europe* (University of Wisconsin Press, 1985), esp. chapter 3; Jordan, *Rare Air.*

15. *Vibe,* vol. 2, no. 4 (May 1994), p. 72. The same article offers these interesting observations about Kelly's living space: "He lives downtown on the Loop, in a sparsely decorated one-bedroom apartment. 'Where I live it's like Batman in Gotham City. No one knows where I live. If you come to my crib, you have to be blindfolded . . . It's not just an apartment to me. I hear my music in there. I never have any company because that's my solitude. My being silent about my personal life allows me to express it in the studio.'"

16. John London, "Competing Together in Fascist Europe: Sport in Early Francoism," in Günter Berghaus, ed., *Fascism and Theatre: Comparative Studies on the Aesthetics and Politics of Performance in Europe, 1925–1945* (Berghahn Books, 1996).

17. See his discussion with Angela Davis in *Transition,* 58 (1992). It includes the following exchange:

> Ice Cube [I. C.]: Did anyone in the Black Panther organization smoke?
> Angela Davis [A. D.]: I'm sure they did.
> I. C.: Did anybody drink?
> A. D.: I'm sure they did.
> I. C.: That ain't loving yourself . . . To me the best organization for black people is the Nation of Islam. It is the best organization: brothers don't drink, don't smoke, ain't chasin' women. They have one job.

18. Paul Gilroy, "It's a Family Affair: Black Culture and the Trope of Kinship," in *Small Acts* (Serpent's Tail, 1994).

19. See *The Source*'s "Annual Car Audio Spectaculars," usually found in the June issue of the magazine.

20. Emmanuel Levinas, "The Transcendence of Words," in *The Levinas Reader,* ed. Sean Hand (Blackwell, 1989), p. 147.

21. Eric Foner, *Nothing But Freedom* (Louisiana State University Press, 1983).

22. Booker T. Washington, *Up From Slavery* (Airmont Books, 1967), p. 27.

23. "No sooner had emancipation been acknowledged than thousands of 'married' couples, with the encouragement of black preachers and northern white missionaries, hastened to secure their marital vows, both legally and spiritually . . . The insistence of teachers, missionaries and Freedmen's Bureau officers that blacks formalize their marriages stemmed from the notion that legal sanction was necessary for sexual and moral restraint and that ex-slaves had to be inculcated with 'the obligations of the married state in civilized

life.'" Leon F. Litwack, *Been in the Storm So Long: The Aftermath of Slavery* (Athlone Press, 1980), p. 240. See chapter 5, "How Free IS Free?"

24. Daniel Miller, "Absolute Freedom in Trinidad," *Man*, 26 (1991), pp. 323–341.

25. Mechal Sobel, *Trabelin' On: The Slave Journey to an Afro-Baptist Faith* (Princeton University Press, 1988).

26. Charles H. Long, *Significations* (Fortress Press, 1986).

27. Lawrence Levine, *Black Culture and Black Consciousness: Afro-American Folk Thought from Slavery to Freedom* (Oxford University Press, 1977).

28. Michael Eric Dyson is again typical of these problems. He notes that in the black vernacular, "personal freedom often is envisioned through tropes of sexual release" but takes this observation no further. See Dyson, *Reflecting Black*, p. 279. It is not solely a matter of "release," though this choice of words has the virtue of making a connection with slavery explicit.

29. Paul Gilroy, *The Black Atlantic: Modernity and Double Consciousness* (Harvard University Press, 1993), chapter 6.

30. On this concept see Paul Connerton's useful book *How Societies Remember* (Cambridge University Press, 1989), section 3, "Bodily Practices."

31. Shahrazad Ali, *Are You Still a Slave?* (Civilized Publications, n.d.).

32. This is powerfully transmitted and its relationship to the problematics of freedom illuminated by several tracks by Ice Cube's crew Da Lench Mob. See, for example, "Capital Punishment in America" and "Freedom Got an A. K.," both from their album *Guerillas in the Mist* (Street Knowledge 7–92206–2).

33. Zygmunt Bauman, *Mortality, Immortality and Other Life Strategies* (Polity, 1993), pp. 187–188. See also Ernst Bloch and Theodor W. Adorno, "Something's Missing," in Ernst Bloch, *The Utopian Function of Art and Literature* (MIT Press, 1988), pp. 5–8.

34. Nas, "Life's a Bitch," from the CD *Illmatic* (Columbia, CK 57684, 1994).

35. Jean Luc Nancy, *The Experience of Freedom* (Stanford University Press, 1993).

36. S. W. V. *It's About Time* (RCA 07863 66074–2, 1992). See also S. W. V., *The Remixes* (RCA 07863–66401–2, 1994).

37. Cornel West, "Nihilism in Black America," *Race Matters* (Beacon Press, 1993); see also Ishmael Reed, "Airing Dirty Laundry," in the book of the same name (Addison-Wesley, 1993).

38. The actor Mr. T anticipated the views of a generation of old-school hip-hoppers when in 1985 he gave this explanation of his flashy taste in jewelry:

> The gold chains are a symbol that reminds me of my great African ancestors, who were brought over here as slaves with iron chains on their ankles, on their wrists, their necks and sometimes around their waists. I turned my chains into gold, so my statement is this: the fact that I wear

gold chains instead of iron chains is because I am still a slave, only my price tag is higher now. I am still bought and sold by the powers that be in this society, white people, but this time they pay me on demand, millions and millions of dollars for my services. I demand it and they pay it ... Yes, I am still a slave in this society, but I am still free by God. "How are you still a slave Mr. T.?" You see the only thing that interests this society is money. And the only thing that it fears and respects is more money.

Mr. T, *An Autobiography by Mr. T* (W. H. Allen, 1985), p. 4. This account of the connection between slavery and identity links personal autonomy with the signs of wealth and the memory of terror. The condition of slavery persists but is changed by divine grace and the very worldly capacity to hire oneself out to others.

39. dream hampton, "G down," *The Source* (September 1993), p. 68.
40. Murray Bookchin, *The Ecology of Freedom: The Emergence and Dissolution of Hierarchy* (Cheshire Books, 1982), p. 272.
41. Frederick Douglass, *My Bondage My Freedom* (Miller, Orton and Mulligan, 1855), p. 50.
42. See June Jordan, "Beyond Apocalypse Now," in *Civil Wars* (Beacon Press, 1981), especially p. 171; Robert C. Solomon, *From Rationalism to Existentialism: The Existentialists and Their Nineteenth Century Backgrounds* (Harvester, 1972), chapter 7. See also the discussion of Albert Camus's *L'Etranger* in Edward Said's *Culture and Imperialism* (Chatto and Windus, 1993).
43. Reporting on his recent performances in London, *Hip Hop Connection*, no. 14 (1995), p. 14, noted this dynamic in operation: "At times this gig resembled a game of Snoop Says . . . 'Throw ya hands in the air,' he'd yell and the audience dutifully obeyed. They were strangely content. It didn't occur to them that Doggystyle's instrumental backing is ideally suited to a live concert. Dre's tuneful production means Snoop's performance should entail musicians, not a cheap impersonal DAT. Unperturbed by this glaring omission, fans avidly sang along to Snoop's casual patter." See also Walter F. Pitts, Jr., *Old Ship of Zion: The Afro-Baptist Ritual in the African Diaspora* (Oxford University Press, 1993).
44. *Hip Hop Connection*, 62 (April 1994), p. 31.
45. Edmund Leach, "Anthropological Aspects of Language: Animal Categories and Verbal Abuse," in E. H. Lenneberg, ed., *New Directions in the Study of Language* (MIT Press, 1964), pp. 23–63.
46. Peter Stallybrass and Allon White, *The Politics and Poetics of Transgression* (Methuen, 1986).
47. Emmanuel Levinas, "The Name of a Dog, or Natural Rights," in *Difficult*

Freedom: Essays on Judaism (Athlone, 1990); Yi Fu Tuan, *Dominance and Affection: The Making of Pets* (Yale University Press, 1984); see also Paul W. Taylor, *Respect for Nature: A Theory of Environmental Ethics* (Princeton University Press, 1986).

48. Hilda Kean, *Animal Rights: Political and Social Change in Britain since 1800* (Reaktion Books, 1998).

49. "The Paradox of Morality: An Interview with Emmanuel Levinas," chapter 11 in Robert Bernasconi and David Wood, *The Provocation of Levinas* (Routledge, 1988), p. 168.

50. It is useful to compare *Doggy Style* with the out-and-out misogyny of DRS and other spokesmen for gangsterdom.

51. Claudia Tate, *Domestic Allegories of Political Desire* (Oxford University Press, 1992), especially chapters 3 and 7.

52. Zygmunt Bauman, *Postmodern Ethics* (Blackwell, 1993), pp. 92–98.

53. Ice Cube, interviewed by Ekow Eshun in *The Face,* no. 65 (February 1994), p. 91.

6. The Tyrannies of Unanimism

1. Edith Sanders, "The Hamitic Hypothesis: Its Origins and Functions in Time Perspective," *Journal of African History,* 10 (1969), pp. 524–526.

2. "A Call to Arms, a Call to Sacrifice," *Nationalism Today* (not dated).

3. Ross Slater, "Revealed: the B. N. P.'s Black Buddies," *New Nation,* June 4, 1998.

4. *The Guardian,* September 11, 1996, p. 5.

5. Marian A. L. Miller, *The Third World in Global Environmental Politics* (Open University Press, 1995).

6. Kierna Mayo Dawsey, "Caught Up in the (Gangsta) Rapture: Dr. C. Delores Tucker's Crusade Against 'Gangsta Rap'" and "Reality Check," both in *The Source* (June 1994).

7. Richard King, M. D., *African Origin of Biological Psychiatry* (U. B. and U. S. Communications Systems, 1990).

8. Douglass S. Massey and Nancy A. Denton, *American Apartheid: Segregation and the Making of the Underclass* (Harvard University Press, 1993).

9. *New York Times Magazine,* April 3, 1994, p. 45.

10. Primo Levi, *The Drowned and the Saved,* trans. R. Rosenthal (Summit Books, 1988), p. 27.

11. Yehuda Bauer, *Jews for Sale? Nazi-Jewish Negotiations, 1933–1945* (Yale University Press, 1994).

12. "Frankly it ain't none of your business. What have you got to say about it?

Did you teach Malcolm? Did you clean up Malcolm? Did you put Malcolm out before the world? Was Malcolm your traitor or was he ours? And if we dealt with him like a nation deals with a traitor, what the hell business is it of yours? You just shut your mouth and stay out of it. Because in the future, we are going to become a nation. And a nation gotta be able to deal with traitors, cutthroats and turncoats. The white man deals with his. The Jews deal with theirs. Salman Rushdie wrote a nasty thing about the Prophet, and Imam Khomeini put a death thing on him." These words were delivered by Minister Farrakhan at a closed meeting in his mosque in February 1993. They are quoted in the film *Brother Minister* made by Jefri Aalmuhammed, Jack Baxter, and Lewis Kesten (phone 516–625–5561).

13. Wilson J. Moses, *The Golden Age of Black Nationalism, 1850–1925* (Oxford University Press, 1988), p. 197.

14. Frederick Douglass, "What Are the Coloured People Doing for Themselves?" in H. Brotz, ed., *African-American Social and Political Thought* (Transaction, 1992), pp. 204–205; Martin Delany, *The Origins and Objects of Ancient Freemasonry: Its Introduction into the United States and Legitimacy among Colored Men* (Pittsburgh, 1853).

15. Prince Hall masonry was the black system of freemasonry in the eighteenth century. See Donn A. Cass, *Negro Freemasonry and Segregation* (Ezra A. Cook Publications, 1957); William A. Muraskin, *Middle Class Blacks in a White Society: Prince Hall Freemasonry in America* (University of California Press, 1975); Harry E. Davis, *A History of Freemasonry Among Negroes in America* (United Supreme Council, Ancient and Accepted Scottish Rite of Freemasonry, 1946); Loretta J. Williams, *Black Freemasonry and Middle-Class Realities* (University of Missouri Press, 1980).

16. Steven Howe's *Afrocentrism: Mythical Pasts and Imagined Homes* (Verso, 1998), is a notable exception to this pattern; see chapter 6, "The Masonic Connection."

17. Claude Andrew Clegg III, *An Original Man: The Life of Elijah Muhammad* (St. Martin's Press, 1997).

18. The important issue of continuities between these movements is complex, with interaction and overlap to be found at different levels, and thus it cannot be settled here. The perils of attempting to deal superficially with the topic are amply illustrated by the failures of Mattias Gardell's *Countdown to Armageddon: Louis Farrakhan and the Nation of Islam* (Hurst and Co., 1996).

19. Nicholas Goodrick-Clarke, *The Occult Roots of Nazism: Secret Aryan Cults and Their Influence on Nazi Ideology* (I. B. Tauris, 1992); and *Hitler's Priestess: Savitri Devi, the Hindu-Aryan Myth and Neo-Nazism* (New York University Press, 1998); Daniel Pipes, *Conspiracy: How the Paranoid Style Flourishes and Where It Comes From* (Free Press, 1997).

20. Georg Simmel, "The Secret and the Secret Society," in *The Sociology of Georg Simmel*, ed. and trans. Kurt H. Wolff (Free Press, 1950), pp. 307–376.

21. Marita Golden, *Saving Our Sons: Raising Black Children in a Turbulent World* (Anchor, 1995); Haki R. Madhubuti, *Black Men: Obsolete, Single, Dangerous? The Afrikan American Family in Transition* (Third World Press, 1990).

22. Roberto Vivarelli, "Interpretations of the Origins of Fascism," *Journal of Modern History*, 63 (March 1991), pp. 29–43.

23. Roger Griffin, *The Nature of Fascism* (Routledge, 1993).

24. Zeev Sternhell, *The Birth of Fascist Ideology* (Princeton University Press, 1993).

25. Max Weinreich, *Hitler's Professors: The Part of Scholarship in Germany's Crimes Against the Jewish People* (Yiddish Scientific Institute, 1948); Henry Friedlander, *The Origins of Nazi Genocide: From Euthanasia to the Final Solution* (University of North Carolina Press, 1995); Hans Peter Bluel, *Sex and Society in Nazi Germany* (J. B. Lippincott Co., 1973); Michael Stolleis, *The Law under the Swastika: Studies on Legal History in Nazi Germany*, trans. Thomas Dunlap (University of Chicago Press, 1998).

26. Alain Finkielkraut, *Remembering in Vain: The Klaus Barbie Trial and Crimes against Humanity* (Columbia University Press, 1992).

27. Anna Bramwell, *The Ecological Movement in the Twentieth Century: A History* (Yale University Press, 1989); Janet Biehl, "'Ecology' and the Modernization of Fascism in the German Ultra-Right," *Society And Nature*, 5 (1994), pp. 130–170.

28. George Mosse, *Toward the Final Solution: A History of European Racism* (University of Wisconsin Press, 1985), and Mosse, ed., *Nazi Culture: Intellectual, Cultural, and Social Life in the Third Reich* (Schocken, 1966); Alison Owings, *Frauen: German Women Recall the Third Reich* (Penguin, 1995); Detlev Peukert, *Inside Nazi Germany: Conformity, Opposition, and Racism in Everyday Life* (Penguin Books, 1993); Jill Stephenson, *Women in Nazi Society* (Croom Helm, 1975); Peter Adam, *The Arts of the Third Reich* (Thames and Hudson, 1992); Michael Kater, *Different Drummers: Jazz in the Culture of Nazi Germany* (Oxford University Press, 1992), and *The Twisted Muse: Musicians and Their Music in the Third Reich* (Oxford University Press, 1997); Robert Wistrich, *Weekend in Munich: Art, Propaganda, and Terror in the Third Reich* (Pavilion Books, 1995).

29. Stefan Kühl, *The Nazi Connection: Eugenics, American Racism, and German National Socialism* (Oxford University Press, 1994); Edward J. Larson, *Sex, Race, and Science: Eugenics in the Deep South* (Johns Hopkins University Press, 1995).

30. C. L. R. James, *A History of Negro Revolt* (Fact Ltd., 1985 [1938]), p. 53.

31. J. A. Rogers, *The World's Great Men of Color* (J. .A. Rogers, c.1947), p. 420;

see also Robert A. Hill, introduction to Robert A. Hill and Barbara Bair, eds., *Marcus Garvey, Life and Lessons: A Centennial Companion to the Marcus Garvey and Universal Negro Improvement Association Papers* (University of California Press, 1987), p. lviii.

32. Robert A. Hill, "Making Noise: Marcus Garvey Dada, August 1922," in Deborah Willis, ed., *Picturing Us: African American Identity in Photography* (The New Press, 1994).

33. Judith Stein, *The World of Marcus Garvey* (Louisiana State University Press, 1986), p. 154.

34. Marcus Garvey, "The Ideals of Two Races," *Philosophy and Opinions of Marcus Garvey*, vol. 2 (Frank Cass, 1967), p. 338.

35. Zora Neale Hurston, *Tell My Horse: Voodoo and Life in Haiti and Jamaica* (Harper, 1990), p. 89.

36. Malcolm X, *The Last Speeches* (Pathfinder Press, 1989), pp. 135–136.

37. Marcus Garvey, Jr., "Garveyism: Some Reflections on Its Significance for Today," in John Henrik Clarke, ed., with the assistance of Amy Jacques Garvey, *Marcus Garvey and the Vision of Africa* (Vintage, 1974), p. 387.

7. "All about the Benjamins"

1. Slavoj Zizek, "Multiculturalism—A New Racism?" *New Left Review* 225 (September–October, 1997).

2. Stuart Elliott, "Spike Lee Tries for Main Street," *International Herald Tribune,* July 10, 1997.

3. James Clifford, *Routes: Travel and Translation in the Late Twentieth Century* (Harvard University Press, 1997).

4. Renato Rosaldo, *Culture and Truth* (Beacon Press, 1989).

5. Annie E. Coombes, *Reinventing Africa: Museums, Material Culture, and Popular Imagination* (Yale University Press, 1994).

6. Vron Ware, "Moments of Danger," *History and Theory* 31 (1992), pp. 115–137.

7. Frantz Fanon, *Wretched of the Earth* (Grove Press, 1963), pp. 254–255.

8. Ibid., p. 30.

9. See my *"Ain't No Black in the Union Jack": The Cultural Politics of Race and Nation* (Hutchinson, 1987), chap. 4.

10. Roger Hewitt, "Us and Them in the Late Space Age," *Young,* vol. 3, no. 2 (May 1995), pp. 23–34.

11. Richard Wright, "The American Problem—Its Negro Phase," in D. Ray and R. M. Farnsworth, eds., *Richard Wright: Impressions and Perspectives* (Ann Arbor Paperbacks, 1971), p. 12.

12. I see strong affinities here with the argument outlined by Rosi Braidotti in "Sexual Difference as a Nomadic Political Project," in her *Nomadic Subjects* (Columbia University Press, 1994).

13. Fanon, *The Wretched of The Earth*, p. 40.

14. Frantz Fanon, *Black Skin, White Masks*, trans. Charles Lam (Markman, Pluto Press, 1986 [1952]), p. 166.

15. Ibid., p. 158.

16. John Hoberman, *Darwin's Athletes: How Sport Has Damaged Black America and Preserved the Myth of Race* (Houghton Mifflin, 1997). This controversial book has been debated in a special review symposium of the *International Review for the Sociology of Sport*, vol. 33, no. 1 (March 1998).

17. Bernard R. Ortiz de Montellano, "Melanin, Afrocentricity, and Pseudoscience," *Yearbook of Physical Anthropology* 36 (1993), pp. 33–58.

18. T. Owens Moore, *The Science of Melanin: Dispelling the Myths* (Beckham House Publishers, Inc., 1995).

19. Carol Barnes, *Melanin: The Chemical Key to Black Greatness*, vol. 1, Black Greatness Series (C. B. Publishers, 1988), p. 53.

20. G. Peart, "More Than the Colour of My Skin," Science Focus, *The Alarm*, 9 (November 1994), p. 25.

21. Moore, *The Science of Melanin*, p. 124.

22. *Image*, vol. 1, no. 3 (January 1995). The image was captioned "The Price of the Dream" and offered for sale as a poster by the photographer and poet Michael Gunn, 12311 Chandler Blvd., Suite 31, North Hollywood, CA 91607.

23. Elizabeth Alexander, "'Can You Be Black and Look at This?': Reading the Rodney King Video," in *Black Male Representations of Masculinity in Contemporary American Art*, ed. Thelma Golden (Whitney Museum, 1994). Also reprinted in *Public Culture*, vol.7, no. 4 (1994).

24. Frank Williams, "Eazy E: The Life, the Legacy," *The Source* (June 1995), p. 56.

25. An alternative account of the significance of Rodney King is articulated by Willie D on *Fuck Rodney King* (Priority Records, 1992). Eric Lott has offered a powerful defense of the record in "Cornel West in the Hour of Chaos in Race Matters," *Social Text*, 40 (1994), pp. 39–50.

26. *The Source*, 69 (June 1995), p. 56.

27. "Gangsta Rap Summit: 'Reality Check,'" *The Source*, 57 (June 1994), p. 72.

28. Ibid., p. 70.

29. Rob Kenner, "Top Rankin'," *Vibe* (October 1994), p. 76.

30. Scott Poulson-Bryant, "Karl Kani—Design of the Times," *Vibe* (October 1994), pp. 59–63.

31. Pnina Werbner and Tariq Modood, eds., *Debating Cultural Hybridity* (Zed Books, 1997).

32. Médecins sans Frontières, *World in Crisis: The Politics of Survival at the End of the 20th Century* (Routledge, 1997).

33. G. W. F. Hegel, *The Philosophy of History*, trans. J. Sibree (Dover Publications, 1956), p. 99.

34. Clifford, *Routes.*

35. Clifford Geertz, "The Uses of Diversity," *Michigan Quarterly Review* (1986).

36. Richard Rorty, *Objectivity, Relativism and Truth* (Cambridge University Press, 1991).

37. Roger Griffin, *The Nature of Fascism* (Routledge, 1993).

8. "RACE," COSMOPOLITANISM, AND CATASTROPHE

1. Saul Friedländer, *Nazi Germany and the Jews, vol. 1: The Years of Persecution, 1933–39* (HarperCollins, 1997), p. 12. See also Stephanie Barron et al., *"Degenerate Art": The Fate of the Avant Garde in Nazi Germany* (Los Angeles County Museum of Art, Abrams, 1991).

2. George L. Mosse, *Nazi Culture: A Documentary History* (Schocken Books, 1981).

3. Max Weinreich, *Hitler's Professors: The Part of Scholarship in Germany's Crimes Against the Jewish People* (Yiddish Scientific Institute, 1946), esp. chaps. 3–10.

4. George Stocking, ed., *Volksgeist as Method and Ethic: Essays on Boasian Ethnography and the German Anthropological Tradition* (University of Wisconsin, 1996); and Suzanne Marchand, *Down From Olympus: Archaeology and Philhellenism in Germany, 1750–1970* (Princeton University Press, 1996).

5. Frantz Fanon's "Racism and Culture," in *Toward the African Revolution: Political Essays*, trans. H. Chevalier (Monthly Review Press, 1967), is an interesting exception to this oversight.

6. Robert Young, *Colonial Desire: Hybridity in Theory, Culture, and Race* (Routledge, 1995) pp. 50–89.

7. Richard Wright, "The Psychological Reactions of Oppressed People," in *White Man Listen!* (Anchor Doubleday, 1964), pp. 16–17.

8. Ibid., p. 64.

9. Emmanuel Chukwudi Eze, "The Color of Reason: The Idea of 'Race' in Kant's Anthropology," in *Anthropology and the German Enlightenment: Perspectives on Humanity*, ed. Katherine Faull (Bucknell University Press and Associated University Press, 1994), pp. 200–241; Berel Lang, "Genocide and Kant's Enlightenment," in *Act and Idea in the Nazi Genocide* (University of Chicago Press, 1990), pp. 169–190.

10. Helmut Bley, *South-West Africa under German Rule, 1894–1914*, trans. Hugh

Ridley (Northwestern University Press, 1971); A. F. Calvert, *South-west Africa: During the German Occupation, 1884–1914* (T. Werner Laurie, 1915), and *South West Africa during the German Occupation* (T. Werner Laurie, 1915); I. Goldblatt, *History of South West Africa, from the Beginning of the Nineteenth Century* (Juta and Co., 1971); L. H. Gann and P. Duignan, *The Rulers of German Africa, 1887–1914* (Stanford University Press, 1977); Jon Swan, "The Final Solution in South West Africa," *Quarterly Journal of Military History* 3,4, pp. 36–55; Everlyn Nicodemus, "Carrying the Sun on Our Backs," in M. Catherine de Zegher, Andrea Robbins, and Max Becher, eds. (The Kanaal Art Foundation, 1994).

11. S. M. Islam, *The Ethics of Travel: From Marco Polo to Kafka* (Manchester University Press, 1996); James Clifford, *Routes: Travel and Translation in the Late Twentieth Century* (Harvard University Press, 1997).

12. L. S. Senghor, "Tyaroye," "Hosties Noires," in *Poèmes* (Seuil, 1984); see also Myron J. Echenberg, "Tragedy at Thiaroye: The Senegalese Soldiers' Uprising of 1944," in P. Gutkind et al., eds., *African Labor History* (Sage, 1978).

13. Sir Charles Lucas, *The Empire at War* (Oxford University Press, 1924).

14. Benjamin Brawley, *Africa and the War* (Duffield and Co., 1918), p. i.

15. David Levering Lewis, *W. E. B. Du Bois: Biography of a Race* (Henry Holt, 1993), p. 556.

16. *The Crisis* (July 1981).

17. Marcus Garvey, "Speech at the Royal Albert Hall June 6th 1928," in *Marcus Garvey and the Vision of Africa,* ed. John Henrik Clarke (Vintage, 1974).

18. John Hope Franklin, *From Slavery to Freedom* (Vintage Books, 1969), p. 480.

19. Arthur E. Barbeau and Florette Henri, *Unknown Soldiers: African-American Troops in World War I* (Temple University Press, 1974), p. 121.

20. Reid Badger, *A Life in Ragtime: A Biography of James Reese Europe* (Oxford University Press, 1997).

21. *St. Louis Post Dispatch,* June 10, 1918, quoted in R. Kimball and W. Bolcom, *Reminiscing with Sissle and Blake* (Viking, 1972). I would like to thank Jayna Brown for bringing this wonderful book to my attention.

22. Peter Jelavich, *Berlin Cabaret* (Harvard University Press, 1993); Michael Kater, *Different Drummers: Jazz in the Culture of Nazi Germany* (Oxford University Press, 1992), p. 8. See also Jurgen Wilhelm Heinrichs, "Blackness in Weimar": 1920s German Art Practice and American Jazz and Dance" (Ph.D. diss., Yale University, May 1998).

23. Nancy Nenno, "Femininity, the Primitive, and Modern Urban Space: Josephine Baker in Berlin," in Katharina Von Ankum, ed., *Women in the Metropolis: Gender and Modernity in Weimar Culture* (University of California Press, 1997).

24. "To the astonishment and distress of many white Americans, dark faces

seemed to be everywhere in the summer of 1929—in the swimming pools of the Normandie and the staterooms of the Queen Mary." David Levering Lewis, *When Harlem Was in Vogue* (Oxford University Press, 1989), p. 255.

25. *The Marcus Garvey and Universal Improvement Association Papers,* vol. 7, November 1927–August 1940, ed. Robert A. Hill et al. (University of California Press, 1990), p. 212.

26. *The Reaction of Negro Publications and Organizations to German Anti-Semitism,* Howard University Studies in the Social Sciences, vol. 3, no. 2 (Howard University, 1942). I would like to thank Laura Yow for pointing out the importance of this text.

27. *Norfolk Journal and Guide,* December 21, 1935, p. 9, col. 4.

28. Michael Kater, "Forbidden Fruit?" *American Historical Review* 94, 1 (1989), pp. 11–43.

29. Wendy Martin, "Remembering the Jungle: Josephine Baker and Modernist Parody," in *Prehistories of the Future: The Primitivist Project and the Culture of Modernism,* ed. Elazar Barkan and Ronald Bush (Stanford University Press, 1995).

30. T. W. Adorno, "On Jazz," trans. Jamie Owen Daniel, *Discourse* 12, 1 (Fall–Winter, 1989), p. 61.

31. Ibid., pp. 45–69.

32. T. W. Adorno, "Perennial Fashion-Jazz," in *Prisms,* trans. Samuel Weber and Shierry Weber (Neville Spearman, 1967).

33. J. A. Rogers, "Jazz at Home," *New Negro,* ed. A. Locke (Atheneum, 1968 [1925]), p. 223.

34. Alain Locke, *The Negro and His Music,* Bronze Booklet no. 2 (The Associates in Negro Folk Education, 1936), p. 72.

35. Ibid., pp. 82–83.

36. Ibid., p. 89.

37. Ibid., p. 38.

38. Michael Kater, *Different Drummers: Jazz in the Life of Nazi Germany* (Oxford University Press, 1994); Eric Vogel, "Jazz in a Nazi Concentration Camp, pts. 1 and 2," *Downbeat* (December 7, 1961), pp. 20–21, and (December 21, 1961), pp. 16–21; Mike Zwerin, *La Tristesse de Saint Louis: Swing under the Nazis* (Quartet, 1985); Horst J. P. Bergmeier and Rainer E. Lotz, *Hitler's Airwaves: The Inside Story of Nazi Radio and Propaganda Swing* (Yale University Press, 1997).

39. Detlev Peukert, *Inside Nazi Germany: Conformity, Opposition and Racism in Everyday Life,* trans. Richard Deveson (Pelican Books, 1989).

40. Karen Pinkus, *Bodily Regimes: Italian Advertising under Fascism* (University of Minnesota Press, 1995); Susan Sontag, "Fascinating Fascism," in *Under the Sign of Saturn* (Farrar Straus and Giroux, 1984).

41. Linda Schulte-Sasse, *Entertaining the Third Reich: Illusions of Wholeness in Nazi Cinema* (Duke University Press, 1996), chap. 10.

42. David Stewart Hull, *Film in the Third Reich: A Study of the German Cinema, 1933–1945* (University of California Press, 1969), p. 182.

43. Ralf Georg Reuth, *Goebbels,* trans. Krishna Winston (Harcourt Brace, 1993), p. 194.

44. George Stocking, *Victorian Anthropology* (Free Press, 1987), p. 106.

45. Yael Zerubavel, *Recovered Roots: Collective Memory and the Making of Israeli National Tradition* (University of Chicago Press, 1995).

46. Lt. Col. Dave Grossman, *On Killing: The Psychological Cost of Learning to Kill in War and Society* (Little, Brown, 1996), pp. 161–162; Grossman speculates about the possible effect of Nazi racial conditioning in raising the casualty rates that were inflicted on British and American forces by German troops. These rates are believed to be 50 percent higher than those the German troops suffered at the hands of their foes. See also Ben Shalit, *The Psychology of Conflict and Combat* (Praeger, 1988).

47. Herbert Kelman, "Violence without Moral Restraint," *Journal of Social Issues,* 29, 4 (1973), pp. 25–61; Henri Zukier, "The Twisted Road to Genocide: On the Psychological Development of Evil During the Holocaust," *Social Research,* 61 (1994), pp. 423–455.

48. Daniel Chirot, *Modern Tyrants: The Power and Prevalence of Evil in Our Age* (Princeton University Press, 1994).

49. Interviews with and about these important figures are contained in David Okuefuna's path-breaking film *Hitler's Forgotten Victims,* made by Afro-Wisdom Productions in 1997.

50. Robert W. Kesting, "Forgotten Victims: Blacks in the Holocaust," *Journal of Negro History,* 78, 1 (1992), pp. 30–36.

51. Mike Phillips and Trevor Phillips, *Windrush: The Irresistible Rise of Multi-Racial Britain* (HarperCollins, 1998), pp. 31–32.

52. *Weekly Journal,* May 4, 1995, p. 5, and *West Africa,* vol. 22, May 8, 1995, p. 778.

53. Lou Potter with William Miles and Nina Rosenblum, *Liberators: Fighting on Two Fronts in World War II* (Harcourt Brace Jovanovich, 1992); see also Brenda L. Moore, *To Serve My Country, to Serve My Race: The Story of the Only African-American WACs Stationed Overseas during World War II* (New York University Press, 1996).

54. Benjamin Bender, *Glimpses through Holocaust and Liberation* (North Atlantic Books, 1995), pp. 161–162.

55. "Escape from Dachau: My Own, Private V-E Day," *Washington Post,* Sunday, May 7, 1995.

56. Tape T-107; Leon Bass of the 183rd combat engineers, T-1241; Robbi Weissman, T-3061; Jacob Boehm, HVT 1357; Harry F., HVT 2761; Tobias

C, HVT 2266; Susan Soffer, T-876. These tapes, in the Fortunoff Archive, Yale University, cover incidents at Buchenwald, Salzwedel, Gunskirchen, and Mauthausen.

57. Graham Smith, *When Jim Crow Met John Bull: Black American Soldiers in World War II* (I. B. Tauris, 1987).

58. William Gardner Smith, *The Last of the Conquerors* (Farrar, Strauss and Co., 1948), p. 105.

59. Leon C. Standifer's memoir relates fascinating details of the activities of black soldiers in postwar Bavaria. It accords closely with the observations made by Gardner Smith. See *Binding Up the Wounds: An American Soldier in Occupied Germany, 1945–1946* (Louisiana State University Press, 1997), esp. pp. 150–173.

60. *U. S. News and World Report,* May 6, 1996.

61. Smith, *The Last of the Conquerors,* p. 35.

62. Ibid., p. 44.

63. Ibid., p. 68.

64. Ibid., p. 108.

65. Ibid., p. 138.

66. Arnold Krammer, *Nazi Prisoners of War in America* (Stein and Day, 1979); and Hermann Jung, *Die Deutschen Kriegsgefangenen in amerikanischer Hand USA* (Verlag Ernst und Werner Gieseling, 1972).

67. Smith, *The Last of the Conquerors,* p. 165.

68. William Gardner Smith, *The Stone Face* (Farrar, Strauss and Co., 1963), p. 115.

69. Ibid., p. 28.

70. Ibid., p. 57.

71. Ibid., p. 105.

72. Ibid., p. 58.

73. Ibid., p. 79.

74. Ibid., p. 93.

75. Ibid., p. 91.

76. Ibid., p. 121.

77. Ibid., p. 122.

78. A new commentary on these events has been generated by the trial of the Nazi collaborator Maurice Papon, who was the chief of police in Paris at the time of the massacre of the Algerian protesters. Testimony by survivors of these events was collected in *Liberation* 18, October 19, 1997; see also *Le Monde,* October 17, 1997, especially "La responsabilité du préfet de police est directe, personelle, écrasante," by Jean-Luc Einaudi.

79. Smith, *The Stone Face,* p. 175.

80. Ibid., p. 205.

81. Ibid., p. 213.

82. *Journal Courier* (New Haven, Conn.), September 3, 1945, reprinted in "In Retrospect: W. Rudolph Dunbar, Pioneering Orchestra Conductor," *The Black Perspective in Music,* vol. 9, no. 2 (Fall 1981), pp. 193–225.

9. "THIRD STONE FROM THE SUN"

1. I. Kant, "On the Different Races of Man," in *This Is Race: An Anthology,* selected, edited, and with an introduction by Earl W. Count Hanery Schuman (New York, 1950), p. 22.

2. I. Kant, "Physiche Geography," appended to J. A. May, "Kant's Concept of Geography and Its Relation to Recent Geographical Thought," translated by the author (University of Toronto Press, Geography Department Research Publications, 1970), p. 262.

3. Bernard McGrane, *Beyond Anthropology: Society and the Other* (Columbia University Press, 1989), p. 94. See also Johannes Fabian, *Time and the Other: How Anthropology Makes Its Object* (Columbia University Press, 1983).

4. Hannah Arendt, *The Origins of Totalitarianism* (Allen and Unwin, 1967), p. 171.

5. Susan Gilman, "Pauline Hopkins and the Occult: African American Revisions of Nineteenth-Century Sciences," *American Literary History,* vol. 13, no. 4 (1992), pp. 57–82.

6. Martha F. Lee, *The Nation of Islam: An American Millenarian Movement* (Syracuse University Press, 1996).

7. Elijah Muhammad, *Message to the Blackman in America* (United Brothers Communications Systems, Newport News, Virginia, 1992), p. 291.

8. Nicholas Goodrick-Clarke, *The Occult Roots of Nazism: Secret Aryan Cults and the Influence on Nazi Ideology* (I. B. Tauris, 1992); Sylvia Cranston, *H. P. B.: The Extraordinary Life and Influence of Helena Blavatsky, Founder of the Modern Theosophical Movement* (Tarcher Putnam, 1993), esp. chap. 7; Richard Noll, *The Aryan Christ: The Secret Life of Carl Jung* (Random House, 1997).

9. John F. Szwed, *Space Is the Place: The Lives and Times of Sun Ra* (Pantheon, 1997).

10. Mattias Gardell, *Countdown to Armageddon: Louis Farrakhan and the Nation of Islam* (Hurst and Co., 1996).

11. Roger Griffin, *The Nature of Fascism* (Routledge, 1993), p. 33.

12. The Ford plant in Cologne stayed open throughout World War II, manufacturing trucks with East European slave labor. Inmates from Buchenwald were purchased to work on the assembly line. See also Neil Gregor, *Daimler-Benz in the Third Reich* (Yale University Press, 1998).

13. Frantz Fanon, *Black Skin, White Masks,* trans. Charles Lam (Markman, Pluto Press, 1986 [1952]), pp. 230–231 passim.

14. Martin Delany, *The Condition, Elevation, Emigration and Destiny of the Colored People of the United States Politically Considered* (George Charles, 1852), p. 213.

15. Georg Wilhelm Friedrich Hegel, *The Philosophy of History,* trans. J. Sibree (Dover Editions, 1956), p. 86.

16. Kenneth R. Manning, *Black Apollo of Science: The Life of Ernest Everett Just* (Oxford University Press, 1983).

17. Richard Wright, *White Man Listen!* (Anchor, 1964), p. 53.

18. "I went out and got some books by this German chick Leni Riefenstahl, Last of the Nuba and People of Kay [*sic*]. There's one motherfucker in one picture looks just like me." Greg Tate, *Flyboy in the Butter Milk* (Simon and Schuster, 1992), p. 34.

19. This essay is discussed at length by Graham Taylor in his Ph.D. dissertation, "Blutopia: Visions of the Future and Revisions of the Past in the Work of Sun Ra, Duke Ellington and Anthony Braxton" (Dept. of American and Canadian Studies, University of Nottingham, 1997). This thesis has been published under the same title in revised form by Duke University Press in 1999, with the author listed as Graham Lock.

20. Duke Ellington, "The Race for Space," in *The Duke Ellington Reader,* ed. Mark Tucker (Oxford University Press, 1993), pp. 293–296.

21. Nichelle Nichols, *Beyond Uhura: Star Trek and Other Memories* (Boxtree Books, 1996), p. 196.

22. Martin Luther King, Jr., *Where Do We Go from Here: Chaos or Community?* (Harper and Row, 1967), p. 86.

23. Nichols, *Beyond Uhura,* p. 164.

24. Richard King, M.D., *African Origin of Biological Psychiatry* (U.B. and U.S. Communications Systems, 1994), pp. 13–14.

25. Milton William Cooper, *Behold a Pale Horse* (Light Technology Publishing, 1991).

26. Ed Vulliamy, "Face-off in Jasper," *Guardian Weekend,* July 11, 1998, p. 14.

ACKNOWLEDGMENTS

This project was completed while I was the beneficiary of a fellowship [SOC/253 (279)] provided by the Nuffield Social Science Foundation. I would like to thank that body for its support, which bought me out of my teaching for a year.

Lots of people in a number of far-flung locations gave up their precious time to help me with different aspects of this labor. They know who they are, and I am honored by their generosity and their friendship. Their names are set out arbitrarily below, but all of them should appear in more than one of my categories. None of them are to be held responsible for my errors and failures.

I must give particular thanks for the friendship, the stimulating dialogues, and the insightful critiques of this project that were provided by Hedda Ekerwald, Vikki Bell, Angela McRobbie, Les Back, Homi Bhabha, Stuart Hall, Greta Slobin, Mark Slobin, Flemming Røgilds, S. M. Islam, Gloria Watkins, and Vron Ware. I appreciate the encouragement and support offered by Chris Connery, Jim Clifford, bell hooks, Mandy Rose, Brenda Kelly, Jon Savage, Michael Denning, Patrick Wright, Hazel Carby, Isaac Julien, Beryl Gilroy, Anne-Marie Fortier, and Iain Chambers.

David Okuefuna, Everlyn Nicodemus, Kristian Romare, Dr. Tricia Bohn, Monique Guillory, Mandy Rose again, Joe Sim, Patrick Hagopian, Graham Lock/Taylor, Ben Karpf, Juergen Heinrichs, Stephanie Sears, and Robert A. Hill helped me with specific items of information, books, tapes, videos, articles, and so on. I must also thank Roman Horak for his help in finding Jean Améry's grave in Vienna; Jaqueline Nassy Brown for material about Josef Nassy; Nina Rosenblum and Bill Miles for informa-

tion about the regrettable fate of their important film *Liberators;* Benita
Ludmer for French press cuttings about the October 1961 pogrom and the
Papon trial; and Larry Grossberg for sending me stuff on POW camps for
the German soldiers in North Carolina. Val Wilmer, Laura Yow, Jayna
Brown, Amanda Sebesteyen, and Nikolas Rose all generously shared materials from their own collections and research projects. This book is better
for their kindness.

Marcus Gilroy Ware and Cora Gilroy Ware were capable cultural ad-
visers and research assistants, especially on matters relating to the
infotainment telesector. They have helped me far more than they realize,
and I want to thank them for their patience, their angular insight, their
sensible sensitivity, their understandable impatience with raciology, and
the precocious wisdom they share.

I should also express my gratitude to the people who came to hear me
talk and engaged me in debate at the various universities and other institutions where I first presented these arguments. The most valuable of these
sessions were at De Balie, in Amsterdam; the English Department of the
University of Pennsylvania; the Center for Cultural Studies at the University of California, Santa Cruz; the University of New Hampshire; the University of Vienna; Stanford University; the Volksbuhne in Berlin; the
Ethnic and Racial Studies conference at the LSE; and the stimulating session organized by Diggante in Stockholm.

I want to thank my colleagues and students at Goldsmiths and at Yale.
My ideas were tested and refined in conversations with Anita Pilgrim,
Eamon Wright, Yoshitaka Mori, Hiroki Ogasawara, Lez Henry,
Giovanni Porfido, and Colin King. My warmest thanks for practical help
go to Mary Clemmey.

The soundscape for this project was supplied primarily by the Creole
modernism of Gonzalo Rubalcaba. He is clearly the greatest ever impro-
vising pianist in the history of what gets called "jazz," and his oblique creativity is both a source of awe and an incitement to reach for something
out of the ordinary. I hear a similar mix of insurgent spirit and relentless
discipline in the equally inspiring work of Edgar Meyer, Victor Wooten,
and his brother Future Man, Marcus Miller, and, of course, Anthony
Jackson. At the risk of sounding sentimental, I would like to think that the
ghosts of Eric Gale, Richard Tee, and Dennis Emmanuel Brown have left
identifiable traces in here somewhere.

INDEX